Father and Son
in Confucianism
and Christianity

Father and Son in Confucianism and Christianity

A Comparative Study of Xunzi and Paul

Yanxia Zhao

sussex
ACADEMIC
PRESS

BRIGHTON • PORTLAND

2 4 6 8 10 9 7 5 3

First published 2007 in Great Britain by
SUSSEX ACADEMIC PRESS
PO Box 139
Eastbourne BN24 9BP

and in the United States of America by
SUSSEX ACADEMIC PRESS
920 NE 58th Ave   Suite 300
Portland, Oregon 97213-3786

British Library Cataloguing in Publication Data
A CIP catalogue record for this book is available from the British Library.

Library of Congress Cataloging-in-Publication Data
Zhao, Yanxia.
Father and son in Confucianism and Christianity :
    a comparative study of Xunzi and Paul / Yanxia Zhao.
    p. cm.
    Includes bibliographical references and index.
    ISBN 978-1-84519-161-0 (alk. paper)
    1. Confucianism. 2. Fathers and sons—China. 3. Fathers
and sons—Religious aspects—Christianity 4. Xunzi.
5. Paul, the Apostle, Saint. I. Title. II. Title: Comparative
study of Xunzi and Paul.

BL1852.Z486 2007
299.5′12563—dc22
                                    2007004314

Typeset and designed by SAP, Brighton & Eastbourne.
Printed by TJ International, Padstow, Cornwall.
This book is printed on acid-free paper.

Contents

Abbreviations

Old Testament (OT)

Gen	Genesis
Exod	Exodus
Lev	Leviticus
Num	Numbers
Deut	Deuteronomy
Josh	Joshua
Judg	Judges
1 Sam	1 Samuel
2 Sam	2 Samuel
1 Kgs	1 Kings
2 Kgs	2 Kings
1 Chr	1 Chronicles
2 Chr	2 Chronicles
Neh	Nehemiah
Mal	Malachi
Ps	Psalms
Jer	Jeremiah
Isa	Isaiah
Job	Job
Mic	Micah

New Testament (NT)

Matt	Matthew
Mark	Mark
Luke	Luke
John	John
Acts	Acts
Rom	Romans
1 Cor	1 Corinthians
2 Cor	2 Corinthians
Gal	Galatians
Eph	Ephesians
Phil	Philippians
Col	Colossians
1 Thess	1 Thessalonians
2 Thess	2 Thessalonians

1 Tim	1 Timothy
2 Tim	2 Timothy
Titus	Titus
Phlm	Philemon

Apocrypha

4 Bar	Baruch
3 Jh	Judith
2 Macc	Maccabees
Sir	ben Sira
Tob	Tobit

Aristotle

Eth. Nic.	*Nichomachean Ethics*
Pol.	*Politics*

Euripides

El.	*Electra Orestes*

Gaius

Inst.	*Institutiones* (Gai Institutionum Commertarii Quattor)

Hesiod

OP	*Homeric Hymns: To Poseidon*

Isocrates

Ad.	*Antidosis*
Ad. Nic.	*Ad Demonicum*
Or.	*Oratores Attici*

Josephus

Ag. Ap.	*Against Apion*
Pseud.-Phoc.	*Pseudo-Phocylides*

Pausanias

Descr.	*Description of Greece*

Philo

Dec.	*De Decalogo*
Ebr.	*De Ebrietate*
Hyp.	*Hypothetica*
Leg.	*De Legatione ad Gaium*

Omn. Prob. Lib.	*Quod Omnis Probus Liber Sit*
Spec.	*De Specialibus Legibus*

Plutarch

Mor.	*Moralia*

Talmud

Sanh.	*Sanhedrin*

Aristea

Ep.	*Epistle*

Preface

This comparative study has come about not only from my own academic interest, but also from the necessity of engaging traditional Chinese and Western cultures. I hope that my endeavours herein will resonate with the call of people's hopes for peace and harmony, and the establishment of world-wide shared values.

Chinese culture has been in intensive contact with Western culture for nearly two centuries, since the later Qing Dynasty (1644–1911) in the first half of the nineteenth century. The influence of Western culture has gradually penetrated every corner of modern Chinese society. Seriously challenged by the dominant world culture, which is based mainly on American and European values and principles, traditional Chinese culture, especially Confucianism, has fallen into a state of crisis. A flood of criticism began to drown the tradition of thousands of years (551 BCE–1911 CE). This deadly attack was begun by the May Fourth Movement, headed by Chen Duxiu, through the 'New Youth' magazine, which used liberty, democracy and science as weapons and took modernization and Westernization as aims. The death of Chinese culture, and in particular Confucianism, was further pursued by the Chinese Communists. The major political critiques and campaigns of the People's Republic of China removed Confucianism from both the government and social custom, enabling scholars to say that, apart from a few fragments, Confucianism had disappeared from Chinese society. The strong criticism of Confucianism continues to the present day, as we can be seen from the studies of both Chinese and Western scholars. Among them, Joseph R. Levensan completely denies the possibility of both Confucian government and life style;[1] Sun Long Ji criticizes Chinese culture from the perspective of 'deeper structure';[2] Yu Yingshi criticizes Chinese Confucianism from an historical point of view;[3] Tu Weiming tries to liberate Confucianism from its feudal and collective context;[4] and Liu Xiaofeng gives his political critique from the viewpoint of a contemporary Christian intellectual.[5]

This crisis of traditional Chinese culture raises many questions: Can Chinese society adapt itself to the Western standard? Can Chinese culture continue to be an independent culture? Does Chinese culture still have the ability to establish a rich, peaceful and harmonious life in the modern world? To answer these questions, it is necessary to determine precisely where the problem of Chinese culture lies, and to evaluate the real power or value of Western culture. One way forward is to engage in comparative study of the two cultures in order to make clear the differences and similarities between them, and to examine the values and disadvantages of Chinese culture found through such a study, in order to identify a possible point for recovery and development.

The increasing ineffectiveness of world-dominant Western culture in achieving the fulfillment of the perfect human life reveals a need to adopt or assimilate some complementary elements and new energy from other cultures. Many scholars have highlighted the possible contribution of Chinese culture to Western culture. For example, the Chinese modern Confucian scholar Qian Mu assumes that the tendency of the world culture is now to take Chinese traditional culture as its suzerain.[6] Thus, in the introduction to their book *Gottfried Wilhelm Leibniz: Writings on China*, the editors, Daniel J. Cook and Henry Rosemount Jr., argue for wider horizons, as did Leibniz himself:

> Three centuries have passed since Leibniz began his effort to promote greater understanding between China and the West, and it is not cynical to suggest that there has not been a great deal of progress toward the goal . . . Given the economic, political, social, and philosophical crises currently facing the Western capitalist democracies, it might well be salutary to look beyond our own cultural traditions for new – or very old – intellectual horizons, as Leibniz did.[7]

Despite the attacks on and criticism of Chinese culture (and especially Confucianism), not only did it survive, but it is gradually growing stronger. As the only one of the three most ancient world cultures still active, Chinese culture still commands the greatest popular following, and remains unshaken in the forest of world cultures. Moreover, it seems that it still has enough internal life force to maintain and prolong its activity: many modern scholars now adopt the view that Confucianism has not only successfully influenced the development of modern East Asian economics, but has also recovered in Modern China.[8] Its great vitality shows that there must be some deep value within, a value that must not only be powerful, but also wonderful. Nonetheless, it is difficult to fully recognize these advantages without a cultural comparison.

A peaceful life is the common hope of all people of the world. Most conflicts between nations are due to the greed and avarice of political careerists obsessed with their own ambitions, but many other conflicts are in fact rooted in the misunderstanding or misinterpretation of different cultures. These terrible conflicts and wars, which are obviously exacerbated by cultural differences, have caused deep world-wide distress, and it is therefore important to initiate immediate dialogue between different cultures in order for them to arrive at fundamental mutual agreement and understanding. It is a common belief that if different cultures were understood correctly, then conflicts would be dramatically reduced. However, the understanding of different cultures must be based on substantial dialogue between them, and such dialogue in turn must be based on cultural comparison. Kant put it this way: 'In order really to form a concept out of mere ideas one must compare, reflect and abstract.'[9]

Although there are different opinions regarding cultural comparison, generally scholars are now in agreement that this kind of exploration is necessary:

> Such a dialogue may not only lead to a better understanding of and respect for people from another culture, thus helping to avoid cross-cultural misunderstandings, but it could also lead to a new way of seeing and understanding ourselves and our culture, because we need the 'other' in order to better understand our 'own' and our culturally conditioned – not determined – point of view.[10]

We are one world, one space-ship earth ecology, one polity, one commonwealth;[11] and this has 'made it necessary to come to a sharing of values'.[12] The establishment of a new, world-shared order of value can be brought about by cultural comparison. Intercultural dialogue can lead to a new openness and sensitivity; namely, a willingness to be informed by another culture. The meeting of different cultures may bear great fruit, as the German physicist Heisenberg pointed out:

> It is probably true quite generally that in the history of human thinking the most fruitful developments take place at those points where two different lines of thought meet. These lines may have their roots in quite different parts of human culture, in different times or different cultural environments or different religious traditions: hence if they actually meet, that is, if they are at least so much related to each other that a real interaction can take place, then one may hope that new and interesting developments may follow.[13]

Thus, the comparison between two cultures is not only necessary but also offers potential unity, as Xinzhong Yao states:

> The possibility of a comparative study of religion arises out of the nature of the human expression of religious vision. Human beings have developed different views of the world and the beyond. At first glance, these views diverge from each other. However, most scholars believe that beneath these views lies some shared vision, which provides a ground for a comparative study of religion. Such a positive philosophy of the religious nature of human beings suggests that, just as tributaries come together to form a single river, so different religious expressions may be integrated into a single comprehensive enterprise, to which individual religions will make their own specific contributions. It maintains that various races, nations and peoples share a fundamental religious framework and that, despite their different approaches, they are moving towards the same, or at least a similar, spiritual goal.[14]

Clearly Chinese and Western cultures are two totally different entities in many ways. Nevertheless, the encounter and ensuing conflict between these opposites may produce new energy. The great ancient Greek philosopher Heraclitus (*c.* 500 BC) famously stated that there will be no development without conflict; different tones can make the most beautiful harmony. Cultural development from this perspective thus needs encounters between different thought patterns. It is also true that for the further fruitful development of both Confucian and Christian cultures, it is vital that comparative investigations between the two are carried out.

However, as the more pessimistic scholars have widely recognized, comparative study between different cultures is no easy task. Special standards are needed for such an undertaking. A comparative study of two cultures not only requires that the scholar has intercultural competence – the ability 'to switch over to another angle of view, acquiring an ability to see the world from more than one culturally conditioned perspective',[15] but it also requires the courage to criticize and analyze one's own culture. It is, however, an enormously inspiring task, in the sense that criticism and analysis not only allows different cultures to understand each other better, but can also lead to the establishment of a new common shareable value system.

With regard to the possibility of comparing Confucian culture and Christianity the Jesuits have provided support and evidence. The famous Jesuit missionary and head of the China mission, Matteo Ricci (1552–1610), believed that there were 'traces of

Christianity' in Chinese culture and customs, including 'evidences of the cross among the Chinese'.[16] By this belief, Ricci confirmed the translatability of Western concepts and ideas into Chinese, the possibility of shared understanding of the notion of God and other spiritual realities across the boundaries of language, geography, culture and time.[17]

In his enthusiastic desire for Europe and China to learn from each other, Leibniz held that 'it would appear almost necessary that Chinese missionaries should be sent to us to teach us the use and practice of natural religion, just as we send missionaries to them to teach them revealed religion'.[18] Thus, by the end of the seventeenth century, as Arthur Lovejoy remarks, 'it had come to be widely accepted that the Chinese – by the light of nature alone – had surpassed Christian Europe both in the art of government and in ethics'.[19] Although there are very many differences between Confucianism and Christianity, in the end, as Julia Ching has firmly stated: 'both Confucianism and Christianity have exercised decisive influence in shaping the beliefs, moral codes and behaviors of large populations in the East and West. A comparative study of Confucianism and Christianity should therefore not only be possible but also fruitful.'[20]

Four main research methods will be used in this comparative work. The essential method used is textual analysis, by which I will turn to the original texts of Xunzi's and Pauline teachings, in order to analyze their direct and indirect meanings and implications. These texts will be taken as the source of truth, and the study of them will reveal the blueprints of their traditions.

However, people have recognized that 'religious texts do not necessarily provide us with a true picture of the origin and early development of a religion'.[21] Hence, there are two textual analysis positions open to us: one is to emphasize light and clarity with nothing left unsaid, while the other is to emphasize darkness and things hidden, outside of conscious awareness.[22] In the former, the meaning of concepts can be understood directly through the language Xunzi and Paul used. Therefore, we can observe the truth through understanding the messages and the meaning of the concept directly presented to us by its distinctive phenomena. In this sense textual analysis can also be called phenomenological methodology. In the latter position, many meanings have become obscured, hidden or beyond language phenomena through the passage of time and the changing of the environment; therefore, we cannot understand their true meaning without discovering their origin and relating them to special historical situations and socio-cultural backgrounds. Thus, when the meaning of a concept cannot be easily understood through phenomenological analysis, hermeneutics as a theory of interpretation is used as a second methodological tool in my study.

Based on hermeneutical interpretation, I intend to carry out a textual analysis by word-structure examination; thus, by observing the structure or constitution of a word, the original meaning of a concept will be explored. In this way, by taking the original meaning of the concept as a foundation, and checking its various extensional meanings, which are scattered throughout metaphysical, and epistemological as well as ethical and religious theories, its general sense will be grasped. Thus, through a combination of historical and linguistic interpretation, the full meaning of a concept will be exposed and contradictions between different interpretations of the text resolved.

The third and most fundamental method employed in this research is that of comparison. Comparison as a research method has been adopted by many scholars in religious and cultural studies during the twentieth century. For example, Liang Shuming uses this method in his book *Dongxi Wenhua Jiqi Zhexue*, as do Julia Ching in *Christianity and Chinese Religion*, Xinzhong Yao in *Confucianism and Christianity: A Comparative Study of Jen and Agape*, and Zhao Dunhua in *Jidujiao yu Jindai Zhongxi Wenhua*. The particular way I use this methodology is to apply it not only in particular case studies, such as the comparison between Xunzi's ideas and Pauline teaching on the Father–Son (F–S) relationship, but also in the broad sense of cultural and religious studies. More precisely, comparison in this work is focused not only on the ethical F–S relationship itself, but also on its social and cultural background; not only on Xunzi's and Pauline theories, but also some of their important concepts. This means that the method of comparison in this research is not used alone, but is combined with a social anthropological approach.

The fourth method I intend to apply in this work is what Martin Heidegger called the 'hermeneutic circle'. From Heidegger's point of view, through using this construct, we can genuinely grasp the positive possibility of the most primordial kind of knowing:

> Only when we have understood that our first, last, and constant task in interpreting is never to allow our fore-having, fore-sight, and for-conception to be presented to us by fancies and popular conceptions, but rather to make the scientific theme secure by working out those fore-structures in terms of the things themselves.[23]

Therefore, our interpretation of a particular message is meaningful only when we have a general sense of the situation overall, while the meaning of the whole text is relevant only when we have fore-projected an initial sense of each individual element in itself.[24] The 'hermeneutic circle' method applied here in this research will start from a general cultural study, go to a specific case study and then from this particular case move back to the general cultural study, where it will end. I will unfold my discussion of the F–S relationship by starting with general cultural definitions, and then apply these to Xunzi and Paul's particular contributions together with specific comparison. However, the discussion will not end at a particular understanding, but will further reflect back to their respective traditions. That is to say, the conclusion of a particular comparison between Xunzi's and Pauline teaching will be taken as a model to guide further cultural transformations. In short, the current comparative studies will begin and end with cultural constructs.

Acknowledgements

First and foremost, I would like to give thanks to Professor Xinzhong Yao, the principal supervisor of both my MPhil and PhD studies. His academic guidance and critical advice are deeply acknowledged.

I owe much gratitude to Professor D. P. Davies and Professor David Cockburn for their thoughtful guidance, stimulating suggestions, theoretical inspiration and encouragement. I am especially grateful to Ms Ruth Russell-Jones, Mr. Michael Morris, Mr. Rodney Aist, Mr. Gareth Jones, Ms Helene McMurtrie-Watson, and Ms June Walters-Aust who have provided invaluable and unconditional assistance in the improvement of my English whist I was writing my PhD thesis, and to Ms Carol Russell-Williams and Ms M. Robson, who painstakingly checked my final proofs for publication.

I am deeply indebted to my dearest husband Guocheng Jiao, and my daughter Yiying Jiao. Without their consistent strong backing and persistent encouragement, I would not have been able to overcome the cultural barriers between the Chinese and Western traditions, nor would I have completed my study and research work.

I wish to take this opportunity to give my wholehearted thanks to my dearest parents: Ms Sulian Lü and Mr. Xuyou Zhao. Without their unselfish love and continuing support to my family, especially in taking care of my husband and my daughter's daily needs when I was studying abroad, I would not have been free to devote myself successfully to academic life. Their deep understanding and unfailing support is a wonderful encouragement to me.

Finally, I am very grateful to Mr. Anthony Grahame, Editorial Director at Sussex Academic Press, for his understanding, assistance and encouragement.

Father and Son in Confucianism and Christianity

A Comparative Study of Xunzi and Paul

The Relationship at the Centre of Confucian Thinking and Christian Ethics

Confucianism and Christianity are the foundations of Chinese and Western culture respectively. The natural father–son (F–S) relationship is at the centre of Confucian thinking; the ethical principle of this relationship is in turn the model for that of other familial, social and political relation patterns. The divine F–S relationship between God and Jesus is also at the centre of Christian consideration and likewise is the model of Christian familial, social and political relationships. The particular aim of this book, then, is to offer a religious and cultural comparative study of this most cardinal and crucial relation pattern.

The Father–Son Relationship

The concept of the F–S relationship implies a physical father and a biological son. It is sometimes extended to the stepfather–stepson, and sometimes even to that between foster-father and adopted son. However, discussion of the F–S relationship in this volume will not be limited in this way, and will be given a more open interpretation. The term will instead be used to describe a broad range of social relationships, involving the natural F–S and its other counterparts in the familial, social political and spiritual realms, such as husband–wife, and elder–younger brothers relationships in the family; the old–young, junior–senior, master–slave and teacher–student relationships in society; the ruler–subject, ruler–ruled and official– citizen relationships in politics; the God–man, Jesus–follower and priest–church member relationships in the Christian religion; and the *Tiandi*–human and sage–common people relationships in Confucian spirituality. The F–S relationship is herein presented as not only a familial, but also a social and political notion; it is not only biological, but also spiritual. The Confucian F–S relationship is a typical *secular* pattern, in which the natural blood kinship and biological physical linkage are the basis and the centre. The Christian F–S relationship is a typical *divine* pattern, in which the universal kinship and spiritual linkage is the foundation and the spiritual relationship between God and Jesus is the centre and starting point. A. Harnack provides us with a clear description of what the divine F–S relationship is:

It is 'knowledge of God' that makes the sphere of the Divine Sonship. It is in this knowledge that he came to know the sacred being who rules heaven and earth as Father, as his
Father . . . Rightly understood, the name of Son means nothing but the knowledge of God.[1]

This broad meaning of the F–S relationship provides an answer to why comparison
should focus on this relationship: in both Confucian and Christian society, the F–S is
the most crucial relationship for both the individual family and society.

Family is the most important element of society: whatever its form, the family
constitutes the core unit in all societies. The relationship between family and society
is reciprocal: 'given a benign governance, to the extent that the family functions well,
the society flourishes, to the extent that the family functions poorly, the society
declines'.[2] In most families of past or present societies, the natural F–S relationship
always occupies the most important place compared to other relationships. Research
has revealed that few societies have escaped from the situation of patriarchy; hence,
patriarchy can be said to be the main form of social organization. In patriarchal societies,
since the son is the certain heir of his father and a potential father in his turn, and again
the father and his heir are the most important figures for both family and society, the
relationship between a father and his son is clearly primordial.

Nonetheless, the importance of the F–S relationship in both Confucian and
Christian society is not the main reason for it being taken as the subject of the comparison. The chief reason for our comparison of the F–S relationship between Confucianism
and Christianity is that it provides a metaphor that can cover nearly all human relationships, including those which are variously familial, social, political and religious or
spiritual, in both Confucian and Christian societies.

The extensions of the F–S relationship in both Confucianism and Christianity are
obvious. Many scholars have realized, for example, that the nature of the well-known
Confucian 'Five Relationships' model is actually family based. Feng Youlan argues that,
in the 'Five Relationships', three of these are family relations; namely, father–son,
husband–wife and elder–younger brothers, while the other two are usually conceived
in terms of the family model.[3] In line with this, Julia Ching indicates that the
ruler–subject relationship resembles the father–son, while friendship resembles brotherliness. Additionally, she states that just as a child owes filial affection to his parents,
so the subject owes loyalty to his sovereign; as the parents are expected to care for their
child, so is the sovereign expected to protect his subject. For this reason, Confucian
society regards itself as a large family.[4] Since all social political relationships are
modelled on the familial relationships and all familial relationships result from that of
the natural F–S, it is reasonable to conclude that the central consideration of
Confucianism is certainly the family and that the centre of the family is no doubt the
natural F–S relationship.

In Confucian society, the kinship family is the cornerstone of society because, in
the traditional Confucian mind, society is itself an enlarged family and the family is
in turn a miniature society. Therefore, the ruler and the father are endowed with the
same function; the king in his country and the father in his home hold the same position. The father is the ruler of his family, while the ruler is the father of the people he
governs. Accordingly, the ruler is the greatest patriarch, officials are the middle rank-

ing patriarchs, and father is the fundamental patriarch. All rulers should love and treat their subjects well, just as a father loves and treats his children well; all subjects and citizens should respect and obey their rulers and officials, just as sons love and respect and obey their fathers. Although some Confucians seem more or less to have realized that there is a certain tension between a son's piety towards his father and his loyalty to his ruler, they have never felt that this difference would destroy their unity. In their mind, the F–S and the ruler–ruled relationships are interlinked and complementary to each other.

Both Hebrew and Greco-Roman cultures have a tendency to give primacy to the natural F–S relationship, and to extend the function of the father to society and the political realm. Early Christianity thus carried on this tradition, and so the metaphor 'God the Father', 'Jesus the Son', 'Children of God', along with a number of other family metaphors, became a means by which to develop and communicate a Christian theology as well as constructing a church community with a certain kind of leadership and certain patterns of interactions between its members.[5] However, in contrast to its cultural background, on the one hand, it takes not the natural but the divine or spiritual F–S relationship as that which is fundamental and the most crucial relationship: 'I kneel before the Father, from whom his whole family in heaven and on earth derives its name' (Eph 3:15); on the other hand, it regards the universal family as the cardinal image of Christian society, in which God is the Patriarch and all the believers in the churches are brothers and sisters; God loves people with a full, mercy-based love, and all believers in turn should believe in him and obey him. The second-century CE Athenagoras acknowledged this understanding by saying, 'According to age, we call some sons and daughters and others we hold brothers and sisters and to the aged assign the honor of fathers and mothers.'[6] To be brothers and sisters under God, and to establish various social relationships according to the pattern of the spiritual F–S relationship between God and Jesus, is the ideal model of people's secular life. In accordance with such a way of thinking, Andrew S. Jacobs further links this 'brethren' relationship among the Christian converts to the ideal of reconstructing the diverse body of believers into a family of God united around the apostle: 'If you desire a friend who supplies goods not of this world, I am your friend. If you desire a father for those who are rejected on earth, I am your father. If you desire a legitimate brother to set you apart from bastard brothers, I am your brother.'[7]

In short, both Confucianism and Christianity emphasize the family. Although Confucian teaching was formed on the natural F–S relationship, and Christian doctrine on the spiritual, both are family-oriented and F–S relationship centered, as well as having a similar tendency to take the central relationship as a model and transfer its function to other familial, social and political extensions, thereby enabling the F–S value-model to permeate the whole of society.

The Ethical Standpoint

Comparisons in this book will be made from an ethical point of view. But why choose an ethical approach in preference to any other? The rational here is first and foremost because 'humanism' and 'ethics' are not only important to Confucianism, but also to Christianity.

To concentrate on human secular affairs and to seek rational rather than divine ways of solving human problems are the main characteristics of Chinese society; furthermore, the moral doctrine of filial piety is fundamental to and is the very essence of Chinese ethics and social life, as Charles A. Moore observes:

> There is the uniquely Chinese concept of spirituality – coupled with, and defining its expression in, the fullest possible development of the ethical character (and innate good-ness) of man, and there is the very famous – and equally fundamental – but usually thoroughly misunderstood doctrine of filial piety, possibly the very essence of Chinese ethical and social life.[8]

According to *The Classics of Filial Piety*, filial piety is 'the root of virtue'; moreover, for David K. Jordan, filial piety is not only the basis of philosophy for the traditional Confucian, but also a guiding value of Chinese society.[9] As morality is the essential character of Chinese society and moral problems are deeply connected to social prob-lems, no problem in Chinese society can therefore be resolved unless the cardinal and central ethical relationships have found their proper solutions.

Although theology is the main characteristic of Christian society, the ethical doc-trine of obedience is the foundation and indeed the essence of Christian religion and its social life; nevertheless, although the divine F–S relationship is the centre of Jesus' doctrine, humanism also plays an important part in his thinking. In Jesus' consider-ation, 'The Sabbath was made for man not man for the Sabbath' (Mark 2:27), therefore 'love your neighbour' is the second greatest law after love of the Lord your God (Matt 22:37–9).

Another important reason for making comparisons from an ethical standpoint is that the *ethical* F–S relationship is the core principle above all others and has supreme value over any other concept relevant to the F–S relationship for both Confucianism and Christianity. For Confucianism, the physical relationship between the father and the son is certainly important, but the ethical relationship is more so: indeed, both Mengzi and Xunzi confirm that the reason for the special importance of humankind is their special possession of morality. Nevertheless, although the spiritual and divine relationships between the Father and the Son are important for Christianity, theolog-ical moral requirements, such as the son's obedience and belief and the father's love, are the most important manifestations of Christian understanding of the divine F–S relation.

All other relationships, such as legal or economic, are based on this *ethical* F–S prin-ciple in both traditional Confucian and Christian societies. In Confucian tradition, legal and economic F–S relationships have never been emphasized as strongly as the ethical element. For Confucianism, the material–satisfying relationship between father and son has no priority for either side; spiritual and moral satisfaction is more important for the father as a father and for the son as a son. For Christianity, the most important thing is to establish a spiritual F–S relationship between God and humans; secular relationships, whether economic or legal, are not as important as the religious ethical principle. Research on both biological and psychological F–S relationships is usually carried out for the purpose of providing a scientifically sound explanation of precisely how the present ethical F–S relationship functions, or else it is advanced to correct the failing or dysfunction of present ethical relationships. In addition, both of these research perspectives provide further biological and psychological possibilities for the establishment of potentially new ethical F–S relationships. In short, for the study of the F–S relationship, neither biological nor psychological patterns are determined by its nature; rather they are subservient to the ethical principle.

In general, almost all scholars of Chinese philosophy and Confucian scholars living in China and abroad agree that this ethical F–S relationship is the touchstone of Confucian ethics. It is argued that the basic characteristics of Confucian ethics are hierarchy and inequality, and that the typical manifestations of hierarchical and unequal relationships are integral to that ethical relationship.[10] It is thus the central expression of Confucian ethics, and people cannot therefore fully understand Confucian ethical theory without an understanding of the ethical relationship between a natural father and his natural son, which lies at its centre.

Although the most important source of the natural father's power and authority comes from the father's imitation of divine creation rather than from his moral activity, the ethical F–S relationship between God and Jesus has a place in Christian society similar to that of the ethical natural F–S relationship in the Confucian tradition. Since no one is perfect except for God, the duty of a natural father is not to be a moral model but rather to guide his son on the road towards the kingdom of God. Nonetheless, the father's power and authority in Christianity are still linked to his duty of education or moral guidance. Moreover, since both the Father God and the Son Jesus Christ are morally perfect, the moral relationship between God and Jesus can be a model for all other relationships in Christian society and the Christian world. Without this moral understanding of the divine F–S relationship, therefore, no Christian ethical theory can be properly interpreted; this understanding is thus a central consideration of both Confucian and Christian ethical doctrines.

This secular ethical F–S relationship is in turn the first important influence on early Confucianism. As many scholars have pointed out, Confucianism, so long dominant in traditional Chinese social and political life, lays great stress upon proper human relationships, especially on proper F–S relationships.

The work of bringing out the importance of human relationships was initiated by Confucius (*c.* 551–479 BC), the founder of Confucianism, and was completed by the later Confucians. It was Confucius who was responsible not only for changing the basis of the virtue of filial piety from the sense of respecting ancestors and producing offspring into the sense of 'respecting one's parents', but also for giving a new value to the position of the physical F–S relationship in society. Since the time of Confucius, the ethical F–S relationship has gradually been given more and more weight in traditional Confucian ethical thinking. Mengzi (*c.* 371–289 BC) did not directly declare that the F–S relationship is the most important of all social relationships, but he did claim that the love between the father and his son is more important than the love found in other relationships. Xunzi (*c.* 298–238 BC) however, not only elevated the F–S relationship but also incorporated into it that of the lord–minister, the elder–younger brother and the husband–wife to form what he termed the 'Great Foundation', and believed that all these four relationships 'share with Heaven and Earth the same organizing principle, and endure in the same form through all eternity' (9.15).

Xunzi developed this idea further and made the importance of the natural F–S relationship more tangible by drawing a parallel with the ruler–ruled relationship, stating that, 'The lord is the most exalted in the state. The father is the most exalted in the family. Where only one is exalted, there is order; where two are exalted, there is anarchy' (14:7). One scholar has even declared that 'if we say the important character of feudal piety is autocracy, then Xunzi was the earliest maker of the infant theory of using filial piety to support autocratic politics'.[11]

After Xunzi, scholars in the Han dynasty actually developed his fundamental principle of elevating the roles of both the father in a family and of the ruler in a state and transferred the expectation of filial piety to the ruler in place of the father, thus, exchanging the functions of father and ruler.

As for the presentation of the divine F–S relationship, this has different forms in the Old Testament and the New Testament. For example, in the OT the F–S relationship is presented in terms of God and human beings, or God and the Kings of Israel, and occasionally in the context of the personal relationship between God and individuals; in the NT, on the other hand, the ethical spiritual F–S relationship, such as the God–Jesus, God–men and Jesus–disciple, is the norm. The ethical F–S relationship between the Divine Father and the Divine Son is thus the most important theme of Christianity. Unlike Confucianism, which provides a moral reason for the hierarchy between father and son, Christianity bases the F–S relationship on theological grounds. For this reason J. D. Cohen argues that 'for Philo the idea of the superiority of parents to their children is in fact separable from, prior to, and indeed more fundamental than its philosophical rationale',[12] while the moral consideration of the F–S relationship remains integral to Christianity. Thus, as I. S. Gilhus states, despite the many possibilities for using family relationships as a metaphor, in mainstream Christianity the dominant model has been the F–S relationship.[13]

As a powerful example, St Paul clearly puts the ethical divine F–S relationship at the centre and foundation of Christian ethical relations, as in Ephesians where he affirms the F–S relationship between God and humans through God and Jesus Christ with the words,

> In love he [God] predestined us to be adopted as his sons through Jesus Christ, in accordance with his pleasure and will. (1:5)
>
> For through him we both have access to the Father by one Spirit. Consequently, you are no longer foreigners and aliens, but fellow-citizens with God's people and members of God's household, built on the foundation of the Apostles and prophets, with Christ Jesus himself as the chief cornerstone. (2:18–19)

In line with the Divine model, Paul directly encourages people to imitate this F–S in developing a relationship with God or Jesus Christ: 'Be imitators of God, therefore, as dearly loved children and live a life of love, just as Christ loved us and gave himself up for us as a fragrant offering and sacrifice to God' (5:1–2). 'Live as children of light (for the fruit of the light consists in all goodness, righteousness and truth), and find out what pleases the Lord' (5:8–9).

In addition, Paul uses the love–obedience relationship between God and Jesus as a model for the religious and secular relationship: Jesus took the Church as his body and gave all his love to it, therefore church members should love and be obedient to Jesus Christ as he was obedient to God; since obedience is Jesus' cardinal virtue, wives should in the same way submit to their husbands (5:22–4), as children should obey their parents (6:1–3) and slaves should obey their earthly masters (6:5–8). As the Father God gives all his kindness and love to the Son Jesus Christ, husbands should love their wives (5:25–32), fathers should bring their children to training and instruction in the Lord (6:4), and masters should treat their slaves justly, and not threaten them, since both have the same master in heaven (6:9).

In short, the ethical F–S relationship is essential in terms of the nature of the relationship itself, as well as for its study in both Confucian culture and Christian tradition; for this reason it necessarily becomes the positional crux of my comparison.

The Value of Comparison

As noted, comparison between Chinese culture and Western culture is necessary and has great significance in terms of developing dialogue as to shared values. Since Confucianism is the mainstream of Chinese culture and Christianity is the cornerstone of Western culture, then Chinese culture cannot be understood without understanding Confucianism, and nor can the Western spirit be interpreted without interpreting the spirit of Christianity. In the process of Confucianism's development, especially in the process of its realization in Chinese society, Xunzi has played a distinctive role; while in the process of Christianity's development within Western civilization, Pauline theory has had a profound influence.[14] In both the Xunzi's and Pauline theory, the F–S relationship can be a fruitful entry point through which to explore the whole of their respective theories. Consequently, comparison between the two expositions of the F–S relationship can pave the way for comparison between Confucian and Christian traditions as well as between Chinese and Western cultures.

Many scholars have expressed views about the core position of Confucianism in Chinese culture. For example, J. K. Fairbank argues that its influence has permeated every fibre of Chinese society through some two thousand years of steady development, with only partial interruption for brief periods. In his view, Confucianism has not only exerted a profound influence on political culture as well as on spiritual life, but has also in fact provided one of the great historic answers to the problem of social stability.[15] Walter H. Slote, in his *Psychocultural Dynamics within the Confucian Family*, states that, although all the societies under consideration have socio-religious derivatives in Buddhism, Daoism, various folk religions and to a lesser extent Christianity, Confucian values have been integrated into psychological substructures of the individual to a far greater degree than those of Taoist or Buddhism.[16] De Bary advances a similar idea in his preface to *East Asian Civilizations* (1988), where he argues that Daoism and Buddhism have exercised less of a role in defining those institutions and ideas most influential in the civil liberties of East Asia as a whole and their modern transformation than has Confucianism. Weiming Tu further states that, although Confucianism is not an organized religion, 'yet, it has exerted a profound influence on East Asian political culture as well as on East Asian spiritual life'. Indeed prior to the entry of the Western powers into East Asia in the mid-nineteenth century, Confucian modes of thought were so predominant in the art of governance, the form and content of elite education, and the moral discourse of the populace that China, Korea and Japan were all distinctively 'Confucian states'.[17]

DeVos's affirmation here is even clearer: Confucianism is an ethical religious tradition that has shaped the culture of China for 2,500 years, following which its influence subsequently spread to Korea, Japan and Vietnam. Moreover, although still not directly visible in the social consciousness of modern Japanese, it still profoundly shapes primary family life experiences.[18] Thus, while the position of Confucianism in modern Chinese society has been challenged greatly since the 'Cultural Revolution', its latter-day influence is still profound, especially since the recovery of Chinese traditional culture from the end of the 1980s. Therefore, the study of Confucianism, for Chinese studies, has not only historical significance, but also modern relevance.

Similarly, the relationship of Christianity in Western culture is a very close one. Before the Enlightenment, for example, everything, including science and philosophy, was the 'maid' and 'servant' of Christian practice. Although the status of human rationality and reason greatly increased as a result of the Enlightenment, the ingrained influence of Christianity on Western society remains very strong. Even the rapid development of science and technology, for example, acts as an affirmation of Christian beliefs, as in the case of philosophers and scientists who have used new discoveries in astronomy as arguments for the existence of God. They have suggested that the scientific theory that the universe exploded into being from nothing some 12–15 billion years ago (the 'Big-Bang' theory) is very readily compatible with Genesis, which describes how God created the universe out of nothing.

Similarly the view that the evolution of the universe seems to be 'finely tuned' for the emergence of life and mind (the anthropic principle) combines with belief in a divine designer.[19] At the same time research into religious experiences suggests that an awareness of some 'other power' above and beyond from everyday life is a surprisingly common feature of human experience.[20] Such issues remain controversial, though it is interesting that both the new arguments in the philosophy of religion and the study of religious experience have recently been included in A Level syllabuses in religion and philosophy. This means that the rapid development of science and technology has not completely eroded the profound influence of Christianity in people's lives.

The high status of Xunzi in Confucianism and of Paul in Christianity is obvious. Many scholars have provided strong evidence for the profound influence of Xunzi on Chinese culture, such as Liang Qichao (1873–1929), for example, who came to this understanding as early as the beginning of the twentieth century. He divided Confucianism into two groups, the Mengzi and the Xunzi Group. He believed that 'all of the masters of classical scriptures, from the paleography to modern script, are all the followers of Xunzi'.[21] From this uniting principle, Liang draws the following conclusion: 'Although academic ideas have changed frequently during the past two millennia, few departed significantly from the Xunzi group.' Another famous contemporary of Liang, Tan Sitong (1865–98), makes a similar comment: 'The system of government, which has lasted for two thousand years, was based on the structure of Qin government (221–207 BC) . . . While the content of the learning of the past two thousand years was based on the theory of Xunzi.'[22] Much earlier, a famous scholar of the Song Dynasty (960–1279), Zhu Xi (1130–1200), had already expressed the same idea: 'Simply because there was no-one who knew with clarity what the true way of humans was, the theory of Xunzi may have been flowed down from one generation to others for thousands of years.'[23] In the same way, modern scholars also realize the importance of Xunzi and his book. For example, Hu Shi identifies the important influence of Xunzi on Han Confucians,[24] while Han Demin demonstrates the influence of Xunzi on the Han political system and Song Neo-Confucian theories.[25] Indeed, it is Xunzi who emphasized that although human nature was evil, it could be corrected by 'moral cultivation of self'. This, together with his absorption of Mohism, Daoism and Legalism, made Confucianism a theory that focused more upon humans and human society, thereby developing further its practical tradition.[26]

Xunzi was not viewed as the second sage after Confucius in Chinese history, and was even unfairly treated as a 'small man' or cruel man after he tried, extremely sharply, to protect Confucius' idea from the misunderstandings of various Confucian groups, especially after the stinging and merciless critique of Mengzi. Xunzi should actually have been regarded as a sage, like Confucius. In the last chapter of the book of *Xunzi*, his disciple left us the following sign:

> Those who offer persuasions say: Xun Qing[27] was not the equal of Confucius. This is not so . . . Xun Qing cherished in his heart the mind of a great sage, which had to be concealed under the pretense of madness and presented to the world as stupidity . . . Students of today can obtain the transmitted doctrines and remaining teachings of Xun Qing in sufficient detail to serve as a model and pattern, the paradigm and gnomon, that establish the standard of the whole world. His presence had an effect like that of a spirit, and wherever he passed by he produced transformation. If one closely inspects his good works, one would see that even Confucius did not surpass him. Because the age does not examine things in detail or judge matters carefully, so it says that he was no sage.

Xunzi devoted all his wisdom and strength to education through Confucianism, his contribution thus significantly shaping Chinese social political structure through his excellent work, in turn influencing the scholars of Confucianism of the former Han Dynasty, as many Western scholars have confirmed. John Knoblack for example, states that:

> Like Aristotle, he [Xunzi] molded successive ages . . . Xunzi taught a whole generation of scholars whose traditions of learning dominated the intellectual world of Han dynasty. Through the filiations of master and student, he determined the Han interpretation of ritual and its role in government, of the Classic of poetry, of the role of music, of the nature, of education and of the lessons of history. More important still, the classical texts, understood within the framework of his philosophy, were the source of inspiration for countless thinkers, government officials, and scholars. Thus, his thought was absorbed into the whole *Weltanschauung* that then shaped the Chinese world, and through its incorporation into the structure of Han dynasty institutions, it persisted for many centuries thereafter.[28]

John Knoblock is not however the only scholar in the West to give Xunzi this elevated position in Chinese philosophy. H. H. Dubs, another English translator of the book of Xunzi, states:

> This philosopher (Xunzi) lived in the latter half of the third century BC. He was the last of the great thinkers of China's earliest period of creative thought. His systematic defense of Confucian ideals against the persistent attacks of varied types of opponents was a significant factor in the ultimate dominance of those ideas in Chinese thought, while the features which he emphasized and the interpretations he gave became determinative influences in the later Confucian orthodoxy. However, this result occurred in spite of other features in his thought regarded as unorthodox by later Confucianists.[29]

Thus Xunzi not only devoted himself to the interpretation of Confucianism, but also tried his utmost to put its principle into practice, in every area of Chinese thought, as Weiming Tu also comments: Xunzi conscientiously transformed the Confucian project into a realistic and systematic inquiry into the human condition with special reference to ritual and authority; his penetrating insight into the shortcoming of virtually all the major currents of thought propounded by his fellow thinkers helped to establish the Confucian school as a forceful political and social persuasion.[30]

The realization of this great project was thus very influential, according to Liu Xiang (77–76 BC), in that Lanling, where Xunzi held a chief position in the local government, has since produced many scholars who were schooled under the influence of Sun Qing. Even today the elders of the city continue to praise Xunzi, saying that the men of Lanling like to adopt the name Qing to honour the example of Sun Qing. In the same way, Liu Xiang valued the book of *Xunzi* highly: 'his book is comparable to the *Records* and *Commentaries*, and it may properly serve as a model,' and goes on to argue that 'if Sun Qing's theory could have been practiced by a lord of men, this lord of men probably would have become True King'.[31]

In the same way, 'Paul remains the pole star for him who would navigate the waters of early Christianity.'[32] He 'has not only been an important influence on Christianity, but in a very real sense he was its founder. He could be called the first Christian.'[33] Although Paul was not a systematic theologian, he laid the foundations for systematic theology, partly by the unwearying mental vitality he brought to every problem he encountered in the course of his Christian activity and thinking, and partly through a natural capacity for seeing both sides of a question and for holding them together, in such a way that they became fused into a unified scheme of thought.[34] Indeed in late antiquity, Augustine energized Christianity through a new understanding of Pauline theology, which came to dominate most of the Middle Ages: 'In turn, few will need reminding that it was preeminently the influence of Paul's theology which shaped the Reformation.'[35] This view is supported by Jeffrey L. Sheler who opines that Paul's 'impact on the shaping of post-Easter faith makes the search for ever clearer portraits of the man a worthy endeavor'.[36]

Pauline teaching thus occupies a fundamental position in the development of Christianity, but it is nevertheless highlighted that 'if the apostle Paul went astray in his theology, then certainly the Protestant church, if not the entire Christian church, is in serious error because it has primarily followed Paul's lead in its theological formulations'.[37] In line with this, some scholars have condemned Pauline ethical teaching, such as, for example, Neil Elliott, who suggests that the basis for the slaves' [South Carolina] catechism is the biblical injunction to slaves to give obedience to their master 'as to the Lord', an injunction that appears in the NT under the name of Paul.[38] His 'I permit no women to teach or hold authority over a man' (1 Tim 2:12) and his admonition to wives to accept subordination to the husband (Eph 5:22) should be held responsible for being the strongest weapon for the Massachusetts Bay Colony's suppression of women Puritan dissenters in 1637. Likewise, his attitude towards Jews became an excuse for the Nazis to kill millions of innocent people. All these events demonstrate that 'the usefulness of the Pauline letters to systems of domination and oppression is nevertheless clear and palpable'.[39]

It has been confirmed that in the early phase of growth of the Christian church, Paul the man had a stature second only to that of Jesus himself.[40] Not only do Paul's extant letters form the main body of the NT outside the gospels and Acts, but they also contain his development of the teachings of Jesus and his elaboration of their application to the church and the individual. He was a pioneer in formulating the doctrines and the ethical implications of the gospel. Many scholars have argued that Paul along with others turned the Jewish prophet Jesus into a Gentile God and made Christianity what it has been ever since.[41]

Written in response to requests, or as solutions to different problematic situations experienced directly or indirectly by their author, and addressed to a variety of readerships, the doctrines and practices proposed in Pauline letters are eminently practical in the real secular world. Some of Paul's letters were general in nature, contributing to the universal understanding of Christianity, while others addressed more particular matters of concern, giving Christian models for action, especially for the application of the general doctrines of Christianity. This double function was crucial for the success of the spread of Christianity throughout the known world. Although not one of the twelve who were direct disciples of Jesus, Paul was actually treated as the thirteenth. After his experience of revelation when he met with the resurrected Jesus on the road to Damascus, Paul, a traditional Jew, previously a persecutor of the followers of Jesus, was transformed into the leading missionary of early Christianity and the founder of churches in Asia Minor and Greece. Once won to Jesus Christ, Paul devoted all his emotion, wisdom, energy and strength to the cause of spreading the good news of Jesus Christ throughout the Gentile world, a cause to which he remained faithful unto death. As he proclaimed, 'I can do all things in him who strengthens me' (Phil 4:12–13).

Nothing could prevent Paul from holding high the banner of Christ, neither the outward turmoil in painful circumstances, nor the – often legitimate – needs and desires of the 'inner man'. In his own words, there was nothing in creation 'able to separate us from the love of God in Christ Jesus our Lord' (Rom 8:39). Paul not only preached the good news of Jesus Christ to his own nation, but also to Gentiles beyond the Jewish pale. His zeal led him not only to the far-flung corners of Europe, but also throughout Asia Minor. The men and women he won to the nascent church included both Jews and Gentiles. Paul's career is so vast that Acts devotes more than half its space to the record of it. Although no other external literary source refers to Paul, the

NT contains a wealth of material on him: 'for we possess not only first hand sources in Paul's own letters to the churches, but also an important and lengthy account of his missionary career by the author of Acts.'[42]

In short, the profound historical influence of Pauline ethical teaching on the F–S relationship is not only of cardinal importance in Christian society, but also in this comparative study where Xunzi and Paul are chosen as its representative components. Many reasons may be listed for this but the following six are the most significant:

First, both inherited deep rooted traditions while bringing them to a new level; in both cases their theories were not entirely appreciated and accepted, and were disliked by some within those traditions. On the one hand, Paul has been the subject of great controversy, has caused much dissension and hatred, and has suffered much misunderstanding at the hands of both friends and enemies.[43] On the other, Xunzi has shouldered an undeserved burden of shame and poor reputation for centuries, when his theory was used and stolen by the later Confucians.[44]

Secondly, both were originally beneficiaries of different cultures in their own age. As a citizen of Zhao, Xunzi left his country and went to Jixia Academic Palace, where he studied the ideas of various groups, thus familiarizing himself with the popular theories of that time, as well as mastering Confucianism. Thus, Xunzi built his theory on the base of Confucianism, with obvious contributions from Daoism, Mohism, the Yin-Yang School, Legalism and other academic schools, resulting in a synthesis of the conflicting currents of interpretation within Confucian circles in his day, as well as a clear portrayal of the non-Confucian theories of the time'.[45] Guo Moruo describes this characteristic of Xunzi very well: 'Xunzi was the last great master among those famous Scholars of the Pre-Qin Dynasty era. He not only made a comprehensive summary of Confucianism, but also of the "Hundreds Schools"'.[46] Paul, on the other hand, was a member of a staunch Jewish family, living in a colony of the Roman Empire with the status of a Roman citizen. He was not only well versed in both Greek culture and the cultural background of Jerusalem, but also well travelled in different cultural areas. According to Acts, Paul was involved in three great missionary journeys, during which he preached to both Jews and Gentiles in Greek and Aramaic (Acts 21:37–40). It was perhaps for this reason that his teaching gained in stature, in that it encompassed or reflected the values of both Jewish and Greco-Roman culture. As Joubert points out, Paul not only shared the common sense knowledge available to most people of his time, but he was also acquainted with the meaning-structures peculiar to the Jews and the Romans.[47] In this sense James D. G. Dunn claims that Paul is one of the most fascinating figures in all Middle Eastern and Western history in terms of his diversity.[48]

Thirdly, both are revolutionary figures despite being conservative and deeply-rooted in their respective traditions. For example, like Confucius, who considered himself a 'transmitter' rather than an 'inventor' of *ru*, Xunzi grafted the new order onto the old, proposing that all the present has roots in the past; that is to say, the roots of humanity both past, present, future are grounded in its deepest needs for belonging and communication. In line with this, we can retrieve the meaning of the past by breathing vitality into seemingly outmoded rituals; thus, in line with Jesus Christ, who declared that he had not come to abolish the Law or the Prophets, but to fulfil them, Paul also intended to transform the traditional values of Judaism into the new movement of Christianity: 'For everything that was written in the past was written to us, so that through endurance and the encouragement of the Scriptures we might have hope' (Rom 15:4). From this perspective, it is clear that Xunzi and Paul tried to keep their own traditions intact, and declared that they were themselves the heirs of their own traditions. In this sense, we can say that, like Xunzi, Paul's personality and theory possessed an element of conservatism.

However, both of them were creative scholars who flew their own colours in their own intellectual histories. The evolutionary nature of their theories is manifested in the following: both tried to break down certain principles of their own traditions. For example, Xunzi took the maxim 'human nature is evil' as the base of his theory – the exact opposite of Mengzi's traditional declaration that 'human nature is good', while Paul's image of Jesus as the elder brother and the head of the church, were also alien to the old tradition. Meanwhile both of them infused new messages into old traditions: Xunzi combined morality and law to create a new conception of *li* (ritual), thereby giving to this conception the characteristics of both Confucianism and Legalism; whereas Paul redefined the relationship between law and faith and made faith more important than the law. Through his new interpretation of the law, the new spirit of Christianity was poured into the traditional framework. By contrasting law with faith, Paul overcame the particularity of legalistic Judaism, using the universal truth of a law-free Christianity.[49]

Fourthly, both were responsible for putting their traditions on a practical platform. Xunzi made a unique contribution to the development of Confucianism, bringing it to a new practical level,[50] based on its systematic and detailed examination and integrating *li* (rituals) and *fa* (law) together. Indeed, according to some researchers, although the ideas of Xunzi did not constitute the dominant source of guidance for government in his contemporary Qin Dynasty (221–207 BC), the Chinese law system from the Han Dynasty (206 BC–220 AD) to the Qing Dynasty (1644–1911) was guided by precisely this integration. This integrating work began from the Han Dynasty, and was further developed in the Wei-Jin Dynasties (220–420), and in the penal code of the Tang Dynasty (618–906); as the model of Chinese law, the penal code of the Tang Dynasty demonstrated that the idea of law was based on the standard of *li*.[51] Similarly there is also a common agreement that Paul is a prince of thinkers and that, without his great efforts, Christianity would not have become a universal religion, as argued by, for example, Gerd Theissen, who suggests that it was Paul and other protagonists who led Christianity from a purely Jewish movement to a movement which involved both Jews and Gentiles. It was Paul who transformed the primitive Christian movement from a rural movement into an urban middle-class movement; and it was Paul who transformed early Christianity from a movement regrouping the homeless poor and excluding the rich into one that appealed to poor and rich alike. It was difficult for the rich to join the early Christian movement before Paul's involvement. Paul and Barnabas are examples of men 'wise, powerful and of noble birth' (1 Cor 1:26).[52] Through a detailed examination of the divergent rankings of Pauline Christian church members, Wayne A. Meeks suggests that it was as an urban cult that Christianity spread through the empire, and that the earliest substantial evidence of its formation comes from the documents associated with Paul. A good number of scholars have argued the importance of the Pauline concept of justification by faith and stressed the extent to which his opinion on law influenced Christianity and the Protestant interpretation of the NT.[53] Meanwhile, C. F. Jones has argued that Paul as a Roman citizen, was fully integrated into the political texture of the Roman Empire and thereby enabled the absorption of Christianity into the fabric of social culture and thus paved the way for its spread throughout the whole world.

Fifthly, both Paul and Xunzi were men of great dedication. Both of them served their own beliefs passionately and selflessly. For them, this was all that mattered, and so no compromise of any kind could be contemplated with those whom they considered their enemies. For this reason, Paul could endure persecution from 'the world' (2 Cor 11:23–33) without any hint of bitterness; but 'when the gospel is attacked directly or indirectly through his own apostleship, he indignantly strikes back';[54] 'especially in Galatians and in 2 Cor 10–13, Paul uses sarcasm, irony, and bitter denunciation, including curses, against those who have attacked him and his gospel'.[55] In short, he let nothing stop him doing the work of Christianity: hard work, exhaustion, suffering, poverty, danger of death' (1 Cor 4:9–13; 2 Cor 4:8f; 6:4–10; 11:23–7).[56] In the same way, Xunzi kept resolute by inner power: 'the exigencies of time and place and consideration of personal profit cannot influence him, cliques and coteries cannot sway him, and the whole world cannot deter him'. He was born to follow the way of Confucius, and he will die following it (*Xunzi* 1.14). He gave those whom he considered to be the enemies of the way of Confucius a severe attack. And indeed his fiercest outbursts of indignation were directed against anybody who tried to turn the way of Confucius to wrong ends. As John Knoblock has recognized, never was criticism so directly aimed at particular heroes of the conventional, officially sanctioned Confucianism of the imperial period.[57] No one criticized other scholars as harshly as did Xunzi, but for this he paid a heavy price: unfair treatment of his own theory for two thousand years, which made Liu Xiang fall into a torrent of tears.[58]

For the sake of the propagation of their teachings, both Paul and Xunxi travelled to many countries, not caring what difficulties they met, living only for the preaching of their ideals for the rest of their lives. According to Liu Xiang's analysis, Xunzi, after finishing his studies in the Jixia Academy of Qi, spent a large number of the subsequent years visiting rulers of different states in order to persuade these men of power and influence them to adopt his theory in their political practices. Paul was born at Tarsus in Cilicia of a Jewish family of the tribe of Benjamin around AD 10. Similarly, around AD 34, after becoming convinced on the road to Damascus that the risen Lord had opened his mind to the truth of the Christian faith and revealed that he had been chosen to be the apostle to the Gentles, Paul dedicated his life to serving the Christ who had personally chosen him as his follower (Phil 3:12).[59] After becoming the servant of Jesus Christ, Paul devoted much time to his missionary travels. Indeed, before he was arrested in Jerusalem and imprisoned at Caesarea Palestinae in AD 58, he had completed three missionary journeys. Thus, up to his imprisonment in Rome and his martyrdom, he had visited different continents: Europe and Asia.[60]

Lastly, both Paul and Xunzi were men of inner struggle as well as men who possessed internal peace. Unlike Mengzi, who considered human nature to be inherently 'good', Xunzi saw it as 'evil', and insisted that this evil could only be eradicated through the full moral cultivation and social education of the populace; therefore, it follows that conflict between 'desire' and 'morality' is inevitable in the life of every man, whether sage, ancient king or commoner. In the same way, Paul viewed human nature as itself sharing the struggle between good and evil; creation itself, he writes, knows the pain and also the hope of a woman in childbirth (Rom 8:22). 'Conflict, struggle in the inward man and outward situations, characterized not only the pre-Christian but also Christian Paul.' 'Whether Rom 7 is to be reckoned as autobiographical or as typical, the chapter shows a profound insight into the struggle between the law as external code and the inward desires and frustrations of an earnest and serious soul.'[61] Moreover, Paul insisted that this cosmic struggle will go on until Christ 'delivers the kingdom to God the Father after destroying every rule and every authority and power (1 Cor 15:24)'.[62] However, both Xunzi and Paul were also men of inward peace. The aim of Xunzi's theory was to establish a harmonious state within the human heart, and a peaceful society and world. For a harmonious body, his focus was the 'art of controlling the vital breath and nourishing the mind' (*Xunzi* 2.4), and for the order of society, the art of government and the way of humanity. In the same way, Paul was a man who knew an inner centre of peace and joy 'in Christ', so that nothing 'in all creation' was 'able to separate him from the love of God in Christ Jesus our Lord' (Rom 8:39).

In short, while there are many differences between Pauline teaching and Xunzi's theory, there are also very many similarities between these two great figures and their doctrines. A comparison between them can therefore only be instructive.

Cultural Comparison from the Religious and Core Ethical Relationship Perspectives

The primary purpose of the present research then, is to present a cultural comparison between Chinese and Western culture from a religious perspective. Religion is not only the expression of human spirituality, but also one of the cornerstones of all cultures; thus no cultural comparison can be done successfully and thoroughly without a comparative study of religion. Comparison between Chinese and Western culture should therefore begin with and focus on the mainstream religions in China and the West. It may be assumed that through religious comparison, not only can the essential differences and similarities between Chinese and Western cultures be discovered, but also the potential conflicts between them. Moreover, a religious comparison, as the necessary primary basis for cultural comparative work, could be of great advantage in producing a new united human culture. Indeed, undertaking a cultural comparative study via the relevant religions is perhaps one of the most effective ways of increasing cultural understanding, and from that, cultural transformation or reformation.

The present research also aims to present a case for religious comparison between Confucianism and Christianity from the perspective of their core ethical relationships. Though there is more than one single religion in both Chinese and Western cultures, Confucianism is nevertheless the dominant stream of thought in Chinese culture as is Christianity in Western culture; so it seems fair to use them to make religious comparisons. Although there are many other important topics in both teachings, the issue of ethics is the essential core of Confucianism and the main thrust of Christianity. It is therefore feasible to draw ethical comparisons between them.

A further aim is to present a case for ethical comparison between Confucianism and Christianity from the perspective of the F–S relationship pattern as presented in the teachings of Xunzi's and Paul, since the practice of both Confucian and Christian ethics is based on its practice in divine or secular contexts. The teachings of both of these great figures resulted from doctrinally and historically validated adaptations of their respective traditions, and the relevance of each has been justifiably introduced in conformity with the spirit of those traditions. Therefore, comparison between Xunzi's and Paul's ethical perspective on the F–S relationship is a major goal of this work. We may assume that comparison of the ethical F–S relationship in the teachings of Xunzi and Paul will help us not only to come to a better understanding of the core doctrines and development of Confucianism and Christianity, but also to further effect linkages between the two traditions.

The final but no less significant aim is to examine both teachings of the F–S ethical relationship to affirm pragmatic attitudes to change, and thence possibly to adjust traditional Confucianism to meet the needs of a developing society in a way that will be beneficial to contemporary Chinese social practice, and at the same time will provide a number of valid arguments for the adaptation of Chinese culture to meet the challenges of the modern age.

Note: for a review of the literature used in this study, please refer to the Appendix, 'Research Scholarship in Christian and Confucian Studies'.

CHAPTER ONE

The Origin of Xunzi's Secular Father–Son Relationship

Xunzi's theory of the secular F–S relationship cannot be separated from its cultural background. It is a synthesis of Confucian and other theories, and has in turn become part of Chinese culture and its later development. This chapter therefore focuses on the cultural background of pre-Xunzi Confucianism as it relates to Xunzi's Secular F–S Relationship, the Pre-Xunzi Confucian Concept of Filial Piety and its development in Xunzi's theory, and the philosophical origin of Xunzi's ethical F–S relationship.

The Cultural Background to Pre-Xunzi Confucian Father–Son Theory

Xunzi was a synthesizer of pre-Qin Dynasty teaching, and there are a great many creative thoughts on philosophical and moral thinking within his teaching. However, his idea of the F–S relationship, despite its creative aspects, was inherited from earlier Confucian thought and has deep roots within it. This can be seen from the development of the status of the F–S relationship and that of the content of filial piety in the pre-Confucianism period.

The father–son relationship in ancient Chinese society before Confucius

In traditional Chinese culture, 'family' was not a term that referred just to the household, but a broad concept that included not only living family members (husband and wife, parents and children and so on), but also deceased former generations, such as distant ancestors and even the originator of the clan; not only dead ancestors – the passing part of a family chain – but also unborn children: the continuation of the family line. In the same way, the F–S relationship was not purely one between a biological father and his son, but also a relationship between forefathers and later generations. In this sense, the father was not an individual person, but a living agent of his ancestors and a guardian of his children; in the same way, the son was not an independent human being, but both the property and the successor of his parents, as well as the producer of the next generation and the continuer of the family chain. This concept is denoted by the use of the Chinese characters *zu* and *jia*.

The Chinese character *zu* means 'ancestor', 'founder' or 'originator', while *jia* refers to the 'family', 'household' or 'home'. In its broad usage, *zu* is primarily presented in terms such as *zuxian* (forefathers), *zuzong* (ancestor of the clan) and *zufu* (one's own grandfather). *Jia* is usually linked to *jiating*, *jiazu* and *guojia*, where *jiating* means one's family and household, *jiazu* one's kinship clan and *guojia* one's country or state. From the meanings of these two words and their phrases, it can be argued that, in the traditional Chinese mind, the ancestor embodied not only the identity of one's own grandfather but also the identity of the originator of one's clan; the family was identified with one's own household as well as with the household of the whole clan, and indeed even with the whole country.

According to Han Demin, the constitutive characteristic of the Three Dynasties[1] is that the state resided in the family, in which the political life of the state was connected with familial consanguineous ethics, which had profound political significance.[2] In fact, in ancient Chinese society, there was no separation either of one's family from one's clan, or of one's own father or grandfather from the clan's ancestors.

> The basic social unit of the Confucian system was the well-ordered family. The family was seen as a microcosm of the socio-political order; the wise father was model for the wise ruler or minister, and dutiful children were the models for properly submissive subjects who knew their place, their role, and their obligations to others.[3]

Nevertheless, from observation of the practices of ancient Chinese religion, it is evident that the position of a father in the ancestral worship rituals before Confucius was never as important as that of the clan ancestor.[4] Indeed, Benjamin Schwartz has described this 'orientation to ancestor worship' as 'central to the entire development of Chinese civilization'.[5] More than that, according to Patricia Buckley Ebrey, in ancient China the ancestor was not only integral to the religious imagination, but also central to the understandings of spiritual realms and of the place of man in the cosmos.[6]

What then is the precise meaning of this concept of the ancestor in ancient Chinese thought? According to Zha Changguo, the object of filial piety in the Western Zhou Dynasty (*c.* 1045–771 BC) involved both *shenzu* (a male ancestor) and *kaobi* (a female ancestor).[7] This in itself provides evidence that in ancient times (even at the time of the early Western Zhou Dynasty) ancestors still included both male and female, demonstrating that female ancestors perhaps had the same status as the male. However, the worship of *bizu* was soon replaced by the worship of *zuxian* or *zuzong* in the later Western Zhou Dynasty, while the female aspect of the ancestor declined, even vanished. This displacement thus indicates the loss of status and power for the female, and the resulting increase of the male in power and social status.

Hence, in the later Western Zhou Dynasty, the male controlled all aspects of authority and honour in life. As the male was the leader of the family, the authority and power of the father became absolute over the mother and the children, so that 'the rights of women and children were minimal'.[8] Although a male-centred *Ru* tradition had existed in China from very ancient times, before Confucius and his followers developed its doctrine, the F–S relationship was less important in social and family life than that of the ancestor–offspring; in parallel with this situation, the father had not yet attained a status in pre-Confucian China that was as important as that of the ancestors. This characteristic can be seen further from the original meaning of *xiao* in the early *Ru* tradition of ancient Chinese society.

The original meaning of xiao

The most important virtue for linking different generations in early *Ru* tradition is termed *xiao* (filial piety) and for linking the same generations *ti* (brother love). Interestingly, the original meaning of filial piety can be seen from observation of the word itself from a pictographic perspective.

The Chinese character of filial piety *xiao* is made up of two parts: the upper part *lao* and the lower part *zi*. The upper part *lao* signifies 'an old man' while the lower part *zi* signifies 'a son' or a child. Moreover, according to *shuowei Jiezi* (the first Chinese dictionary that was edited in AD100) this character indicates that an old man is supported by his son. Meanwhile, according to its implied meaning, *xiao* has an equal meaning with *fang*, which means 'following' or 'obeying'; filial piety therefore implies that a child follows his elder.

Based on these two interpretations, it is clear that the original meaning of filial piety is not merely defined as the virtue of serving one's parents, but also of serving the old. Nevertheless, from He Ping's viewpoint, this concept was not presented in this way until the Zhou Dynasty,[9] where its meaning was further extended from a family notion to a socio-political term, viewing society and the state as an 'enlarged family'. Filial piety had thus been related to the living parents,[10] although its primary focus was first and foremost upon the ancestors. Accordingly, serving one's parents (whether alive or dead) had not yet become a virtue, and hence it is different from the father-central notion that was advocated by Confucianism.[11]

Another element of 'filial piety' is connected with posterity, and with reproducing successive generations. Thus, according to Zhou Yutong, the concept is closely related to worship of the sexual organs,[12] as is also argued by Song Jinlan, who states that the meaning of filial piety is equal to *yao*, and that *yao* can be changed to *jiao*. As *jiao* implies sexual intercourse, 'the original picture of *xiao* gives the meaning of intercourse between the male and the female, and also of the reproduction of posterity'.[13] In line with this, Guo Moruo examines the original meaning of *zu* and *bi* in the oracle inscriptions of the Shang Dynasty (*c.* sixteenth to eleventh century BC), concluding that the pictographic character of *bi* represents the vulva of the female, and that of *zu* the penis of the male. Therefore, it is possible that the custom of the worship of *bizu* in ancient China reveals an important historical fact: the worship of female and male ancestors developed from the worship of the vulva and penis, which was due to their role as organs from which new life can be produced; consequently, the spiritual meaning of ancestor worship is 'respect for life and the power of life'.[14]

It is clear that two meanings were included in the original content of filial piety. The first of these was virtue (moral duty) in worshipping the ancestor and showing respect to the originator of the clan; the second meant 'to have' or 'to produce' posterity. We can see this character from the *Ru* classic *Shi Jing*, or *The Book of Songs*, for example. According to Xiao Qunzhong, filial piety has three basic meanings in *The Book of Songs*: (1) reproducing children and emulating the ancestor's meritorious achievements, (2) connecting one's behaviour to the continuity of the family line with moral virtues, and (3) offering sacrifices to one's ancestors to ask their blessing on the flourishing of one's descendants.[15] These three meanings can actually however be summarized as two: on the one hand, filial piety was linked to the root of the family by which ancestral worship was under focus; the songs 'O, my great deceased father, I will devote my filial piety to you forever and ever'[16] and 'Now I lead them to appear before my enshrined father, to sacrifice and present their offerings'[17] belong to this aspect. On the other hand, filial piety was connected with the continuity of the family, with posterity production as its content; the songs 'Thou hast backers and helpers – they are men of filial piety and moral integrity'[18] and 'Ah! Ah! Our Meritorious ancestor! Permanent are the blessings coming from him, repeatedly conferred without end . . . They have come to you in this place'[19] are in line with this meaning.

Shi Jing reflects the beliefs and customs of the pre-Confucius era. With typical conservatism, pre-Xunzi Confucianism carried on both meanings of the original concept of filial piety: first, 'having more male posterity in order to carry on one's family continuity' is still the most important task of a filial son: 'There are three things which are no part of filial piety, and not providing for posterity is the greatest of them.'[20] Notwithstanding that ancestor worship was also a very important part of filial piety. *Li Ji* (*The Book of Rites*) gives a good summary of this: 'All things originate from heaven; man originates from his (great) ancestor . . . in the sacrifices at the border there was an expression of gratitude to the source (of their prosperity) and a going back in their thoughts to the beginning.'[21]

However, some developments, namely connecting the father with the ancestor, had already taken place in pre-Xunzi Confucianism, which on the one hand brought the dead father into the line of one's ancestors, and on the other suggested that a son was supposed to treat his living father as a potential ancestor. Hence, the father's authority is not conceived of as originating from the father himself, but as springing from the ancestor and as being strongly reinforced by that ancestor. This is because in the unending chain of generations the father represents to the son the immediate link in the ancestral chain.[22] Thus, the father, while alive, acts as agent of them; upon death he becomes one of the ancestors, whose influence remains the most potent factor in guiding the son's life. Even if the content of filial piety is occasionally linked with the serving of parents, in that service the parents are the living agent of the ancestor; this means that filial piety is never consciously treated as a virtue of a son.

The Cultural Background of Xunzi's Secular Father—Son Relationship

Therefore, the original meaning of filial piety was neither linked to reverence of one's own parents nor a particular virtue of a son subordinate to his father; it was Confucius himself who started to connect filial piety to the virtue of a son. After Confucius' advocacy of the doctrine of serving one's parents, especially one's living parents, these ideas became embedded in the Confucian doctrine of filial piety, and gradually became part of the daily life of traditional Chinese society. Moreover, there was a clear intention to use filial piety as not only the duty to serve one's biological parents, which is to interpret filial piety in a familial context, but also the conduct of serving older generations in general (interpreted in a social context). Indeed, according to Hsieh Yuwei, Chinese society was built up on the basis of filial piety, which has penetrated into every corner of Chinese life and society, permeating all the activities of the Chinese people:

> The doctrine of filial piety was recognized as primary among Chinese ethical principles, with the virtue thus shaped also taking the paramount position in Chinese morality . . . One can hardly understand Chinese ethics, and to some extent even Chinese political activities, if one cannot grasp the true importance of this filial doctrine with its practical application in Chinese society.[23]

Pre-Xunzi Confucianism and the father–son relationship

The effect of Pre-Xunzi Confucianism on the F–S relationship can be seen in the first two great figures of early Confucianism, Confucius himself and Mengzi, who linked filial piety to the virtue of a son, and took the natural F–S relationship as the basis of the other four relationships of *Wulun* (Five Relationships). As we have already seen, filial piety is not merely a familial notion used in connection with the parent–child relationship, but is also a clan and social notion used with reference to the old–young relationship before Confucius. The following description from *Li Ji* (*The Book of Rituals*), for example, was the reflection of the Ancient Golden Age: 'When the Grand Course[24] was pursued, a public and common spirit ruled all under the sky . . . Thus men did not love their parents only, nor treat as children only their own sons.'[25] Confucius thus not only inherited the spirit of Zhou rites, but further changed its focus in accordance with new requirements resulting from the changing social environment.

When the Spring and Autumn Era (770–476 BC) entered its later period, the base of the old patriarchal system was almost lost: the kinship clan increasingly declined in power, while the power of the father became stronger, and finally became unparalleled among all the family relationships. Following the changes in society, Confucius (551–479 BC) reflected on changes in family relationships and extended the content of filial piety from its original emphasis on the dead clan ancestor to a new emphasis on the living parents. Through focusing the contents of filial piety in its familial meaning and putting filial piety as a special virtue of a son, Confucius promoted the F–S relationship to a very high status:

> A man of all-comprehensive virtue does not transgress what is due from him in all the spheres beyond himself, and it is the same with a (truly) filial son. Therefore, a son of all-comprehensive virtue serves his parents as he serves Heaven, and serves Heaven as he serves his parents. Hence a (truly) filial son does all that can be done for his parent.[26]

Unlike the Buddha and the Christ, who focused their attention on how to enable humankind to attain the divine state, Confucius focused his whole attention on how the perfect state can be reached in a secular society. He taught humanity to respect spiritual beings but to keep aloof from them, saying that this 'may be called wisdom' (6:20). It is said, 'The subjects on which the Master did not talk, were – extraordinary things, feats of strength, disorder, and spiritual beings' (7:21). Confucius no longer stressed the subject of an afterlife and minimized filial piety to the dead: 'While you are not able to serve men, how can you serve their spirits? . . . While you do not know life, how can you know about death?' (11:11). Instead, he devoted all his attention to the continuity of regular family life by focusing on the secular relationship between parents and children, especially between father and son (2:6; 4:18; 4:19). It is notable that in some places where Confucius mentions filial piety the objective of the relationship is not only always focused on the F–S element, but also that of the ruler–minister and the older brother–younger brother, with particular reference to the son:

> Zi Xia asked what filial piety was. The Master said, 'The difficulty is with the countenance. If when their elders have any troublesome affairs, the young take the toil (burden) of them, and if, (when) the young have wine and food, they set them before their elders, is this to be considered filial piety?' (2:8)

At other times, however, the emphasis is directly upon the F–S relationship: 'While a man's father is alive, look at the bent of his will; when his father is dead, look at his conduct. If for three years he does not alter from the way of his father, he may be called filial' (1:11). Consequently, the rites for the dead, such as three years' mourning, were in Confucius' opinion no longer for the remote ancestor, but for one's own dead parents: 'When Mang I asked what filial piety was, the Master told him, "It is not being disobedient". He further explained: "That parents, when alive, should be served according to propriety; that when dead, they should be buried according to propriety; and that they should be sacrificed according to propriety"'(2:5).

Mengzi continued Confucius' emphasis on the secular F–S relationship and further enhanced it as the basis of the other four relationships of the *Wulun*; namely, the five relationships of ruler and minister, father and son, husband and wife, elder brother and younger brother, and friends. Unlike other later Confucians, whose emphasis on these five relationships was directed mainly to the first three, Mengzi gave to the F–S relationship the most important place: 'Of services, which is the greatest? The service of parents is the greatest' (4A:19.1). He even used the virtue of the filial piety of a son to judge whether that man was a man or not. He says, 'If one could not get the hearts of his parents he could not be considered a man, and that if he could not get to an entire accord with his parents, he could not be considered a son' (4A:28).

When Mengzi talked about filial piety, however, usually the emphasis was not particularly directed at the F–S relationship but that of the child–parent. His emphasis on the F–S relationship can be seen clearly from the following: it is to be noted that first, there was no particular discussion of other parent–child relationships, such as mother–son or father–daughter, but rather discussions which particularly point to the F–S pattern. For example,

> Between father and son, there should be no reproving admonitions (as) to what is good. Such reproofs lead to alienation, and in alienation, there is nothing more inauspicious. (4A:18)

> Of all (that) which a filial son can attain, there is nothing greater than his honouring his parents. And of what can be attained in the honouring of one's parents, there is nothing greater than the nourishing of them with the whole empire. (5A:4)

Secondly, although he did not directly stress the first three male relationships of the *Wulun*, he did give greater attention to them in saying:

Ministers will serve their sovereign, cherishing the principles of benevolence and right-eousness; sons will serve their fathers, and younger brothers will serve their elder brothers, in the same way . . . and so, sovereign and minister, father and son, elder brother and younger, abandoning the thought of profit, will cherish the principles of benevolence and righteousness, and carry out all their intercourse upon them. (6B:5)

All this suggests that the role of mother, although important to the children, is not as important as that of the father. Many scholars have reached a similar conclusion regarding the importance of the F–S relationship. As Jiao Guocheng points out, for example, it is the *Ru* tradition that puts the heaviest emphasis on kinship relation-ship and family love; nonetheless, among these kinship relationships, the most important is the parent–child relationship, especially that of father and son.[27] Further, a modern Chinese sociologist, Fei Xiaotong, states, 'The developing line of the Chinese family is solely along the single father's side.'[28] Slote here provides an expla-nation: 'In its traditional format, Confucianism was rigidly authoritarian and bolstered by a social matrix that was essentially totalitarian. As such, the legal power of the male and rulers approached the absolute.'[29] Although Slote refers here to Confucianism after rather than before Han times, as Han Confucianism was the devel-opment of former Confucianism, this can nevertheless be taken as a reference to pre-Qin Confucianism. Han Demin on the other hand demonstrates the importance of the father rather than the mother from a more reasonable perspective: the Chinese family regards a father as its representative; consequently, the Chinese familial relationship is centred around the F–S relationship.[30]

All this is evidence that in the traditional Confucian mind, the relationship between father and son was more important than the mixed gender relationship, such as the mother–son or father–daughter relationship. While the mother was the origin of life in a biological sense, and this made her an object of the son's filial piety, the family was nevertheless formed in terms of its original social element, which regarded the father as its representative; therefore, in referring to the wider socio-political significance of filial ethics, the main concern was manifested in the F–S relationship. In short, Mengzi not only carried on Confucius' linking of filial piety to the F–S relationship, but placed it as the basis of *Wulun*.

Xunzi's development of the father–son relationship and the concept of filial piety

Following the route of his Confucian predecessors, Xunzi carried on the tradition of emphasizing the living parent aspect of filial piety and devoted more attention to the F–S relationship, further exalting the position of the living father to the highest place. According to Xunzi, it is a law of nature to distinguish the higher from the lower (9.3). Therefore, in a relationship between two things, one element needs to be exalted. The higher status in the F–S relationship is that of the father and the higher position in the ruler–ruled relationship is thus that of the ruler: 'The lord is the most exalted in the state. The father is the most exalted in the family' (14:7). In Xunzi's belief, 'Where only one is exalted, there is order; where two are exalted, there is anarchy' (14:7). Therefore, there must be a division between the father and the son, and between the ruler and the ruled. Some scholars have even declared that 'if we say the important character of feudal piety is autocracy, then Xunzi was the earliest maker (originator) of the infant theory of using filial piety to support autocratic politics'.[31] After Xunzi, scholars in the Han dynasty actually developed his concept of emphasis on the twin roles of the father in a family and of the ruler in a state, further completing the transfer of filial piety to the ruler from the father, and the exchange of the function of the father with that of the ruler.

In the same way, there must also be a distinction between the forefather and the father, which is realized by giving the higher status to the father. In focusing solely on living parents, Xunzi implicitly denied the existence of ghosts and spirits. From this perspective, he argued that to offer a sacrifice to one's forefather was the correct way to express one's emotion in relation to the memory of the deceased parents and that this displayed the virtues of affection and reverence, but with no sense of praying for a protection or for blessing from the departed ghosts:

> That sacrifice originates in the emotions stirred by remembrance and recollection of the dead and by thinking of and longing for the departed, expresses the highest loyalty, faithfulness, love, and reverence, and is the fulfillment of ritual observances and formal bearing. If it were not for the sages, no one would be capable of understanding the meaning of sacrifice. (19:11)

It is obvious that, for Xunzi, serving the dead is only useful for the better service of the living; sacrifice to the dead deepens emotion for the living. In other words, serving the living father is the aim, while serving the dead is only a tool for reaching this aim. As a further development of Xunzi's idea, the later Confucian work, the *Classic of Filial Piety*, further consolidated the father's position through associating the deceased father with a transcendental power that deserves worship: 'In filial piety there is nothing greater than the reverential awe of one's father. In the reverential awe shown to one's father there is nothing greater than making him the correlate of Heaven.'[32]

Thus from Confucius to Xunzi and from Xunzi to the later Confucians, the father was gradually promoted to the highest position above all other social relationships either within or beyond the living world. More than that, starting from Xunzi, the filial piety of a son to his parents not only gained in moral reinforcement but also in legal assurance. In line with this point of view, Xunzi advocated the following laws:

> In a family with an octogenarian, one son does not do corvée labour. In a family with a nonagenarian, the whole family is excused from it. For those who are cripples or ill and have no one to feed them, one man does not serve. During the mourning for father and mother, for three years the son does not serve. (27.57)

Filial piety of the son to the father also came to be exalted in the Han (202 BC–AD 220). In *Li Ji*, for example, Tseng Tzu is quoted as saying, 'Set up filial piety and it will fill the space from heaven to earth; spread it out and it will extend to the four seas; hand it down to future ages and from morning to night it will be observed;' thus, in the *Classics of Filial Piety*, filial piety has become the root of all virtue and the source of all teachings.

The Pre-Xunzi Confucian Concept of Filial Piety and Xunzi's Development

Here the earliest and most outstanding moral norm was filial piety.[33] Many changes took place during the transformation of the strong Confucian relationship between ancestors and posterity to that between father and son, but the most important of these was in the understanding of the content of filial piety.

The first important change in this content of filial piety was in the associating of filial piety with *ren* (benevolence and humanity); *Ren* is a cardinal principle and the most fundamental virtue of Confucianism, a term for which there is no counterpart in English. Different scholars have therefore translated it in different ways: some as 'magnanimity', 'benevolence' or 'perfect life' (James Legge); some interpret it to denote 'true manhood' and 'compassion' (Lin Yutang), while others translate it as 'human-heartedness' (Derek Bodde). Thus, although there is no consistent translation for *ren* as a perfect or supreme virtue for describing positive efforts for the good of others, it represents not only humanity, but also encompasses the sense of a correct and proper way for men to conduct themselves. Confucius did not discuss whether human nature was 'good' or 'evil', but rather regarded 'benevolence' as the most important virtue in the sense of being 'truly human', and in turn creatively associated this quality with filial piety: '*Xiao* (filial piety) and *ti* (respect for and love of the elder brothers) are the roots of *ren* (benevolence)' (1:2). His association of *ren* with *xiao*, on the one hand, indicates that if filial piety is an element of true humanity, then *ren* has its true meaning of being 'humane to each other'; without which it loses its fundamental sense. On the other, the abstract 'benevolence', through associated with filial piety, has been transformed into a concrete concept and therefore stands still on a practicable basis.

Mengzi further developed this idea. On the one hand, he took 'benevolence' to denote the 'tranquil habitation' of man (4A:10); on the other, he regarded filial piety as a necessary part of benevolence, thereby connecting the two concepts in a closer way: 'there never has been a man trained to benevolence who neglected his parents' (*Mengzi* 1A:1).

For Mengzi, the first reason for this unity between benevolence and filial piety is because of the nature of benevolence itself: 'the benevolent man loves others' (4B:28), while the deepest love comes from the love between parent and children: 'if one could not get the heart of his parents he could not be considered a man, and that if he could not get to an entire accord with his parents, he could not be considered as a son' (4A:28). Hence 'virtue' in the parent–child relationship cannot be divorced from 'benevolence'. Mengzi's second justification for yoking filial piety with benevolence is that 'the richest fruit of benevolence is in the service of one's parents and the richest fruit of righteousness is the obeying of one's elder brother' (4A:27). Thus, from his viewpoint, every son must serve his father in line with the principle of benevolence and righteousness (6B:4); therefore, 'Filial affection for parents is the working of benevolence' (7A:15).

With the connection of filial piety and *ren*, filial piety itself in Mengzi's thinking became rooted at the base of human nature: 'the exercise of love between father and love, the observance of righteousness between sovereign and minister . . . these are the appointment of Heaven. But there is an adaptation of our nature for them' (7B:24). Following Mengzi's intention to take benevolence as the root of virtue, Xunzi also regards benevolence as the very basis of morality. However, in contrast to Mengzi, who took benevolence to be the 'content' of morality alone, Xunzi combined not only benevolence, but also ritual as being essential elements of morality. Thus, like Confucius and Mengzi, Xunzi regarded benevolence as 'humane', as something linked to justice and morality; since, for him, justice and morality are always bound up with ritual, the close linkage between these three is therefore emphasized:

> Only after the gentleman has dwelt with humane principles through justice and morality is he truly humane; only after he conducts himself with justice and morality through ritual principles is he truly just and moral; and only where he regulates with ritual principles, returning to the root and perfecting the branch, is he truly in accord with ritual principles. (27.21)

Indeed, Xunzi accentuated ritual over and above benevolence, stating that: 'Thus, a man without ritual will not live; an undertaking lacking ritual will not be completed; and a nation without ritual will not be tranquil' (2.2). In this way, through emphasis on ritual, Xunzi transmuted the chief elements of filial piety from benevolent affection into discernment between morality and ritual: 'To be able to employ ritual and moral principles in serving one's parents is called "filial piety"' (9.16a).

Being bound up with justice and morality, 'benevolence' in Xunzi's understanding hence differs from that in both Confucius and Mengzi. If we say that 'benevolence' in Confucius' understanding is *zhong* (sincerity and loyalty) and *shu* (do not do to others what you would not have others do to you), and that in Mengzi's interpretation it becomes affection and love, then in Xunzi's consideration it is 'discernment':

> To elevate the worthy and employ the able; to place them in a ranked hierarchy, (from) eminent to base; to distinguish between near and far relatives; and to assign precedence according to age from old to young . . . Hence, one who is humane will be humane in regard to these matters. (24.5)

As the essential nature of ritual is discernment, so that it is also forms part of morality and justice is the same: 'if their sense of morality and justice is used to divide society into classes, concord will result. If there is concord between classes, unity will result; if there is unity, great physical power will result' (9.16a), thus, discernment too is an integral part of benevolence:

> The graduated scale of humane conduct is to treat relatives in a manner befitting their relation, old friends as is appropriate to their friendship . . . The gradations of position in moral conduct are to treat the noble as befits their eminent position, the honorable with due honor, the worthy as accords with their worth, the old as is appropriate to their age, and those senior to oneself as is suitable to their seniority. (27.21)

Thus, filial piety, as either the root of virtues or as the virtue of a son itself, has to take discernment as its basic characteristic.

The second important change to Pre-Xunzi Confucianism in the context of filial piety is to regard 'respect' as the essential base of filial virtue. According to Heiner

Roetz, most of the explications of the term 'filial piety' in early Confucianism centre are around the concept of *respectful care*.[34] For Confucius, it is important to satisfy the material needs of one's parents (physical care), but material support for one's parents alone is not enough for the true filial son. The most important thing for him is thus to respect his parents from the 'bottom of his heart' to render his parents' personalities esteemed and their spirits consoled (spiritual care). This is why when Ziyou asked the Master about filial piety, Confucius answered: 'The filial piety of nowadays means the support of one's parent. But dogs and horses likewise are able to do something in the way of support . . . without reverence, what is there to distinguish the one support given from the other?' (2:7).

There are many elements involved in the consideration of respect for one's parents: first of all, one has to regard one's parents' anxieties as one's own anxiety, as Confucius declared: 'Parents are anxious lest their children should be sick' (2:6). Or again, the son should try trying his best to keep a happy countenance when he meets his parents: thus, when Zixia asked what filial piety was, the Master said: 'If, when their elders have any troublesome affairs, the young take the toil of them' (2:8). Moreover, one has to protect one's parents' honour and try to shield them from being shamed in a public place. For the sake of protecting parental honour, a son should even conceal his father's shame or crime as much as possible. Here a typical story of concealment is provided in *The Analects*:

> The Duke of Sheh informed Confucius, saying, 'Among us here there are those who may be styled upright in their conduct. If their father has stolen a sheep, they will bear witness to the fact.' Confucius said, 'Among us, in our part of the country, those who are upright are different from this. The father conceals the misconduct of the son, and the son conceals the misconduct of the father. Upright is to be found in this.' (13:18)

On the other hand, Confucius never advocates a son's blind obedience to his father. On the contrary, he suggests a son must remonstrate with his parents when they do something wrong. However, he insists that this remonstration should be practised in a proper way, that is, with reverence: 'In serving his parents, a son may remonstrate with them, but gently; when he sees that they do not incline to follow his advice, he shows an increased degree of reverence, but does not abandon his purpose; and should they punish him, he does not allow himself to murmur' (4:18). Xunzi carried on this Confucian point of view that filial piety involves both material support and spiritual respect of one's parents by taking reverence and love as the spirit of *li* (rituals or rites): 'Ritual principles include treating the eminent in a respectful manner; fulfilling one's filial duties to the old; behaving with fraternal courtesy toward one's elders; treating the young with affection; and being kind to the humble' (27.16). Nonetheless, unlike Confucius who especially stressed the importance of a true filial son keeping his father in an honoured position, Xunzi put more emphasis on the justifiable disobedience of a filial son in the sense of doing *dayi* (greater justice). For Xunzi, respecting and honouring one's parent was certainly important; however, it was more important for a true filial son to act according to righteousness and justice. If conflicts arise between either respecting one's parents or exalting their long-term benefit or between a private or public benefit, then one should follow the requirement of long-term benefit for one's parents or choose the public justice rather than blind respect and following one's parents. This topic will be discussed in detail in Chapter 5.

The third change in the concept of filial piety was to connect it to ritual (rites and propriety). For Confucius, the priority for a benevolent person is to constrain himself with ritual; it therefore follows that a true filial son is to treat his parents according to ritual: 'That parents, when alive, should be served according to propriety; that, when dead, they should be buried according to propriety; and that they should be sacrificed to according to propriety' (2:5).

What is the precise meaning of 'ritual or propriety'? According to Confucius, the essential purpose of the unbreakable rules of ritual is to keep 'statutes in order': 'There is government, when the prince (ruler) is prince (ruler), and the minister is minister; when the father is father, and the son is the son' (12:10); otherwise, if the ruler and the minister are out of order, there will be usurpation and chaos in the state; and if father and son do not maintain their rightful position, there will be inharmonious conflict in the family. This principle of letting everybody keep his proper role or status and perform his proper duties according to the requirement of that place and status is what Confucius called *zhengming*. Xunzi developed this Confucian ideal and further regarded ritual as the core norm of his social theory. From his standpoint, both filial piety (the important principle used in dealing with the father–son relationship) and loyalty (the important principle for dealing with the ruler–minister relationship) is subordinate to ritual. This is why he declares that:

> Ritual principles provide the footing men tread on. When men lose this footing, they stumble and fall, sink and drown. When observance of small matters is neglected, the disorder that results is great. Such is ritual. (27.40)

> To be able to employ ritual and moral principles in serving one's parents is called 'filial piety'. To be able to use them in serving one's elder brother is called 'brotherly affection'. To be able to use them in serving one's superiors is called 'being lordly'. (9.16a)

Xunzi thus developed Confucius' idea that the essence of ritual is order, while from the importance of social order he further elaborated the principle of social differentiation or division.

Xunzi discussed the necessity of social order and peace. He said that if a society is formed without social divisions, strife results; if there is strife, disorder ensues; if there is disorder, fragmentation results (9.16a). He also discussed the necessity of social division in terms of personal potentiality and intelligence, declaring that when 'various grades of human beings live together', although they have the same desires, they have different degrees of awareness concerning those desires. For example, although in approving of things the wise and stupid are the same, since what they approve is different, the wise and stupid are in this way separated. Therefore, proper distinctions between the wise and stupid, between lord and subject and between superior and subordinate are necessary.

Moreover, because of the imbalance between human desires and the potentiality for social satisfaction, social division is also necessary: 'All people desire and dislike some thing, but since desires are many and the things that satisfy them relatively few, this scarcity will necessarily lead to conflict' (10.1); consequently, gradation and division between different relationships are necessary.

In addition, Xunzi discussed this necessary social division in terms of human nature itself. The acquisition of human nature in itself denotes order and gradation; the unequal relationship between the superior and the inferior thus expresses itself through this natural order.

Thus, the ideal of the graded position was imported into the relationship between father and son not only from the perspective of moral requirements, but also from that of human nature.

Another change in the concpet of filial piety in pre-Xunzi Confucianism was to extend the concept of filial piety from being a family term into a socio-political term. Although there are different opinions as to whether or not Confucius started to link family filial piety with political loyalty,[35] one fact is clear: he did parallel filial piety with loyalty in itself. Two examples can be provided here: (1) 'When Ji Kangzi asked how to make the people revere their ruler and be faithful to him, the Master replied: "Let him preside over them with gravity . . . then they will reverence him. Let him be filial and kind to all . . . then they will be faithful to him"' (2:20). (2) 'When people asked Confucius, "Sir, why are you not engaged in the government?" the Master replied: "What does the *Book of Documents* say of filial piety? . . . You are filial, you discharge your brotherly duties. These qualities are displayed in government"' (2:21). These two examples show that if extending the common practice of filial piety to parents into all social relationships can be achieved, the respect of the subject to the ruler would follow, and therefore there would be no need for particular political action. This suggests that in Confucius' opinion there should be a deep relationship between filial piety to parents and political benevolence and honesty: 'When those who are in high stations perform well all their duties to their relations, the people are aroused to virtue' (8:2). If the practice of filial piety towards one's parents is applicable also to political benevolence and honesty, then filial piety is not only the essence of individual virtue, but also the essence of political ethics; accordingly, the code of the F–S relationship can not only be practised in social relationships, but can also be extended into political relationships.

The reason why Confucius wanted to connect filial piety with loyalty, or family virtue with social political virtue, is perhaps due to the merging of family and state. Since the ancient Chinese never distinguished state from family, it was therefore natural for a person who declared himself an inheritor of tradition, such as Confucius, to consider the family to be the microcosm of the state, and the state to be the macrocosm of the family. Thus, it seems reasonable to Confucius, in relation to the family and the state, to regard the virtue of filial piety and the virtue of loyalty as different aspects of the same thing.

The connection between familial filial piety and political loyalty was for this reason recognized by connecting together filial piety and *ti* (brotherly love) in the statement that: 'The superior man bends his attention to what is radical. That being established, all practical courses naturally grow up. Filial piety and fraternal submission! – are they not the root of all benevolent actions?' (1:2). Since filial piety is the root and source of all other virtues, it is expected that a youth who is filial at home will be respectful to his elders abroad and will be an earnest and truthful person who can cultivate friendship well (1:6); therefore, it seems natural for Confucius to draw the following conclusion: They are few who, being filial pious and fraternal are prone to offending against their superiors. They have none who, not wishing to offend against their superiors, have been disposed to stir up confusion (1:2).

Thus, the essence of brotherly love is to respect and love one's brother, because such a brotherhood is not only confined to a kinship family but also extends to the different social relationships between the old and young within the whole of society, then brotherly love is not limited by its family sense; it is also a social notion. Hence, through the link of filial piety with brotherly love, filial piety has become a virtue for dealing with both family and social relationships.

In turn, Mengzi completed the link between the family and the society with his *Wulun* (Five Relationships): 'Between father and son, there should be affection; between sovereign and minister, righteousness; between husband and wife, attention to their separate functions; between old and young, a proper order; and between friends, fidelity' (3A:4.8). It is easy to see that these five relationships are not purely about family affairs, but are blended into social relationships. And in this mixture the relationship between old and young is the linking point. This is because, according to Weiming Tu, the precedence of the old over the young governs more than sibling relationships. Tu further indicates that Confucianism 'underscores age as a factor in organizing human relationships' so that it 'is thus an ordering and sequencing principle'. Thus, a distinctive feature of Confucian ethics is to accept seniority as a value in setting up social hierarchy.[36]

Following from the link of family relationships with social political relationships, the characteristic of hierarchy or gradation between ages and between genders in the family gains a profound political significance. It paves the way for the realization of the transformation of the state into an expanded family, and for that family to be in turn an instrument of the state in Chinese society.

By connecting the family and socio-political virtues, the status of ruler, father and elder brother are in this way tightly linked together; family thus became the place where the principles and rules of two of the 'Three Bonds' were applied. This can be seen from Zengzi's (*c.* 505–436 BC) classification of the two opposite groups: father and elder brother, together with the husband, elder and ruler in one, and the son with the younger brother, wife, junior and minister in the other:

> What are 'the things which men consider right?' Kindness on the part of father, and filial duty on that of the son; gentleness on the part of the elder brother, and obedience on that of the younger; righteousness on the part of the husband, and submission on that of the wife; kindness on the part of the elders, and deference on that of juniors; with benevolence on the part of the ruler, and loyalty on that of the minister – these ten are the things which men consider to be right.[37]

Thus, through such classification, Zengzi had in fact prepared the way for Confucianism ultimately to 'transfer filial piety into loyalty' and merge the ethical F–S relationship with that of the political ruler and the ruled. Hence, in the later Confucian society, the emperor was commonly regarded as the 'father' of the state and his people, with the local officials being viewed as 'father–mother officers'. This is the reason why Lin

Yusheng states that 'Confucian political philosophy did not regard the realm of politics and the realm of the family as separate domains.'[38]

Xunzi inherited these two traditions and in turn discussed the F–S relationship not only in a natural and family sense, but also in a social and political sense; he not only extended the natural F–S relationship over other family relation forms, such as the brothers and the husband and wife, but also socio-political derivatives, such as old–young, teacher–disciple in society and the ruler–ruled in politics. More than that, Xunzi further extended the F–S relationship to spiritual relation forms, such as that between the sage and the common people and Heaven and humans. The concept is thus becoming a universal mode of conduct for every occasion: using it in serving the ruler, one will be certainly successful; using it in conducting benevolence, one will surely become wise (7.4).

What, then, is this universal code? Xunzi declares it thus: 'That the young should serve the old, the base the noble, and the unworthy the worthy–(this) is the pervading moral rule throughout the world' (7.5). This universal principle can be also seen in his description of the common character of a *Ru* person:

> The *Ru* model themselves after the Ancient Kings; they exalt ritual and moral principles; as ministers and sons they are careful to esteem their superiors to the highest degree . . . When they lived in Quedang,[39] youngsters of the village apportioned the catch of their nets so those who had parents took more, because their cultivation of filial piety and fraternal submission so transformed them. (8.2)

After the social change in both the 'Period of Spring and Autumn' and the 'Period of Warring States', both the form of society and of government were far different from that of the Zhou Dynasty. The connection between the state and the family was no longer as close as before, and the separation between them was more and more obvious. In such circumstances, Xunzi's idea of integration between family and political ethics could not be the natural reflection of the social and political reality, nor could it conform exactly to the idea of Confucius. In fact, Xunzi's attitude towards the historical legacy was creative rather than conservative. On the one hand, Xunzi inherited the spirit of Confucian ethics, which took the love between the father and the son as its basis; on the other hand, he re-constituted the consanguineous moral code which was the basis of his political ethics so that it was no longer a pure rule system based on the reflection of the spontaneous affective action between father and son. He thus introduced a greater emphasis on social justice, thereby making the F–S relationship the base as well as the servant of the ruler–minister relationship.

In this way, Xunzi expanded the identification of the function of filial piety in both family and state, and extended the control–obedience model of the F–S pattern to the political ruler–ruled relationship. He was the first person not only to draw a direct parallel between the father and the ruler, but also to tilt the balance in favour of the ruler, thus making filial piety the basis of political autocracy. He put it thus: 'The father can beget the child, but he cannot suckle it. The mother can suckle the child but is unable to instruct and correct it. The lord not only is able to feed his people but is adept at teaching and correcting them'; therefore the lord 'is the father and mother of his people'; he is, of course, worthy to be mourned for three years in exactly the same way as a parent (19.10). Moreover, in Xunzi's mind, the lord who takes care of every detail of all his subjects' welfare in fact contributes more than a parent; therefore, three years' mourning for him may indeed not be enough to display the magnitude of the people's affection and debt. Thus, as Han Demin has realized, following from emphasis of the importance of the F–S relationship, Xunzi extends this to the importance of the relationship between the ruler and the minister and, thence, from the authority of the father to the authority of the ruler.[40] In accordance with this relationship set, Han Demin concludes that although Xunzi took the consanguineous ethic as the base of political life, he nevertheless seldom talked of the type of filial piety which was directly presented as a natural, instinctual feeling; rather, he promoted this concept on the social entity level, thereby enhancing it to the point where it is open to political and organizational management activity.[41]

This analysis of Xunzi's ideal of the F–S relationship is quite sound. In fact, he actually paid more attention to a conceptual F–S pattern in the political ethical dimension than the natural F–S relation form itself. Indeed, his considerable energy is devoted to discussion of the relationship between ruler and subject, the responsibilities of a gentleman or a sage, the duty of the teacher and so on, but is seldom directly referred to the natural F–S pattern.

However, Xunzi's political theory never departed substantially from its consanguineous base; all his political extensions of the F–S relationship are founded on a biological relationship bedrock: for example, his political relationship between the ruler and ruled simply replicates the natural F–S pattern. He expresses it thus:

> No superior fails to love perfectly his subordinates who governs them according to rituals. The relation of the superior to his subordinates is analogues to that of 'tending and caring for a small infant' . . . Hence, the closeness between subordinates and their superior will cause rejoicing 'as though he were their parents. (11.9a)

Hence, the F–S relationship and the ruler–minister relationship are described as identical:

> The relation between lord and minister, father and son, old and younger brothers, husband and wife, begin as they end and end as they begin, share with Heaven and Earth the same organizing principle, and endure in the same form through all eternity. Truly this may be described as the 'Great Foundation'. (9.15)

In this way, by stressing the similarity of father and ruler, Xunzi framed the F–S relationship within the discussion of the ruler–minister relationship. This concept was in turn absorbed in its totality by the author of *Li Ji*:

> If a man in his own house and privacy be not grave, he is not filial; if in serving his ruler, he be not loyal, he is not filial; if in discharging the duties of office, he be not reverent, he is not filial; if with friends he be not sincere, he is not filial; if on the field of battle he be not brave, he is not filial.[42]

From this perspective, Xunzi shifted the focus from instinctive affection between the natural father and his son to the distinction and grade between them. This is not however because Xunzi consciously retreated 'from the Confucian standpoint of the consanguineous patriarchal clan system',[43] but because of his unique stress on ritual.

This emphasis on the ritual element of filial piety resulted in an ethical theory which stressed the 'principle' rather than the human element. The obedience of the son to his father and the minister to his ruler is hence due to the requirement of ritual rather than to personal obligation. It is true that Xunzi emphasized the importance of person, in the sense that every principle must be fulfilled by that person, but there is a clear difference between his idea of kingship and that which is central to Confucius' political ethics. Xunzi's emphasis on ritual has the advantage of avoiding the pitfalls of the traditional Chinese idea of loyalty to the person, which may lead directly to political collapse; in contrast, loyalty to a principle or law can, on the one hand, prevent political collapse and, on the other, be more easily transformed into a law-ruled social system.

The Classics of Filial Piety confirmed Xunzi's ideal through its declaration that 'filial piety commences with the service of parents; proceeds to the service of ruler; and is completed by establishment of the person's good character'.[44] Thus, the Confucian norm of filial piety not only formed the moral rules and conduct for the family itself, but also had a direct political function;[45] it served not only as a fountainhead of wisdom, but also symbolized the mature state of Chinese morality as a whole.[46]

The Philosophical Base of Xunzi's Father–Son Relationship

Xunzi's father–son relationship has not only cultural and historical origins, but also philosophical roots. As a typical Chinese scholar, truth for Xunzi is not understood as something revealed from above or an abstract principle with logical consistence, but as a discoverable and demonstrable principle in human affairs.[47] He believed that the way for human society to evolve, as devised by the ancient sage kings, was the reflection of a deeper pattern within the universe itself, namely, the most 'fitting' or 'proper' way to be; he also thought that the ordinary moral rules and standards of civilized society, which the sage likewise created, are truths that are universally binding on us rather than merely conventions.[48] Therefore, Xunzi tried to locate his ethical doctrine harmoniously in a greater cosmic order and discussed it from the perspective of the nature of human beings.

The cosmological origin of Xunzi's interpretation of the father–son relationship

In order to affirm that human nature is good and to enforce the power and authority of social norms, the ancient Chinese proposed the concept of the 'Way of Heaven' (*tiandao*). The founder of Daoism, Laozi, declared that: 'Man takes his law from the Earth; Earth takes its law from Heaven, Heaven takes its law from the Tao. The law of the Tao is its being what it is.'[49] This tradition Xunzi inherited and thence rooted his ethical F–S theory into a cosmological origin, as Paul Goldin has has recognized:

> In the term *dao*, or Way, Xunzi postulates a single and universal ontology. The Way is the way of the Universe, and the 'plan and pattern' [*jingli*] of reality, and theories are 'heterodox' if they do not conform to it. The exalted rectification – or rectification of names – is a tool

that philosopher can use to distinguish lewd antinomies from truths compatible with the Way.[50]

In line with this, a similar view was proposed by Robert Eno in 1990:

> When the Xunzi slices the world into pieces and principles, it does so not only for objective entities but for life conceived as situation and roles. This analogous structure between natural and ethical worlds allows the Xunzi to make an implicit but clear claim to the effect that ritual *li* embody intrinsic principle of ethical existence fundamentally equivalent to principle of natural existence, or '*li*' pattern.[51]

In the same way, Kurits Hagen provides evidence for the cosmological root of Xunzi's ethics via discussion on his conception of *Zhengming* (correcting of names):

> Take names (*ming*) and categories (*lei*) to represent privileged groupings, their ontological status being assured by virtue of their correspondence with the deep structure of the universe. Names and categories are grounded in *li* taken as 'principles of natural existence' or the Way as the 'plan and pattern' of reality.[52]

Furthermore, according to Li Shenzhi, the unity of Heaven and Man is the most ancient concept of Chinese philosophy and Chinese culture and the one with the broadest implications; it is fundamental not only to Confucianism, but also to all other systems of intellectual thought. Therefore, the seeking of a cosmological root for Confucian moral theory actually began before Confucius.[53] Confucius inherited this ancient tradition and declared, 'Great indeed was Yao as a sovereign! How majestic was he! It is only Heaven that is grand, and only Yao corresponded to it' (8:19). Similarly, Mengzi further connected human nature to the nature of heaven, affirming that: 'He who has exhausted all his mental constitution knows his nature. Knowing his nature, he knows Heaven' (7A:1). To associate humanity with *tian* (heaven) is thus the beginning of what later scholars called the theory of *tian ren he yi*, which integrates heaven and human beings together and regards humans as sharing the same nature as the universe.

It is a common idea in Confucianism that heaven is the progenitor and ancestor; humans are the descendants. Heaven and Man are therefore united, act in unison, and respond to one another. Heaven does not speak, but conveys its messages through natural calamities and omens,[54] which interact with, and can also be influenced by, each other. This character is reflected in the commentaries of the *Book of Changes*,[55] in which the relationship between Heaven and humans is described in identical terms to the relationship between father and son:

> Qian is heaven, so means father; Kun is earth, so means mother.[56]

> Heaven and earth exist. Then the myriad entities are produced.
> There are myriad entities; then there are man and woman.
> There are man and woman; then there are husband and wife.
> There are husband and wife; then there are father and son.
> There are father and son; then there are prince and retainer.
> There are prince and retainer; then there are high and low.
> There are high and low; then property and rights can be arranged.[57]

Unlike this traditional Confucian view of human society and nature as a unified whole, Xunzi had a strong inclination to split them into separate entities. He declared that: Heaven does not halt the winter season because people dislike cold; Earth does not diminish its wide expanse because people dislike great distances (17.5); 'The Course of Heaven is constant; it is not preserved by Yao, nor is it destroyed by Jie (17.2).[58] In his view, the way of humanity is differentiated from the Way of Heaven and there should therefore be no moral interaction between nature and human society; therefore whoever is enlightened with respect to this division can be called a 'supreme person' (17.1).

This division, however, was nevertheless itself rooted in cosmological logic. From Xunzi's standpoint, because there is a division between the Way of Heaven and of humans, there is no moral influence between Nature itself and human society since the constancy of Heaven represents universal truth; it is unchangeable and knowable, and should therefore be both a guide and model for humankind. Humans' behavior towards each other within the social and physical circumstances they encounter must thus match the Way of Heaven and be a replica of it; this also extends to the moral principle of the F–S relationship.

Guocheng Jiao describes this cosmological naturalization process as the merging of inevitability of nature with unchangeable hierarchy. This 'merging' in itself, produces 'transformations' and 'order,'[59] as Xunzi stats:

Heaven and Earth are the beginning of life. (9.15)

Heaven and Earth are the roots of life. (19.2a)

When Heaven and Earth conjoin, the myriad things are begot; when the Yin and Yang principles combine, transformations and transmutations are produced; when inborn nature and conscious activity are joined, the world is made orderly. (19.6)

In fact, Xunzi not only occasionally affirmed the generative function of Heaven and Earth, but also professed the potential transforming union between Heaven and humans, proclaiming that:

Heaven did not create the people for the sake of the lord, Heaven established the lord for the sake of the people. (27.68)

When everything is unified and there is no duality, one can communicate with the Spiritual intelligences and form a Triad with Heaven and Earth. (8.11)

Thus, rituals serve Heaven above and Earth below, pay honor to one's forebears, and exalt ruler and teachers, for these are three roots of ritual principles. (19.2a)

Thus, this generative communing between Heaven and humans is an interactive process: Heaven and Earth give birth to the *junzi* (sage, gentleman), and he in turn provides the organizing principle for Heaven and Earth (9.15). Over and above this, within Xunzi's worldview, the function of the 'sage' (wise and moral man) in this process of natural regularization was integral to the principle of order:

Heaven is able to beget the myriad things, but it cannot differentiate them. Earth can support man, but it cannot govern him. The myriad things under the canopy of heaven and all those belong among living people depend upon the appearance of the sage, for only then, is each assigned its proper station. (19.6)

This passage tells us that although Heaven itself begets humans, order, perfection and sufficiency is achieved only through the wise and moral man. This is why John Knoblock observes that, 'Xunzi, in agreement with most of his contemporaries, accepted that Heaven/Nature "produces" (literally, "bears"), but he denied that Nature acts to seek anything. He thus denies to nature the conscious intentions the traditional view granted to Heaven.'[60]

Thus, how can we classify precisely the cosmological root of Xunzi's F–S relationship? On the one hand, Xunzi adopted the Daoist ideal of constancy to describe the unchangeable character of the 'fundamental principles' and 'general principles' (15.1c) so as to give heavenly sanction (*tiandao*: the Way of Heaven) to his moral system: 'Heaven possesses a constant Way; Earth has an invariable size; the gentleman has constancy of deportment' (17.5); on the other hand, he incorporated the Mohist concept of *Tiande* (heavenly virtue) to express both the inevitability and importance of the distinction between ruler and subject, father and son, and husband and wife.[61]

In the Mohist tradition, this concept of the heavenly virtue is used to refer to the moral power inherent in nature, which exerts power over human society. For Xunzi, 'heavenly virtue' is thus a mandatory power against which humankind cannot rebel; it is hence a natural power with full ordained authority and stability. In line with Xunzi's account, its most important element is *Cheng*, which means 'truthfulness', 'loyalty', 'sincerity' or 'honesty', with the most important characteristic of the Way of Heaven being the unchangeable natural order of gradation. For him, 'sincerity' is an instrumental virtue which upholds 'the principle of humanity and conduct itself with justice'; it is also a virtue which compels action according to the natural order, which is the original and highest justice and therefore possesses the ultimate power. In this he proclaims that,

> For the gentleman to nurture his mind, nothing is more excellent than truthfulness. If a man has attained perfection of truthfulness, he will have no other concern than to uphold the principle of humanity and behave with justice. If with truthfulness of mind he upholds the principle of humanity, it will be given form. Having been given form, it becomes intelligible. Having become intelligible, it can produce transmutation. If with truthfulness of mind he behaves with justice, it will accord with natural order. According with natural order, it will become clear. Having become clear, it can produce transformation. To cause transmutation and transformation to flourish in succession is called the *Tiande*, the power of nature. (3.9a)

According to Xunzi, this inevitability of nature can be applied to everything, everywhere; it forms part of the universe, and human society cannot therefore evade this mandatory distinction. What, then, is this natural order? His argument was that all things on Earth and under Heaven are unequally born, belonging to different groups, with their own respective status. For all things in a higher position there must exist equivalents in a lower position as a counterbalance. This is the inevitability of nature, or the Universe. Therefore, if human society is to be in harmony with the natural order, it must follow the consequent principle of gradation; it is therefore in accordance with this principle to categorize society into different classes, and different people into graded social positions. Specifically, it is necessary to separate noble from humble, worthy from unworthy, governor from commoner; consequently, the authority of fathers, husbands or the ruler must also be differentiated, as must the obedience of sons, wives or subjects. Without this differentiation, society will not maintain its equilibrium, as Xunzi affirmed:

> Where the classes of society are equally ranked, there is no proper arrangement of society; where authority is evenly distributed, there is no unity; and where everyone is of like status, none would be willing to serve the other. Just as there are Heaven and Earth, so too there exists the distinction between superior and inferior . . . Two men of equal eminence cannot attend each other; two men of the same low status cannot command each other – such is the norm of Heaven. (9.3)

John Knoblock discerns this aspect of Xunzi's worldview clearly and further indicates that this feature is derived from his developmental background within the academic school of Confucianism, which he describes thus:

> In the view of *Ru* philosophers, the nature of society is hierarchical and inheres in the natural inequality of things, but Heaven, which produced the 'teeming masses', also provided an appropriate station of life that is the due lot of each. Those highest in ability, wisdom, intelligence, and inner power, by general assent, become rulers . . . Those of lesser talents become feudal lords, grand officers, and officials. Each serves an appropriate role in the structure of human society. The responsibility, income, and prestige of each are commensurate with the position he occupies.[62]

The most significant cosmological fact of Xunzi's ethical F–S relationship is also traceable to elements of Zhuangzi's theory that the power of Heaven is associated with the 'wise ones' or sages. This concept is not found in Mozi, however, although he created an identical concept of heavenly virtue, there was no attempt to connect this power to the sage. It was Zhuangzi who first drew a parallel between this power, which is intrinsic to heaven, and the power inherent in the *Dao*, and he further associated it with the Daoist sage:

> Heaven and Earth have the greatest beauty, but they do not speak of them; the four seasons have clear laws, but they do not discuss them; the myriad things have intrinsic principles of order that complete them, but they do not explain them. The sage seeks the source of the beauty of Heaven and Earth and penetrates into the intrinsic principles of all things. For these reasons, the Perfect Man acts with assertion, and the Great Sage does not create. This is called observing Heaven and Earth.[63]

Xunzi accepted Zhuangzi's theory and viewed the system of ritualistic moral principle as being derived from the profound insights of the sage in observing the Way of Heaven and of Earth:

> Heaven and Earth are the beginning of life. Ritual and moral principles are the beginning of order. The gentleman is the beginning of ritual and moral principles. Acting with them, actualizing them, accumulating them over and over again, and loving them more than all else is the beginning of the gentleman. Thus, Heaven and Earth give birth to the gentleman,

and the gentleman provides the organizing principles of Heaven and Earth. The gentleman is the triadic partner of Heaven and Earth, the summation of the myriad of things, and the father and mother of the people. (9.15)

Xunzi argued that the task of the sage was to lay out before him all the myriad of things and set himself to match precisely how each settles on the suspended balance (21.5a). Here Guanzi's affirmation that 'The sage alters with the times, but is not transformed; he accords with things, but is not moved'[64] seems to concur with and explain this interpretation of the sage's task, which was not to create a new way for human society, but rather to apply the Way of Heaven to the human society. That is to say, the rituals and moral principles, or the feudal moral code system, was not procreated but instead invented by the ancient sage kings, themselves according to natural order; this natural code or order, in turn, conferred authority and power upon both the moral codes and the sage as their originator.

Because authority and power reside within the sages and their moral teachings, hence the ordinary people ought to learn from them, and put into practice these principles. This is the process of learning and self-cultivation, in which the potential of the father and son and their derivatives are revealed.

Xunzi's view of human nature and his interpretation of the father–son relationship

To understand better the philosophical base of Xunzi's interpretation of the F–S relationship, we need to explore his theory that human nature is inherently evil. Here he differed from Mengzi, who held the view that the capacity to understand and apply moral principles distinguishes humans from animals, and that this was intrinsic to human nature: 'the feeling of commiseration belongs to all men; so does that of shame and dislike; and that of reverence and respect; and that of approving and disapproving.' He declared, 'Benevolence, righteousness, propriety, and knowledge are not infused into us from outside; we are certainly furnished with them' (6A:6). Xunzi, however, did not regard this moral sense as an innate element of human nature. On the contrary, he believed that there was a serious flaw in Mengzi's commitment to the goodness of human nature, that was the practical consequence of neglecting the necessity of ritual and authority for the well-being of society. However, Xunzi did not deny the importance of morality for human beings; in contrast, he used morality as a standard with which distinguish human beings from animals:

What is it that makes a man human? I say that it lies in his ability to draw boundaries . . . Even though wild animals have parents and offspring, there is no natural affection between them as between father and son, and though there are males and females of the species, there is no proper separation of sexes. (5.4)

Some argue that what Xunzi stressed here is this concept of 'boundary', and that was not clear whether or not it referred to morality; therefore it does not follow that he adheres to this moral distinction between humans and animals. Nevertheless, taking into consideration other arguments, such as 'regarding learning and not learning as the boundary that distinguishes men from animals', the conclusion that morality is the distinguishing factor seems to be clear. Xunzi declares that, 'those who undertake learning become men; those who neglect it become as wild beasts' (1.8). Thus, learning becomes the key to this distinction in his view. Moreover, learning must 'start with the recitation of the Classics and conclude with the reading of the rituals' (1.8); and since both the context of the Classics and the contents of rituals are *li* and *yi*, which are the parallel words for morality, hence morality is equivalent to the boundary to distinguish humans from animals. From this perspective, Xunzi actually held a similar opinion to that of Mengzi in viewing morality as representing this distinguishing and dividing line.

Yet instead of judging morality to be inherent within human nature, Xunzi interpreted it as being the essence of the 'acquired' human nature, or *wei*, the 'man-made' human nature; this 'man-made' human nature is a concept that differs entirely from that of nature. Nature, in Xunzi's account, refers to the nature of Heaven itself, which is an attribute that people cannot learn or acquire by practice. On the contrary, ritual and morality, which were 'invented' by the sages, represented the essence of the 'man-made' nature that could be acquired through learning and practice, and which obviously does not belong to that which is innate in nature. Moreover, unlike graded and acquired elements, the original human nature is common at all:

> In natural talent, in born nature, awareness, and capability, the gentleman and the petty man are one. In cherishing honor and detesting disgrace, in loving benefit and hating harm, the gentleman and the petty man are the same. Rather, it appears that the Way they employ to make their choices produces the difference. (4.9)

> All men possess one and the same nature: when hungry, they desire food; when cold, they desire benefit and hate harm. Such is the nature that men are born possessing. They do not have to await development before they become so. (4.11)

However, this common human nature is not good, but inherently evil: the essential nature of man is his desire to eat meat instead of grain and vegetables; to dress in decorative rather than simple, dull clothes; to travel by horse and carriage instead of on foot; to be as honoured as the Son of Heaven and to be as wealthy as if one possessed the whole world. These desires are evil because they tend to lead to corrupt consequences. Thus, because of this inherent evil, it became necessary for the ancient kings to propose principles of morality and justice.

> Accordingly, the Ancient Kings acted to control them with regulations, ritual and moral principles, in order thereby to divide society into classes, creating therewith differences in status between the noble and base, disparities between the privileges of age and youth, and the division of the wise from the stupid, the able from the incapable. All of this caused men to perform the duties of their station in life and each to receive his due; only after this had been done was the amount and substance of the emolument paid by grain made to fit their respective stations. This is the Way to make the whole populace live together in harmony and unity. (4.14)

On examining Xunzi's logic, however, one encounters a problem: if there is no good but only evil in human nature, why then is humanity considered to be the highest and most developed species in the world? For Xunzi, this represents no question at all: what makes a man essentially human lies not in his being a featherless biped, but in his *zhi* and ability to 'draw boundaries' (5.9). This term *Zhi* translates into English as 'intelligence, intellect or wisdom'; Xunzi believed that, from birth, the distinction between human beings and animals does not depend on the possession of virtue, but on the faculty of intelligence or wisdom. This human being possesses, by which he is able to discern between good and evil; between what is useful and what is useless; between what is right and what is wrong; between what will lead to benefit and what is harmful.

Why, then, do human beings organize themselves into a society instead of living in individual isolation? From Xunzi's point of view, this is a direct result of the faculty of intelligence, by which human beings know that it benefits them more to live in society than to live separate individuals. Why, too, do human beings learn and practise rituals and morality in order to use them to curb their evil nature? This is because they know that the restraint which results from rituals and morality will bring them great reward. Why, further, are humans considered to be the noblest beings in the world? This is because human beings can use their intelligence to manage and control themselves and the world. This is also the reason why, although their natural bent is towards greed they can nevertheless learn how to act according to the requirements of morality. Thus, it is the faculty of intelligence that enables people to develop prudence and foresight, and in turn consider the consequences of their actions (4.11).

Opinions differ regarding Xunzi's theory that human nature is evil and Mengzi's opposite view.[65] However, increasingly, scholars are coming to believe that there are nevertheless some points of agreement between the two: (a) They both looked to Confucius as the source of and the authority for their own views, and their objective in each case was to perpetuate the value system of Confucianism. (b) Each turned too to the past in order to build on it, just as Confucius had before them and as Confucians after them would also do.[66] (c) In terms of their ethical philosophy, they did not on the fact of it disagree about the character of moral action, but similarly emphasized its importance for the human being. (d) Both had the political ideal of maintaining order and harmony and encoraging the accumulation of wealth. Lu Debin demonstrates the similarities and differences between the two scholastic theories on human nature in the following four respects: first, Mengzi regards virtue as the distinguishing factor which divides human beings from animals. He not only takes virtue to be the manifestation of human nature and its value, but also views it to be the origin of morality; Xunzi on the other hand, attributes this difference to human intellect, which perceives the benefit of personal morality, and hence the value of cultivating moral virtue. Thus, Mengzi's theory of virtue was built on the ideal of the morality of human beings, while Xunzi in contrast founded his theory on the concept of *zhi*, as the faculty to 'acquire' this morality and perceive its benefits. Nevertheless, neither the single quality of virtue nor that of intelligence in itself can account for the essential nature and significance of human beings; on the other hand, both of them as a single whole play an important part in traditional Confucianism. Secondly, Mengzi's theory of human nature leads directly in his view to the need to cultivate inherent goodness, while Xunzi's theory of *Zhi* resulted in the need to 'adapt' to offset inherent evil. The former thus aims at the expansion of human virtue, while the goal of the latter is to limit or restrain the human tendency to sin. Both regarded the defence and promotion of the Confucian ideal as their task. The essential difference between them is that while the one focuses on 'setting up the biggest', the other pays attention to 'destroying the smallest', but they are nevertheless interrelated and complementary to each other. In the third place, Mengzi's theory led to emphasis on moral cultivation from inside human consciousness and the ideal of morality, whereas Xunzi's theory resulted in an emphasis on the practice of external principles to acquire this morality. Mengzi's ideal could thus provide people with a will to act in accordance with this morality as cultivated, but did not safeguarding them against outside temptation, while Xunzi's concept of an authoritative external principle with penalties could restrain people from sinful activities, in this way accentuating the best in each.

Finally, Mengzi's emphasis on the essential goodness of human nature gave a metaphysical basis to human virtue and human life, and therefore assumed great significance. Nevertheless, Xunzi's emphasis on the faculty of human intelligence provided for the development and evolution of human nature and the ultimate manifestation of human value; in this sense perhaps outweighed Mengzi's theory. For surely, without the faculty of human intelligence, the nature of human virtue would be stifled since the realization of the moral ideal depends upon the intellect.[67] Interestingly, here Mou Zongsan (?–1995), the famous Neo-Confucian scholar in contemporary times, argues that the shortcoming of Chinese culture is just this lack of attention to human intelligence:

> According to individual practices, if the application of learning through intellect not developed, then long-lived traditional religious role played by the sage in cultural life in perceiving and reaching profound moral insights is threatened, and immorality may result. Thus, if this keen intellect is not present in those with a priestly function, then it is hard to realize the ideal of real King.[68]

An important point here is that the strong emphasis on human morality at the expense of intelligence has made Chinese culture less advanced in both the natural physical and man-made world. In contrast, the great advantage of the West is its strong awareness of the nature and critical application of human intelligence. Xunzi's theory of the development of intelligence, it seemed to him, was therefore good medicine to remedy the sickness of Chinese culture.

This concept is significant in that the application of intelligence in human nature not only has significance for overcoming the shortcomings of Chinese culture, but also provides a philosophical base for his ideal of the F–S relationship. First, Xunzi's conception of the evil inherent in human nature provides a logical basis for the father's authority over his son for distinguishing the role and duty of the father in educating the son to overcome this through moral virtue. Because of this evil nature, moral virtues can be cultivated only after birth, and moral knowledge can be acquired only through self-learning and social education. For Xunzi, the ruler should be a sage; as the representative of the Way of Heaven, he has the duty to apply his highly developed intellect to draw up moral principles in accordance with the natural order, and use his profound insights to educate and to guide people to be 'perfect humans'. This duty of the ruler was the basis of composed his authority and power. Thus, in the same way, the father as the head of the family also has a duty to guide and educate his son through the teachings of the sages. This role of the father as 'agent' of the sages fulfils his paternal duties and justifies his authority over his son.

Secondly, in this sense, the application of *zhi* to moral education of the son and the father himself guarantee the authority of the father, since both the father and the son in both their moral cultivation and education develop their wisdom to know what is the right moral path for them and know naturally through their study and education that following the teachings of the sages is the way to maintain both their family harmony and in turn the social solidarity. Thus, it becomes their desire to fulfill their different roles, and to carry out the teachings of the sages: the father will desire to teach his son the insights of the sage, and in turn it will be the son's pleasure to treat his father as the agent of the sage, and to learn from his father as from the sage. Consequently, the authority of the father and the obedience of the son are enhanced through the strength of these teachings. From this standpoint, the following argument of Weiming Tu is right: if the cognitive function of the mind (human rationality) is singled out as the basis for morality, even if morality is alien to our nature, even if we do not wish to voluntarily harness our desires and passions in order to act for both survival and well-being in accordance with societal norms, the faculty of intellect nevertheless perceives the benefits of morality for social cohesion.[69]

Thus, Xunzi's theory that human nature is inherently evil has paved the way for the ethical relationship between the father and the son. This in turn is the foundation of his social ideals. In his view, the most effective way to set humans apart from animals is to organize them into a society. At the same time, if the evil in human nature is allowed to reign, chaos and conflict result. It is for this reason that 'ritual' and 'morality' must be so formulated as to avoid such disorder by distinguishing between social levels and ranking them appropriately to achieve harmony. This is what Xunzi termed *fen* and *bian*. Thus the function of ritual and morality is, on the one hand, to create such distinctions and, on the other, to create social harmony. Nevertheless, according to the research of Hui Jixing, division in hierarchy is not the goal of Xunzi's concept of rituals; social gradation ranks well below the value of creating a harmonious relationship among social relationships.[70]

This idea, in a sense, has captured the spirit of the Confucian norm of *li*, since from the time of Confucius, the need to maintain harmony has been paramount in Chinese social order, as Youzi affirms: 'in practising the rules of propriety, a natural ease (harmony) is to be prized. In the ways prescribed by the ancient kings, this is the excellent quality, and in things small and great we follow them' (1.7). Xunzi in turn incorporated this ideal into his theoretical construct, designating rituals and music as the most important instruments for achieving social harmony and for reducing collective conflict. Thus, *li* (ritual) and *yue* (music) were yoked together, and the blend viewed as a way of achieving harmony within human relationships. These theoretical constructs in turn influenced the author of *The Book of Li Ji*, in which *li* is viewed as the direct means to bring closer and harmonize the relationship both between father and son and older and young: 'Generally speaking, that which makes man [a] man is the meaning of his ceremonial usages . . . When the relation between ruler and subject is made correct, affection secured between father and son, and harmony shown between seniors and juniors, then the meaning of those usages is established.'[71]

If ritual and moral principle create order as well as harmony, then the ethical relationship between humans is also necessary as social foundation; consequently, the ethical relationship between father and son is essential for well-balanced human life. Therefore, if we say that the establishment of meaningful rituals and standards of morality is essential to resolve the problem raised by the evil inherent in human nature, and that the establishment of the ethical F–S relationship arises from the desire to heal the conflict between a father and a son caused by that inherent evil, then this is also true of relationships between ethical ruler–ruled, elder brother–younger brother, teacher–student and husband and wife, as affirmed by Tu Weiming:

> Hsun Tzu underscored the centrality of self-cultivation. He outlined the process of Confucian education, from noble man to sage, as a ceaseless endeavor to accumulate knowledge, skills, insight, and wisdom. He believed that unless social constraints are well articulated, we are prone to make excessive demands to satisfy our passions. As a result, social solidarity, the precondition for human flourishing, is undermined. The most serious flaw in the Mencian commitment to goodness of human nature is the practical consequence of neglecting the necessity of ritual and authority for the well-being of society. By stressing that human nature is evil, Hsun Tzu singled out the cognitive function of the mind (human rationality) as the basis for morality. We become moral by voluntarily harnessing our desires and passions to act in accordance with societal norms. This is alien to our nature but perceived by our mind as necessary for both survival and well-being.[72]

To sum up, Xunzi's view that human nature is evil can lead to status divisions between father and son and their derivatives and thence to unequal or unbalanced relationships between them. The inherent evil in human nature leads to greed and covetousness, and to increase in damaging personal desire. These features of the human condition in turn raise a problem: if all humans are permitted to give free rein to their desires, then the society will neither have enough wealth to satisfy those desires, nor can it provide enough honour and status to satisfy the demands of the individuals within it. How then can society deal with such a problem? In Xunzi's view the most effective counterbalance is to separate people into different rankings and to require them to complete their moral duties according to the demands of their social status or position. He puts it thus:

> If people live in alienation from each other and do not serve each other's need, there will be poverty; if there are no class divisions in society, there will be contention. Poverty is a misfortune, and contention a calamity. No means are so good to remedy misfortunes and eradicate calamities as causing class divisions to be clearly defined when giving form to society. (10.1f)

Consequently, these social distinctions are essential for harmony and order, even for the peaceful distribution of profits. Indeed, Xunzi stressed the necessities of gradation and disparity between different classes or different social ranks in order to regulate the appropriacy of political treatment as well as economic distribution. However, the gradation and distinction are characteristics of human moral ethics rather than human nature; hence Xunzi declared that every individual is equal in regard to their nature:

> All men possess one and the same nature. When hungry, they desire food; when cold, they

desire to be warm; when exhausted from toil, they desire rest; and they all desire benefit and hate harm. Such is the nature that men are born possessing. They do not have to await development before they become so. (4.9)

They have similar natural talents, awareness, faculties and capacities: 'In natural talent, inborn nature, awareness, and capability, the gentleman and the petty man are one. In cherishing honor and detesting disgrace, in loving benefit and hating harm, the gentleman and the petty man are the same' (4.8). This original parity alongside human evil results in equal opportunity to change those evil tendencies through moral education. Thus, all share the wisdom to recognize the depth of their evil nature, and to know how to build up a strong moral foundation. All of these factors have a strong bearing on Xunzi's perception of the actual features of the F–S relationship, as will be discussed in detail in Chapter Four.

CHAPTER TWO

Sources and Background of the Pauline Divine Father–Son Relationship

Christianity grew out of Judaism and was initially developed by Jewish Christians who were living in the Roman Empire; its cultural environment was thus dominated by 'syncretism' – that 'quickened pace of contact between peoples and cultures that produces the mutual influence and intermingling'.[1] This biblical/Jewish background to Christianity is vital to an understanding of the Pauline letters, as is acquaintance with the Greco-Roman background; both are crucial for an understanding of the specific situations to which Paul directed his religious and ethical instructions.[2] Early Christianity – a Jewish movement in a Greco-Roman environment – is therefore inseparable from both Greco-Roman and Jewish culture, as Joseph Klausner, author of *Jesus of Nazareth*, affirms: 'An eclectic system like this could be acceptable to early Christianity, which also was a combination of Judaism and Hellenism and likewise was uprooted from its historical soil.'[3]

Paul was not only a Jew born of a Jewish family and educated by a traditional Jewish culture, but also apostle to the Gentiles, who used Greek to preach the new Christian message; in this sense, Judaism and Hellenistic cultures were root sources for his ethical ideas and teaching. Nonetheless, the immediate source of Paul's understanding of the divine father–son (F–S) relationship was the teaching of Jesus of Nazareth, which in turn was embedded in the Old Testament (OT). Taking these into account, this chapter will discuss the background to the Pauline concept of the F–S relationship from three perspectives: its Jewish and Greco-Roman cultural backgrounds and its theological source.

The Ancient Jewish Cultural Background

There exists a continuing debate on the general influence of Judaism on Pauline teaching, as William S. Campbell, for example, has discussed in detail.[4] Adolf von Harnack too saw Pauline Christianity as the Hellenization of the Palestinian Jewish message preached by Jesus of Nazareth, thereby placing Paul closer to Judaism.[5] James D. G. Dunn claims that whatever later Christians made of what he wrote, Paul himself would certainly have wanted to affirm that his Christology remained within the matrix of Jewish monotheism.[6] Wayne A. Meeks further states that though the use of family terms to refer to members was not unknown in pagan cult associations, particularly in Rome and in areas where Roman customs influenced Greek associations, the early Christians took their usage from the Jews.[7]

Other scholars, such as Ferdinand Christian Baur, prefer to differentiate between Christianity and Judaism, but nevertheless acknowledge that the deepest root and origin of Christianity is in the OT. Paul himself, as increasing numbers of scholars have recognized, simultaneously told his readers he was advancing in Judaism beyond many Jews of his own age and was extremely zealous for the traditions of his fathers (Gal 1:14). It may be that Paul himself wanted to have it both ways: 'to understand himself as an apostate in relationship to his Gentile converts but as a loyal son of Israel in relationship to Jews.'[8]

The crucial status of the father–son relationship in ancient Jewish culture

The influence of Jewish culture on the Pauline divine F–S relationship can be first seen from the supreme status of the parent in ancient Jewish society, which was paramount. Evidence regarding the parent–child relationship as the most fundamental is provided in the book of the *Wisdom of Ben Sira*, in which honouring one's parents (Sir 3:1–16) as instructed by the fifth commandment and the consequences of obeying or disobeying them are highlighted: 'Respect for a father atones for sins, and to honor your mother is to lay up a fortune' (Sir 3:3). According to Peter Balla, the expectation that children should honour their parents was expressed in numerous texts many centuries before the Christian era.[9] J. D. Cohen's research demonstrates that for some ancient Jewish teachers, 'to honour one's parents' was second only to honouring God (Josephus *Ag. Ap.* 2.27–206; *Pseud-Phoc.*8); and for others the honour due to one's parents was as significant as that due to God.[10]

Honouring one's parents requires that both minors and adult offspring to be responsible for the care and material support of their aged parents. Indeed, from a Jewish standpoint, whoever abandons their parents in their old age is the equivalent of a blasphemer (Sir 3:16). Again, some Jewish sources claim that the punishment for a son who fails to provide for his parents, should be death by stoning (Josephus *Ag. Ap.* 2:28–206).

Since children are expected to respect, honour and obey their parents (Exod 20:12), in this way, the nature of the F–S relationship in ancient Jewish culture is thus one of authority and obedience: 'Jewish wisdom emphasized honoring and obeying one's parents (Sir 3:1–4) in deeds as well as words (Sir 3:8), serving them as one's masters (Sir 3:7).'[11] For this reason, it was common for ancient Jewish theorists to use a hierarchical model to describe these family relationships: 'Only children who learned the discipline of obedience would understand how to exercise authority over others' (Isocrates *Ad. Nic.* 57; *Or.* 3.37).

The Jewish belief was that the hierarchical F–S relationship was determined by the father's role and function. Fathers were expected to provide for their children (Aristea *Ep.* 248) and this became the model for other relationships. One of the father of the house's main duties was to teach his children, and this teaching role is the basis of the requirement for a son to make reparation: as parents are benefactors in that one is reared by them in early life, and educated and guided by them in spiritual and religious life; in return, this debt must be repaid (Hesiod *OP*. 18–89). Therefore, one of the son's responsibilities is the duty of parental care.

This duty to care for aged parents also functions to ensure personal well-being, since Jewish wisdom stressed that as a result one's own old age would be blessed (Sir 3:12–15), and proposed that those who honoured their parents would have a long life (Exod 20:12) and would be rewarded in the world to come. By contrast, those who dishonoured their parents risked meeting the same fate at the hands of their own children.[12]

Honour and respect are due not only to parents but also to elderly people in general. An understanding of this fundamental status of the parent–child relationship as determining other social roles can be gained from the observations of the prominent Jewish philosopher Philo[13]of Alexandria (a contemporary of Paul), writing of the fifth commandment: 'In the fifth commandment on honoring parents we have a suggestion of many necessary laws drawn up to deal with the relations of old to young, rulers to subjects, benefactor to beneficiary, slaves to masters' (Philo *Dec.* 165).

In Philo's view the parent–child relationship was crucial because it was the model and basis for all other relationships: 'For parents belong to the superior class of the above mentioned pairs, that which comprises seniors, rulers, benefactors and masters, while children occupy the lower position with juniors, subjects, receivers of benefits and slaves' (Philo *Dec.* 166). It is clear that in Philo's mind there were parallels to be drawn between the parent–child relationship and that between seniors and juniors, rulers and subjects, benefactors and receivers, and masters and slaves; namely, a hierarchical similarity existed, where one element of the relationship was of higher rank than the other. Thus, the principles relating to the parent–child relationship are not only a fitting model for social relationships, but also offer practical suggestions for political networks. In this sense, the parent–child is not only the fundamental relationship of family, but also of society.

However, it is not the similarities between the parent–child relationship and that between senior–junior, ruler–subject, benefactor–receiver and master–slave relationships that are the primary reason for its use as a model and guide pattern. Indeed, its most fundamental purpose is to represent the parent's direct imitation of God's functions regarding generation and immortality. Thus, from Philo's viewpoint, the father fulfils the role of 'creating a new life' through begetting a child. Through his imitation of God's act of generation, a father can transcend the limitations of his perishable body and thereby propagate lineage to the next generation.[14] In this sense, the father has physically paralleled God's power of creation and immortality:

> Since just as He achieved existence for the nonexistent, so they in imitation of His powers, as far as they are capable, immortalize the race. (Philo *Spec.* 2.225)

> We see that parents by their nature stand on the borderline between the mortal and the immortal side of existence, the mortal because of their kinship with men and other animals through the perishableness of the body; the immortal because the act of generation assimilates them to God, the generator of the All. (Philo *Dec.* 107)

In imitating God's function in creation and in immortality, the parents thus possessed authority and power over their children; in the same way, in replicating the authority and power of parents, other relationships in society and politics became their counterpoints. From this perspective, the essential of legislation dealing with relationships between old and young, ruler and subject, benefactor and receiver and masters and slaves are derived entirely from the core relationship between parent and child.

From the emphasis on God and the fathers' imitation of God came the centrality of the spiritual character of the F–S relationship: thus a father is commanded to provide love for his children: 'Jewish piety, as understood by the Rabbis, rested on the fulfillment of a very large number of approved acts, *mitzvoth*, of either a ritual or an ethical character; it was indispensable that these be performed in a spirit of love.'[15] Interestingly, this outworking doctrinal principles reappears in Pauline religious ethics.

Nevertheless, although parents possess authority and power in the parent–child relationship, it is the F–S relationship that is fundamental. This is seen for example in the reference to 'true-born sons' to define the proper connection between ruler and subject, for which the model is just this F–S relationship:

> The ruler should preside over his subjects as a father over his children so that he himself may be honored in return as by true-born sons, and therefore good rulers may be truly called the parents of states and nations in common, since they should show a fatherly and sometimes more than fatherly affection. (Spec. 4.184)

The fact that the reference is to this F–S band in particular (rather than that of the parent and child in general) is affirmed in the special terminologies used for 'father', 'son' and 'parents', whereas this is not the case for 'daughter' or 'mother'. This usage of *ho pater* and *huios* or *pais* in Philo's work is well expounded J. D. Cohen:

> In most of Philonic discussions, the terminology for parents is *hoi goneis*, which is a term of masculine plural; and the terminology of father is *ho pater*. When speaking specifically of sons, Philo often uses the masculine *huios* . . . In numerous passages, however, the masculine forms of *pais* are used interchangeably with *huios* or its plural, to denote male children specifically.[16]

Two observations are apposite here: on the one hand, there is no specific term for 'mother' or 'daughter', while the terminology used for 'parents' takes its masculine plural form. Taken together, this implies that the position of the male is higher than that of the female in Philo's understanding. In the same way, the F–S relationship may be taken as more central and indeed higher status than that between mother and daughter.

Some scholars, however, insist that compared to Greco-Roman culture, Jewish culture accorded mothers a high status – even a position equal to that of the father. Two arguments are often used to reinforce this view. First, in most circumstances, it is the parents in general rather than the father specifically that is discussed, as, for example, in Philo, *Spec. Leg.* 2.42:234–6; *Ebr.* 5:17 and *Omn. Prob. Lib.* 12:87. Secondly, at times, the mother is mentioned alone: for example, in Apocrypha, *Tob* 4:3–4, it is said that one should honour and please one's mother, because she has not only experienced pregnancy and given birth to her children, but also endured great pains both in this and in their upbringing.[17]

However, although this argument may be valid with regard to the higher status of women in Israel as against Greco-Roman culture, the ancient Jewish mother did not have equal status with the Jewish father. In particular the mother–son or mother–daughter relationship did not rank with the F–S relationship. Indeed, according to Ross S. Kraemer's research, Hellenistic Jewish sources give little attention to mother–daughter relationships, while literary sources in general furnish only the most minimal representations of this, in contrast to the depiction of fathers and sons, mother and sons, and even fathers and daughters.[18] Thus, while sole references to the mother may indicate that she was also important in Jewish culture, it does not necessarily follow that her status was equal to that of the father. Individual reference to the father is not only greater in Philo than that to the mother, but also, as stated, specific terminology used for father and son is absent in the case of the mother. Therefore, it can be argued that the occasional emphasis upon the mother does not of necessity undermine the dominant position of the father. Similarly, while references to the parents rather than the father singly may be more frequent, this merely demonstrates the important role of both mother and father; it does not lead us to the conclusion that the mother's position is equal to the father's.

Indeed, there is ample evidence to the contrary: the position of the father is higher than that of the mother. There is first Philo's affirmation as already discussed of the F–S model above all others as the pattern for the ruler–subject relationship. Moreover, while there is no a clear expression of equality between father and mother, there is firm declaration that man is superior to woman: 'The woman, says the law, is in all things inferior to the man. Let her accordingly be submissive – for the authority has been given by God to the man.'[19] Given this 'superiority' of the male, it therefore logically follows that the F–S model specially should form the basis of familial and thence socio-political relationships.

Nevertheless, some feminist theologians propose opposing views of women in Jewish culture. For example, on the basis of a detailed study of nineteen Greek and Latin inscriptions of varying or sometimes unknown dates, in which without exception a woman is named as some type of community or synagogue leader, Bernadette Brooten argues for the existence in the Diaspora of a form of Judaism which allowed women an active role in the religious life of the synagogue.[20] However, as Tessa Rajak has recognized, there is a problem regarding Brooten's statement: her conclusion, based on the women's presence among the office-holders, fails to account for the presence of children among the office-holders. These children can hardly be regarded as having been functional in their posts, as leaders of the synagogue. Accordingly, it is not valid to posit women's leadership from their being named as leaders in these various inscriptions. Moreover, 'There too, at any rate in Asia Minor, women and children were to be found, among a vast preponderance of men.'[21] Therefore, this is a shaky basis on which to conclude that women had an equal position to men.

This traditional Jewish view of the status of the male and the father is fully visible in Pauline teachings. Although there is a debate here on the position ascribed to women in these teachings, with some scholars holding to the idea that the position of women in the fledgling Christian church under Paul's guidance was quite high,[22] the out-working of Paul's doctrinal principles on the relationship between men and women is obvious upon the superiority of male: 'Wives, submit to your husband as to the Lord' (Eph 5:22); 'Now I want you to realize that the head of every man is Christ, and the head of the woman is man, and the head of Christ is God' (I Cor 11:3); 'A man ought not to cover his head, since he is the image and glory of God; but the woman is the glory of man. For man did not come from women, but woman from man; neither was man created for woman, but woman fro man. For this reason, and because of the angels, the woman ought to have a sign of authority on her head' (I Cor 11:7–10).

This higher esteem of men can also be shown by the fact that (a) God is portrayed as male: for example, He is the Father of Jesus Christ as well as the Father of all believers; (b) God created the male (Adam) in His image and made the female (Eve) from the rib of the male for the male; (c) it is a male – Abraham – who is recognized as the father and model of many nations and of all God's believers; and (d) it is also a male – Jesus Christ, the Son of God – who was sent to be the saviour of human beings and to be exalted as the king of kings. For Paul, everything is through him (Jesus), in him and for him. Jesus being the head of all creation implies that the male in turn is the head of all things, and that everything is through the male, in the male and for the male.[23] Because of this, certain feminist critics still hold Paul responsible for leading Christianity toward patriarchy.[24] On the other hand, it is to be remembered here that the supreme status of father in Pauline thinking is not manifested through the centrality of the natural, but rather the spiritual F–S relationship.

The central status of the spiritual father–son relationship in Jewish culture and its influence on Pauline ethical thinking

It was common in ancient Jewish culture to use kinship terminology based on a social rather than a genetic relationship. Thus, for the ancient Jew, 'father' implied not only biological origin, but was also a title of great respect, such as, for example, titles like 'father of the Jews' (2 Macc 14:37) and 'father of the world'. There were also various texts applying F–S terminology to teachers and their disciples, who were called 'children of their teachers' (4 *Bar.* 7:24; 3 *Jh.* 4), while their teachers were 'their fathers' (2 Kgs 2:12; 4 *Bar.* 2:4, 6, 8; 5:5; Matt 23:9).[25] Moreover, kinship relationships in Jewish culture are redefined in spiritual terms; the corollary of such spiritual kinship is that Philo regarded God as 'Father' (Philo *Spec.*1.318).[26]

This deep-rooted concept was in turn fully inherited by the NT authors, including Paul himself. This is affirmed by Moxnes, who claims that terms used by Philo and Josephus of the Essenes and the Therapeutae such as 'spiritual kinship' or 'spiritual household' are similar to those used of Christian groups by various NT authors, as well as in Gnostic scriptures. Thus, household and kinship/family metaphors provided a powerful idiom for 'chosen' groups, as well as for the larger context.[27] For Paul, then, the term 'father' not only denoted the natural begetter of the son, but could also be applied to any respected elder (Acts 7:2; 22:1; 1 Tim 5:1), to the apostles, people with authority, and especially God himself as the creator. The authority and power of the father, and the obedience and submission of the son not only pointed to the natural kinship relation, but also to all the relationships between authority and the powerless, such as apostle–disciple, priest–Christian believer, and especially the God–Jesus relationship.

The spiritual concepts of Jewish culture in terms of honouring and obeying parents as well as elders are integral to Pauline moral teaching, in which the authority–obedience and mutual love relationships become the main themes not only of the divine and the natural F–S relationships, but also that of husband–wife and master and slave in the family; Jesus–believer, God–man, apostle–disciple and priest–church member relationships in Christian religion; and ruler–citizen or patron–client, and old–young relationships in the socio-political field.

The centrality of the spiritual F–S relationship in Jewish culture is at the same time bound up with an understanding of the origin of paternal authority and power. In contrast to Chinese culture, the authority and power of the Jewish father were not naturally developed from a biological or secular paradigm, but rather had a theological underpinning. In other words, the power and authority of the father do not come from his natural generative power or productive capacity, but instead from the fact of his creation in the image of God. For the Jewish people, it is this role as Creator of the universe and humankind, and the function of creation itself, that defines God's absolute power; similarly, it is thus the begetting function of the parents that give them power over their children.[28]

Two conclusions can be drawn here: on the one hand, God transcended by far both natural father and parents in ancient Jewish thought; therefore, ultimate obedience to God Himself came first, while the honour due to one's parents flowed logically from that obedience.[29] On the other hand, the parental role, especially that of the father, was so profound that it was second only to God Himself; therefore paternal authority and power were so fundamental as to provide the model for other relationships in secular society.

This deep-rooted Jewish tradition concerning the primacy of God was further developed in the great Pauline doctrinal expositions; on the one hand, Paul, the Apostle lays extreme emphasis on the authority and power of God and Jesus Christ, and thence outworks the 'power versus submission' paradigm of the Father's relation to the Son, and the Son's relation to the Believer; on the other hand, he took this powerful metaphor of F–S to describe the God–Jesus relationship, and expounded for the young Christian churches in his care the profundity of this relationship as being above all other social, political and familial ties. Hence the religious F–S relationship between God and Jesus becomes the centre and model for all other ethical relationships, including that of the natural F–S.

The Greco-Roman Cultural Background to the Pauline Divine Father–Son Relationship

Thus, the influence of ancient Jewish culture upon the principle of daily life in the NT Christian household is profound; some scholars, however, emphasize the influence of Hellenistic Judaism as well as Greco-Roman household codes on the NT. For example,

Andrew T. Lincoln asserts that it is not sufficient simply to trace the origin of the Pauline house code to Philo and Josephus, but it needs to be situated in the broader context of the discussion of household management in the ancient world that goes all the way back to the classical Greek philosophers.[30]

As the cultural pattern and philosophy of the dominant Greco-Roman power of the first century, it is almost inconceivable that Hellenism did not have some shaping influence on Paul's thought.[31] This was certainly the case for Philo, for example, for whom Hellenic culture was the foundation of his epistemology, as Paul van Buren states, Israel's view of knowledge was in the same way moulded by its influence.[32] Therefore, Paul's interpretation of the 'Christ event' under 'Hellenistic culture' should be understood as a term for a culture that results from mixing what were originally Greek cultural elements with originally non-Greek cultural elements.[33] In fact, few would deny that there is a connection between ancient Jewish and Greco-Roman cultures, especially in relation to the Pauline idea of household codes. It is not surprising therefore, that Aune argues that the Hellenistic Jewish household codes were developed from Greco-Roman culture.[34]

Paul was a Jew by race and by practice (Rom 11:1; Gal 1:14–15; Phil 3:3), and therefore yearned for the ultimate inclusion of the Jews in God's gracious purpose (Rom 9–11). His message was proclaimed in terms familiar to them – the law, faith, the promises, the righteousness of God, judgment, the Spirit and so on. It was a Hellenistic world where he wrote in Greek, used the Greek translation of the OT, and, at times, exhibited the strong influence of this world. Above all, however, Paul was a Christian; thus in his eyes, Jews and Greeks alike were only custodians 'until Christ came' (Gal 3:24; 1 Cor 1:4–17); for this reason, he felt himself to be obligated both to Greeks and to Gentiles to preach the gospel (Rom 1:14–15).

Paul's primary source is the OT, but nevertheless the impact of the larger world around him can be discerned both conceptually and stylistically. Working as he was within a cultural melting pot, Paul was a figure detached from any given context, his wide-ranging vision encompassing whatever came from outside and using, shaping and integrating these influences according to his own roots or purposes:[35]

> Paul was a unique person. Just as aunts see now the father and now the mother in the child, so we see now the Jew and now the Hellenist in Paul. But the child is not his mother or his father; he is himself. Paul was emphatically himself. His letters to the churches of Galatia, to Thessalonica, to Corinth or Philippi, are not just the serious communications of a Christian theologian; it is Paul writing, and the unmistakable flavor of his personality pervades them.[36]

Nevertheless, although to outward appearances Paul is a 'wanderer between two worlds', his theological thinking displays an astonishing unity.[37] In this sense, the relationship between the father and the son in Pauline teaching shows a merging of old and new traditions, at the same time developing a strong and practical cultural base for Christian living.

The status of the father in Greco-Roman culture

The position of the father in Roman antiquity was very high – much higher than in

Jewish society. This resulted from the high status of males in ancient Greco-Roman society, and the power of the *paterfamilias* and *patria potestas* in the family.[38]

The powerful status of the male in Greco-Roman society can be shown first from their sense of social honour and from their sensitivities to all that might cause their shame or dishonour. Thus, as affirmed by Carolyn Osiek and David L. Balch, male honour in ancient Greco-Roman society consisted of maintaining the status, power and reputation of the male members of a kinship group over and against the threats posed against them by outsiders, in return receiving an absolute loyalty and deference from different members according to their proper role in the hierarchy of authority within the family.[39] From this perspective, hierarchy is integral to each familial structure: by nature, men command and women, slaves and children obey. The quality of male rule is adapted in each case, but is decisive.[40]

The powerful status of the male can also be seen from the social construction of gender. Greco-Roman society believed in the inherent superiority of male over female in nature, strength and capacity for virtue or courage; the dangerous power of women to bring shame upon the family was thus of paramount concern to the male, women therefore had no equal position with men and were, for this reason, controlled, enclosed and guarded by them.

According to Roman tradition, the family was the heart of pagan society,[41] as is reflected in special terminologies linked with its members and the authority accorded to them. The Greco-Roman word for family unit itself, for example, is *familia*, while its formal head was termed the *paterfamilias*.[42] Many differences exist however between the English understanding of the word 'family' and its Latin counterpart, for which according to Richard P. Saller, there are two meanings: *familia* as *res* and *familia* as *personae*. Moreover, there are a variety of meanings of *familia* used in respect to *personae*. The first is the strict legal sense of all *personae* in the *potestas* of the *paterfamilias*, either by nature or by law, including the *paterfamilias*; namely, sons, daughters, adopted children, grandsons and granddaughters. However, in its strict legal sense, the wife or the mother is not included in this concept, but instead in that of *domus*, which also covers a broad semantic range. The term is used with regard to household and kinship to mean (a) the physical house; (b) the household, including family members and slaves; (c) the broad kinship group, including agnates and cognates, ancestors and descendants; and (d) the patrimony. All these meanings are thus related to and merge into one another.

An important difference between *familia* and *domus* however is that the latter also acts as the symbol of both status and family, as affirmed by Saller: 'the *domus*, apart from kinship, was central to Roman construction of social status'; this is because 'Domus in the sense of human household, as well as physical house, was a focus of honour for Romans: the honour of the *paterfamilias* depended on his ability to protect his household, and in turn the virtue of the household contributed to his prestige.'[43] Hence in the concept of *familia*, the father actually possessed the highest position in both his *familia* and *domus*.

Further, there are two expressions of the father's authority – *paterfamilias* and *patria potestas*. The first of these refers to the position of primary authority in the household, and is the male head of the home as addressed in the household codes. *Patria potestas*, on the other hand, denotes the father's authority of life and death over his son and other family members. This concept was a central organizing principle of Roman law concerning persons and property, and was regarded as a characteristically Roman feature, often dominating historical familial interpretations in terms of its nearly absolute legal power of the father over his wife and his children.

This absolute authority was further defined by the Roman word *pietas*, a core virtue of the Roman ideal of family relations, defined in the *Oxford Classical Dictionary* as 'the typical Roman attitude of dutiful respect toward gods, fatherland, and parents and other kinsmen'. As Saller notes, although there are several layers of meaning commonly associated with *pietas* incorporated in this definition, its emphasis is on duty rather than affection or compassion.[44] The Greek commentator, Dionysius of Halicarnassus, detailed the lifelong power that Romulus granted to fathers over their children: the power to imprison, to beat and even to kill their sons,[45] while Sextus Empiricus placed the Roman father's power in a wider, mythical-historical context:

> Cronos decided to destroy his own children, and Solon gave the Athenians the law concerning things immune by which he allowed each man to slay his own child; but with us the laws forbid the slaying of children. The Roman lawgivers also ordain that the children are subjects and slaves of their fathers, and that power over the children's property belongs to the fathers and not the children, until the children have obtained their freedom like bought slaves; but this custom is rejected by others as being despotic. (3.211)[46]

Not surprisingly the Greeks therefore regarded the Romans as cruel and harsh, as is evident in the following description: (a) A Roman master could sell a slave only once, but if a father sold a child who subsequently attained freedom, then the father was entitled to re-sell him or her; (b) the disposal of children was a widely known custom (Pausanias, *Descr.* 2.26.4); a father could not only refuse to rear a newborn, even against the mother's objections (Gardner, p. 6), but (c) also, sometimes, order a deformed infant to be killed (Denboer, pp. 98–9, 113, 116).[47]

This harshness has also been evoked by P. Veyne in *A History of Private Life*, where the Roman family and household of the Republic are described as units bounded not by affection but by the limits of the father's power. Moreover, Veyne sees the son's position as similar to that of a slave, in terms of being treated virtually as a chattel: 'Children who were moved about like pawns on the chessboard of wealth and power were hardly cherished and coddled.' Consequently, for children the father's death 'signaled the end of a kind of slavery'.[48] It is clear that paternal authority over life and death of family members had declined in the period of the empire to the extent that in practice fathers could not kill their children; while it is not difficult to find examples of fatherly love, tenderness, affection, care, distress, or warmth,[49] his authority over the family still permeated the fabric of Roman society.

The position of the father–son relationship in Greco-Roman culture

It naturally follows from this that the relationship between the parent and the child in Greco-Roman culture is central: 'The literary records of the Greco-Roman world are replete with portrayals of or references to parents and children.'[50] Indeed, as Halvor Moxnes affirms, 'family metaphors played an important role in Roman society; especially important was the metaphor of F–S. It is significant that the Romans saw themselves not as a society of mothers and daughters or of brothers, but of fathers and sons.'[51]

Balsdon further notes that Roman society was built on the idea of deference in the family as in the state: 'Whatever their age, sons and daughters owed deference to their father, who had the sanction of power over them; their wholehearted and sincere submission was an exaltation of *obsequium*; it was *pietas*.'[52] Hence, the father image assumes particular significance in the title *pater patriae* as used of the emperor. In this sense, then, the family of the emperor became the 'state family' and reinforced the image of the emperor as the father and head of the state. Here Eva Marie Lassen notes how Caesar made use of this strongly entrenched father metaphor to assist his rise to power; by representing his own family as a 'state family', Augustus effectively reinforced the image of himself as both state leader and father-figure.[53] Saller's research also affirms that for centuries the Roman *paterfamilias* has served as a paradigm of patriarchal authority and social order; *patria potestas* was viewed as the embodiment of arbitrary, even tyrannical power, rather as the sort of power a master exercises over his slave, a power more or less unaccountable to higher principles or formal procedures.[54]

From the above analysis it can be seen that family relations in ancient Roman society acted as a kind of 'barometer' to measure moral and social well-being. In Roman antiquity a father was expected to extend his skills of household governance to those needed to rule a city, since these were regarded as synonymous (Euripides, *El.* 386–7; Isocrates *Ad Nic.* 19; *Or.* 2; Plutarch *Dinner of Seven Wise Men* 12; *Mor.* 155D). From this perspective, it was natural to also extend the F–S relationship itself from private to public affairs, as Cicero indicates: 'Roman authors believe family formation and the organization of the household to be natural steps in social evolution, rather than a matter of culturally specific development susceptible to historical analysis.'[55]

This is a tradition which can be traced to its source in the thought of ancient Greek philosophers. Aristotle, for example, believed that order in the household would produce order in society as a whole, since societal norms and household norms were inextricably linked. Although there were differences between these codes (see, for example, Aristotle *Pol.* 1.1.2, 1252a; 1.5.6, 1260a), the principles of household management could be nevertheless be linked with the broader category of advice on city management.[56]

The rationale for this fluid translation of 'household' into 'political' power (and *vice versa*) is at least threefold. One significant aspect is its character of strict hierarchy, with rigid distinctions of status stretching from the honorable citizen to his bondservants, and outwards to fine divisions within the ranks of citizens themselves; these 'divisions' in turn governed socio-political interactions between propertied Romans, as observed by Saller.[57]

The second reason for this easy transference of principle is grounded in the character of family itself. Romans considered the bonds of family and kinship to be biologically based, but not biologically determined. As Saller argues, this meant that Roman law offered citizens a flexibility in restructuring their kinship bonds that was remarkable by later European standards, because divorce and remarriage were very easy in the classical period. Adoption was also common, although 'apparently not so common as to vitiate a model of the kinship universe based on biological reproduction',[58] which in itself permitted of no change of filiations; an adoption built on a non-biological base gave kinship bonds much flexibility. Hence, status distinctions coupled with the flexibility of kinship bonds and the mobility of loyalty within the family itself provided the perfect pattern for socio-political hierarchies.

The third aspect is that the familial conceptions of both *paterfamilias* and *pietas* are extended in the same way to the principles of political action: 'Loyalty to master, patron, and emperor (as the supreme commander of the army) was undoubtedly an important mobility factor in Roman Hellenistic society.'[59] Osiek and Balch explore this key notion of the 'patron', and demonstrate that the Roman family and household were shaped in line with its influence; indeed, one important element of the demonstration of male honor was this function of patronage and hospitality. From this perspective, 'patronage' itself was primarily a form of extended kinship, in which an extension of familial loyalty is applied to other relations neither related by blood, law, or other traditional ties; in this sense, the patron functions as a kind of 'surrogate father', and the patronage system is as thus defined in fact a way of replicating the kinship system. By ascribing to the patron the function of a father, the paternal role is extended and enlarged from a familial to a social notion.[60]

Powerful indications of this relationship between 'household management' and 'politics' come from the Romans themselves, particularly in the work of Arius Didymus', Augustus Caesar's friend and philosophical teacher, whose viewpoint can be extended to Greco-Roman society in general.

The essential point made here is that since humans are by nature political animals, then this should be linked with 'household management', as developed in the '*politeia*'. This primary association (*politeia*) was taken to be the legal union of a man and a woman for the begetting of children and for sharing life; this union is termed the 'household' and is in turn the basis for the foundation of the city. In what sense, then, can the 'household' represent the basis of the 'city'? This is because the household can be compared to any small city; if, as intended, the marriage flourishes, and children mature and marry, they then pair off; so, another household is founded, and eventually a third and a fourth are formed. From these, a village and finally a city emerge. So just as the household yields seeds for the formation of the city, it also yields the stuff of the constitution (*politeia*).

What, then, are the founding principles for this 'household'? Here Didymus likened the patterns of monarchy, of aristocracy and democracy with the relationship of parents to children, of husbands to wives, of children to one another, respectively. It is the principle of the authority and power of the male leader rather than any other principle that is implied in the household: the male uniting with the female is in accordance with a desire for begetting children and for continuing the race, which provides an opportunity for man being responsible in ruling his household by nature. Speaking precisely, since the deliberative faculty in a woman is inferior, in children does not exist, and in the case of slaves is completely absent, therefore, the need for governing both the household itself and those things related to the household, is naturally more fitting for the man. In turn, it is natural to conclude that this characteristic of the father's authority over his children is comparable to that of a ruler over his subjects (Aristotle *Eth. Nic.* 8.11.2, 1161a), and in the same way to extend paternal power to political power.

From this analysis it is apparent that the nature of the F–S relationship in Greco-Roman culture was closely akin to that of master and slave, with the patriarchal power of the father consistently extending to political hierarchical power. Unlike the modern family, for whom the domestic hearth is primarily a place of retreat or refuge from the world of work and education that lies outside the home, the Roman household was not merely dwelling-place; instead it assumed many functions. It was a place of constant social, economic, and indeed often political intercourse, where family relationships were structured as the basis of patriarchal order rather than affection. Although there is a debate about the real function of this patriarchal order,[61] it seems reasonable to conclude that in the Greco-Roman world, such a system was synonymous with hierarchy, and that in turn familial authority linked closely with state authority, as observed by Eva Marie Lassen: 'Family metaphor flourished in Roman society and helped to underline its hierarchical nature.'[62]

The influence of Greco-Roman culture on the Pauline divine father–son relationship

The religion of Christ has been regarded as something wholly new, except in so far as it had roots in the OT, and in the sense of an absolute antithesis to the pagan world in which it so rapidly propagated itself.[63] Nevertheless, such a view seems as false as the opposite extreme, which would hold that Christianity is simply the fortuitous concourse of religious atoms already in existence without the intervention of any divine providence.[64] In this regard, David E. Aune has observed that despite some remaining questions about the influences on Pauline teaching raised by recent theory on the origin of the form of the NT household codes, a consensus has nevertheless been reached that their form is derived from the Hellenistic discussion of 'household management',[65] as is found for example in the following five views on their sources. Martin Dibelius here discussed Paul's Epistle to the Colossians (in particular chapters 3 and 4) where he suggested that verses 18 in Chapter 3 to the first of chapter 4 'Christianise' the Stoics code as presented in such phrases as a popular handbook pattern like that of Hierocles, especially in 'as is fitting' (Col 3:18) and 'acceptable' (3:20), which are typically Stoic, and were inter-Christianized by the expression 'in the Lord' (3:20).[66] In this Karl Weidinger follows Dibelius, reaffirming the view that the household code schema has its origin in Stoic–Cynic philosophy, but that it is used also in Hellenistic Judaism.[67] Later Klaus Thraede further proposed that the NT Code is not only influenced by Stoics, but also by Plato.[68] Balch adds to this with the statement that 'Aristotle developed household codes to advise aristocratic men about the various ways they should rule their wives, children and slaves' (Aristotle *Pol.* 1.2.1–2, 1253b; 1.5.3–4, 1259b; 3.4.4, 1278b).[69] Berger, on the other hand, combined these two suggestions.[70] As for the origins of the Pauline F–S relationship itself, Aune explores its potential political applications.[71]

Thus, despite the general 'consensus' discussed, divergence of opinion also exists as to specific influences on Pauline teaching. It seems that while each scholastic view has caught some aspect of the truth, none of have caught the whole: 'Every step in the development of the New Testament is understandable in the light of Philonic, Stoic, and other types of Jewish and Hellenistic thought and practice.'[72] Notwithstanding apparent contradictions, however, one fact is clear – NT and Pauline household codes were influenced by a variety of sources; that is, the principles of Christian daily life as advocated by Paul not only embodied Judo-Hellenistic values to encourage Christians to sever familial, social and religious ties with pagans, but also integrated those of the Greco-Roman culture into social patterns in the early Jesus movement.

To elaborate more precisely, first, since 'kinship and its set of interlocking rules formed the central social institution'[73] the divine F–S relationship became the centre of the Pauline ethical relationship. Secondly, since political factors were another major consideration, this concept extended to the Roman Empire itself, which became one big family with the emperor as the *paterfamilias* of its multiple members.[74] In line with this analogy, the emperor thus embodied absolute power over the Roman world, equivalent to that of a father over his children.[75] The authority–obedience relationship between the divine Father and Son can thus in this sense be equated with the political relationship in Pauline thinking. Thirdly, because the early Mediterranean world was demarcated in terms of power, gender and social status, and males were generally well educated and well situated in the institutional hierarchies of the Christian church,[76] the need for hierarchical familial and social structures thereby naturally became interwoven with the theme of 'serving God as Master' to become one of the central themes of Pauline religious ethics. In the further place, patronage also dominated the Mediterranean world, both as an ideology and as a social relation, and originated in the social sphere of the family;[77] this in turn paved the way for establishing a patron–client relationship in Pauline Christian religious society. lastly, although the *paterfamilias*'s lifelong power over his slaves, adopted and biological children formed the backbone of Roman society, a more 'sentimental idea of the family' flourished in the later Roman republic, which not only emphasized the ideal of harmony between husbands and wives, but also stressed the principle of affection towards the children of the family.[78] It is thus possible that Pauline concept of *agape* between God the father and the Son, reflected in the affection between the natural father and son, has its roots in all of the foregoing.

In short, the Pauline F–S metaphors communicated a well-known set of ideals within Roman society. This content was not however solely limited to the F–S, but also included the concept of brotherhood: 'In the light of the Roman tradition of describing society as a "father–son" relationship, it is striking that the most popular term to describe interrelationships among the first Christians was "brothers".'[79] Thus, it could be argued that through the metaphor of brotherhood, Pauline teaching successfully promoted equality, but without destroying the hierarchical social fabric.[80]

The Theological Sources of the Pauline Divine Father–Son Relationship

This being so, it is nevertheless the case that many of Paul's paternalistic traditions derived from Jewish sources; W. D. Davies argues in *Paul and Rabbinic Judaism* that Christ himself provided the wellspring of Pauline teaching: 'it was the words of Jesus Himself that formed Paul's primary source in his work as ethical *didaskalos*'.[81] Indeed, on this point, some scholars go so far as to claim that the household codes have a purely Christian origin.[82] Thus, the theological sources of the Pauline F–S relationship merit exploration, and will be discussed from three perspectives: the biblical sources of the Pauline *divine* F–S relationship, the term 'Abba' as invoked in the prayers of Jesus to the Father and the designation of God as 'Our Father' in the NT.

Biblical sources of the Pauline divine Father–Son relationship

As some scholars have recognized, basic to the ethical teaching of the Bible is the insistence that the final measure of human conduct cannot be devised by humans themselves, but stems from the nature of God, from the quality of His love for mankind, and from the character of His redemptive activity.[83] That the Pauline interpretation of the F–S relationship is strongly rooted in its biblical source therefore seems beyond question. Many scholars have their own different contributions to make on the divine roots of Pauline teaching in the OT. For example, Robert M. Grant claims:

> To a Jewish Hearer, Paul's proclamation would make sense because the Old Testament prophets had proclaimed the moral demands of God, had insisted that his wrath was due against disobedience, and had spoken of a mysterious 'servant' who would suffer on behalf of the people and win God's forgiveness. Jews had heard of God's creative and caring actions for the people. God was obviously real and living, and announced himself as the only God. He chose individuals, addressing them as sons; he promised resurrection; and he took the prophet Elijah up into heaven at death. (1 Kgs 2:11)[84]

According to Jeremias, from earliest times the Near East was familiar with the mythological concept of deity as the father of humankind. Ancient peoples, tribes and families thus consistently pictured themselves as the offspring of a divine ancestor. Consequently, whenever the word 'father' is used for a deity in this context, it implies a fatherhood of unconditional and irrevocable authority. This is even truer of the OT,[85] in which God has been called as the Father.[86]

In the OT, God is referred to as 'Father' only fourteen times. However, each of these references is integral in establishing the framework of the divine F–S relationship, and three significant aspects of the relationship between God and humankind are established among them. The first of these is that between the creator and the created: 'Is he not your Father, your Creator, who made you and formed you?' (Deut 32:6). 'Have we not all one Father? Did not one God create us?' (Mal 2:10). Here, it is implied that (a) God is the Great Being with power and authority to make all things, and (b) that God created humanity and endowed them with the gift of reason together with 'free will'. As a Creator with full power and authority, God not only expects to be honoured as the Lord, but also expects reverence: 'A son honours his father, and a servant his master. If I am a father, where is the honour due to me? If I am a master, where is the respect due to me?' (Mal 1.6).

In short, the OT has made us familiar with the Hebrew concept of fatherhood as implying a relationship of care and authority on the one side and love and obedience on the other (Deut 1:31; 8:5; 14:1; Isa 1:2; Jer 3:19; Mal 1:6).[87]

Secondly, in the OT, God is a merciful Father of those who fear him: 'As a father has compassion on his children, so the Lord has compassion on those who fear him' (Ps 103:13). Although Israelites, as his chosen people, were a stubborn and obstructive nation, being their Father, God still poured all His affection on them:

> How gladly would I treat you like sons, and give you a desirable land, the most beautiful inheritance of my nation.
>
> I thought you would call me 'Father' and not turn away from following me. But like a woman unfaithful to her husband, so you have been unfaithful to me, O house of Israel. (Jer 3:19)

For Israel, this is because mercy is the nature of God as father: 'Where are your zeal and your might? Your tenderness and compassion are withheld from us. But you are our Father, though Abraham does not know us or Israel acknowledge us; you, O Lord, are our Father, our Redeemer from of old is your name' (Isa 63:15–16). Therefore, God's mercy exceeds all human comprehension: 'Is not Ephraim my dear son, the child in whom I delight? . . . Therefore my heart yearns for him; I must great compassion for him, declares the Lord' (Jer 31:20). Thus, God's fatherly love becomes his first and his last word, regardless of the guilt of his children.

Finally, in the OT, although God represents love, mercy and forgiveness, he is also a severe Father; he will punish rebels and reward obedient: 'for I, the LORD your God, am a jealous God, punishing the children for the sin of the fathers to the third and fourth generations of those who hate me, but showing love to a thousand generations of those who love men and keep my commandments' (Exod 20:5–6). In this respect it thus seems that He differs from a natural father; in the case of the natural F–S relationship, there is a sense that biological ties decide the attitude of each towards the other: since he is my son, I will recognize him as such and love him, whether or not he obeys. Hence, by distinguishing from such a biological sense, an absolute authority–obedience relationship between God and people in the OT has been established.

Paul thus takes the twin qualities of 'forgiveness' and 'severity' as forming an integral part of God's nature, but emphasizes *agape* as balancing the reverence and obedience which are due to Him as 'Father' of the Jewish Nation.

The divine Fatherhood in the OT hence has distinctive characteristics. First, God as Father is not the ancestor or progenitor but the Creator with full power, knowledge and perfect virtue, with authority not only over humans but also over the whole physical universe. Secondly, God's divine Fatherhood is related to Israel alone in a quite unparalleled sense: 'The second characteristic of Jewish statements of this period about God's fatherhood is that God is repeatedly spoken of as the father of the individual Israelite.'[88] God is the Father of the Israelite nation: its people are His first-born, chosen out of all peoples (Deut 14:2) and Israel is called 'my son' (Hos 11:1); as a consequence, God's love, in the OT, promised salvation exclusively for Israel.

Although this relationship was nationalistic rather than 'individualistic', God as Father had strong and intimate individual connections with the Israelite kings, each of whom could in this sense be conceived of as an individual son of God. This means that collective fatherhood did not therefore exclude the idea of an individual relationship.

This prepared the way for the idea of an individual relationship between God and Man, which would be fully developed in the Pauline divine F–S relationship.

Abba in the prayers of Jesus

The character of divine Fatherhood had changed by the time of Jesus Christ. The Christian view of God's parenthood brings an unparalleled element of intimacy into the human relationship with God, which we see from the use of the word *abba* in the prayers of Jesus. According to Jeremias's examination of the prayers of Jesus, God is almost always addressed as *abba* (my father). He writes:

> To his [Jesus] disciples it must have been something quite extraordinary that Jesus addressed God as 'My Father'. Moreover not only do the four Gospels attest that Jesus used this address, but they report unanimously that he did so in all his prayers (note: 21 times, 16 times if parallels are counted only once). There is only one prayer of Jesus in which 'my Father' is lacking. That is the cry from the cross: 'My God, my God, why hast thou forsaken me?' (Mark 15:34, Matt 27:46, quoting Ps 22:1). Still, we have not yet said everything. The most remarkable thing is that when Jesus addressed God as his father in prayer he used the Aramaic word *abba*.[89]

As identified in this examination, *abba* is a form of the word 'father' in Aramaic. Jewish prayers did not contain a single example of *abba* as an address for God, yet Jesus consistently used this term when he prayed; the notion *abba* reveals beyond doubt the very basis of Jesus' communion with God; the Son speaks to the Father in terms of great intimacy and closeness. From here we can conclude that father is a designation for God in Jesus' mind.

Nevertheless, this depiction of the *abba*-terminology has been challenged by Martina Gnadt[90] and James Barr in their separate articles entitled 'Abba Isn't Daddy'. According to the latter scholar, *abba* 'was not a childish expression comparable with "Daddy"; it was more a solemn, responsible, adult address to a Father'. Moreover, while it is possible that all cases in which Jesus addresses God as 'Father' connected with *abba*, it is impossible to prove that this is so, for there are alternative hypotheses which seem to fit the evidence equally well. Lastly, although the use of *abba* in addressing God may have first originated with Jesus, it remains difficult to prove how constant and pervasive this element was in his expression of his divine relationship with God; it is therefore difficult to demonstrate that this divine relationship is central in our total understanding of him.[91]

Thus, Barr's opinion has at first galnce challenged Jeremias' interpretation of '*abba* is daddy'. On the other hand, Paul R. Smith argues that this challenge is unsuccessful, since even Barr would have to concede that *abba* was a word used both by the young child, and in fact was one of the first words spoken by an infant, as well as being used by older children as a term of respect. In line with this, to claim that *abba* does not mean 'daddy' in any sense is to ignore this use by the infant, while to place too much emphasis on the 'daddy' may perhaps be to ignore its use by adults as a term of respect.[92] It could also be said that Jeremias' interpretation does not challenge but rather confirms that 'Jesus used *abba* to point to God as his "Father" or as the "Father"'. For in the first place, it does not matter whether *abba* is Aramaic or Hebrew, or whether it existed before Jesus' time; what is important is that Jesus uses it in addressing God. Again, it does not matter whether *abba* is a babyish or adult address to a father; the issue here is that Jesus uses this term to address God as his Father. Whatever the ultimate meaning of *abba*, this cannot change the fact that Jesus addresses God Himself as his Father, and that thereby an intimate relationship between Jesus and God as Son communing with Father has been established.

There are two kinds of contexts in which Jesus refers to God as 'Father'. In the first, he speaks to others of God as 'your Father'; in his own personal communion, the appellation is 'my Father'. The 'your Father' sayings thus picture God as the Father who knows what His children need (Matt 6.32 par. Luke 12.30), who is merciful (Luke 6.36) and unlimited in goodness (Matt 5.45), who can forgive (Mark 11.25), and whose good pleasure is to grant His kingdom to His flock (Luke 12.32).[93] It therefore follows that two distinctive Christian features arise here: God as the Father of Jesus Christ highlights the God–Son relationship; while God as the Father of the disciples of Jesus establishes the individual relationship which because of salvation thereby becomes possible between God and His believers. This also provides a precedent for the apostles and leaders of the churches to adopt the title of 'Christian fathers'. In this sense, Paul sometimes regards himself as the father of other Christian fellowships for which he is spiritually responsible, as his Epistles to the fledgling Christian churches show.

The designation of God as 'Father' in the New Testament

In contrast with the OT, then, the relationship that is most spoken of in NT texts is that between father and son as affirmed by Peter Balla; the texts of the four Gospels testify, for example, that Jesus and his disciples shared the norms of their environment: parents are to be honoured; they are to be obeyed; and, when they grow old, they are to be cared for. Balla's research additionally shows that to speak evil against parents was widely condemned in the New Testament world, which is further rooted in OT: 'Whoever strikes his father or his mother shall be put to death' (Ex 21:15 MT).[94] Some parables also highlight this relationship (Matt 21:28–32, 33–40; Luke 15:11–32) with emphasis upon the obedience that a son owes to his father and the filial right to inherit not only the paternal estate, but also its associated authority. All of these aspects of the F–S relationship form an integral part of the relationship between God and Jesus as described in John's Gospel.[95]

The designation of God as father attained its full development in the later writings of the four Gospels and can be specifically traced between the Gospels of Mark and John: 'There is a noticeable increase in F–S language as one moves through the canonical Gospels beginning with Mark and ending with John. There is no earthly father, but all response to the paternal image is fixed on God.'[96]

This exclusivity of the divine relationship also creates a tension between the divine and the natural F–S relationships. Indeed, Jesus asserts himself declares that he came 'not peace but a sword', which will be driven between son and father, daughter and mother, and daughter-in-law and mother-in-law. In Matt 10:34–6 and Luke 12:51–3, this is an allusion to the prophetic lament in Mic 7:6. Matt 10:37, Luke 14:26 and Mark 10:29 extend this to include the command for a man to leave his children for Jesus' sake and 'for the gospel'. In this sense, the message of Jesus would divide believer from unbeliever, with absolute loyalty to God and His Christ even deny his/her own family: 'Who ever comes to me and does not hate father and mother, wife and children, brothers and sisters, and even his own life, cannot be my disciple' (Luke 14:26). For the Christian, following Jesus and his truth came before all things – before family, worldly positions and indeed life itself. Therefore, obeying God's will demands a total re-birth from one's former life; since 'the coming kingdom disturbs the patriarchal family'.[97] When Jesus proclaims 'Let the dead bury their own dead, but as for you, go and proclaim the kingdom of God' (Luke 9:60a; cf. Matt 8:22b), he not only shifts the focus onto his living ambassadors, but also replaces the 'biological' family by the sense of spiritual union and fellowship which ties all believers: 'Whoever does the will of God is my brother, and sister, and mother' (Mark 3:35). Indeed, as a physical enactment of this principle, Jesus' own family ties are replaced by this relationship with his disciples.[98]

Jesus' understanding of the family was almost shockingly revolutionary in contrast with the former notion of family with its patriarchal head; but in the new fellowship 'brother will betray brother to death, and a father his child. Children will rebel against their parents and have them put to death. All men will hate you because of me, but he who stands firm to the end will be saved' (Mark 13:12–13), whereas, in the new family, God is the mighty spiritual Father in heaven (Matt 23:9), and 'all are brothers' (Matt 23:8) who must worship in spirit and in truth (John 4:24).

For the authors of the Gospels, the response to this tension between the divine and the natural F–S relationship is clear: the believer must follow God's will and sever one's F–S natural familial ties. Further, as Gerd Theissen observes, there is a need for renunciation of worldly possessions, as well as of the self: 'The sayings' tradition is characterized by an ethical radicalism that is shown most noticeably in the renunciation of a home, family, and possessions.' Indeed it could be said that Jesus' preaching on ethics is based on the feature of homelessness: 'The Ethic of the sayings excludes family ties as well. Giving up a fixed place of abode means breaking with family relationships. To hate father and mother, wife and children, brother and sister is one of the conditions for discipleship.'[99] Such radicalist ethics can be practised and passed on only under extreme living conditions; they are not pertinent to everyday life. Therefore, as Theissen concludes, 'the breach with the family was probably hardly ever put into practice consistently'.[100] In fact, many men took their wives with them on their wanderings (1 Cor 9:5).

It seems, then, that prior to Paul's Epistles, it was not specifically commanded that Christian identity required the creation of a Christian household.[101] As an apostle of Jesus, it was for this reason that Paul set himself the task of adding to the Christian Doctrines practical principles for daily living.

To this end, Paul embedded the brotherhood-like nature of Christian fellowship outworked in a household hierarchical structure. Nevertheless, some NT scholars, such as Karl Olav Sandnes, perceive household and brotherhood as separate models of fellowship.[102] Klaus Schafer in particular views household and brotherhood as contrasting models in Pauline ecclesiology: for him, the household represents the patri-archal model, while brotherhood represents the egalitarian and participatory. The Pauline familial paradigm is thus considered an antitype of that which typified antiq-uity.[103]

In the course of rooting the brotherhood-like nature of the Christian fellowship within a hierarchical household structure, however, there were far fewer occasions refer-ring to tensions in the family in the Pauline letters than in the Gospels. Peter Balla notes however that in the Pauline corpus there are fewer texts addressing issues of real child–parent relationship, the Epistles rather reflect issues which emerged in the embryo Christian churches for whose guidance Paul was responsible, and which threat-ened to wreak the purity of Christ teachings; thus the term 'father on earth' refers not only briefly to fathers as family members, but also in a spiritual and figurative sense to leaders in general.[104] In this way Paul redefined and transformed the *divine* F–S and the *natural* F–S relationships, at the same time embedding the new model in its socio-polit-ical context.

How, then, should we understand the character of Pauline teaching? Different scholars here provide different perceptions. E. Schüssler Fiorenza, for example, claims that there is a theory of 'decline' implicated within these contrasting divine and worldly models, arguing that as the early church was an egalitarian community embodying no patriarchal elements, this egalitarian character was destroyed as the church gradually replaced these forms of community by patriarchal structures.[105] From this jucture later Christian codes tended to compromise in favour of social reality and to merge Christian relationships with existing social relationships.

Other scholars, such as Franze Laub, hold that those codes which give guidance for household slaves, such as those contained in Colossians, Ephesians and 1 Peter, do exclude any reference to class status, but instead stress specifically Christian ideas, such as *agape* (Col 3:19; Eph 5:21–33) and the equalizing lordship of Christ (Col 3:24–5; 4:1; Eph 6:9). This integrating power across class structures is something entirely new in ancient social history: to conceive of masters and slaves as having the same Lord and judge (Col 3:25b) was an extremely radical concept.[106] Indeed, Karl Olav Sandnes comments here that 'what we see in the New Testament is not an egalitarian commu-nity which is being replaced by patriarchal structures', but rather that 'in the family terms of the New Testament, old and new structures come together'. There is hence a convergence of household and brotherhood structures, in which the brotherhood-like nature of the Christian fellowship is the catalyst, embedded in household structures.[107]

It should be noted here that these opposing arguments are based on a similar assumption, resulting in something of a contradiction. Yet the coexistence of equality and hierarchy is neither a manifestation of a compromise with existing social relation-ships nor a contradiction between a new structure and an old structure.

To emphasize the authority of a father is the logical consequence of Christian theo-logical deduction. The *natural* F–S relationship is in this sense an imitation of the *divine* F–S relationship, just as the Jesus–disciple, apostle–believer and ruler–subject relation-ships are also imitations of that relationship. Therefore, the attributes of the divine Father and Son, such as the *agape* of the Father and the obedience and submission of the Son, are in turn applicable to all other relationships.

However, because these imitational relationships in family, society and politics are all under the authority of God, and since all are sons of God, and therefore equal before God with no gradations in their status in His kingdom, 'equality' is paradoxically their defining element. Thus, 'equality' as well as 'obedience' together becomes one of the essential aspects of the F–S relationship. Just as Theissen states, in Paul, the relation to Christ was marked by differences in 'human mobility'; through drawing his images of redemption from partly social experience and partly from the natural world, and through the bond with the one Lord 'Jesus Christ', from this perspective 'early Christianity offered everyone opportunities for a change for the better and made these opportunities experienceable for everyone in the congregation'.[108]

No one will deny that, for Paul, there are two distinct concurrent roles for any Christian: one as a man (or woman) of the people of God, and the other as a member of a particular secular society, two roles which are too distinct to be confused. One is the role fulfilled in the human relationship with God Himself, while the other concerns that with other human individuals. This is in essence the duality of the human role. In the God–Man relationship, the highest virtue is that of obedience or submission; in human relationships, on the other hand, it is 'equality' which takes priority in dealing with others, because within such a relationship, 'Paul accepts a differentiation of roles and functions, but not a status differentiation.'[109]

Following this line of thinking, the interrelationship between the doctrines of obedience and equality is understandable. Following the perfect model of the F–S relationship between God and Jesus, sons, wives and slaves should in the same way show respect and obedience to their fathers, husbands or masters in their secular life. Each has a different role to play. However, since all are God's people, no matter who the father and who the son may be, both have an equal position in faith in God and Jesus Christ; their individual status is therefore of the same importance to God.

It is clear, then, that both equality and obedience are necessary qualities within the Christian father–son relationship. This being so, we can neither conclude that the two doctrines of equality and patriarchy are contrary to each other, nor argue that there is no interrelationship between them. What we can however establish is that, by working out the practical applications of these two doctrines, Pauline teaching has actually brought together theological theory and social reality, and thereby put Christian theology on a workable level. In other words, his teachings not only provide spiritually sound and order principles for the maintenance of society and its structure, but also offer a distinctive Christian way of life. It is for this reason that Paul uses several kinship terms when describing relations within the Christian communities or towards God or Christ. For example, he may designate himself 'father' in the address and in the same Epistle address them as 'brothers'.[110] It is for this reason too that some feminist interpretations of Romans argue that Paul 'was motivated by a Hellenistic desire for the One, which among other things produced an ideal of a universal human essence, beyond differences and hierarchy'.[111]

In short, the combination of Christian 'patriarchy' and 'equality' not only makes of Christianity an organization suited to a world mission, but also keeps Christianity in a level of transcendence. There thus exists no contradiction between the Pauline concepts of patriarchy and equality – they are rather a logical development of Pauline interpretative theology and religious ethics, in the sense that Paul successfully integrated Christ's teaching into Greco-Roman and Jewish social ideals:

> The social structure as 'household' is found here also, but the main focus is upon the household as a pattern of authority structures and relations between various members of the household. Moreover, the household is not viewed as an ideal in contrast to elite or political authorities; rather, the household with its patriarchal structure is portrayed as an integral part of the macrocosms, ruled over by the emperor. Slaves are members of the household as a matter of fact, although their relationship to their master is different from that of husband and wife or father and son.[112]

Thus, Paul not only inherited the spirit of Jesus Christ, but he also carried out the mission assigned to him by Christ of creating a practical foundational base for the realization and universal expansion of Christianity.

The Philosophical Basis of the Pauline Divine Father–Son Relationship

The philosophical base of the Pauline divine F–S relationship can be viewed from two perspectives: the paternity and the original creation of God and their continuity in Jesus Christ, and sinful human nature.

From the ontological angle, Paul takes God as the source and origin of all things in the universe; the Pauline F–S relationship is therefore based on the noumenon of the masculinity and paternity of God. Like other authors in the NT, Paul, inherited on the one hand the Jewish tradition of the masculinity and paternity of God, as Creator of the whole universe, including human beings. On the other hand, he took God's nature to be that of a living Creator whose creation never ceases and which is renewed through Jesus Christ, his Beloved Son. This aspect of 'rebirth' from previous sin into new spiritual life through Jesus Christ and his gift of the Holy Spirit were uppermost in Pauline teaching. From the co-creation of new human life Jesus Christ had a position of being a one with God; thus the divine status of Jesus Christ was confirmed.

In the Gospel of John the affirmation of Christ's divinity is very clear, while in the Pauline letters the emphasis is often more upon his humanity – as the 'first-born Son of God'. To all who believe in him is given the right to become a child of God. Nevertheless, there are also a number of occasions where Paul refers to Jesus as God. For example, 'he will oppose and will exalt himself over everything that is called God or is worshipped, so that he sets himself to be God' (2 Thess 2:4). This is not only because the original creation of God was for him and through him, but also because the New Creation of God is through him as heir to the kingdom of God, but also as Co-Creator.

Why then do both God the Father and the divine Son continue to offer rebirth to humanity? In other words, why does God offer salvation? By way of an answer to this difficult question perhaps if we say that as the son is the favourite one of a father, the father will offer him all his love, even if he is not worthy, as in Christ's parable of the 'Prodigal Son' for example. Genesis also tells us that at the creation of the universe, God created humanity in His own image, bestowing not only free will, but also intelligence. Although humans (from Adam thereafter) did not use this free will and intelligence wisely, thereby causing the fall of humanity, as a Father God still did not cease to give mercy and forgiveness to humans, offering them salvation and redemption through Christ's sacrifice for their sins in their place.

This Paul stresses endlessly; God's love is so deep that for the sake of saving humans, he even sent his beloved Son Jesus Christ to die on the cross. Thus the gift of this *'agape'* or 'divine love' comprises both the beginning and the end of God's relationship with humankind. By self-giving love under the name of the F–S relationship, Paul made the Christian community a type of fictive kin group shaped by norms of the prevailing kinship institution:

> Given the kinship labels used by Paul, for example, his would clearly be fictive kin groups. On the other hand, the social movement organization set up by Jesus was based upon loyalty and solidarity towards Jesus himself and his cause rather than among the recruits. Thus, while the Jesus faction was elective in its recruitment, it did not have the qualities typical of the fictive in groups of the Christian movement organization.[113]

Why does humanity need God's salvation? This is because the tendency of human nature is towards sin: all are sinners: 'All men, both Jews and Greeks, are under the power of sin' (Rom 3:9); people are slaves to sin (Rom 6:17, 20; 7:14); sin is the constant pattern and principle of human life on earth (Rom 7:25; 8:2), which can be removed only by God. In Christian theory, no human effort can attain salvation; rather, it is a precious gift from God. Thus, Robert L. Reymond urges Christian missionaries to continue to proclaim and teach Paul's above doctrine, because it is only if 'men by God's enabling grace see themselves as they truly are – as sinful, incapable of saving themselves, and guilty before God – that they will see their need of Christ's saving work'.[114]

What, then, is the sin? Sin, for Paul, is not defined in terms of an ethical standard or code, although he is convinced that sin bears evil ethical fruit. Sin is falling 'short of the glory of God' (Rom 3:23). It is isolation from God, but above all it is 'pride' in one's own ability and wisdom.[115] However, sin is not only an act or an attitude of rebellion against God; it is also an objective condition or status, even when one is not guilty or responsible (Rom 6:12–14). In short, sin is the objective condition of humanity after the fall of Adam; it is the human condition and results in death.[116] Because rebellion against God represents the greatest sin, humility therefore becomes one of the main themes of Paul's preaching. He thus not only praised the obedience of Jesus Christ to God, but he also believed himself to be a slave of Jesus Christ. In line with this, he not only urges men to obey the will of God and to have faith in Jesus Christ, but he also counseled wives to obey their husbands, sons their fathers and slaves their masters.

If human nature is sinful, then, how can human beings receive God's salvation? For Paul, an authentic moral being is not purely a physical creation possessing a soul; human nature is essentially pluralistic and dualistic with both spirit and flesh. The Holy Spirit can work on our hearts, on the one hand, to awaken our intelligence to seek and to follow God's will and on the other hand, to guide our free will to respond to God's call.[117]

This representation of human nature opens the way for a discussion of Pauline religious ethics[118]and provides the philosophical grounds for an exploration of the Pauline divine F–S relationship and its principle. First, sinful human nature cannot be overcome without faith in Jesus Christ; it is for this reason that Paul urges the human quest for spiritual life within the secular or earthly life, following the model of Jesus Christ. Thus, in the relationship between a natural father and a son, they should, on the one hand, imitate this divine relationship and, on the other, they should treat each other as brothers; this they should do as 'sons of God'. In this way, the principles of the divine F–S relationship between God and Jesus Christ are strengthened and systematized in Pauline teaching.

Secondly, since the imitation of God and the God–Jesus relationship is so emphasized, compared with the four Gospels, Pauline teaching focuses not only on the divine F–S relationship between God and Jesus, but also on the spiritual F–S relationship between God/Jesus and Men, between apostles and church members, even the social, political and familial secular relationships. This characteristic of Pauline teaching can be seen from Chart 1: different presentations of various father–son relationships in the four Gospels and Pauline letters.

Chart I

Position	Number of Occurrences				
	Jesus as the Son of God	God as the Father of Jesus	Jesus as the Son of Man	God as the Father of Men	Human Father and Son
Matthew	15	21	29	2	7
Mark	8	3	13		5
Luke	10	9	26	2	15
John	25	98	12		1
Pauline letters	28	21	3	17	9

From Chart 1 it can clearly be seen that as in the Gospel of John, the divine F–S relationship between God and Jesus is also a major theme in the Pauline letter. However, unlike any of the four Gospels, Paul put much more emphasis on the F–S relationship between God and Men, and the natural F–S relationship also occupied him a good deal. Through emphasis on the God–Jesus and God–Men relationship, the brotherhood between Christian believers and even that between Jesus and God's people is built up; by highlighting Jesus' Sonship, his virtues of obedience, submission and humbleness were enhanced and this paved the way for the function of the *divine* F–S as a model for all the other *secular* relationships.

In this way, Pauline teaching links the divine world with secular society, thereby giving Christianity a greater chance of spreading more widely into society and making Christian doctrines more practicable.

CHAPTER THREE

Classification of the Father–Son Relationship

There are two ways to classify the F–S relationship: according to the father's and the son's function, and the characteristics required in an ideal relationship or according to the actual manifestation of this relationship in both Christian and Confucian doctrines and practices. This chapter is divided into four sections: discussing the nature of the F–S relationship, and examining the functions and characteristics of a father and a son through the exploration of texts; describing the three main functions of the F–S relationship that are the bases from which its classification of patterns proceed; explaining the two dimensions – secular and divine – of the F–S relationship; and demonstrating the similarities and differences between these two dimensions.

The Nature of the Father–Son Relationship

The origin of the Pauline F–S relationship located in Greco-Roman and Jewish cultures and the source of that of Xunzi's in early Chinese culture have been engaged in Chapters 1 and 2. In both early Chinese and Hellenistic cultures, the concept of the F–S relationship was neither limited to the natural or biological sense nor limited to the kinship[1] family, but was broadly employed in connection with the various social and political relationships within the whole secular as well as the spiritual world. This characteristic can be seen first from the definitions of both father and son respectively, and then the content of their relationship.

Father and son in Judeo-Christian

The Greek word for 'son' is νιος. From the Homeric epic onwards νιος stands alongside παις, although νιος is not exclusively restricted to the legitimate descendant. Apart from the literal meaning, there are five meanings for νιος in Hellenism: (1) a title in the style of oriental and especially Egyptian rulers, for example, in 'Son of God'; (2) a type of honorary title for leading citizens; (3) although this is rare, sometimes νιος occurs for people who are not relatives but are close, for example, pupils; (4) among the Stoics, the idea of divine 'sonship' was suggested by doctrines of the unity of humankind; (5) finally, νιος is also regarded as the exalted title of Jesus in the early Christian period.[2]

These Greek meanings of 'son' may be compared with the rich usage of 'son' in the OT, in which three basic and six broader senses of son are found. The three basic meanings are: (1) a term for physical descendants and relatives. In this sense, 'son' conveys a meaning of personal status: 'son' here not only means the male child begotten by the father and born of the mother; it is also used for other degrees of relationship, for example, the son's brother, grandson, nephew, cousin of son and daughter, daughter-in law and descendants. (2) In most instances it is a patronymic term to denote personal status. The most significant use of 'son' in this sense is to reveal that the individual is not isolated. He is seen in the organic context of his family and tribe. (3) Even in the earliest times adoption played a big part in Mesopotamia. It served to give childless couples descendants, who would produce care in old age and gifts at death and to accomplish the freeing of slaves. Equality with physical sons was conferred by adoption as a legal act by which someone of alien blood was recognized to be a child with full rights and duties.[3]

The six broader terms for 'son' are: (1) used to mean 'young men', 'youths', 'children', or 'the slaves born in house' (Gen 17:12); (2) used as an intimate address for younger companions, students or listeners to whom the one speaking stands in the relation of a father; (3) more rarely 'son' expresses the fact that the one speaking regards the one addressed as subordinate, or that the speaker is calling himself subordinate; (4) son as a term of relation to a collective society, a country or a place, a group; the term also denotes sharing a nature or quality or fate, being taken captive and bound; (5) son as a term is an expression which relates to a particular age; and (6) son also acts as a term for relationship to God.[4]

The idea of a physical F–S relationship between Yahweh and other divine beings or angels, such as one finds elsewhere in the ancient Orient, is alien to the OT and is nowhere suggested. The term 'son' is used in relation to God in two senses: first, to mean kings who have been chosen by God: three times in the OT the king is called God's son (2 Sam 7:14; Ps 2:7; 89:26–7). Far more often, the F–S relationship is used to denote the relationship of Yahweh to Israel or to the Israelites. This kind of meaning can be seen when Yahweh speaks of Israel as his first-born son (Exod 4:22; Jer 31:9), whom he has called as his dear child (Jer 31:20) out of Egypt (Hos 11:1) and given a special place among the nations as the other sons (Jer 3:19).

From the definition of 'son' described above we can see that the term is found in the following relationships: natural father–son; foster father and adopted son; master–slave; ancestor–descendant; elder–younger between relatives; adults–children; ruler–citizen; authority–subordinate; teacher–student; God–man; God–King of Israel and God–individual believer. It is therefore obvious that the F–S relationship in the OT is employed in a very wide sense. We can also see the wide usage of this term in the definitions of father in both Greco-Roman-Jewish and Chinese culture.

In accordance with the *Theological Dictionary of the New Testament*, the Greek word for 'father' is πατηρ.[5] Generally speaking, πατηρ has the following meanings: (a) The father of the family. (b) Very occasionally the grandfather can also be called πατηρ. This use is possibly because πατηρ can reach further back and be used for 'forefather' or 'progenitor', since forefather can be taken spiritually as the initiator of an occupation, trend or group. (c) πατηρ does not have to denote blood relationship and its projection in the past. In fact, a foster father is also one's legitimate father. (d) The word can also be used to represent a stage of life: 'the old or honorable man' – this is because a man can be called 'father' because he reminds us of our physical father; thus πατηρ is a term of respect in addressing the aged and honorable. (e) In the Greco-Roman world, father is head of the house. (f) He can also be teacher. (g) He can be 'God'. (h) He can also be a ruler. (i) Plato even used 'father' in the cosmological sense, while Stoicism used 'father' as the begetter.

We can also see the wide usage of the 'father' from the meaning of *kathegetes*. The Greek word for guide, teacher and master is the same word for teachers, masters, fathers or headmasters. 'The three terms used are equivalent and mean "master-teacher", even *kathegetes*, which can have the sense of "guide, conductor" and thus would mean "educator, spiritual director".'[6]

The use of 'father' for teacher, master, educator and so on is seen not only in the OT, but also in the NT. For example, in Matt 23:8–10, when Jesus addresses his disciples, he pronounces a threefold injunction that has no parallel in the other Gospels: 'But you must not be called "Rabbi", for you have only one teacher (*ho didaskalos*), and you are all brothers. Neither shall you call anyone on earth "father", for you have only one heavenly father. Neither shall you be called *kathegetai*, for you have only one *kathegetes*, the Christ.'

In the OT, the concept of 'father' has a certain sacred aspect, even when it is used as a basic element in the family concept. The father is the head of his house as well as the priest of the house. Because of this sacred aspect, according to the *Theological Dictionary of the New Testament*, the dignity of the father as the priestly head of the house can be transferred to priestly officials who do not belong to the tribe, then to the prophets, who are called "father" by their pupils (2 Kgs 2:12) or the king (2 Kgs 6:21), and finally to administrators, those who bear trustworthy authority, or benefactors, the 'fathers of the poor' (Job 29:16). Not only the sacred but also other basic features of 'father' could be transferred to non-tribal persons. Thus the figure of the 'father' is a kind of ideal when it represents the side of the priestly office which should evoke respect, or when it stands for the even higher authority of the prophet with its demand for unconditional acknowledgment.[7]

Paul and his successors carried on this tradition and used the F–S relationship in a sacred and very wide sense. There are ten usages in Paul's teaching: (1) God as the father of our Lord Jesus Christ (1 Cor 8:6, 15:24; 2 Cor 1:3, 11:3; Col 1:3). (2) God as the father of men (Gal 1:1; Eph 2:18, 3:14, 6:23; Rom 1:7, 8:5; 1 Cor 1:3; 2 Cor 1:2, 6:18; Gal 1:3–4, 4:6; Eph 4:6, 5:20; Phil 1:2, 4:20; Col 1:2; 1 Thess 1:3, 3:11, 3:13; 2 Thess 1:1; 2:16; Phlm 3). (3) God as the father of all believers: because those who are led by the Spirit are sons of God (Rom 8:14) and by him (the Spirit) we cry, 'Abba, Father' (Rom 8:15); 'The Spirit himself testifies with our spirit that we are children of God' (Rom 8:16). (4) 'Father' is used to describe a former believer and later believer relationship; for instance, Abraham as the father of Israel and father of later believers.[8] (5) Father is used to illustrate the apostle–disciple or apostle–church member relationship. Horrell argues: 'In these later letters it become clear that the "household" pattern of instruction becomes the pattern for the whole church and for the behaviour of its subordinate members in relation to the church's leadership.'[9] (6)

Father is used to describe a teacher–disciple relationship: in Acts 23:6, when Paul describes himself as son, it hardly refers to his ancestors, but rather to his teachers.[10] (7) Father is used to describe the master–slave relationship in which the master is father and the slave is son: Paul uses this pattern to describe Jesus–disciple (1 Cor 3:5; 2 Cor 2:14; 3:6; 4:5), Jesus–believer (1 Cor 7:22; Rom 12:11; 14:4, 18), and even God–Jesus relationships. As Stowers has recognized, though Christ Jesus was in the form of God, he did not regard equality with God as something to be exploited; he emptied himself, taking the form of a slave, being born in human likeness, and being found in human form; he humbled himself and became obedient to death on a cross.[11] From this we can see that master, teacher and father have a parallel meaning in Pauline thinking. (8) The F–S relationship is used also to describe the elder–younger church member relationship.[12] (9) It is also used to describe a ruler–citizen relationship. Referring to the relationship between community and household or the social hierarchy and domestic hierarchy, Horrell concludes that the church community is shaped according to the household model; indeed, it is described as the *oikos theou* (1 Tim 3:15), hence the ecclesiastical hierarchy mirrors the domestic and social hierarchy.[13] (10) Paul also used another F–S-type relation, the patron–client relationship, to describe the religious relationships, such as God–Jesus or Apostle–Christian believer. According to Stephan J. Joubert, 'Paul, in his role as apostle, presented himself as broker on behalf of God, Jesus and the Holy Spirit (the heavenly patrons) to the Corinthians (the clients).'[14] Thus, the urban context, with its institution of the household within a system of patronage and structures of personal authority, provided the setting for the first Christians and circumscribed their social behaviour.[15] In short, as MacDonald has pointed out, 'the role of leaders as relatively well-to-do householders who act as masters of their wives, children, and slaves is inseparably linked with their authority in the church'.[16] Hence, there is the clear linkage between the religious and familial authorities in Pauline thinking.

Father and son in Chinese culture

The Chinese parallel of the English word father is *fu*. *Fu* has two different tones, fù and fu. Fù has two meanings; one is male parent, the other is the form of address for all former generations, for example, forefathers, uncles, uncles in law and so on. Fu has three different meanings: (1) an honorary title for an older male; (2) an honorific term for addressing males; and (3) and the meaning of origin. In contrast, the Chinese parallel of son is *zi*, which has six basic usages: (1) children of the parents, either including or excluding female offspring; (2) the young prince who will be the king; (3) one of the five conferred titles of nobility; (4) a common address for males; (5) teacher; and (6) with reference to the works of some scholars of the pre-Qin dynasty.[17] The wide usage of 'father' can be seen from the meaning of *lao*, of which there are six usages: (1) opposite to young, it means older in age; (2) old people; (3) a gentle word for the death of people; (4) someone who has rich experience; (5) contrary to 'new', to name a thing that has existed for a long time; and (6) original or former. In the Chinese language, there are only nine words linked with *lao*; among them, five are for old people. Among the other four, one is for the older generation, one is for an adult male, one is for father and another one is for a virtue for dealing with the old, with one's father and one's former generations. This implies that the father has the same meaning as that of old in both age and generation.

From the meaning of 'father', 'son' and *lao*, it can be seen that there are six relationships included in the traditional Chinese F–S relationship: natural father–son; foster father and adopted son; ancestor–descendant; uncle–nephew; older–younger, and predecessor–successor. In addition to the ancient Chinese regard of the state as an enlarged family, and the ruler and sage as the father all the people, the ruler–ruled, educator–student and heaven–man relationships are also presumed to be demonstrations of the F–S relationship.

Although there are some differences of interpretation of 'father' and 'son' in Greco-Roman and Chinese cultures, some common points emerge. First, father or son is a term for naming the male. Secondly, 'father' usually has two essential meanings: one is the male parent, and the other is former generations. 'Son' also has two basic meanings, one is the direct biological offspring of parents; the other is younger or later generations. Sometimes, the F–S relationship is not designated by age or blood lineage but by social status: the senior or the one who is of higher status is the father and the junior or the one who is of lower status is the son; this is an extension or demonstration of the F–S pattern in the political field.

This characteristic has been inherited in modern languages as can be seen from usages such as in *Chambers Twentieth Century Dictionary*, where 'father' is defined as a male parent; an ancestor or forefather; respect applied to a venerable man, to confessors, monks, priests, etc.; a member of certain fraternities; a member of a ruling body; the oldest member, or member of longest standing, of a profession or body; one of a group of ecclesiastical writers of the early centuries, usually ending with Ambrose, Jerome and Augustine: the first person of the 'Trinity'. While the 'son' is defined as a male child or offspring: formerly extended to a son-in-law; a descendant, or one so regarded or treated; a disciple; a native or inhabitant; the produce of anything; a familiar (sometimes patronizing) mode of address to a boy or to a male younger than oneself.[18]

It is clearly indicated that the content of the F–S relationship in both Chinese and Western culture is used not only in the sense of a physical born-birth relationship, but in a broad and functionary sense, namely, he is a begetter, a producer, a creator; he also is a protector, a benefactor, a patron, a guide and an educator of his son. His age is older than his son's, his knowledge is supposedly richer than his son's, and in addition, his morality is presumed to be higher than his son's, and thereby he is a person with not only legal, but also moral authority and power over his son. Consequently, the F–S relationship is one between a creator and a created, or between a begetter and begotten; it is also a relationship of benefactor–beneficiary, of giver–receiver, of patron–client and of protector–protected. Moreover, the F–S relationship is that between an elder and a younger, a former generation and a later generation, a senior and a junior, an authority and a subordinate, even an educator and an educated. Accordingly, the F–S relationship in both Chinese and Western culture is not only a family notion, but also a social, even political notion. These characteristics form the basis of its classification and will be explored in the following section.

Basis of Classification

There are three main functions of the F–S relationship: creation, benefaction and age distinction. These three functions are the bases from which its classification of patterns can be revealed.

Classification on the basis of creation

Father and son can be formed in a relationship between the creator and the created; therefore, the F–S relationship can be fulfilled through a process of creation which is from 'nothing' to something. There are two kinds of creation in this world: physical and spiritual. In the physical creative process, both creator and progeny are visible, as in the case of the biological father creating his son. We call this visible creation a 'natural creation', as in the case of physical or biological F–S pattern being called as the natural F–S relationship.

In a natural F–S relationship, the blood tie is of primary importance; the son's quality of flesh is closely related to that of the father. The order of lineage is of secondary importance: the begetter is the senior and former, and the born is junior and later. Such an absolute order cannot be changed. This means that if one male and another are in a relationship of flesh birth and born, they are in a natural F–S relationship, no matter whether the person involved admits this relationship or not.

In spiritual creation, the creator is invisible spirit, and the created is visible physical flesh with an invisible mind. Both the creator and the process of this creation are invisible, although it can be felt and understood by the created. Paul describes this characteristic of spiritual creation clearly in his letter to the Romans: 'For since the creation of the world God's invisible qualities – his eternal power and divine nature – have been clearly seen, being understood from what has been made, so that men are without excuse' (Rom 1:20). The spiritual creation belongs only to God or the God-like. For Christianity, God's spiritual creation is the original creation, which is far before any kind of creation; the natural father's creative work is only an imitation of the original creation. It is God who initiated and completed the original creation, thereby allowing men, other creatures and the universe to be created from nothing; therefore this spiritual creation is a divine creation, and the F–S relationship between God the creator and his creatures is a divine relationship pattern.

There is a similar description of this in the Confucian tradition, that is, the idea that 'heaven gives birth to thousands of people' (*tian sheng zheng min*). For the ancient Chinese, the creation of life was completed by two pairs of primary elements in cosmology: the Heaven and Earth, along with the Yin and Yang principle. Yin and Yang principally account for change in Nature, whereas Heaven and Earth are the materials of which life is composed.[19] Although Xunzi denied the moral personal character of Heaven and Earth in its influence on human society, he never denied the creational character of them, for as he declared: 'Heaven and Earth are the beginning of life' (9.15). However, there are substantial differences between the Christian God's creation and Confucian 'Heaven produces people'. For Christians, divine creation is the intentional action of God, while for Confucians, the spiritual creation of Heaven and

Earth is a natural process without any intention. *The Doctrine of the Mean* elucidates this function of Heaven and Earth:

> The heaven now before us is only this bright shining spot; but when viewed in its inexhaustible extent, then the sun, moon, stars, and constellations of the zodiac, are suspended in it, and all things are overspread by it. The earth before us is but a handful of soil but when regarded in its true breadth and thickness, it sustains mountains like the Hwa and the Yo, without feeling their weight, and contains the seas and rivers, without their leaking away.[20]

Dong Zhongshu, the most famous Confucian of the Han Dynasty, considered Heaven 'the most spiritual'[21] and believed that it was the great-grandfather of all humans: 'Humans cannot produce themselves, because the creator of humans is Heaven. That humans are humans derives from Heaven. Heaven, indeed, is the great-grandfather (*zeng zufu*) of humans.'[22]

Although there is a difference between the physical creation and the spiritual creation, that is, the spiritual creation is presented in a symbolic sense rather than in terms of physical creation and cannot therefore be totally fulfilled by physical creation, we cannot consider spiritual creation without considering its physical counterpart. Just as the spiritual creation is a necessary part of a natural father's physical creation of a son, so the natural relationship is the physical base of the imagination of a spiritual F–S relationship. Even the God–Jesus relationship is revealed by Jesus' physical body; likewise, in the pure physical F–S relationship, there is nevertheless a spiritual element. The difference is only that some traditions pay more attention to the kinship set while others put more stress on the spiritual relation.

The creational F–S relationship can be classified into two different types in practice, according to the following figure:

Creational father–son relationship ⟋ physical creational father–son relationship
 ⟍ spiritual creational father–son relationship

From stressing the physical creation between the natural father and his biological son, a tradition is brought forward which sees the biological F–S relationship as crucial and treats it as the centre and the model of all other relationships. This natural F–S centered tradition is regarded as the secular relationship pattern between the father and son, as follows:

The physical creational F–S relationship ⇒ the natural F–S relationship ⇒ the secular F–S relationship

By emphasis on the spiritual relationship between God and his divine creature, another F–S relationship pattern is brought forward: within this pattern, the God and his Creature relationship is not only put at the centre but also regarded as the model of other relationships. We call this kind of spiritual or God centered tradition the divine F–S relationship, as in the following figure:

The spiritual F–S relationship ⇒ the God–Creature relationship ⇒ the divine F–S relationship

The Confucian F–S pattern is no doubt a secular tradition, while the Christian one is divine. For a traditional Confucian, the most important thing is to keep his family in order and in harmony. Within this process, it is of primary importance for him to deal with his relationship with his father or forefathers and with his sons or grandsons. This is because the family is a miniature of society. The relationships in either social or political life are believed to be copies or transformations of the natural F–S relationship: in society, a senior is likened to a father, a junior to a son; the leader acts in the manner of a father and those that are led behave like sons; the ruler is treated as a father, and his subjects are regarded as his sons etc. The skill needed for controlling a country is the same as for running a family: if the individual can manage his family well, he can govern his society or state well. And as discussed previously, this idea also has its echoes in Greco-Roman culture.

For Christians, the spiritual creational relationship between God and Jesus is the base and center of their religious life. The aim of all Christians is to build a new relationship with God the Father through his first-born Son Jesus Christ, which is the sign of starting of their new life in God's Kingdom. This new established F–S relationship between God and human is a copy and imitation of the divine F–S relationship between God and Jesus; hence, unlike in the life of Confucianism, the most important thing in Christian life is not the natural F–S relationship and family life, but rather the divine life based on the creational spiritual F–S relationship.

Classification of father–son relationship on the basis of benefaction

In all cultures, it is the legal, dutiful and moral responsibility of a father to provide basic maintenance for his children, which includes both material and spiritual beneficial supports.[23] In a secular culture the burden that is laid on the shoulders of the physical creational father for providing for his family is mainly focused on the material aspect, even if it also has a spiritual dimension, whereas in a religious culture the task of the spiritual creational father is mainly focused on providing for his children's spiritual requirements, although material support is supplied as well. Thus, although the survival, happiness and salvation of his children is the most important work of the spiritual father God, his spiritual support is actually never separated from his economic support; in the same way, although supplying his children's material needs is more fundamental for a physical father, his spiritual support is also important to them. And just because of this, the spiritual relationship between Heaven and the sage and between the sage and the humans are included in the Confucian the secular F–S relationship, while in the Christian divine F–S relationship the natural F–S relationship between a biological father and his son is also an element within its doctrine.

In line with the economic function of the secular pattern, there come analogous patterns of the natural F–S relationship; while on the model of the spiritual satisfying function of the divine pattern, there come extensional demonstrations of the spiritual F–S relationship in the religious and secular world. Chart 2 provides a classification of the beneficial F–S relationship pattern:

Chart 2

F–S relationship based on benefaction	Economic supply pattern	Fictive F–S relationship	Stepfather–stepson Foster father–adopted son
		Beneficial F–S relationship	Patron–client Master–disciple Master–slave
	Spiritual satisfactory pattern	Spiritual guidance F–S relationship	Sage–people Jesus–disciples Apostle–Christian believer
		Educational F–S relationship	Teacher–student Priest–church member

As the patterns set out in Chart 2 are partly fulfilled by some aspects of the beneficial functions between the father and son, all of them can therefore be given the name 'father–son relationship'.

The father–son relationship based on age and authority

As noted, there is an absolute order in the natural F–S relationship, in that the father is always older than the son, and the son can never be older than his father.[24] This being so, the F–S relationship is extended into an age analogy. In such a situation, the elder is usually to be treated as a father, and the younger may be treated as a son; former generations are always to be regarded as fathers and later generations are always to be regarded as sons. This kind of analogical extension not only occurs in family kinship between close or distant relatives, but is also applied to the relationship between neighbours, members of the same society or groups and so on. The age analogue of the F–S relationship in a family and between kinship relatives is called a kinship familial F–S relationship; in different social situations the social analogue of the F–S relationship. Chart 3 provides a classification of the F–S relationship based on age.

Chart 3

F–S relationship based on age	Kinship familial F–S relationship	Between relatives	Grandfather–grandson
			Uncle–nephew relationship
			Elder brother–younger brother relationship
	Social father–son relationship	Between former generations and later generations outside of the family and relatives	Old–young relationship

In the same way, the F–S relationship can be formed according to different social status. The higher status or authority side will play the role of father, and the lower status side, or the side without authority, will play the role of son. The most obvious of this kind of F–S in a traditional society is first the ruler–subject relationship and then the official–citizen relationship as well as the senior–junior relationship. However, since the authority is not only a political concept, but also a religious norm, then the prophet with power enabling understanding all mysteries and all knowledge is also an authority (see Chart 4).[25]

Chart 4

Father-son relationship based on social status or authority	Social life	Senior–junior relationship
	Political life	Ruler–subject/ruled relationship
		Official–citizen relationship
	Religious life	Prophet–common believer

To extend the F–S relationship to the political field, and to transfer the function of father to the ruler and the function of son to the ruled, is not alien to ancient Chinese or Greco-Roman culture. For both, the transferring of the F–S relationship from the familial sense to the social and even political sphere is a matter of its nature. Such a transformation will be discussed in the next section.

We can therefore see that, although F–S relationships may be classified in terms of creation, they can also be classified according to a beneficial and age differentiation. However, in terms of their nature, all the manifestations of the F–S relationship can be reduced to two dimensions: the spiritually based and the biologically based. The dimension derived from biological creation can be called the secular F–S dimension; the dimension derived from the spiritually based constitutes the dimension of divine F–S relationship. Now we turn our attention to the two dimensions of the F–S relationship.

Two Dimensions of the Father–Son Relationship

According to the different emphases of the physical or spiritual function of creation, two dimensions of the F–S relationship can be identified: the secular and the divine. Perhaps it is better to use the spiritual instead of the divine when we consider the application of the spiritual create-created F–S relationship to Chinese understanding. There is nothing like the Christian understanding of divine in Chinese thought. However, Xunzi's understanding of the spiritual relationship between Heaven and human is different from that of Mengzi, so even if we use the spiritual F–S to define the spiritual create-created relationship, we still cannot achieve a completely similar identity. Therefore, for stressing the different characteristics of Christian and Confucian F–S relationship, in order to emphasize the transcendental character of the Christian ethics,

I choose divine rather than spiritual to define the spiritual creational or functional relationships.

What we have called the secular relationship is one in which the focus is on the physical and worldly material functions between the father and son. It is a human-centered relationship in which the biological birth–born relationship, the material benefit and the secular moral responsibilities of the father and son are made the central concern. By contrast, the divine relationship is one centered on the spiritual creational function between father and son. In it the spiritual birth–born relationship, the divine authority and power over human life before and after one's death, and the religious responsibility and moral duties of obedience to the divine father of the human son are taken as the central point of consideration.

There are two types of relationship in the secular F–S pattern; one is the *father-centered* and the other is the *individual-centered* pattern. The *father-centered* F–S pattern is hierarchical and the father's right and authority and the son's obedience and responsibility to his father are at the centre of the relationship. The *individual-centered* F–S pattern is one in which individual rights (including both the father's and the son's) are the central concern; equality between father and son is therefore its chief characteristic.

The *divine* F–S relationship is one which places God at the center. Here, God's authority and power, which elicit the human son's fear and obedience, are absolute and definitive. A comparison of characteristics between the two secular and between the secular and divine F–S relationships is set out in Chart 5.

Chart 5

Dimensions of F–S relationship	Further division	Emphasizing point	Ideological ideal	Relationship between father and son	Representative
Secular F–S relationship	Father centered F–S relationship	Emphasis on father's authority and power and son's obedience and subordination	Enhancing of moral responsibility and duty	Unequal	Traditional Chinese and Ancient Greco-Roman F–S relationships
	Individual centered F–S relationship	Emphasis on the individual's rights	Stress on legal rights of individuals	Equal	Modern Western F–S relationship
Divine F–S relationship	God centered F–S relationship	Emphasis on God's power and authority	Advocating religious faith	Unequal	Christian F–S relationship

At least three main F–S relationship patterns exist in modern societies. Since the individual-centered F–S pattern is not the target of the current discussion, the equal F–S

relationship will not be considered. Consideration will focus here mainly on the similarity and difference between the father-centered and the God-centered F–S
relationships. For convenience of discussion, we will still call the father-centered F–S
relationship *secular* and the God-centered one *divine*.

Constitution of the secular father–son relationship

As the secular F–S relationship mainly focuses on real society in the earthly world, its
foundation and main features are manifested in family life. However, as noted earlier,
the Confucian secular F–S relationship is not only a single familial notion, but also a
social, even political notion.

The natural F–S relationship is based on biological blood ties, in the sense that the
father is the son's physical begetter, and the son is his father's progeny. In such a
relationship, although to act according to one's ethical responsibilities is important for
a well-ordered relationship, the physical birth relationship between father and son is
recognized as its beginning; identification, of father or son, is appreciated through the
biological link. Thus, it is not important whether or not a father loves his son: he cannot
escape from the situation of being his son's father; it does not matter whether or not a
son has actually fulfilled his duties, for the son cannot deny the fact that he is his father's
offspring and his father his generator. In other words, it does not matter whether the
F–S relationship is running well or badly, the blood lineage between them cannot be
broken by their personal will or desire.

In Confucian society, the natural F–S relationship is the cornerstone of its other
familial analogues. Because family in Confucian understanding is not merely a nuclear
family but a clan, hence not only the natural father and son, but also their kinship surro-
gates are included within the familial sense of F–S relationship.

The basic Confucian family is a group of people who live together and share the
same property. Most of the ancient Chinese people living in a family would come from
the same ancestors; however, people without the same lineage can also live together to
form a family by adoption or patronage. This indicates that family life was not always
as simple as in the natural sense; sometimes, by being engaged in more than one
marriage for men, and transferring a male child from a close relative to a non-boy
family, the concept of the F–S relationship in the family can be extended to a fictive or
kinship relationship. Thus, as in Greco-Roman antiquity, the family in a traditional
Confucian society 'can be understood as a diachronic and synchronic association of
persons related by blood, marriage, and other social conventions, organized for the dual
purpose of enhancement of its social status and legitimate transfer of property'.[26] In
such a situation, not only the natural and the adopted, but also the kinship pattern
should also be taken into account in the familial sense of F–S relationship.

The kinship father–son relationship is a relationship between an older generation
and a younger generation of relatives. In this sense, all the male cousins of the father
will be treated as fathers, and all male cousins of the son will be treated as sons. Thus,
all the kinship uncles are the surrogate fathers of their nephews, while all nephews are
the surrogate sons of their uncles. The kinship F–S relationship is the centre, but not
the target of Confucianism. The target is to extend this relationship to the whole of

society, and to let that whole become an enlarged family. Consequently, the familial notion of the Confucian F–S relationship has to be extended to a social and even a political sphere.

The social sense of secular F–S relationship is an extension of the natural pattern in Confucian social life. The transformation of this relationship from the familial sense to the social and political sense began with Confucius, the founder of Confucianism. This transformation is realized through the connection of the F–S to the brothers relationship by linking *xiao* (filial piety, the virtue of loving and respecting one's father) with *ti* (the virtue of showing one's love and respect to one's elder brother). Through the connection between *xiao* and *ti*, the F–S relationship is linked to the relationship between the elder and the younger brothers. *Ti*, therefore, from being a notion of dealing with the blood brotherhood only becomes a concept used for dealing with neighbours and even strangers. This is why Zengzi says, 'Let there be a careful attention to *perform the funeral rites* to parents, and let them be followed when long gone *with the ceremonies of sacrifice*; then the virtue of the people will resume its proper excellence' (1:9).

The social manifestations of the secular F–S relationship involve a series of beneficial patterns, such as patron–client, master–slave or master–disciple. Unlike ancient Greco-Roman society, in which the patron–client relationship was popular,[27] the master–disciple relationship was more important for Chinese society. In this relationship, the master provided a potential material or spiritual benefit to his disciples by teaching them skills or knowledge for making a good life; the disciples in turn gave their respect and necessary obedience to their masters for their professional instruction. The master–slave relationship was also a very important reflection of the natural father–son relationship, even if the authority and power of the master over his slave and the obedience of the slave to his master were of the utmost importance, and more important than any other requirement of the natural F–S relationship.

If we say that the love in a natural F–S relationship is due to an instinctive force, the love between parent and child, generally speaking, is sacrificial love. However, traditional Confucian ethics was, at least partially, a sort of pragmatism. Speaking concretely, some of the principles used to deal with various social relations are utilitarian: one shows goodness to somebody because of fear that if one does not do so other people will not show goodness to oneself, and in the hope that if one shows goodness to others, others will return such goodness.

If we say that this is a part consideration of the 'golden rule', we are open to the accusation that the golden rule has been oversimplified; however, the compensatory character of Confucianism is obvious and it was in fact criticized by the legalist Hanfeizi thousands of years ago. The most significant thing is that Confucian ethical theory is never totally utilitarian. Confucianism has something that has transcended utilitarian calculations to become a noble love, that is, a selfless and benevolent love. To apply such a benevolent love in a social relationship, one should treat one's own generation as brothers and sisters, former generations as fathers and mothers, and future generations as sons and daughters. It is in this sense that we say the F–S pattern can be applied to older–young relationship, and the relationship between elder and younger brothers.

Confucians lay special emphasis on social life, and this naturally cannot be separated from material considerations. However, from the standpoint of Confucianism, there is something more important than the material for a person as a human, and that is to live a moral and harmonious life. To live such a desirable life one must behave according to the tenets of morality. Morality is not something purely secular or earthly-like, but something spiritual linked to the Way of Heaven and Earth. Because the Way of Heaven and Earth is recondite and cannot be seen and understood properly by ordinary citizens, the task of revelation and interpretation of the Way of Heaven and the Earth must fall upon the shoulders of the sages. This means that, although in terms of the physical body of humans are created by their parents; in terms of their spiritual character, such as moral sense and inspiration etc., they are the creation of the sages. It is the sages who discovered the way of Heaven and Earth and employed it into human society in terms of morality and justice, which is regarded as the way of human society. Because the spiritual creation of human beings can only be completed through the sages with the assistance of the social government and teachers, the governor or teacher could be seen as another important kind of father for the common people. From this follows the political and then the spiritual manifestation of the F–S relationship.

Of the Confucian understanding of the relationship between family and state, the F–S and ruler–ruled, John Knoblock has an impressive description. He says,

> The ancient Chinese conceived the state on the model of the family. The ruler occupied the position of a parent. He was to treat his subjects with the solicitude of a parent, loving them, caring for them, nurturing them, teaching them, leading them. His subjects were like children. They were to admire him, emulate him, follow him, respect him . . . (and) obey him.[28]

The political manifestation of the F–S relationship is of two kinds: one is the ruler–minister/subject and the other is the governor–governed pattern. Three issues need to be considered in discussing the political sense of the F–S relationship:

First, the political F–S relationship is not a pure spiritual relationship, but a mixture of the material and the spiritual relationship. For Confucianism, the ruler has a mandated authority, which is given by Heaven; therefore, he is the agent of Heaven, and is certainly the spiritual leader of his people too. However, as the governor of his people, he must not only be in charge of the connection between human society and Heaven, but also in charge of his people's living affairs. Thus he must provide both material and spiritual benefits to the people. This is what Confucianism calls benevolent government.

Although the ruler has a mandated authority, the ruler is not the ultimate authority, but merely an agent of the authority upon earth. His function is only that of mediator between Heaven and human beings. Consequently, if the ruler is not good enough, that is, if he cannot behave according to the will of Heaven and bring benevolence to the people, he will lose his position as the agent, and also lose his power and authority. This is because the 'will of Heaven' is viewed by some Confucians, such as Mengzi, as the same as the 'will of the people': Heaven listens to the call of the people, and Heaven sees what the people see.

Secondly, it is necessary to consider the situation that the political manifestation of the F–S relationship was not apparent until the Spring and Autumn Period.[29] According to some researchers, the character *zhong*, which is used to mean political loyalty, does not appear in earlier documents, such as the *Book of Documents*, the *Book of Poetry* and the *Book of Changes*. It is believed that the application of this word in political fields did not become prevalent or popular until the time of the Spring and Autumn Period (770–466 BC). [30]

It was only from the time of Confucius and Mengzi that *zhong* started to refer to the inner virtue in oneself in dealing with other people. In the context of Confucius, the word *zhong* means sincerity. Confucius often links *zhong* with trust (*xin*). Similarly, in the *Book of Mengzi*, both *zhong* and *xin* are used simultaneously and associated with other virtues, such as 'benevolence, dutifulness, sincerity, and truthfulness' (6A:16) or kindness: 'The imparting by a man to others of his wealth, is called "kindness". The teaching to others what is "good", is called "the exercise of fidelity (*zhong*)". The finding of a man who shall benefit the kingdom, is called "benevolence" (The *Books of Mencius* 3A:4).' Therefore, in the teachings of Confucius and Mengzi, *zhong* is usually interpreted as meaning sincerity, conscientiousness, or the exhaustion of one's self in the performance of one's moral duties. However, *zhong* is also used in a different context in the *Analects* and the *Book of Mengzi* with strong political connotations: 'A prince (ruler) should employ his ministers according to the rules of propriety (rules of conducts, rituals, rites and propriety); ministers should serve their prince with faithfulness (*zhong*)' (3:19).

Like Confucius and Mengzi, Xunzi usually associated *zhong* (loyalty and honesty) with *xin* (trustworthiness and keeping one's word). Nonetheless, for yielding the importance of ritual principles, Xunzi laid great stress on the addition of the virtues of respect and reverence to the virtues of *zhong* and *xin*. For him, as a minister or lower rank, mere loyalty and honesty to the ruler or superior are not enough; along with loyalty and honesty, giving precedence and polite refusals are also needed (13:1–9). Thus, unlike Confucius and Mengzi, who pay more attention to the mutual responsibility of ruler and ministers, Xunzi especially requests ministers to conduct themselves well.

Thirdly, according to Confucians, the analogy of the natural F–S relationship can not only be extended to the social and political life, but also to the spiritual life. In spiritual life, the F–S relationship is manifested as Heaven and humankind, in which Heaven is like a father and humankind a son. In Confucian minds, it is beyond doubt that there are potential connections between Heaven and Earth and humankind. The human spirit can integrate itself with the Way of Heaven and Earth or, to use a Western notion, the natural law; consequently, humans can understand the route of natural operations and discover the rules of natural organization. The men who discover the rules of natural operation are called sages, who should not only be the kings of society, but also the sons of Heaven. Thus, the secular F–S relationship began from a physical relationship of birth, but ended in a spiritual relationship.

There are three levels of the spiritual F–S relationship in a Confucian context. The highest level is the relationship between the universal way (the Way of Heaven) and the individual human. In Confucian thought, the Way of the Sages is so important that it is the only standard for organizing society; without the Way of the Sages, human society cannot stand; however, the Way of the Sages is only an imitation of the Way of Heaven. It was the ancient sage-kings who discovered the Way of Heaven first and then achieved the Way of the Sages through the imitation of it. This, on the one hand, tells us that the Way of the Sages is so important in the senses that (a) it is the copy of the inevitable and unchangeable Way of the Heaven, and (b) humans must follow it without any hesitation and suspicion. On the other hand, it tells us that there is an objective ultimate truth waiting for people's observation; if people can, like the sages, explore it carefully and wholly, it can be found by any person. The difference between the sage and people is just that the one has cultivated his morality fully and developed his intelligence wholly, but the other has not yet done so. Thus the Way of Heaven, discovered by the ancient sage, can also be explored by the individual person. The way of approaching one's perfect nature is known as self-enlightenment, and the process of exploring the Way of Heaven is named as the process of self-cultivation.

From the relation between the Way of Heaven and the Way of Sages comes the second level of spiritual relationship, the sage–common people relationship. As noted earlier, Confucians firmly believe that human society would never have existed without the sages' discovery of the principles of *Li* and *Yi*. According to the common ideas of Confucianism, the sages were not only the original organizers of human society, but also the original teachers of humankind. Hence, they are the spiritual creators of human beings, and the later humankinds are all their spiritual offspring.

The last level of spiritual relationship in the secular F–S relationship is the teacher–student relationship. For Confucians, the function of the sage is to interpret the Way of Heaven and thereby to invent social principles for the form and development of society; the function of teachers is to interpret the Way of the Sages and to teach the citizens to acknowledge and understand the Way of the Sages. The reason for a teacher to be a teacher is that he is the one who is skilled in understanding the way of the sage-kings. Without the teacher's interpretation of the Way of the Sages, people cannot help but misunderstand and confuse the Way of Heaven and Earth. The teacher is the key and cornerstone to right understanding of both the Way of Humanity and the Way of the Universe.

The constitution of the Confucian secular father–son relationship is presented diagrammatically opposite.

The constitution of the Christian divine father–son relationship

As a God-centered spiritual relationship, the central concern of the Christian divine F–S relationship is the relationship between God the divine father and Jesus Christ the divine son. However, as noted, the spiritual centered divine F–S relationship does not exclude secular elements; not only the pure spiritual relationship between the divine father and the divine son and the spiritual relationship between the apostle and Christian members, but also the mixture of spiritual and material relationship in its religious and political implications are also included. Thus the constitution of the Christian divine F–S relationship will be discussed in relation to the following four related aspects: the creational, the spiritual, the social-political and the familial.

The creational manifestation of the divine F–S relationship is a relationship between the creator God and his creatures. While it may be alien for Christians to talk of this relationship in the sense of Yahweh creating other divine beings or angels,

Chart 6

Confucian secular F–S relationship	Familial sense of F–S relationship	Natural F–S relationship	Created flesh of his son only	According to blood tie
			Flesh created and material support	
			Flesh created, material support and spiritual guidance	
		Fictive F–S relationship	Stepfather and stepson	According to legality
			Foster-father and adopted-son	
		Kinship F–S relationship	Uncle–nephew Elder–younger brother	According to consanguinity
	Social sense of F–S relationship	Social analogical F–S relationship	Elder–younger	According to age
			Senior–junior	According to social status
			Patron–client	According to benefit
			Master–slave	According to power and authority
		Political analogical F–S relationship	Official–citizen	According to political status
			Ruler–subject	
	Spiritual sense of F–S relationship	Spiritual guidance F–S relationship	Teacher–student	According to knowledge
			Sage–common people	According to spiritual guidance
			Universal Way and individual	According to the power of truth

Christians do indeed use it to describe the creational relationship between God and his creatures.

There are three levels of this creational aspect of the divine relationship in Christian theological thinking: the highest level of the spiritual creational relationship is between God and Jesus. God's beloved Son Jesus Christ, although a man born of a human, is believed to have been born from a virgin without any sexual relationship with her husband. Thus Jesus was created by the spirit of God and had no physical relationship with an earthly father. It was the spirit of God who descended into the womb of the Virgin Mary and thus Jesus Christ was created. Consequently, Jesus Christ, for Christians, is the direct progeny of the Holy Spirit. The process of the creation of Jesus Christ was a totally spiritual creational process. By his spirit, God created Jesus Christ from nothing to be a real king of both the dead and the living, the heir of his kingdom in both Heaven and Earth, and the executor of his salvation.

The middle level of the creational divine F–S relationship is that between God and Adam or Man in general, which can be called the humankind creational divine F–S relationship. God created Adam the ancestor of humans on the sixth day and rested on the seventh day; Adam and humans in general were the final created creature made in God's image and likeness: 'Let us make man in our image, in our likeness' (Gen 1:26) and with a mandate of right to rule: 'and let them rule over the fish of the sea and the birds of the air, over the livestock, over all the earth, and over all the creatures that move along the ground' (Gen 1:26). Since man is assumed to be the highest creature of God's creation and was created in God's own image, the divine F–S relationship between God and men is established.

The lowest level of creational divine F–S relationship is between God and the whole world, which can be called the cosmic creational F–S relationship. Since not only human, but also all other living creatures in this world, and even the world itself, have been created by God, God is the father of the world.

For Christians, the most important creational F–S relationship is that between God and Jesus Christ; this is said to be the sign of the start of the new covenant, and a sign of the agreement between God and humanity – a sign of God's new salvation and great forgiveness. From this creational divine F–S relationship is derived the spiritual divine F–S relationship.

The cosmic and humankind creational divine F–S relationship is the analogue of the spiritual creational divine one, especially the God–Jesus one, in the theological thinking of Christianity. According to the theology of Christianity, the God–Jesus' F–S relationship pattern has been realized through the following five forms: God and his believers, Jesus and his disciples, Jesus and Christians, the Apostles and early Church members and the priest and Church members. All these five forms are based upon faith and *agape*, the divine love. In terms of faith, the spiritual divine F–S relationship is supposed to be one of authority–obedience; in the case of love, because all are God's children, the spiritual father (except for God himself) and spiritual son should treat each other like kinship brothers. This means that equality and hierarchy coexist in the divine F–S relationship.

Although the divine and spiritual F–S relationship is the central concern of its doctrine, Christianity, especially Pauline religious ethics, does not stop with the spiritual concern of this relationship; when it focuses its attention on the spiritual F–S relationship, it never overlooks the social political life outside Christian society. Therefore, the social and political implications of the divine pattern are also part of its consideration. Thus, the relationships between master–slave, elder–younger and ruler–ruled have an important place in Pauline discussion of the divine F–S relationship (see Chart 7).

Chart 7

Christian divine F–S father-son relationship	The divine creational F–S relationship	Spiritual creational relationship between God and Jesus
		Human creational relationship between God and Adam
		Cosmic creational relationship between God and creature
	The spiritual F–S relationship	Jesus–disciples
		Apostle–Christian believer
		Priest–Church member
	The political F–S relationship	Ruler–ruled
		Official–citizen
	The social F–S relationship	Old–young neighbours
		Senior–junior strangers
		Teacher–student
	The familial F–S relationship	Father–son
		Husband–wife
		Master–slave

There was an apparent conflict between Christian faith and secular social life. Jesus' way of resolving such a conflict was to 'give to Caesar what is Caesar's, and to God what is God's' (Matt 22:21). Paul tried to offer a more practicable understanding of the relationship between the ruler and the ruled, the master and the slave. From his standpoint, the governor was chosen by God and acted as the agent of God in the secular world, and the law is the manifestation of the will of God; so that both the ruler and the law was endowed with God's authority and power. Thus, both obedience to the governor and following the requirements of the law are necessary: the ruled must listen to the ruler and obey his command as a son obeys and listens to his father; the slave has to follow the requirement of the law to obey his master, even if the master and the slave are both the sons of God and have an equal position before God.

According to the law, a Christian believer also needs to respect the older in age and senior in position. According to Theissen, there are four motives for the Christian to practise *agape*: imitation, differentiation, reciprocity and eschatological reward. Theissen's four motives theory can be employed to explain the Christian action that treats an elder stranger as his father and a younger stranger as his son.

First, respecting the older stranger is sovereign behaviour, which makes human beings godlike. For Christians, as the sun shines on good and evil alike, people should love their enemies the same as their loved-ones; therefore, Christians should love and respect the older stranger just as one loves one's aged parents. This is the imitation motive.

Secondly, practising the command of loving one's enemy is special to Christianity; respecting the older stranger should be what sets Christians apart from other groups. As you are God's people, you should 'Let your light so shine before men, that they may see your good works and give glory to your Father who is in heaven' (Matt 5:16). This is the motive of differentiation.

Next, although respecting an older stranger is not offered in expectation of returned love, which would make it like lending money without ever getting it back, it may result in making people stop being strangers. Reciprocity, as the motive, is powerful enough to push people to love and to respect. For example, if you want young people to treat you like a father, you should treat elders as your father first, and if you want the old to treat you as a son, you should treat the young as a son first. For Christians, this mutual love derived from the reciprocity motive; although repayment in this world is not the most important thing for a Christian.

The most important reward for the Christian is eschatological reward.[31] This characteristic can also function in the familial manifestations of the divine F–S relationship. Since the divine and the spiritual F–S relationship is the reflection of its natural pattern, Christianity, especially Pauline teaching, also emphasizes the familial sense of this relationship, albeit that the Christian divine familial F–S relationship is not the same as the Confucian secular one.

The divine F–S relationship is not like the secular one which assumes all its other analogues as imitations of the natural F–S pattern; by contrast, it takes all other analogical relationships as an extension and imitation of the divine pattern. Although the idea of the divine F–S relationship must clearly have been derived from its natural sense, that is not inconsistent with saying that, for Christians, the natural relation, rather than the idea of it, is an imitation of the divine relation. This is to say, in Christianity, the emphasis of the F–S relationship is not on its biological aspects but rather its spiritual aspect. In other words, the biological F–S relationship is merely the imitation of the divine pattern in its creator-created function. Thus we can conclude that the spiritual F–S relationship actually started from the divine and ends with the secular natural F–S relationship.

Differences and Similarities between These Two Dimensions

Chart 8 identifies the differences and similarities between Confucian secular father–son relationships and the Christian divine F–S relationship.

Chart 8

	The originator	The track of extension	Nature of extension	The virtue of extension
Secular F–S	Biological F–S relationship	biological–familial–social– political–spiritual–divine	Moral transcendent	Benevolence
Divine F–S	Divine F–S relationship	Divine–spiritual–political– social–natural/biological	Holy descent	*Agape*

We can draw the following conclusions: there are at least six differences between the secular and divine F–S relationships: first, they have a different linkage and basis. The secular pattern is based on blood kinship and biological and physical linkage, while the divine one is based on universal kinship and spiritual linkage.

Secondly, they have a different meaning and different directions. The secular F–S relationship is started from a natural biological relation, extending to the familial kinship, and then spanning various social imitational F–S patterns, until it arrives at its political guise. In due course it transcends itself to assume the form of the spiritual and is finally transformed into the religious divine sense. By contrast, the divine F–S relationship originates from the divine relationship between God and his only Son Jesus, God and Adam (mankind in general), God and his creatures, and then passes over into its spiritual form between Jesus and his believers, priests and church members and so on. Such a spiritual relationship is further transformed into the various political and social imitational analogous relationships, in which the relationship between neighbours in society and the imitational F–S relationships between king and government officials, and between government official and citizen in the political field, are its main manifestations. In the same way, the divine F–S relationship moves on its familial kinship forms, and finally ends with the biological sense.

Thirdly, they have different foci and core concerns. The focus of the secular F–S relationship is on its biological form, in which the duties and responsibilities and rights of the biological father and son to each other are its main concern. The family kinship F–S relationship and its extensional analogies in a secular society are derived from its biological pattern; consequently, the existing duties and responsibilities and rights in the various analogous F–S relationships are all reflections of the biological father and son. Similarly, the position and influence of the analogous father and son in society are the reflection of biological fathers and sons in a family. By contrast, the focus of attention in the divine F–S relationship is upon the relationship between God, the divine Father, and his beloved Son. Spiritual F–S relationships, such as Jesus and his disciples, apostles and church members in the religious world and the relationship between neighbours in secular society, and officials–citizen relationships in politics, although they have their physical source in the natural F–S relationship, they are apparently in nature imitations and reflections of this divine relationship. Of course, the duties and rights of God and his Son are the most important issues in the divine relationship.

The secular F–S relationship is mainly focused on the physical relationship, while the divine one is mainly focused on the spiritual relationship; the secular F–S relationship is focused on the earthly secular world, while the divine one is focused on the divine world.

Fourthly, the approach adopted in the secular F–S relationship is different from that of the divine pattern. The direction of the human F–S relationship is from the secular world to the transcendent world; more specifically, it starts from the physical birth relationship and ends with the transcendent spiritual fictional relationship. On the other hand, the direction of the divine F–S relationship is from the divine world to the secular world; more concretely, it starts from the divine spiritual relationship between God and Jesus and ends with the physical F–S relationship.

Fifthly, the means of transferring from the secular F–S relationship to the divine one is different from the transferring from the divine to the secular. In the former, the transformation from secular to the divine can be fulfilled by a human being's moral effort. It is the process of moral cultivation through individuals' observing of ordered love, which helps the natural affection between a biological father and his son to be extended from one's family to one's clan, and then to the society and even to the universe; this is a process of development from the virtue of filial piety to the virtue of benevolence. In the divine F–S relationship, the descent from divine love to secular love can only be fulfilled through the revelation of the Holy Spirit. The transfer from the secular to the divine can only be completed through faith. The process of change from universal love to kinship love is a process of salvation, and the process of transfer from the kinship form to the divine form is a process of faith in God and Jesus Christ.

Finally, the way that they deal with the tension between honoring the earthly father and the heavenly father is different. It seems that Confucius and Xunzi have different emphases so that contradictions occur between social justice and familial justice. For example, Confucius insists that, if the father or the son commit some wrongdoing or some crime, the father or the son should conceal it for each other and so social justice should give way to the harmony between father and son; Xunzi, on the other hand, insists that the greater *Yi* should replace the lesser *Yi*, and social justice should be regarded as more important than familial justice. However, both of them devote all their attention to secular society rather than to divine affairs. It seems that Heaven and the Will of Heaven are just instruments for realizing human aims and their humanity. By contrast, in the Christian emphasis on the divine F–S relationship there can be a tension between serving the heavenly father and honoring the earthly father. The suggested way of dealing with this tension is to give up the earthly father and approach the heavenly father. This can be seen in more than one example in which Jesus does not allow the disciples to escape discipleship by appealing to filial piety in the Gospels. However, some scholars insist that there is still an agreement with the unconditional affirmation of the fifth commandment: sons should be obedient to their fathers. Many passages in the Gospel suggest that discipleship was owed to Jesus above all the duties of piety. Others believe that this contradiction is only superficial, because no one would deny that the eschatological outlook is an essential consideration when dealing with those contradictory conditions.

Although there are so many differences between the divine F–S and the secular F–S relationships, we can nevertheless make some essential connections between these two types of relationships. Both are based on an emotion of automatic mutual love between the father and the son, and both link to the moral duty requirement for both the father and the son of material as well as spiritual care. There are more similarities between the Pauline divine and Xunzi secular F–S relationships. For example, both start from a creational relationship, and then run through the whole of human life, in which both the secular and the divine worlds are included. Neither of them focuses exclusively on the secular or the divine world. Xunzi's secular F–S relationship starts from family life, and through its extension, reaches social and political life, and finally moves up to divine life, whereas the Pauline spiritual F–S relationship starts from the divine relationship, then moves down to various religious, political and social lives and is finally realized in family life. This implies that there is no unbridgeable gap between human secular life and divine life for either Paul or Xunzi. Human beings can transfer themselves from the secular world to the divine world by their personal efforts, and this effort is based on morality or on faith.

More than that, both the Confucian secular and the Christian divine F–S relationship take social life as not only an aim in itself, but also the means of reaching their own aims. Confucian F–S relationships aim at the perfect secular family life, while Christian F–S relationships aim at future spiritual life. Social life for both is important only in that it acts as the 'way' or the 'path' for people to reach their final purpose and aims. The final goal of Confucianism is to build an orderly and harmonious kinship through the F–S relationship, and of Christianity to build a harmonious spiritual relationship. However, just as 'The state was to them only the means, though the only means, to individual perfection,'[32] so society is always a necessary path and means for establishing an orderly and harmonious individual relationship. This is the reason why both Xunzi and Paul pay considerable attention to the discussion of relationships.

In addition, neither Xunzi's secular nor the Pauline divine F–S relationship draws a narrow boundary. Both further extend their dialogue to wider matters. Explicitly, the Confucian F–S relationship does not stop at the biological relationship, but transcends its secular dimension to the divine one, where Heaven and Earth act as the parents and humans as the children. It is believed that by the communication and integration between the way of humanity and the Way of Heaven and Earth, the secular sense of the F–S relationship is linked up with the divine sense one. Similarly, the Christian divine F–S relationship is not confined to the spiritual world. The spirit has descended from heaven to the secular world, and naturally, the spiritual F–S relationship has influenced the biological one. Accordingly, the spiritual world has been linked together with secular society; and the spiritual relationship with the physical relationship by the descending of the Holy Spirit. In fact, the divine F–S relationship of Christianity has never been separated from its secular pattern from the very beginning. Speaking plainly, the divine F–S relationship is initially copied from the physical F–S relationship. Without the pattern of the natural sense, it is difficult to understand the concept of the divine F–S relationship.

Last, although Xunzi and Paul have different beginnings and travel by different roads, they finally arrive at the same point. In the following chapters, we shall see that the secular F–S in Confucianism and the divine F–S relationship in Christianity come to a similar conclusion: mutual love between father and son; a definite distinction between the father's authority and the son's obedience; and a hierarchical and orderly society.

CHAPTER FOUR

The Pauline Ethical Divine Father–Son Relationship

Chapters 2 and 3 presented a general discussion on the constitution and different presentational forms of the divine F–S relationship. In this chapter discussion will focus on the nature and ethical manifestations of the Pauline divine F–S relationship.

When speaking of Paul's ethics, Brian S. Rosner suggests that we should simply have in mind 'his ways which are in Christ' (1 Cor 4:17); his 'instruction as to how one ought to walk and please God' (1 Thess 4:1); 'that pattern of teaching' to which he committed the early Christians (Rom 6:17).[1] These excerpts from Paul's writings indicate that Paul's moral reflections cannot be separated from his theological understanding.[2] Since Paul customarily rests his moral imperatives on the basis of God's prior action on behalf of believers in Christ, exploration of the Pauline ethical understanding must start from the centre of the Pauline divine F–S relationship. However, as Wayne A. Meeks has pointed out, understanding the ethics of early Christianity must begin with a rigorous attempt to describe the culture of the time, and with its religious, social and familial *mores*.

The Centre of the Pauline Ethical Divine Father–Son Relationship

The centre of the Pauline divine father–son relationship is focused on the relationships with God,[3] in which not only the God–Jesus, but also God–humans and Jesus–believer relationships are included. Since Paul's ethical injunctions and prohibitions are rooted in the redemptive acts of God,[4] of the three relationships related to God, the God–Jesus relationship is the centre and base of the other two. We therefore presume that this relationship is not only the centre of the Pauline theology, but also his ethical divine F–S relationship.

There are four reasons to support the statement that the God–Jesus relationship is the centre of the Pauline theological divine F–S relationship: first, the God–Jesus relationship is a keystone in defining the divine nature of the Pauline F–S relationship. 'Divine' is a term pertaining to, proceeding from, the nature of God or god and of the sacred. It is also a notion to be attributed to God in service or adoration, or offered to something religious and holy.[5] Thus, a divine F–S relationship has two preconditions: it must be a spiritual relationship beyond a physical or a biological linkage; and also, it must be a holy relationship with reference to God.

In Christian theology, there are three main meanings included in the notion of 'holy': it is something associated with God; a relation to something regarded as sacred or consecrated; a situation devoted to the service of God, or a condition of being morally and spiritually pure. There are two meanings implied within the conception of 'spirit': one is of the human spirit or soul, the other is something of or from or like God. The F–S relationship between God and Jesus, like the relationship between God and humans, is a relationship based on the spirit of God: 'those who are led by the Spirit of God are sons of God' (Rom 8:14); 'For the father–son relationship is neither necessary nor physical as based on the creator–creature status: it is ethical and spiritual, based on God's unmerited choice and man's response in faith' (Rom 8:14–17). Unlike the God–Adam relationship that is based on biological creation, the creation of God in the relationship between God and Jesus is beyond biological and based on the spiritual linkage.

Indeed, Paul talks about Jesus Christ as the 'first-born' over all creation in Col 1:15. However, since many scholars do not hold to Pauline authorship of Colossians, and again the phrase 'first-born' here is used more in a spiritual than a physical sense, there is no strong evidence to prove that Paul thought that Jesus Christ was the physical creation of God. There is more evidence for confirming the status of God for Jesus Christ: 'Yet for us there is but one God, the Father, from whom all things came and for whom we live; and there is but one Lord, Jesus Christ, through whom all things came and through whom we live' (1 Cor 8:6). 'He will oppose and will exalt himself over everything that is called God or is worshipped, so that he sets himself up in God's temple, proclaiming himself to be God' (2 Thess 2:4). Therefore, it is safe to say that, even if there is a begetter–begotten relationship between God and Jesus Christ, this relationship is not the same as the creator–created relationship between God and Adam, the ancestor of mankind. It is a purely spiritual creational relationship. Therefore, there is no problem in taking the God–Jesus relationship as a divine F–S relationship.

However, according to Paul, the divine fatherhood is not limited to Jesus Christ but open to all Christian believers: God is, first of all, the Father of the Lord Jesus Christ (Rom 15:6; 1 Cor 1:9; 2 Cor 1:3); then through Jesus Christ, the Father of all Christian believers (1 Cor 8:6; 2 Cor 1:3; 6:18); thus the divine F–S relationship is also definable for the God–human relationship.

Moreover, because the divine title is not limited to God, but also shared by Jesus Christ, Jesus Christ is not only the Son of God, but also the rescuer as well as the deliverer of Christian believers;[6] he is not only the beloved Son of God, but also one of the Trinity and the Co-operator of God in the process of creating the universe and the new world. Therefore, the Jesus–Christian believer relationship can also be defined as a divine F–S relationship.

It is true that on most occasions, Paul would rather separate God from Jesus Christ by calling God the Father and Jesus Christ the Lord. The evidence can be found in the sentence, 'Grace and peace to you from God our Father and from the Lord Jesus Christ', which is found at the beginning of most of Paul's letters (1 Cor 1:3; 2 Cor 1:2; Gal 1:3; Eph 1:2; Phil 1:2; Col 1:2; 1 Thess 1:1; 2 Thess 1:2; 1 Tim 1:2; 2 Tim 1:2; Titus 1:4; Philm 1:3). Moreover, the tendency to distinguish God from Jesus can be also seen in his distinction between the Spirit of God and the Spirit of Jesus Christ in Rom 8:9–11:

You, however, are controlled not by the sinful nature but by the Spirit, if the Spirit of God lives in you. And if anyone does not have the Spirit of Christ, he does not belong to Christ. But if Christ is in you, your body is dead because of sin, yet your spirit is alive because of righteousness. And if the Spirit of him who raised Jesus from dead is living in you, he who raised Christ from the dead will also give life to your mortal bodies through his Spirit, who lives in you.

The strongest distinction between God and Jesus Christ can be found in 1 Cor:

Now when it says that 'everything' has been put under him, it is clear that this does not include God himself, who put everything under Christ. When he has done this, then the Son himself will be made subject to him who put everything under him, so that God may be all in all. (1 Cor 15:27–8)

James D. G. Dunn points out that the acclamation of Jesus Christ as Lord involved no heavenly coup or takeover, no replacement of God by Christ. Not because the one was identified with the other, but because the one God had chosen to share his sovereignty with the exalted Christ.[7]

However, he was not always exempt from the ambiguities; sometimes, he declares Jesus Christ to be the image of God: He is the image of the invisible God, the first-born over all creation (Col 1:15); occasionally, Jesus is described directly as God: 'He will oppose and will exalt himself over everything that is called God or is worshipped, so that he sets himself up in God's temple, proclaiming himself to be God' (2 Thess 2:4). 'There is one body and one Spirit – just as you were called to one hope when you were called – one Lord, one faith, one baptism; one God and Father of all, who is over all and through all and in all' (Eph 4:3–6). This is because in Christ all the fullness of the Deity lives in bodily form, and you have been given fullness in Christ, who is the head over every power and authority (Col 2:9–10). Therefore, for Paul, divine father-hood is identified not only with God the Father of Jesus Christ (Rom 1:1–4; 1:9; 5:10; 8:3; 8:29; 8:32; 15:6; 1 Cor 15:24; 2 Cor 1:2;1:3;11:31; Gal 1:1; Eph 1:3; 1:17; 3:14; 6:23; Phil 1:2; 2:11; Col 1:3; 1:12; 3:17; 1 Thess 1:1, 3:11, 3:13; 2 Thess 1:2; 1 Tim 1:2; 2 Tim 1:2), but also with Jesus Christ, the Son in that it is related to the relationship between God and men or God and Christian believers (Rom 1:7; 8:14; 8:15; 8:16; 8:17; 8:19; 8:21; 8:23; 9:26; 1 Cor 1:3; 1:9; 8:6; 2 Cor 1:2; Gal 1:3; 1:4; Eph 1:2; Phil 4:20; Col 1:2; 1 Thess 1:1;1:2; 2 Thess 1:1; 2:16). More than that, 'Trinitarian' theology does exist, for example, 2 Cor 13.

Although in line with the above demonstration, the Jesus–Christian believer relationship can also be defined as a divine F–S relationship. Similar to the God–believer relationship, it must take the God–Jesus relationship as its source and model. This is the second reason for regarding the God–Jesus pattern as the centre of the Pauline divine F–S relationship.

To ascertain that the God–Jesus relationship is the centre of the Pauline divine F–S relationship, it is first necessary to confirm the central position of the God–Jesus relationship among the three divine F–S models: without the God–Jesus relationship, other divine relationships have no formation because Jesus Christ was the first-born Son of God. Through his crucifixion he became the heir of the kingdom of God, and through him all Christian believers become the adopted sons of God. Jesus Christ is the only way to enter the kingdom of God. Thus, the F–S relationship between God and men can never be established except through Jesus Christ and the divine F–S relationship between Jesus and Christian believers can never exist without regarding Jesus Christ as the Son and the trinity of God. The Gospel, as Paul understands it, is 'about the Son of God, who was descended from David according to the flesh, and was proclaimed as Son of God in power according to the Spirit of holiness by the resurrection from the dead' (Rom 1:3f). More importantly, the F–S relationship between God and Jesus was established before any other relationship existed.[8] Consequently, in Pauline Christianity, this relationship is the most fundamental relationship not only for suggesting, but also establishing, other divine relationships.

The third reason for regarding the God–Jesus relation as the centre of Pauline divine F–S relationship is because the essential nature of this pattern has been determined by the God–Jesus relationship. The distinctive characteristic of the Pauline divine ethical F–S theory is to put emphasis on equality as well as hierarchy between the two parts of the relationship, which is decided by the nature of the God–Jesus relationship. As the Son of God, the distinctive virtue of Jesus Christ is to obey and fear God, and to humble himself in dealing with others. However, being in human form, he was exalted to be the heir of the kingdom of God by his faith in, and obedience to, God. Two possibilities are implicated here: if Jesus Christ can be the heir of the kingdom of God through belief in and obedience to God by his human body, people who have been the brothers of Jesus Christ through faith in him can also be heirs of the kingdom of God. Thus, the special divine F–S relationship between God and Jesus has paved the way for the possible connection and transformation between the holy and secular relations and thereby provided a possibility for realization of equality among believers, between Jesus and believers, and even between God and Jesus Christ.

Finally, the reason that the God–Jesus relationship is central to the divine F–S relationship for Paul is also because the relationship between God and Jesus Christ is the model and guide of its secular analogues. All the presentations of the secular F–S relationships are imitations of the God–Jesus relationship; the God–Jesus relationship is not only the model and guide of Christian familial relationships, such as natural father–son, husband–wife, but also of social relationships, such as master–slave or teacher–disciple; it is not only the model and guide for religious relationships, such as apostle–follower or priest–church member, but also for political relationships, such as the ruler–subjects or senior–junior.

The ethical relationship between God and Jesus is the centre of the Pauline divine F–S relationship. P. T. Forsyth confirms the moral centre of social Christianity. According to him, the main work of the church is determined by the nature of the Saviour's work on the cross, and this work was a condensed action of His whole personality. The Saviour's work, being personal, was therefore ethical, and not official. Therefore, the essence of Christ's work was securing once and for all the kingdom of God in the real world. The divine F–S relationship between God and Jesus is mainly focused on its theological sense; it was not concerned with purely human relationship, but rather with the relationship between humankind and God, with men and women in their relationships with each other, and subsequently with Christ as God's response to the human plight. However, ethics in the West is defined as 'the study and philosophy of human conduct with emphasis on the determination of right and wrong and the basic principle of right action',[9] and as the study and philosophy of perfect and harmonious human relationships in Chinese tradition. While 'Paul's theology is relational' and Paul's anthropology defined persons by their relations, the divine F–S relationship between God and Jesus though could not be regarded as the same as a normal ethical relationship, for it belonged to religious ethics; it is indeed a religious ethical relationship. This defines the ambiguous character of the Christian movement in its attitude to family life and the relationship between the household and the faith, notwithstanding the two distinctive trends within Pauline F–S doctrine, namely, a spiritual trend and frequent attempts to re-embed Christian discipleship within the household.[10] Consequently, the particular characteristic of the Pauline ethical F–S relationship can be demonstrated from its special manifestations of the divine dimension.

People may perhaps argue that the qualities of the divine father and the divine son do not belong to the ethical but to theological virtue. However, theological virtue can be treated as ethical virtue because they cannot be separated from each other; they need to be viewed as complementary elements of an individual's life. As D. D. Newman Smyth argues, 'Ultimately they belong together. Each originally implies the other, and in the perfected life both are made one.'[11] William Wrede proposes a similar argument and states that NT theology can be called NT ethics as well because it 'makes doctrine out of what itself is not doctrine' but mostly 'practical advice, direction for life, instruction for the moment'.[12] James D. G. Dunn further discusses the connection of divinity and morality in Pauline teaching. He comments that it is clear that for Paul 'the wrath of God' denotes the inescapable, divinely ordered moral constitution of human society. God's reaction to evil and sin has determined that human actions have moral consequences.[13] If God's final judgment will be completed from the moral constitution of the world he created, it is reasonable to conclude that both the quality of God the Father and Jesus the Son belong to religious ethics. If Pauline theology can be equally treated as religious ethics, then Pauline theological virtue can be regarded the same as ethical virtue. In addition, in the divine F–S relationship, 'the Christological element and the ethical element stand in close relation to each other; what we are speaking of here is Christological ethics'.[14] Thus, although for some scholars it would not be appropriate to try and construct a Pauline ethic of parenthood based on his metaphor,[15] it seems to me that the best way to discuss Pauline divine ethics is from his metaphor of the divine F–S relationship.[16] This is because love, as the foundation of Pauline ethics and central meaning of the ethical orientation of the church,[17] can be reflected fully from this relationship.

The Ethical Manifestations of the Pauline Divine Father–Son Relationship

The Pauline ethical divine F–S relationship is a reflection of its pagan and Jewish environment; indeed, the general rule in early Christianity was a kind of child–parent relationship, seen in its pagan and Jewish environment as honouring one's parents, which was strongly expected from children. According to Peter Balla, texts affirm that Jesus and his disciples shared the norm of their environment: parents are to be honoured; they are to be obeyed, and when they grow old they are to be cared for.[18] Paul's conversion had not changed his belief in and about God. It was the Creator God of Genesis who had also enlightened him; it was the God who had called Jeremiah who had also chosen him; it was the grace of this God which made him what he was.[19] Therefore, the core elements of the Pauline divine F–S relationship will be demonstrated from the ethical manifestations of both divine fatherhood and divine sonship.

The ethical manifestation of the Pauline divine fatherhood

The ethical manifestation of Pauline fatherhood can be partly identified in the following five ethical qualities of divine fatherhood: (1) God is the father of holiness; (2) God is the father of glory; (3) God is the father of grace; (4) God is the father who is merciful; and (5) God is the father of justice and righteousness.

(1) God is the Father of holiness. First, God is the only one who created men and the universe.[20] God is independent[21] and possesses eternal power and divine nature: 'For since the creation of the world God's invisible qualities – his eternal power and divine nature – have been clearly seen, being understood from what has been made, so that men are without excuse' (Rom 1:19–20). Since God is one, he is invisible and un-image-able.[22] Therefore, God the Father is a holy and divine being (Acts 17:29).

God is a living God, who not only created the universe and men in the past, but whose recreating work will continue through the renewing of human life. Dunn connects this new creation with salvation. He states that it is no surprise that God's act in raising from the dead, the climax of his salvation, is of a piece with his act in creating: 'He who gives life to the dead' is 'he who calls things that have no existence into existence.'[23]

This new creation work of God was designed to be fulfilled through his Son Jesus Christ. As the image of the invisible God and the first-born over all creation, God was pleased to have all his fullness dwell in him, and through him to reconcile to himself all things both on Earth and in Heaven and to make peace with humans. It is clear that this image is not of God as an angry opponent having to be cajoled or entreated, but of God the injured partner, actively seeking reconciliation.[24] Thus, it is also clear for Paul that as a living God, the divine father not only demonstrated his new creational work through sending Jesus down to earth and raising him from the dead, but also by giving people a new perfect spiritual immortal life through Jesus Christ: 'Just as Christ was raised from the dead through the glory of the Father, we may live a new life' (Rom 6:4).

(2) God is the Father of glory. Paul confirms that God is the almighty Father, not only can he create all things from nothing and make them exist from non-existence, but he can also raise life from the dead:

> That (incomparably great power) is like the working of his mighty strength, which he exerted in Christ when he raised him from the dead and seated him at his right hand in the

heavenly realms, far above all rule and authority, power and dominion, and every title that can be given, not only in the present age but also in the one to come. (Eph 1:19–21)

It is in the obedience of Jesus that God is to be known and it is in the suffering of Jesus that God is glorified.[25] Because Jesus Christ can be raised from the dead by faith in God, we also can be given an eternal new life by faith in Jesus Christ:

Don't you know that all of us who were baptized into Christ Jesus were baptized into his death? We were therefore buried with him through baptism into death in order that, just as Christ was raised from the dead through the glory of the Father, we too may live a new life. (Rom 6:3–4)

From these statements we can see that in Pauline theology, the power of raising life from the dead is the main content of God's glory, and that to earn eternal life in heaven by faith in Jesus Christ is the main theme and aim of the Christian life. In this sense, to earn eternal life in heaven by faith is not only the theological purpose but also the secular moral purpose of people.

(3) God is the Father of grace. According to Brad Eastman, Paul's Christianity is seen to be a religion in which one is 'justified' solely by divine grace, which is merely 'received' by human faith.[26] James D. G. Dunn points out that 'more typical of Paul's experience of God was a sense of grace and power which were transforming and sustaining his daily living'.[27] This is because, first, God is the only one who is perfect with full beauty and virtue; he not only has a 'good, pleasing and perfect will' (Rom 12:2), but is also a 'God of peace but not disorder' (1 Cor 14:33). This perfect nature is the source of human encouragement and hope: 'May our Lord Jesus Christ himself and God our Father, who loved us and by his grace gave us eternal encouragement and good hope, encourage your hearts and strengthen you in every good deed and word' (2 Thess 2:16–17).

Secondly, God is the only one who has the highest authority and whole ability. God not only created the beautiful and ordered the universe, but has also destroyed ugly death and will bring immortal life to his believers: 'This grace was given us in Christ Jesus before the beginning of time, but it has now been revealed through the appearing of our saviour, Christ Jesus, who has destroyed death and has brought life and immortality to light through the gospel' (2 Tim 1:9–10). Therefore, God not only possesses all power and authority in the past and the present, but will therefore also have all power and authority in the future.

Moreover, God is the only one with full knowledge and true wisdom. God is a wise Father with full knowledge and wisdom that human wisdom and knowledge can never reach: 'Although they claimed to be wise, they became fools and exchanged the glory of the immortal God for images made to look like mortal man and birds and animals and reptiles' (Rom 1:22). God's wisdom is on the one hand revealed through Jesus Christ, because Christ is 'the power of God and the wisdom of God' (1 Cor 1:24), but on the other hand it can be seen through the capacity of humans to know and understand the signs of God: 'We have done so not according to worldly wisdom but according to God's grace. For we do not write to you anything you cannot read or understand' (2 Cor 1:12–13). God not only created humans, but created humans in his own image, therefore humans receive their intelligence as well as their free will from being created in the image of God.[28] This is what makes humans different from other creatures. Although this free will of humans often leads them to choose sin, it can also lead them to choose faith in Jesus Christ and reach salvation. However, to say that humans have intelligence is not the same as saying that humans have the same wisdom as God. The wisdom of God is not only different from the wisdom of humans, but is also higher than the wisdom of humans: 'For the foolishness of God is wiser than man's wisdom, and the weakness of God is stronger than man's strength' (1 Cor 1:25). The most important aspect of the wisdom of God, in Pauline teaching, is to appreciate the weak and the lowly, and to exalt those who put themselves in a humble, lower position:

> But God chose the foolish things of the world to shame the wise; God chose the weak things of the world to shame the strong. He chose the lowly things of this world and the despised things – and the things that are not – to nullify the things that are, so that no-one may boast before him. (1 Cor 1:27–30)

According to Brian S. Rosner, Aristotle argues that whatever prevents the development of virtue makes the spirit 'humble', 'humility' and 'to humble oneself' and so on are never viewed positively in Greek ethics, so that Paul's seeing humility as a virtue would have been revolutionary in the world of many of his converts.[29] This is why Jesus' ethic is strictly opposed to every humanistic ethic and value ethic; Christian ethics are the 'ethics of obedience'[30] and the ethics of weakness. As Moltmann states that God (Jesus) is not greater than he is in humiliation; God (Jesus) is not more glorious than he is in this self-surrender. God (Jesus) is not more powerful than he is in this helplessness; and he is not more divine than he is in this humanity.[31]

From Paul's point of view, no one can boast before God, either in knowledge or in wisdom; God is the highest one over any kind of human being, even himself presented in Jesus' form of humanity. Only when human beings humble and lower themselves before God can they be promoted to a noble and higher position by God. Otherwise, they remain humble and lower beings forever.

(4) God is the Father of mercy (2 Cor 1:3). For Pauline belief, God is the Father with a whole heart of love as well as forgiveness; his love is greater than his anger. God is a Father with compassion and love: God is 'the Father of compassion and the God of all comfort, who comforts us in all our troubles so that we can comfort those in any trouble with the comfort we ourselves have received from God' (2 Cor 1:3–4). In short, when we are in trouble, God comforts us; when we are suffering, he gives us salvation. For Paul, although salvation must be completed through Jesus Christ, it begins and ends with God the Father. It begins with the Father's foreknowledge and predestination of the elect, is carried on by his calling, justification and adoption of them, and terminates with his glorification of them in the Eschaton.[32]

God's love is expressed not only in his special creation of humans in terms of being different from other creatures by having free will and intelligence, but also in his riches of kindness, tolerance and patience to men (Rom 2:4). It is God's kindness and love that have saved us; it is God's mercy rather than the righteous works we have done that have 'saved us through the washing of rebirth and renewal by the Holy Spirit, whom he poured out on us generously through Jesus Christ our Saviour' (Titus 3:4–6).

Nonetheless, the greatest love that God gives people is expressed in his forgiveness of men's sin: 'When we were still powerless, Christ died for the ungodly' (Rom 5:6); 'while we were still sinners, Christ died for us' (Rom 5:8); 'when we were still God's enemies, we were reconciled to him through the death of his son' (Rom 5:9–10). More precisely, although 'all have sinned and fallen short of the glory of God', God still keeps his forbearance and even further has presented Jesus Christ as a sacrifice of atonement in order to show that 'he had left the sins committed beforehand unpunished' (Rom 3:25).

(5) God is the Father of justice and righteousness and he will execute the final judgment on everybody, both the living and the dead, to punish the evil and reward the good:

> God "will give to each person according to what he has done". To those who by persistence in doing good seek glory, honour and immortality, he will give eternal life. But for those who are self-seeking and who reject the truth and follow evil, there will be wrath and anger. There will be trouble and distress for every human being who does evil . . . but glory, honour and peace for everyone who does good. (Rom 2:6–10)

Paul had a deep belief that 'God is just'. In his view, God understands clearly what to love and what to hate, knows exactly who is worthy to be rewarded, and who deserves to be punished. However, God's rewards and punishment are not according to one's moral behaviour, but depend on whether people believe in God and obey the gospel of Jesus Christ: 'He will punish those who do not know God and do not obey the gospel of our Lord Jesus' (2 Thess 1:8). This religious ethical point of view is totally different from that of normal ethical requirements.

From the above analysis we can see that there is some continuity between the Pauline concept of divine fatherhood and the OT's concept of fatherhood. For example, God is the creator who is perfect with total power and full knowledge; the nature of God is justice and righteousness; therefore, there will be a just judgment executed in the future, not only to reward, but also to punish. However, there are new concepts present in the ethical qualities of the Pauline divine father compared with the divine fatherhood of the OT: first, there is more emphasis on God's immortality and the capacity to raise the dead and give people eternal life. Secondly, there is more focus on the glory of God through Jesus Christ. Thirdly, there is more emphasis on the love and forgiving nature of God. Fourthly, Paul gave nearly all his attention to God's new salvation project and, finally, there is a particular emphasis on the weakness and the obedience of the Son.

The ethical manifestation of the divine sonship

The notion of divine sonship in Pauline thought has two meanings: one is the special calling of Jesus Christ; the other applies to all Christian believers. Accordingly, the ethic of divine sonship is expressed from two perspectives: the ethical qualities of Jesus Christ and the ethical qualities of Christian believers. Since the ethical qualities of Christian believers are an imitation of those of the Son of God, the ethical qualities of Jesus Christ will be our main focus.

As the Son of God and the brother of Christian believers, Jesus Christ is said to have demonstrated two kinds of qualities: his virtuous relation with God and his ethical qualities in relation to Christian believers.

For Paul, there are three important ethical qualities in Jesus Christ's dealing with God: love, fear and hope. Since medieval times virtues have been divided into ethical and divine ones: ethical virtues refer to courage, wisdom, temperance and justice while divine virtues are love, faith and hope; and here arises a question: are love, fear and hope really ethical virtues? All virtues referring to human relationships are to be considered normal ethics, while all virtues relative to the relationship between divine and human belong to religious ethics; since whatever virtue, if it is related to familial, social, political and spiritual relationships, is an ethical virtue, love, fear and hope, since they are not secular ethical virtues, are religious ethical virtues.

The Son fears the Father because he possesses the most powerful force and the highest authority; the Son also loved the Father because he is holy and glorious; the Son hoped in the Father because he is justice and forgiveness, as well as being a love giver. All these three moral virtues inspire the same conduct, that is, faith in God and obedience to the will of God.[33] Jesus' ethic is an ethic of obedience. Obedience not only indicates whom one obeys, but also what one obeys. For Paul it is clear that obedience is to be governed by God's will and that God's revealed will provides the specific norms or standards. Paul sees the meaning of human action not in the development towards an ideal of man, which is founded on the human spirit; 'he sees only the individual man standing before the will of God'.[34] Thus, absolute obedience to the will of the Father becomes the most important virtue that Jesus displayed in dealing with God.

The virtue of obedience can be seen particularly in two events: one is Jesus' descent from Heaven to Earth and the other is his death on the cross for the purification of sins. From Paul's point of view, there is a close relationship between Christ's descent and his death, and between the death and the power of Jesus Christ. For Paul, the mortal nature of human form is a kind of sin linked closely with death; the descent of Jesus into human form thereby causes him to become subject to the power of death. However, it is the death and resurrection of Jesus Christ that cleaned the sin of human form, which made Jesus become the king of kings. Gustaf Aulen has reminded us that the classical doctrine of the Atonement represented the death of Christ neither as a satisfaction paid to God nor as a moral influence on men, but as a victory over evil powers.[35] Two forces determine the two facts: God's self-giving divine love and Jesus Christ's absolute obedience. It is God's self-giving divine love that made him send his beloved Son down to earth in the sinful form of human flesh; it is Jesus' absolute obedience that made him receive this mission of being sent in the likeness of sinful flesh to be the sacrifice by his death on the cross. Paul declares that the love of God is incredibly great:

> In Love he predestined us to be adopted as his sons through Jesus Christ, in accordance with his pleasure and will . . . to the praise of his glorious grace, which he has freely given us in the One he loves. In him we have redemption through his blood, the forgiveness of sins, in accordance with the riches of God's grace that he lavished on us with all wisdom and understanding. (Eph 1:5–8)

For Pauline Christians, the obedience of Jesus Christ is absolute: as an heir of the kingdom of God, Jesus Christ was the image of God, and had been endowed with the same power and authority as God. Thus, Jesus was not only supreme over everything, but also had the power and ability to escape from crucifixion. However, for the realization of God's salvation, he was absolutely obedient to the will of God: not only in being sent to Earth in a sinful human form, but also in not seeking to escape from crucifixion, the curse of the law. For God's salvation plan, Christ, 'who, being in very nature God, did not consider equality with God something to be grasped, but made himself nothing, taking the very nature of a servant, being made in human likeness' (Phil 2:6–7), and in order to complete the eternal salvation of humankind, Jesus was happy to appear as a man: 'he humbled himself and became obedient to death – even death on a cross!' (Phil 2:8) and allowed God to make him who had no sin be sinful for humans (2 Cor 5:21). Since it was the virtue of obedience that made Jesus Christ choose to descend and die on the cross, the descent and death become the signal of Christ's faith in and obedience to God. Accordingly, Morna D. Hooker concludes that the death of Christ demonstrates not God's displeasure but the Son's obedience; in other words, by the death of Jesus the loving purpose of God is achieved through the obedience of his Son Jesus.[36] Using Robert L. Reymond's phrase, Paul teaches that Christ's entire work of salvation is founded in and flows out of his obedience.[37]

Why is the virtue of obedience the fundamental character of the Christian divine sonship? Paul's answer is: 'For just as through the disobedience of the one man the many were made sinners, so also through the obedience of the one man the many will be made righteous' (Rom 5:19). Since obedience is linked to righteousness and disobedience to sin, therefore, all sons of God who intend to be free of sin are supposed to enjoy their submission to God and the condition of being slaves of God: 'Don't you know that when you offer yourselves to someone to obey him as slaves, you are slaves to the one whom you obey – whether you are slaves to sin, which leads to death, or to obedience, which leads to righteousness?' (Rom 6:16). Why would Christians want to be the slaves of God? From the Pauline standpoint, this is because, first, humankind, in the natural state, is morally depraved. Paul asserts that humankind has become filled with every kind of wickedness, evil, greed and depravity (Rom 1:29); moreover, they are darkened in their understanding and separated from the life of God (Eph 4:17); therefore man has a moral inability to please God or to save himself.[38] Only through Jesus Christ's obedience to death and through the sacrifice of himself can human sin be expiated, God's propitiatory love and reconciliation be shown, and the redemption of humans and the destruction of the evil kingdom be completed.[39] Obedience can not only cleanse sin and connect to righteousness and justice, but also bring redemption and salvation; thus, it is only in the condition of being 'free from sin and having become slaves to God' that the human race can reap the benefit of being led to holiness, and the 'result is eternal life' (Rom 6:22).

Paul believed that all these virtues that Jesus demonstrated in his relationship with God are what the followers and believers of Jesus should learn from him, and that these virtues can influence Christian believers through the Holy Spirit by leading believers to a perception of Jesus as Lord (1 Cor 12:3) and to a filial consciousness of God as their Father (Rom 8:15–16; Gal 4:6). Therefore, in relation to God, all Christians should have an attitude of love, fear and hope and keep their faith through obedience.

Everybody should fear God: 'Continue to work out your salvation with fear and trembling, for it is God who works in you to will and to act according to his good purpose' (Phil 2:13). God is so powerful and capable that no other forces in this world are comparable with God and therefore nobody can escape from God's power. To avoid God's punishment, one ought to show fear through one's conduct of obedience: 'Do everything without complaining or arguing, so that you may become blameless and pure – children of God without fault in a crooked and depraved generation' (Phil 2:14–15).

It is indicated here that there is a close relationship between fear and obedience. Fear is the cause of obedience and respect is the result of human fear. Therefore, both fear and obedience are necessary for people approaching the condition of being saved by God. It is true that, compared with the rich discourse on love and forgiveness, Paul has less to say on fear and punishment; however, he devotes much attention to discussing obedience, both the factual obedience of Jesus Christ and the necessary obedience of humankind to God. Ordinary Christian believers should first be holy or righteous; secondly, obey God's commandment and finally respond to God's love. However, since both love and obedience are connected to God's power and authority, fear of God is a necessary virtue for all Christians.

In accordance with Paul's emphasis on God's love and forgiveness, hope in God is also important for Christian believers. There are two chief aspects to hope: hope in God's glory, which means hoping that he will give Christians an eternal spiritual life through their faith in Jesus Christ; and hope in God's mercy, which is hope that God can compromise his wrath and give people his love, forgiveness and salvation: 'And we rejoice in the hope of the glory of God' (Rom 5:2); 'May the God of hope fill you with all joy and peace as you trust in him, so that you may overflow with hope by the power of the Holy Spirit' (Rom 15:13). However, the result of hope is still faith and waiting: 'We also rejoice in our sufferings, because we know that suffering produces perseverance; perseverance, character; and character, hope. And hope does not disappoint us, because God has poured out his love into our hearts by the Holy Spirit, whom he has given us' (Rom 5:3–5). As sons of God, the most important virtue Christians ought to learn from Jesus Christ the Son of God is his virtue of love. Paul says that of the three virtues a Christian should show – faith, hope and love – the greatest one is love (1 Cor 13:13). Since Jesus' love not only fulfils the law but is also an expression of God's love of righteousness, therefore love is the goal and aim of Christian ministry and the Christian life. He urges Christians to pay more attention to *agape*: 'Be imitators of God, therefore, as dearly loved children and live a life of love, just as Christ loved us and gave himself up for us as a fragrant offering and sacrifice to God' (Eph 5:1–2).

What is love? From the Pauline point of view, love is patient and kind. It does not envy, it does not boast, it is not proud. It is not rude, not self-seeking, not easily angered, and keeps no record of wrongs. Love does not delight in evil but rejoices with the truth. Love always protects, always trusts, always hopes, and always perseveres (1 Cor 13:4–7). In other words, 'Love must be sincere. Hate what is evil; cling to what is good' (Rom 12:9).

Where does divine love come from? Xinzhong Yao has given us a summary: '*Agape* is essentially and fundamentally understood in terms of the being and character of God. Without the succour of God's sovereignty and grace, the great tree of Christian love cannot grow.'[40] As the divine creation, *agape*, on the one hand, is a completely self-giving and self-affirming love. Because of the identification of God with Jesus Christ in creation, this self-giving and self-affirming love not only includes the original creation of God, but also the recreation of Jesus Christ. On the other hand, since the realization of his love can be seen only in the universal order of creation, in human history and in human love, therefore, God's love is involved with, and is realized by, the love of his creatures, especially human beings created in the image of God himself.

Jesus' virtue of love can be seen more clearly from his obedience to God and his humility in relation to humans, the sinners. Paul states that, as the Son of God, and especially the image of God, Jesus Christ, like his Father, loves sinful men very much and very deeply too. However, the manifestation of Jesus' love is different from that of God. God's love is presented through his glory and mercy, while Jesus' love is presented through his obedience to God and humility towards men. For the purpose of the love of God, he would even like to be used as a tool in the process of God's salvation. Because he so loved mankind, he wished to contribute his perfect life to reconcile the wrath of God; for the purpose of the redemption of men, he wished to use his innocent blood to cleanse the sin of men and make a new contract with God. Thus, Jesus Christ not only made himself nothing before God, but also made himself a servant of people, a slave, even a sinner, in the secular world. He chose a weak, soft and humble nature in order to present his love of both his Father and his followers: 'And being found in appearance as a man, he humbled himself and became obedient to death – even death on a cross!' (Phil 2:6–9). However, through his manifestation in humility, Jesus eventually fulfilled his mission of salvation and became the king of both Earth and Heaven. Therefore, the adopted sons of God, who are led by the Spirit of God and believe in Jesus Christ, will know the joy and satisfaction in which the will of God is brought to fruition in the day-by-day life of obedience.[41] Thus, all Christians are vigorously urged and commanded to obey God because God's will not only enables them to obey and to give love to God and Jesus Christ, but also to show their love to each other. As the followers of Jesus Christ, the sons of God and the brothers of Jesus Christ, humans demonstrate love in their response to the command of loving one's neighbour: 'Whatever other commandments there may be, are summed up in this one rule: "Love your neighbour as yourself." Love does not harm your neighbour.' Accordingly, F. F. Bruce argues that the believer is not under law as a rule of life, unless one thinks of the law of love.[42]

According to Paul, 'loving one's neighbour' is a mutual love for each other, which includes at least six meanings: (1) entertaining hospitably, even strangers who need your help; (2) 'Rejoice with those who rejoice and mourn with those who mourn' (Rom 12:15); (3) 'Live in harmony with one another' and do not put any stumbling-block or obstacle in your brother's way (Rom 14:13); (4) 'Do not be proud, but be willing to associate with people of low position. Do not be conceited' (Rom 12:16); (5) 'Therefore make every effort to do what leads to peace and to mutual edification' (Rom 14:19); and (6) to humble yourself: 'Do nothing out of selfish ambition or vain conceit, but in humility consider others better than yourself' (Phil 1:3). In sum, love means 'Be devoted to one another in brotherly love' (Rom 12:10); honour one another above yourselves (Rom 12:10); and never be lacking in zeal, but keep your spiritual fervour, serving the Lord. Be joyful in hope, patient in affliction, and faithful in prayer. Share with God's people who are in need and practise hospitality (Rom 12:11–13).

For Christians, there is a close connection between love of neighbour and a parent's love for a child. Because neighbours are an extension of the parents, the child always expects the same love from neighbours as from their parents, and also tries to give to neighbours the same love as to their parents. The love between parent and child and the love between neighbours are on the same level. This is why Pauline teaching regards loving parents and loving neighbours as the same.

However, *agape* is not completed at this level of love; it includes a higher level of love, that is, 'love your enemy': 'Bless those who persecute you; bless and do not curse' (Rom 12:14). 'Do not repay anyone evil for evil. Be careful to do what is right in the eyes of everybody. If it is possible, as far as it depends on you, live at peace with everyone' (Rom 12:17–18). It is obvious that this Christian love has a religious base; it is communicated through and out of a 'pure heart and a good conscience and a sincere faith'.[43] As Theissen has recognized, these requirements to renounce violence and to love people who are hostile to us radically call into question our normal behaviour. So it is quite understandable that these demands should themselves continually be called into question.[44] In the realm of human emotion, it is reasonable to love one's lover and to hate one's enemy. This is why people exact revenge as an action of justice in the secular world. However, Paul, like his Master Jesus Christ, requires Christians to practise *agape* not only to their neighbour, but also to their enemy. This fully demonstrates the divine character of his notion of love.

Two things must be noted in regard to Pauline understanding: one is that to 'love your enemy' does not involve giving up the Christian faith; the other is that to 'love your enemy' does not mean submission to evil and giving up the fight against the enemy. In Paul's mind, there is nothing as important as faith in the gospel and the Lord Jesus Christ: 'You stand firm in one spirit, contending as one man for the faith of the gospel without being frightened in any way by those who oppose you' (Phil 1:27–8); 'Be strong in the Lord and in his mighty power. Put on the full armour of God so that you can take your stand against the devil's schemes' (Eph 6:10–11). For the sake of Christian faith, one has to stand 'against the rulers, against the authorities, against the powers of this dark world and against the spiritual forces of evil in the heavenly realms' (Eph 6:12). From this we can see that, although Paul put love as the first command above all other commands, compared with faith and fighting evil, secular love, especially love for the enemy, is secondary. In other words, from the Pauline point of view, the most important thing we ought to learn from Jesus Christ is his faith and obedience to God, consequently, to be the prisoner or slave of God and Jesus Christ is very important for all Christians. Paul many times talked about himself as the slave of God or the prisoner of Jesus Christ. To express the importance of faith, Paul even put faith above one's personal effort in works: 'For it is by grace you have been saved, through faith – and this not from yourselves, it is the gift of God – not by works, so that no-one can boast' (Eph 1:8–9). Because of this, some scholars have separated Pauline theology from its Jewish tradition.

Moreover, for Paul, faith in Jesus Christ is even more important than blindly following the law. The law is given by God. However, it is the law which put the innocent Jesus Christ to death, and it is the law which restricts men from knowing the truth. So law is not as important as faith. For Paul, law is no more than the knowledge of what is right and what is wrong. It can only reveal the sin of men; therefore, it relates to sin rather than truth. Crucial to a proper understanding of Paul is his doctrine of God.[45] Because Jesus is the only way to reach God's truth, and Jesus is the power and wisdom of God, only faith in Jesus Christ can enable men to be rid of sin and approach the truth – by believing from the heart you are made righteous (Rom 10:10).

The Essential Nature of the Pauline Father–Son Relationship

In recent years scholars have frequently highlighted the issue of contradictory statements within one letter or between different letters. C. H. Dodd regards Paul as a man full of contradictions. According to him, Paul, though freed from his past in his 'conversion', now and then falls back into his Jewishness, especially when he is worrying about his brothers and sisters in the flesh. Then, he seems to become overwhelmed by emotion, losing for moment the clarity of truth in Christ![46] It is true that there appear to be contradictions within the Pauline letter or letters; however, if the Pauline religious ethics are interpreted from their essential nature, these contradictions can be fully understood.

From the ethical qualities of both the Father and the Son, we can summarize the following main characteristics of the Christian divine F–S relationship as seen in Pauline teachings. First, it is a relationship of mutual love. This mutual love, on the one hand is an equal love: the Father loves the Son, and the Son loves the Father; and on the other hand, it is a conditional love: because the Father loves the Son, the Son in response loves his Father. However, because God's love is an infinite self-giving love, and there is no condition of being short of love, this, on the one hand, makes this conditional love unconditional and, on the other hand, love becomes one of the driving forces of the Son's obedience to the Father.

Secondly, it is an authority–obedience relationship. The F–S relationship is actually like the master–slave relationship, since not only the power and authority of the Father but also the obedience of the Son is absolute: 'For it is shameful even to mention what the disobedient do in secret' (Eph 5:12). There is neither bargaining nor compromise between them. It is quite clear that in terms of power and authority, there is no equality but rather patriarchy and hierarchy in the F–S relationship. This patriarchy and hierarchy are established on the basis of the Father's love, power, justice and righteousness; because God's love is self-giving and unconditional and his power and justice is absolute, the patriarchy and hierarchy based on them are absolute.

Thirdly, it is an absolute relationship of the powerful and the weak. The Father is powerful, in creation, in salvation and in wisdom; the nature of the Son before the Father is weak; even though he possesses the same power over other creatures, compared with the power of his Father, it is still weak (2 Cor 13:4). This is not only because the power of the Son was endowed by the Father, but also because the power of the Son is for the realization and manifestation of the power of the Father. Therefore, humility is the right attitude when the Son faces the Father.

Fourthly, it is a relationship between the glorious and the humbled. The Father is almighty and full of goodness, but he is merciful and forgiving. Apart from his humility, the Son has nothing to do in the face of the glory of God. Therefore, he prays, he cries; he has faith in the Father and has confidence and hope in the Father's salvation. As Brian S. Rosner states, Paul valued humility because he served Jesus Christ who humbled himself and took the form of a servant and became obedient unto death; and because the God of the Jewish Scriptures humbles the proud and raises the humble.[47]

Finally, it is a relationship between the just and the sinner. The Father is righteousness and justice, but the Son, because of his human flesh, which is a form linked to sin, has to be sent to death. It is true that he has become judge in the name of justice and righteousness after being raised from the dead; however, this justification of the Father was made after the Son's crucifixion and after the Son's incarnation.

From the above analysis, it is clear that the relationship between the Father and the Son, in Pauline thought, is a relationship of patriarchy as well as subordination in terms of command and obedience. Therefore, inequality and order are its nature; no kind of equality existed in the relationship between the Father and the Son while the Son was in the secular world. Yet there is equality between the Father and the Son, but this equality only happens after the resurrection of the Son:

> What I am saying is that as long as the heir is a child, he is no different from a slave, although he owns the whole estate. He is subject to guardians and trustees until the time set by his father. So also, when we were children, we were in slavery under the basic principles of the world. But when the time had fully come, God sent his Son, born of a woman, born under law, to redeem those under law, that we might receive the full rights of sons. Because you are sons, God sent the Spirit of his Son into our hearts, the Spirit who calls out, 'Abba, Father.' So you are no longer a slave, but a son; and since you are a son, God has made you also an heir. (Gal 4:1–7)

In short, there is clear subordination, yet the complex status and role of Jesus Christ actually means that there is a potential equality between the Father and the Son: since in Heaven they possess the same power and authority and have the same task to save and judge the world – in this sense, they are equal to one another. This consideration of the equality between God and Jesus Christ not only leaves room for equality between Jesus and believers, but also among people of different genders, different races and different status. In this sense, Carolyn Osiek says:

> Paul draws upon the language of the city-state . . . to imply that all Christians, female and male, have the responsibility of full participation in the commonwealth in which they belong most appropriately. This is the basis for any vision of a discipleship of equals in the Pauline churches. In a world of social inequalities, Christians are to live in the consciousness of their heavenly equal citizenship here and now.[48]

As the model and basic relationship, the Pauline divine F–S relationship was not manifested merely in the relationship between God and Jesus Christ or between God and Man, but also spread its influence onto the secular world. The essential term of the divine relationship becomes the guiding principle of both its religious and its secular analogues.

The Ethical Extensions of the Pauline Divine Father–Son Relationship in the Secular World

According to Max Weber, there are three ideal 'types of legitimate domination': rational–legal, traditional and charismatic.[49] This Weberian typology has been carefully and critically applied to the structure of authority in the primitive churches by Bengt Holmberg and Martin Hengel. From a Weberian perspective, Jesus is the charismatic leader of the Christian movement and Paul, among others, may be regarded as a 'minor founder'[50] whose authority is secondary but nonetheless charismatic. However, as the three characteristics had all been applied to the Pauline Christian church and Christian society, the charismatic character which derived from mutual love and the hierarchical character which derived from the authority–obedience, powerful–weak and glory–humble relationships should both become characteristics of Pauline secular and religious ethics. This can be demonstrated from two facts: the existence of leadership in the Pauline Christian church and the emphasis of Paul on the notion of imitation.

The consensus view that there was no leadership in the early Pauline church has quite rightly been challenged as being defective at the level of presupposition and method in recent years. As G. Horrell has argued: 'a considerable number of itinerant missionaries exercised some form of authority and leadership in earliest Christianity . . . It is also clear that certain forms of resident leadership did exist within the various Christian communities.'[51] Alastair Campbell argues that leadership in the earliest churches was provided by the householders in whose house the congregation met.[52] Although Paul's understanding is that Christian leadership is to be task-orientated, that is, on the one hand, leaders are to be considered no more than servants who function under the Lord and, on the other hand, the focus is not on who they are, but rather on what their task is, by the unity of church leader and householder, there is still an authority transformation: the authority of the Father in the divine F–S relationship is transferred to the church leader and in turn the religious power of the apostle or priest is transferred into the secular power of the householder.[53] There is a theoretical process of transformation of the Pauline divine F–S relationship: it is first extended to a religious relationship in the Christian church, then to the political relationships of secular society and finally to the natural relationships of a family. David G. Horrell gives a description of the process of the first transformation:

> Within the canonical Pauline corpus, then, a clear trajectory can be seen in which the locus of power and authority shifts from the itinerant apostles, Paul and his co-workers, to the male heads of households resident in the Christian communities, though this resident leadership is still legitimated in Paul's name and through the implied agency of some of his most prominent co-workers.[54]

All the extensions in part imitate the function or the character of the divine F–S relationship. These extensions, no matter whether functional imitations or the character simulations of the divine relationship, all have some common characteristics: all have a patriarchal as well as a hierarchical feature. According to Kathy Ehrensperger, the notion of imitation is closely linked to questions of power and authority and Paul's self-understanding as an apostle. From her research, the concept of imitation has produced a wide-ranging spectrum of solutions which are seen as a call to obedience, humility, self-giving, self-sacrifice for the sake of Christ and salvation of others.[55] Horrell puts it this way:

> The pattern seen most clearly in the Pauline epistles, then, in which a resident structure of leadership develops, based upon the structure of the household and with prominent men as the overseers at the top of the ecclesiastical as well as domestic hierarchy, becomes established broadly as the dominant pattern of leadership in what later emerges as 'orthodox' Christianity.[56]

Accordingly, some of the new voices in biblical studies insist that Pauline letters and Pauline interpretation have played a fundamental political role in support of slavery and the subordination of women.[57] Nonetheless, the theme of equality is never far away. Robert Atkins concludes that Pauline churches are high-group/low-grid communities characterized by strong group boundaries but with 'little concern for internal division or hierarchy'.[58] Robin Scroggs argues that in the Christian society members are completely equal to one another, no matter how much status distinction the 'world' might assign:

> While the world continues to humiliate the outcasts, within the society, where each is equal to the other, mutual love and acceptance are joyfully experienced . . . In the community the member knows not only that God loves him but that other people can do as well. The sect, in fact, is the true family of the participant.[59]

In such a true family of participants, a hierarchical structure of organization is absent, people become leaders by virtue of their ability, and authority stems from the Spirit. James D. G. Dunn offers the same suggestion in saying that the call for masters to treat their slaves 'with justice and equality' assumes a higher degree of equality than was normal. Moreover, he further points out that the repeated reference to the primary relationship to the Lord (for both slave and free) highlights a fundamental criterion of human relationships, which in the longer term was bound to undermine the institution of slavery itself.[60] Both these characteristics will be examined in turn.

The ethical manifestation of the Pauline divine father–son relationship in its religious extensions

The manifestation of the divine F–S relationship in its religious extension can be demonstrated from the patron–client relationship in which three relationships – Jesus–disciple, apostle–believer and priest–church member – are included. The common ethical manifestation of the Pauline divine F–S relationship in these three extensions can be seen in the following three aspects: (1) all the religious extensions of the divine F–S relationship are based on mutual love; (2) the hierarchical as well as the patriarchal characteristics are the main characteristics of the religious extensions of Pauline divine F–S relationship; and (3) there is a coexistence of both equality and hierarchy in these extensions. These are essentially the stock characteristics of decent and respectable well-to-do persons in Greco-Roman society. Patronage is also an integral part of the social structure of early Christianity. According to Stephan J. Joubert, God in the Pauline letters is described as the heavenly patron and his believers as the clients:

> Paul described the invisible world of God in terms of the first-century Mediterranean institutions of kinship and politics. According to him God was at the head of the cosmos as the heavenly *paterfamilias* (1 Cor. 8:4). Not only was he the father of Jesus (1 Cor. 1:9; 2 Cor. 11:31) who had put all things in the cosmos in subjection under his son (1 Cor. 15:27–8), but he was also the father of the new family of believers (1 Cor. 8:6; 2 Cor. 1:3).[61]

Carolyn Osiek and David L. Balch also regard the Pauline church as an explicitly fictive kinship patronage system: the system of financial support that provided for the travel needs of itinerant missionaries like Paul and his companions, the hospitality provided by prominent church members in their houses, the growing concentration of patronal power in the hands of church leaders in the second and third centuries: 'all of these were elements and adaptations of the patronage system.'[62]

Patronage is a mutual relationship between unequal partners for the exchange of services and goods, in which the patron and the clients enter long-standing mutual obligations that bind them either legally or socially or both. There are two characteristics in the patron–client relationship: the first is a personal relationship based on informal and friendship ties, though it serves ends that exceed the personal domain. Because family, religion, politics and business are not clearly distinguishable spheres of life, personal, familial, political and business affairs are not distinct, but fold into one another. The second is that the patronage relationship is vertical; it necessarily fosters unequal relationships and undermines horizontal ones. The patronage system is therefore a good way to keep social inferiors dependent on their superiors, who are unable or unwilling to establish horizontal social solidarity.[63] According to David G. Horrell, in the Pastoral Epistles, the leaders of the churches are resident members of the communities, specifically male heads of households. Duties are listed for them: each 'must manage his own household well, keeping his children submissive and respectful in every way – for if someone does not know how to manage his own household, how can he take care of God's church?' (1 Tim 3:3–5). Deacons likewise must 'manage their children and their households well' (1 Tim 3:12). This wording is surely an indication also that such households often included slaves as well as a wife and children.[64]

The patriarchal characteristic in the religious extension of the divine F–S relationship is obvious. It can be seen from the fact that God was imagined as a male and all his believers were called sons of God in the Pauline letters. It has been suggested, however, that the members who formed the Pauline church included not only males, but also females, and some females even undertook important roles in the church. In 1 Cor 16:19 and Rom 16:3–5, the missionary couple Prisca and Aquila have a Christian assembly in their house; an otherwise unknown Nympha hosts a church in her house in Laodicea (Col 4:15). Rom 16:1 mentions Phoebe the deacon and patron, and Rom 16:7 Junia, an apostle presented as a powerful figure. From Paul's great warning to the leadership of women and their active participation in the worship of early Pauline assemblies, it can be seen that female leadership in Pauline churches was active and influential; nevertheless, all the believers, whether they were males or females, were called sons. This indicates that Paul actually included the female in the category of the male. Because only the word 'son' is used to describe the position after people have faith in Jesus, it is reasonable to conclude that Paul actually put males in a higher position.

Secondly, the only one who is named as the father of all God's believers (Rom 4:18), including both circumcised and uncircumcised (Rom 4:11–2), is Abraham, the first person to be chosen to receive God's blessing through his impregnable faith in God. 'What does the Scripture say? "Abraham believed God, and it was credited to him as righteousness"' (Rom 4:3). 'Against all hope, Abraham in hope believed and so became the father of many nations' (Rom 4:18). Because Jewish culture was formed in a male dominant environment, it is understandable that it used a male figure rather than a female to be the model of faith. Paul's enhancing of Abraham as the father of all Christian believers clearly indicates that he carried on the Jewish patriarchal tradition. In Paul's mind, it is the imagery of the Father/Man God who not only chose a male (Abraham) as the model of his believers and the origin of all later Christians; he also sent his 'Son' Jesus Christ, a male king of kings, to descend to the earth as the saviour of the whole world. Not only the creator, but also the origin figure and saviour are also males. This provides strong evidence for the dominance of patriarchy in Paul's thought.

Moreover, there is a patriarchal system in the Pauline church. The most important evidence is that all the leaders of the church in Paul's discussion are men. Although he uses female imagery in describing the apostle's work (1 Thess 2:7–8), and although a number of female figures were respected by Paul individually, for example, Timothy's grandmother and mother (2 Tim 1:5), Phoebe (Rom 16:1), Priscilla (Rom 16:3), Euodia (Phil 4:2), and although there were even some female leaders actually in Pauline churches, the Pauline tradition still preferred to use men rather than women as examples in discussing the responsibilities of church leaders, such as elders of the church (Titus 1:6), priests (1 Thess 2:6–8; Col 1:28; Titus 3:1–2), overseers (Titus 1:7; 1 Tim 3:2) and deacons (1 Tim 2:8–10; 2:12–13), with the qualifications that includes 'have only one wife' and 'can manage his family well'; all these requirements are for male fathers rather than for females. This reflects the belief in Paul's mind that it is the male rather the female who should be the foundation of the church constitution.

Paul's view in the household code that a husband should love his wife was actually contrary to Greco-Roman culture, where the wife merely functions as a producer of children; indeed, Paul is labelled as 'the first century feminist' by W. Klassen.[65] However, against such a feminist picture, Paul produces a hierarchical argument for male superiority through the famous household codes that wives should submit to the husbands while sons and slaves ought to obey fathers and masters. Through such a contradiction, the character of patriarchy in the Pauline church is once again clearly exposed.

Finally, although Paul on occasions used the metaphor of mother to describe his relationship with the Christian community, more often he used the metaphor of father to introduce himself to his followers: 'To Titus, my true son in our common faith' (Titus 1:4), and when discussing the relationship between himself and his church members: 'Even though you have ten thousand guardians in Christ, you do not have many fathers, for in Christ Jesus I became your father through the gospel; therefore, I urge you to imitate me' (1 Cor 4:15–16). People may argue that it is because Paul himself is a male that he uses the father metaphor more, but in fact Paul's F–S metaphor for describing the relationship between him and his disciples is very much like the F–S relationship between God and Jesus, or God and his people. If Paul uses F–S to describe the apostle–disciple relationship because he is male, would we also say that the God–Jesus relationship is described as F–S relationship due to God being male? If God is regarded as a male, then the patriarchal character of Christian ethics is clear. If God is not regarded merely as male, why did Paul use the F–S metaphor to describe this religious relationship?

Apart from patriarchy, hierarchy is also an important characteristic of the religious extension of the Pauline divine father–son relationship. Paul quite often used the F–S relationship to describe the relationship between God's former and later believers, and gave power and authority to the former God–believers. As noted he used the F–S relationship to describe the relationship between Abraham and later Christian believers (Rom 4:16–21). For Paul, the former believer can not only be the father of later believers, but also as the father possesses power over his son, the former believer possesses authority over the later believer. As he presented himself as a broker on behalf of God, Paul not only took himself as the *paterfamilias* of church members,[66] but also ascribed to himself supernatural authority, thereby claiming the highest rank for himself within the *ekklesia*.[67] He reminded the Corinthians of his fatherhood. This has been taken as an indication of Paul's claim of absolute power and authority over his converts on the analogy of the power and authority of the *paterfamilias*, particularly in Roman society.[68]

Paul also argued that the apostle would become the father of his church members and gain power and authority over his church members. The hierarchical character of the church community can be manifested through different relationships such as the model–imitator and the guider–follower. All these relationships follow a teach–obedience model. The priest must teach everyone with all wisdom in order to present everyone perfect in Christ (Col 1:28); the imitator must be obedient, be ready to do whatever is good (Titus 3:1–2). In Eph 4:15–16 Paul clearly describes the hierarchical constitution of the church. He uses the words 'the body of the Christ' to describe the Christian church. In his mind, there is a hierarchy in this body: Christ is the head; thus other supporters (which included both those who were doing management or administrative work for the church, such as the overseer and the deacons, and those who were doing spiritual work for the church, such as the apostles, prophets, pastors, teachers, workers of miracles, and so on) are the ligaments: all other things grow up through them and build themselves in love.

> And in the Church God has appointed first of all apostles, second prophets, third teachers, then workers of miracles, also those having gifts of healing, those able to help others, those with gifts of administration, and those speaking in different kinds of tongues. (1 Cor 12:28)

> It was he (Christ) who gave some to be apostles, some to be prophets, some to be evangelists, and some to be pastors and teachers, to prepare God's people for works of service, so that the body of Christ may be built up until we all reach unity in the faith and in the knowledge of the Son of God and become mature, attaining to the whole measure of the fullness of Christ. (Eph 4:11–13)

From the distinction of the different jobs and their responsibilities in the church, we can see that there is a rank or order moving from God and Christ to the normal Christian believer: in this rank, God and Jesus Christ are the highest; they are the source and head of the church. The apostle and prophet are the second level; they are the witnesses of God and Jesus Christ. The pastor or priest and teacher are the third level; they preach and spread the new message of Christ. These first three levels of rank belong to the spiritual leadership of the church; they undertake the spiritual function of the church. The fourth level is the administrative level, which is composed of the church elders, the overseer and the deacons; this is the institutional side of the church, and it undertakes the organizational function of the church. Finally comes the normal Christian believers' level; this is the bottom rank, and it is also the outward appearance of the church; without them, the body of Christ's church cannot be built.

However, the hierarchy, which was established between the apostle and community, was based on imitation of the power and authority of God; in other words, the fatherhood of the apostle or the priest corresponds to the authority and power of God, and the power and authority are manifested through weakness, 'I came to you in weakness and fear, and with much trembling. My message and my preaching were not with wise and persuasive words, but with a demonstration of the Spirit's power; So that your faith might not rest on men's wisdom, but on God's power' (1 Cor 2:3–5). This makes the Christian hierarchy closely related to equality. From the Pauline standpoint, equality is based first on common sinful nature: 'There is no difference, for all have sinned and fall short of the glory of God, and are justified freely by his grace through the redemption that came by Jesus Christ' (Rom 3:23–4). Sin has come down to men through Adam, and nobody can escape from their sinful nature; all men have to die to their flesh by this sin and cannot be saved until their sin has been cleansed by the blood of Jesus Christ, until their sinful nature has been conquered by the resurrection with Jesus Christ, and until God's justice has been realized in the world. There is no favourite before God; everybody will receive God's justification according to their due: 'God "will give to each person according to what he has done". To those who by persistence in doing good seek glory, honour and immortality, he will give eternal life. But from those who are self-seeking and who reject the truth and follow evil, there will be wrath and anger' (Rom 2:6–8). The difference between Christian believers is only the difference between God's fellow-workers and God's building or God's field (1 Cor 3:9).

As the theme of love is one of the most important topics of the divine F–S relationship, the virtue of love is essential to both sides of the Jesus–disciple, the apostle–believer and priest–church member relationships. As noted Paul calls God the 'Father of compassion and the God of all comfort, who comforts us in all our troubles' (2 Cor 1:3–4), and also calls everybody in the church to 'be imitators of God', as dearly loved children and to live a life of love: just as Christ loved us and gave himself up for us as a fragrant offering and sacrifice to God (Eph 5:1–2), to be devoted to one another in brotherly love (Rom 12:9). 'Share with God's people who are in need, practise hospitality' (Rom 12:13); 'Let no debt remain outstanding, except the continuing debt to love one another, for he who loves his fellow-man has fulfilled the law' (Rom 13:8). For him, between all Christians, as the different parts of one body of the church (1 Cor 12:20), there should be no division; the parts should have equal concern for each other

(1 Cor 12:25); if one part suffers, every part suffers with it; if one part is honoured, every part rejoices with it (1 Cor 12:26). Paul especially emphasizes the importance of love for the high-rank people in the church:

> If I speak in the tongues of men and angels, but have no love, I am only a resounding gong or a clanging cymbal. If I have the gift of prophecy and can fathom all mysteries and all knowledge, and if I have a faith that can move mountains, but have no love, I am nothing. If I give all I possess to the poor and surrender my body to the flames, but have no love, I gain nothing. (1 Cor 13:1–3)

These ethical requirements of the Pauline divine F–S relationship are manifested not only in its religious, but also in its social political analogues.

The ethical manifestation of the Pauline divine father–son relationship in its social and political extensions

Since Paul and the Pauline letters have long played an important role in shaping political and cultural affairs,[69] studies of the Pauline ethical F–S relationship must be understood as an activity with political implications and responsibilities. The manifestation of hierarchy in political life is embodied chiefly in the relationship between the ruler and the ruled. In Pauline understanding, it is necessary to submit to the authorities, not only for fear of possible punishment, but also because of conscience (Rom 13:5). He says, 'Everyone must submit himself to the governing authorities' (Rom 13:1). Why? In Paul's opinion, this is because, first, there is no authority except that which God has established; 'Therefore, to rebel against authority is to rebel against what God has instituted, and those who do so will bring judgment on themselves' (Rom 13:1–2).

Secondly, because the authorities are God's servants who are given full time to governing (Rom 13:6). The rulers are God's vice-regents, God's deacons for praising those who are doing good and punishing those who are evil-doers.[70] Because the authority of leaders and the ruler has been established by God, and because they are servants and agents of God, rulers should not be a source of terror for those who do right, but only for those who do wrong (Rom 13:3).

Finally, though 'the fruit of the Spirit is love, joy, peace, patience, kindness, goodness, faithfulness, gentleness and self-control' (Gal 5:22–3), because of their evil nature human beings cannot control their behaviour, so the power of rulers is needed for both society and the individual to punish wrongdoing.

It is clear that in Pauline understanding, the hierarchy in the political field is not only necessary, but also reasonable. Its existence is not only for the sake of keeping society in order and securing harmony, but also for the fulfillment of God's commandment. The same things are true of the master–slave and the male–female relationships. For many scholars, the Pauline letters have given a divine sanction for the hierarchy between the master and the slave and between the male and female:

> Slaves, obey your earthly masters with respect and fear, and with sincerity of heart, just as you would obey Christ. Obey them not only to win their favour when their eye is on you,

> but like slaves of Christ, doing the will of God from your heart. Serve wholeheartedly, as if you were serving the Lord, not men. (Eph 6:5–7)

> Wives, submit to your husbands as to the Lord. For the husband is the head of the wife as Christ is the head of the church (his body), of which he is the Saviour. Now as the church submits to Christ, so also wives should submit to their husbands in everything. (Eph 5:22–4)

> Wives, submit to your husbands, as is fitting in the Lord. (Col 3:18)

Amy-Jill Levine states that 'the later Pauline texts offer the New Testament's most problematic treatments of women's roles and household systems'.[71] According to the Apostle's attitude to the institution of slavery and women, some scholars classify Paul as essentially a social conservative. Some scholars even hold the idea that, to a degree, these letters served a dependable and systematic function within the institutionalized brutality of American slavery; the canonical Paul was made complicit in the whipping of slaves.[72] In the same way, other scholars insist that Paul is no less indispensable to the Christian ideology of patriarchy in our own time. For example, Faludi observes: 'In their sermons, the New Right ministers invoked one particular biblical passage with such frequency that it even merited press attention: Ephesians 5:22–4 . . . "The husband is the head of the wife, even as Christ is head of the Church" – became an almost weekly mantra in many pulpits'.[73]

However, as Justin J. Meggitt has recognized, an examination of the relevant evidence in its appropriate social context reveals Paul to be more radical than is usually supposed.[74] Paul actually tried his best to give women an equal position to men: 'In the Lord, however, woman is not independent of man, nor is man independent of woman. For as woman came from man, so also man is born of woman. But everything comes from God' (1 Cor 11:11–12); the wife has similar rights to the husband (1 Cor 7). Paul specially emphasizes the love between husband and wife:

> Husbands, love your wives, just as Christ loved the church and gave himself up for her to make her holy, cleansing her by the washing with water through the word, and to present her to himself as a radiant church, without stain or wrinkle or any other blemish, but holy and blameless . . . After all, no-one ever hates his own body, but he feeds and cares for it, just as Christ does the church – for we are members of his body. (Eph 5: 25–30)

Although there is no direct discussion of the equality and love between ruler and ruled, there are discussions on the equality between master and slave: 'And Masters, treat your slaves in the same way. Do not threaten them, since you know that he who is both their master and yours is in heaven, and there is no favouritism with him' (Eph 6:9). By the same logic, we can conclude that there is no lack of equality in the Pauline ruler–ruled relationship. Maybe some will argue that these household codes relate to the domestic structure of the Greco-Roman household and display no explicit connection with church leadership and structure or the ruler and the structure of the state. Nevertheless, as MacDonald points out: 'The Colossian and Ephesian *Haustafeln* represent a placing of power more firmly in the hands of the rulers of the households (husband, fathers, masters), ensuring that leadership positions fall to members of this group.'[75] James D. G. Dunn also argues: 'The *Haustafeln* may indicate a greater concern to demonstrate the good order of the Christian households and a consequent commitment to maintaining the orderly structure of society.'[76] Accordingly, the ethos of the instruction – the coexistence of the equality and the hierarchy in the household relationship, which has been appropriately labelled as 'love-patriarchalism' by Theissen[77]and MacDonald[78] – should be applicable in the same way to the ruler–ruled, or the authority–governed relationship.

Moreover, the Colossian and Ephesian *Haustafeln* address the same social groups in the same order: wives, husbands, children, fathers, slaves, masters. Women, children and slaves are instructed to be submissive; husbands, fathers and masters are urged to be loving and just in their actions toward those under their care.[79] Therefore, the common characteristics which prevailed in social and political relationships are the same as those portrayed in the natural F–S relationship.

The ethical manifestation of the divine father–son relationship in its familial extensions

The hierarchical character of the natural F–S relationship is also distinct. As noted, Paul linked the natural F–S pattern with the master–slave one. He used the word 'obey' for the son as well as for the slave: 'Children, obey your parents in everything, for this pleases the Lord' (Col 3:20). 'Slaves, obey your earthly masters in everything' (Col 3:22). 'Children, obey your parents in the lord, for this is right' (Eph 6:1). 'Slaves, obey your earthly masters with respect and fear, and with sincerity of heart, just as you would obey Christ' (Eph 6:5). It is clear in Paul's mind that, although the son is different since he is the heir of his father's house, before he becomes an adult he is no different from the slave: 'as long as the heir is a child, he is no different from a slave, although he owns the whole estate' (Gal 4:2).

Many sources have provided strong evidence of the low position of children. Sometimes, as we have seen in Chapter 3, the position of children in ancient Roman society could be worse than that of slaves, since slaves could be offered for sale only once, but a child could be sold repeatedly by his father. The implication is that Paul not only regards obedience as the most important virtue of a son but also regards disobedience towards one's parents as wicked and evil (Rom 1:30). This characteristic of the Pauline ideal of Son can be seen in the parable where a father sent his son to collect the rent for the vineyard he had let out to tenants. In all three synoptic Gospels it is assumed in a self-evident way that the son obeyed his father. Joachim Gnilka expresses a majority view in affirming that the story is to be assigned to a Hellenistic Jewish-Christian congregation[80] as a model of the obedience of Jesus, the Son of God.

As the Christian family is the metaphor of the kinship family, the divine F–S relationship is a metaphor of the natural F–S image. Peter Balla clearly sees the connection between people failing to honour God and being disobedient towards their parents, and argues that from this negative formulation it is clear that Paul affirmed the duty of honoring God and, in relation to it, children's duty of honoring their parents.[81] An interesting issue arises: how do the metaphor of divine F–S in the religious family and the natural F–S image in the natural family interact with each other? Invild S. Gilbus gives a possible answer. He argues that, since family relations are close to

human experience and symbolically rich, it is to be expected that the semantic potential of the family used as a symbol is always greater than its realization in the actual
texts. Connotations will abundantly contribute to making family a fruitful religious
symbol. Further, it is possible that when mythological family structures transcend
normal family relations they will have more power in generating religious meaning.[82]
Gilbus's argument is acceptable if the Pauline ethical F–S relationship is taken into
consideration.

Pauline ethical doctrine in relation to the natural F–S relationship can be more
clearly seen in the households that are presented in Colossians and Ephesians in which
the hierarchical character of this relationship is very clear: the father is the head, the
authority, and the power; under the authority and power of the father, the son can do
nothing except obey him: 'Children, obey your parents in the Lord, for this is right.
"Honor your father and mother" – which is the first commandment with a
promise–"That it may go well with you and that you may enjoy long life on the
earth"' (Eph 6:1–3). 'Children, obey your parents in everything, for this pleases the
Lord' (Col 3:20). Peter Balla attempts to use one sentence to summarize such a
relationship: 'Honor can cover the whole area of children's duties in the Fifth
Commandment; the same is true about the warning to sons to obey their parents in
the wisdom literature'.[83]

The patriarchal character of the Pauline natural F–S relationship is also evident. It
is true that we cannot prove that the position of the father is higher than that of the
mother from the above quotations. But, as we have noted, though Jewish culture,
unlike Greco-Roman culture (which gave the father an absolute power and authority
over his son), paid attention to the mother and, sometimes, it seems that the mother
has the same position as the father in terms of power over her children, it actually gave
a higher position to the father, and so, as an heir of both Jewish and Greco-Roman
cultures, Paul gave a higher status to the father, too. The evidence for this conclusion
can be seen from the command: 'Sons obey your father' and from his ethical advice to
the father: 'Fathers, do not exasperate your children; instead, bring them up in the
training and instruction of the Lord' (Eph 6:4). 'Fathers, do not embitter your children,
or they will become discouraged' (Col 3:21). The above suggestions to the father come
just after the commands of obedience for children. After this declaration of the duty of
children, Paul did not present the duty of parents, but the duty of the father only. This
means that it is quite clear in Paul's mind, that it is the father rather than both father
and mother who is in charge of the disciplining and instruction of children. Some might
argue that the father rather than both parents together is highlighted here because of
the particular character of the father – he is quick to be angry and has a tendency to be
violent. However, as some scholars have recognized:

> It is not without reason that Paul addresses not parents but fathers in Ephesians 6:4: a father
> held the primary authority in the household as the *paterfamilias*, the male head of the home
> addressed in household codes. By contrast, despite the authority inherent in their role,
> mothers held no legal authority over their own children. (Gaius, *Inst.* 1.104)[84]

It is important to recognize that it is the particular role rather than the particular
character of the father that made Paul offer the above suggestion. Because it is the father

who is in charge of children's training, instruction and discipline, there is a greater like-lihood that he will exasperate his children.

It is clear, then, that both hierarchy and patriarchy are characteristics of the Pauline natural F–S relationship. This Pauline idea was inherited from Greco-Roman culture, and further influenced Western society profoundly. For example, Blackstone wrote in his book *Commentaries on the Law of England* that 'in marriage, husband and wife is one person, and that person is the husband'.[85] Ivy Pinchbeck and Margaret Hewitt proclaim that a father's rights over the custody of his children were paramount. At common law, a mother had no rights over her children during the lifetime of the father, nor was her position necessarily improved by his death, since the father had a right to appoint a testamentary guardian who, at the father's death, took priority over the mother, who had no right to interfere with his powers. 'Indeed, the rights of the father as against the mother were so absolute that the courts did not in fact have the power to grant a right of access to her children to a mother whose husband had not granted it himself.'[86] However, this is not the worst:

> The children were, at common law, in a much worse position than the mother. Parents were under a moral duty to support and educate them; they might be held guilty of manslaughter if they allowed their children to starve or perish for lack of proper medical attention. But in practice, this was a very imperfect obligation, since there was no power of enforcing these duties except through the Poor Law, which laid down the duties of parents and grandparents to maintain poor children . . . Thus, in effect, children had little right against their parents at common law either as to maintenance or to education, or, indeed, to protection against cruel treatment from their parents.[87]

However, as noted earlier, equality in the F–S relationship, as in other social political relationships, is not completely covered by these patriarchal and hierarchical characteristics. There is a mutual moral responsibility between the natural father and his natural son. Paul discusses the responsibilities of both sides, and is not inclined to emphasize merely the father's right or the duty of the sons. For Paul, father and son both have their own roles to play, their own jobs to do; this means that the moral responsibilities of both the father and the son are in symmetry. In the sense that both have their own moral responsibility, they are equal. Moreover, although the father and the son play different roles in the family, their positions before God are the same: as in Christ 'there is neither Jew nor Greek, slave nor free, male nor female, for you are all one in Christ Jesus' (Gal 3:28), there is no favour for the father or the son before God and Christ. They are independent individuals; God can receive their prayers and they can contact God personally. Consequently, they have equal rights and an equal status, because God loves them all at the same level and for the same purpose. In God's sight, there is no father and son, they are all offspring of God; they are all in the same situation of being sinners and waiting for God's salvation; they all have to gain entry into the kingdom of God through faith in Jesus Christ. Howard Thurman's own belief is apparently informed by the Western spiritualizing interpretation of Paul: 'It is my belief that in the Presence of God there is neither male nor female, white or black, Gentile or Jew, Protestant nor Catholic, Hindu, Buddhist, nor Muslim, but a human spirit stripped to the literal substance of itself before God.'[88] The Pauline idea itself made it possible for modern churches and theologians to establish contemporary religious ethics by retaining and developing the aspect of equality.

From the above analysis we can see that equality as well as patriarchy and hierarchy are part of Pauline thinking. This situation is not easy to understand; it is confusing. How can equality and hierarchy exist in the same frame at the same time? Is it true to say that 'Paul contradicted himself and any attempt to reconcile the various statements produces forced harmonization'? However, as Schreiner has concluded, the claim that Paul contradicts himself in law is not valid.[89] Gerd Theissen uses the term love-patriarchalism to explain this aspect of Pauline teaching.

According to Theissen, in the congregations of the Pauline churches there developed an ethos obviously different from that of the synoptic tradition; namely, the ethos of primitive Christian love-patriarchalism. This love-patriarchalism takes social differences for granted, but ameliorates them through an obligation of respect and love, an obligation imposed upon those who are socially stronger. From the weaker are required subordination, fidelity and esteem. Whatever the intellectual sources feeding into this ethos, with it the great part of Hellenistic primitive Christianity mastered the task of shaping social relations within a community which, on the one hand demanded of its members a high degree of solidarity and brotherliness and, on the other hand, encompassed various social strata. He states that it is this love-patriarchalism that produced the church's fundamental norms and fashioned lasting institutions. It solved problems of organization and prepared Christianity to receive the great masses. Members of the upper classes could find a fertile field of activity, so that ancient Christianity never lacked for distinguished leadership figures – beginning with Paul. But the lower strata were also at home here. They found a fundamental equality of status before God, solidarity and help in the concrete problems of life, not least of all from those Christians who enjoyed a higher station in life.[90]

Theissen has given us a clear picture of the great significance of what he called the situation of love-patriarchalism. However, what he describes is the advantage and value of the situation where equality and hierarchy existed at the same time; he did not explore the reason why Paul could put equality alongside patriarchy and hierarchy in the frame at the same time. Jacques Gernet argues that the distinction between the spiritual and the temporal or between the body and the soul makes it possible for a person to be both a good Christian and at the same time a loyal subject.[91] This argument can perhaps give us a clue. At least four reasons can support Paul's combination: first, as noted, though Paul did not work out the idea of the Trinity clearly, the germ of the idea already existed in his thought. He actually treated Jesus the same as God and so gives Jesus a status equal to God's.

Next, it is the human nature of Jesus Christ before his crucifixion and the possibility of humans becoming holy that made Paul produce the patriarchy/hierarchy combination. In the Pauline mind, though Jesus Christ is the only Son of God, he became a whole man when he descended to Earth from the Father. He was born from a woman with the same sinful flesh form, and had the same emotions and desires as every man. There is no difference between Jesus and other men except for his faith and obedience to God. However, he became the king of kings after his crucifixion, and had an eternal life after being raised from the dead. This means that all men in the sinful flesh form have the potential of being saved by faith in Jesus Christ; they can die with him through baptism and have a new life by believing in him. Therefore, in Paul's thought, there is equality between Jesus and common believers. Through faith in Jesus Christ, not only can men become the sons of God like Jesus Christ, but also they can walk side by side with Jesus Christ in the kingdom of God after justification by God. If men have become part of the same body of Jesus Christ, then they will also share the same honor and grace as Jesus Christ.

Thereafter it is the command of love that makes the link between the hierarchy/patriarchy and equality possible. Why did God give his Son the power of salvation? Why did God let Jesus be his heir and even have the same position as himself? It is because of his self-giving love. Why did God let his believers be saved through faith in his Son Jesus Christ and why does Jesus Christ want to share his own glory and honour with his followers? This is because of *agape*, holy love. It is the love that made the rich become poor in order to let the poor become rich; love that made the holy humble in order to make the humble holy; it is also love that made the pure die for the sinful in order to change their sinful nature. Therefore, it is love that makes it possible for equality to exist together with hierarchy at the same time.

Last, the idea that 'weakness, and humility are the true wisdom and power' made the link between hierarchy and equality a reality. Because God's wisdom is to value weakness and devalue pride, to enhance humility and despise the complacent, and to use the weak to shame the strong, then power and authority are not linked with strength and force, but with weakness and humility. If two contradictory attitudes, such as weakness and humility, can be linked together, then the linkage between hierarchy and equality is also reasonable and can be realized in the practice of human life.

CHAPTER FIVE

Xunzi's Ethical Father–Son Relationship

Xunzi's thinking on the secular F–S relationship demonstrates totally different features from the Pauline idea of the divine F–S relationship. The ethical characteristics of Xunzi's secular pattern will be discussed in terms of three aspects: its centre, its ethical manifestations, and its characteristics and nature.

The Centre of Xunzi's Secular Father–Son Relationship

Xunzi's F–S relationship is a typical secular pattern. A relationship is secular rather than divine usually because of its character, namely, the relationship is established in accordance with secular needs. Two things are relevant to secular needs: one is the physical birth link, and the other is the material benefit relation. As a typical secular model, Xunzi's F–S relationship is focused on physical humanity rather than the spiritual divinity of human life. For Xunzi, although there is a model–follower relationship between the 'Way of Heaven' and the 'Way of Humans', this guider–guided relationship is not intentionally built up by a divine being. This is because, in contrast to some earlier streams of the Chinese tradition, where Heaven and humans can morally influence each other, Heaven and Earth in Xunzi were merely natural phenomena; thus, the Way of Heaven is equal to the Way of Nature, or the Natural Law. As natural phenomena, Heaven and Earth are neither intended to guide people, nor have any divinity, but are constantly unchangeable but knowable forces. Though the relationship between humans and Nature is a relationship between humanity and the existence beyond human beings, their relationship is not regarded as a spiritual but as a natural relationship. Accordingly, ethical consideration of the divine relationship is excluded from Xunzi's ethical thinking, and his ethical thinking on the secular F–S relationship is focused tightly on the human sphere.[1]

As discussed in Chapter 1, Xunzi's ethical F–S theory is based on the secular kinship, in which the natural F–S relationship is central. All other relationships within and outside the family are regarded as extensions of this relationship.

First of all, the relationship between the natural father and the biological son has actually been taken as the model and exemplar of other familial relationships. As discussed previously, there are only three family relationships on the agenda of Xunzi's discussion: that is, father–son, husband–wife, and elder–younger brother. Other familial relationships, such as father–daughter, mother–son, fictive father–adopted son, and uncle–nephew were never on his discussion list.

The natural F–S relationship is at the centre of these three family relationships. Although the older–younger brother relationship is also stressed by Xunzi, it is the F–S alone that is at the centre. This is due to the fact that there is no essential difference between the above two relationships in Xunzi's thinking. Indeed, the essence of the older–younger relationship is exactly the same as that of the father–son, and the code for dealing with the two is nearly the same. Some examples provide evidence. In the chapter of *Contra Twelve Philosophers*, when talking about the demeanour of the father, the son, the elder brother and the younger brother, Xunzi says:

> When he plays the role of a father or elder brother, his cap should protrude straight out and his robes be full, his demeanor should be relaxed and his manner should be dignified, grave, inspiring, correct but comfortable to be around, noble and imposing, broad-minded, enlightened, and calmly at ease. When he plays the role of son or younger brother, his cap should protrude and his robes should be full, his demeanor should be attentive, and his manner should be temperate, confident, helpful, honest, constantly striving, respectful, exemplary and unassuming. (6.13)

Xunzi clearly identifies the role of the father and that of the older brother, and similarly the response of the son and that of the younger brother. In addition, in talking about the virtue of the father and the elder brother, Xunzi used a series of similar words to describe them: what makes a person a father is to be generous, to be kind, and to possess ritual principle; while what makes a person an elder brother is to be affectionate, loving and overtly friendly (12.3); when Xunzi talked about the virtue of the son and younger brother, he even used the same words of reverence to describe them (12.3). This indicates that there are no essential differences either between the virtues of the father and those of the elder brother or between the virtues of the son and those of the younger brother: the requirements of the son and the younger brother are virtually identical. As a son, he should defer to his father, while a younger brother should defer to his elder brother; a son should relieve his father of work and a younger brother should relieve his elder brother (23.1e). The rights and responsibilities of both the father and the elder brother are also the same: on the one hand, they should be respected and revered (12.3); on the other hand, they are expected to love and take care of their son and younger brother as well.

Here a question arises: if there is no essential difference between the F–S relationship and the brother relationship, why is it that the F–S rather than both the F–S and the brother relationships are privileged? To answer this question, we must understand Xunzi's concept of *li*.

Xunzi's concept of *li* is derived from Confucius, where *li* was regarded as the means by which to correct people, and the main support and regulator of a state,[2] which was developed into the most important concept by Xunzi. There are two meanings of *li*: one is gradation and the other is harmony.[3] Xunzi contended that the ancient kings had set up ritual regulations with distinctions according to rank, seniority and role to keep people from competing for things they all desire.[4] Nevertheless, 'rites can only reach their highest perfection when both emotion and form are fully realized and order and harmony prevail'.[5] Xunzi pays some attention to the aesthetics of rituals, to details of rubrics as well as to a sense of balance and beauty: 'Rites trim what is long and stretch out what is too short, eliminate surplus and repair deficiency, extend the forms of love and reverence, and step by step bring to fulfillment the beauties of proper conduct.'[6]

This tells us that although Xunzi insists on distinction of rank, his understanding is not as a repressive limitation but as a differentiation that allows society to function smoothly;[7] although he enhances harmony, his understanding of harmony is not only the equal balance of two things, but the order or distinction between two ranks: 'harmony is extended to mean an orderly combination of different elements, by which a new unity comes into being.'[8] In other words, his distinction is combined with the principle of harmony and his content of harmony is based on gradation. Though there is gradation between the older brother and the younger brother, as the sons of the father, on most occasions they have equal status and position. Actually, the value of brotherly love is not on the same basis as filial piety. An elder brother is only a leader among equals, with no authority to regard his younger brothers as subordinates. And so the behavioral content of brotherly love underscores its cooperative nature: affection and kindness on the part of elder brothers, respect and deference on the part of younger brothers. Essentially this means that brothers should compromise and not quarrel.[9] This is not like the F–S relationship, in which gradation is definite and absolute; equality between the father and son is only manifested in their moral cultivation. In this sense the F–S relationship is privileged.

It is also true that the relationship between a husband and a wife is given particular attention by Xunzi. Moreover, the requirements for the husband and wife are quite different from those of the F–S relationship. For example, more rejoicing and love are included. Nonetheless, what is more significant is that Xunzi wants to emphasize order in the husband–wife relationship rather than mutual love and rejoicing:

> The rules generally forbid a wife to assume power over her husband, although a wife will be highly praised for assuming family responsibility, taking care of the family's needs, and raising her sons from childhood when her husband happens to be stupid, ill-behaved, or dead. The stipulation against a wife's assuming power under normal circumstances is dictated by the very nature of family organization. She must be made to subordinate herself to her parents-in-law and to get along well with her sister-in-law for the sake of family order and harmony.[10]

In this sense, the ethical requirement for the husband–wife relationship is not much different from that of the F–S relationship. In Xunzi's opinion, the male is a person of power and positive strength, therefore his status is superior; the female is a person of weak and passive aspects, hence her status is naturally inferior (27.38). From this understanding it can be seen that what Xunzi really wanted to emphasize was the higher and stronger position of the husband in comparison to the lower and weaker position of the wife; this is the superiority–inferiority content of this pattern. In other words, the husband–wife relationship is also a reflection of the relationship between the powerful father and the humble son. Accordingly, there is no reason to say that it is the husband–wife rather than the F–S relationship that is the centre of Xunzi's secular theory.

Secondly, Xunzi not only takes the natural F–S relationship as the fundamental relationship of the family, but also transfers its function to social and political life.[11] Therefore, he draws parallels between the F–S, the older–younger brother and the husband–wife and the ruler–subject relationships: 'Where ritual is not obtained, between lord and minister there is no honored position, between father and son no affection; between elder and younger brother no submissiveness, and between husband and wife no rejoicing' (27.41). In fact, the F–S relationship was taken as the fundamental model of the political ruler–ruled relationship by Xunzi.

This means that the F–S relationship is extended not only to the political, but also to the social field. From the extension of the natural F–S relationship in familial, social and political life we gather that the natural F–S relationship has been regarded as essential and fundamental pattern by Xunzi in his thinking of the secular human life.

Finally, the natural F–S relationship is also the centre of Xunzi's image of the divine F–S relationship. The manifestation derives mainly from the relationship between the *tiandi* (Heaven and Earth) and the *shengren* (sage) and between the *shengren* (sage) or *junzi* (gentleman) and the common people.[12]

To understand this relationship, it is necessary to illustrate them by outlining the following concepts: *tiandi*, *dao* and *shengren* or *junzi*.

Tiandi is composed of two separate words – *tian* and *di*. *Tian* means heaven or sky and *di* earth. To put them together in a Xunzi context signifies nature or natural force and natural order. From our discussion 'on the cosmological root of Xunzi's F–S relationship' in Chapter 1, we concluded that for other Confucians, especially Mengzi, *tian* was a powerful impersonal moral force, whose essential nature is shared by human beings. Moreover, this essential human nature is knowable, so humans can know the way of *tian* through individual moral cultivation. Xunzi inherited the Confucian impersonal and knowable characteristics of *tian* into his conception of *tiandi*. Nonetheless, Xunzi's Heaven and Earth are not integrated with, but separated from, humans. Xunzi proclaimed that there was no interference or interaction between Heaven and human society. Heaven and Earth are impersonal and emotionless: 'Heaven does not suspend the winter because men dislike cold weather. Earth does not reduce its broad expanse because men dislike long distance' (17.5). He did not consider Heaven a divine power, and he therefore denied the efficacy of worshipping it.[13] And there was no special moral meaning behind unusual natural events: the Heaven does not reward good government, nor does it perish because of misgovernment (17.1). Therefore, fortune and misfortune are linked with man's own action rather than the will of a personal god; in other words, the divine relationship between a personal God and humanity does not exist for Xunzi. However, *tiandi* is still one of the most important concepts for Xunzi; it is the cosmological root for his moral theory.[14] The impersonal nature of *tiandi* could not guarantee the presence of righteousness – the sage-kings who were capable of establishing the norms or mode of society were necessary.[15] Since *tiandi* has an unchangeable and invisible but knowable characteristic, it paves the way for the importance of another two concepts: *dao* and *junzi*.

In Chinese the character for *dao* is composed of two parts: head and walk. In the bronze inscription, it was composed of three parts: head, foot and path to describe a person walking along a path; it also meant a theoretical principle. From the pictograph of *dao* it can be seen that *dao* in Chinese actually has two different but relevant meanings: the real path and the constant theoretical principle. For most early Confucians, *dao* is the depiction of methods, principles and doctrines that lead to the ideal order of society; it is the right way of life within human society which is observed by the *junzi* (gentleman) or *shengren* (the sage) – a path followed by ancient kings. However, in Xunzi's thinking, *dao* is elevated into the principle by which the whole of Nature operates. As Knoblock states,

> The *Dao* for Xunzi is thus not merely the right way to conduct oneself, nor is it just the way by which the ancient sages organized human society; rather, it is a cosmic principle that operates according to certain invariable principles that can be grasped by the mind since the mind shares the fundamental qualities of the *Dao*.[16]

The English translation of *junzi* is gentleman, or noble man, and it characterized by two main meanings: usually it is the name of an ideal man with higher moral qualities; sometimes, it is equal to the concept of sage, especially when *junzi* is used for ancient sage-kings. The sage in the Chinese language is *shengren*, which means the sort of men who invented *li* (rituals) and *yi* (moral principles), and told people what righteousness and justice were. In the book of Xunzi, *shengren* and *junzi* are mostly distinguished from each other, but sometimes they are used interchangeably. For example, in 'The Great Compendium' and the 'Discourse on Ritual Principles', Xunzi used the sage juxtaposed with Heaven and Earth:

> Thus Heaven and Earth produce it and the sage perfects it. (27.31)

> Heaven is able to beget the myriad things, but it cannot differentiate them. Earth can support man, but it cannot govern him. The myriad things under the canopy of heaven and all those who belong among living people depend upon the appearance of the sage, for only then is each assigned its proper station. (19.6a)

But in 'On the Regulations of Kings', Xunzi used gentleman instead of sage: 'Thus, Heaven and Earth give birth to the gentleman, and the gentleman provides the organizing principle for Heaven and Earth' (9.15). From this it is reasonable to claim that the concept of sage and the concept of gentleman were treated in the same way, especially when linked to a cosmological context.

A question arises: why is the relationship between *tiandi* and the sage to be regarded as a spiritual or divine relationship? It is because *tiandi*, or Heaven and Earth, are thought of as the begetters of *shengren*; they are the source of the merits of a *shengren* or *junzi*. The fulfillment of the *shengren*'s glory and honour is based on the contribution of the '*Dao* of Heaven and Earth'. Without Heaven and Earth, *junzi* cannot come into being; and without the '*Dao* of Heaven and Earth', the achievements of the *shengren* in organizing society and differentiating between humans and animals cannot be successfully accomplished. Therefore, Heaven and Earth are the divine parents of *shengren* or *junzi*.

Why is the relationship between the sage and the common people regarded as a spiritual divine relationship? A sound reason is because, for Xunzi, the sage or gentleman is the triadic partner of Heaven and Earth, the summation of the myriad things, and the father and mother of the people (9.15). From this we can see that the *shengren* (sage) or *junzi* (gentleman) has two important functions: in relation to Heaven and Earth, the sage is the assistant: the sage scrutinizes Heaven above and establishes on Earth below; 'he fills up and puts in order all that is between Heaven and Earth; and he adds his work to the myriad things' (9.16c). From the human side, it is a *junzi* who gives significance to people's lives:

> Heaven is able to beget the myriad things, but it cannot differentiate them. Earth can support man, but it cannot govern him. The myriad of things under the canopy of heaven, and all those who belong among living people depend upon the appearance of the sage, for only then is each assigned its proper station. (19.6)

The Way of Heaven and Earth can be neither realized by the people nor practised by human society without the right interpretation of the sage or gentleman. As Xunzi noted, if there were no gentleman, Heaven and Earth would lack the principle of order; ritual and moral principles would have no guidelines. There would be no proper recognition of lord and leader above and no proper relationship between father and son, older and younger brothers, husband and wife below (9.15). As a perfect person with full capacity, ability and virtue in general, the sage can practise and know things without limit (2.10). In other words, the sage in Xunzi has a dual character, partly spiritual and partly human, in some sense like Jesus, who is both the Son of God and the Son of Man. The sage not only works on human society, but is also the assistant of Heaven and Earth. Therefore, although he is a human personality, which anyone can potentially achieve, because he is a person with full knowledge and morality, he is actually beyond the common people, and this makes the relationship between the sage and the common people a sort of spiritual divine F–S relationship.

However, the spiritual divine relationship between the sage and the common people is not the same as the divine relationship between Jesus and the Christian believer. This is because, although the sage is a person who is beyond normal or common people, he is still a human being, not different from other people in the composition of his physical structure and his mind:

> In natural talent, inborn nature, awareness, and capability, the gentleman and the petty man are the same. In cherishing honor and detesting disgrace, in loving benefit and hating harm, the gentleman and the petty man are the same. Rather, it appears that the Way they employ to make their choices produces the difference. (4.8)

Therefore, the F–S relationship between the sage and the common people is not like the divine relationship between Jesus and believers, which is an entirely divine relationship in the sense that Jesus has the same function as God. The sage–common people relationship is based on a human relationship, even if it is a spiritual human relationship. This is because, although the sage has recreated the nature of human beings in the sense of spiritual transformation, this transforming function is no more than the natural father's instruction of his son. In addition, the affection of the ancient sage-king in loving his people and his way of taking care of them are the same as parents in relation to their children. This is why Xunzi says, 'This amiable and fraternal gentleman is the father and the mother of his people. Here the term "gentleman" assuredly has its meaning as his acting as the father and mother to his people' (19.10).

In short, the natural F–S relationship is not only the foundation for understanding familial and social political relationships, but also the basis for understanding the Chinese sense of divine relationships; therefore, it is the centre and base for Xunzi's secular F–S relationship. By transforming and extending the function of this relationship, the union of the family and society and the state is built up, and the union between the *tiandi* and the human is also established. By sharing the same natural principles of order with Heaven and Earth (22.3e), it is natural that the relationships between the lord and the minister, the father and the son, the older and the younger brother, and the husband and the wife should possess similar characteristics (9:15).

The Ethical Manifestation of Xunzi's Secular Father–Son Relationship

The ethical manifestation of Xunzi's secular father–son relationship will be discussed under two headings: the ethical manifestation of the natural F–S relationship and its familial analogies; and the application or extension of the ethical natural F–S relationship to its social, political and spiritual divine patterns.

The ethical manifestation of the natural father–son relationship and its familial analogues

As the natural F–S relationship is representative of other familial relationships, the ethical manifestations of other family relationships can be illustrated through the interpretation of the F–S pattern. What, then, is the ethical manifestation of Xunzi's natural F–S relationship?

The chief ethical manifestation of the relationship can be shown through the hierarchical order between them: the father commands with power and authority, and the son obeys without power and authority.[17] The father is noble and powerful, and the son is humble and weak. Therefore, the father is superior and above, and the son is inferior and below. The son has nothing to bring to his father except respect and submission: if you are straightforward and diligent, obedient and respectful of your elders, you are properly called a 'good youth' (2.12). Otherwise, 'to be young and yet unwilling to serve one's elders, misfortune will follow' (5.3). In such a condition, even if a son can persuade his father what he does is wrong, he can only do this with an attitude of sincerity and respect; he cannot do it in a direct way with any sign of opposition.

Another ethical manifestation of the natural F–S relationship can be seen in Xunzi's stress on the absolute rights of a father over his son and the seemingly endless responsibilities of a son to his father. There are only a few places where Xunzi discusses the morality of the father (e.g. 12.3; 19.16; 27.18), in which a 'strict' feature of the father is posed (19.16). For example, the virtue of the father is 'being generous, to be kind and possessing ritual principles, while the moral principles he uses to deal with his son are that he 'loves him but does not show it in his face', 'assigns his son tasks but does not change expression in his assignment', and 'guides him using the Way but does not use physical compulsion'. By contrast, there are a number of passages that directly point to the moral requirements of a filial son. Xunzi discussed such requirements from many angles: emotion, appearances, attitudes and speech, as well as conduct. However, all these can be interpreted by one word, namely, 'respect'. He said, 'What makes a person a son? I reply: To be reverent, loving, and the perfection of good form' (12.3).

Why is respect the most important virtue for a filial son? Xunzi used a story to explain why: Zilu questioned Confucius: Consider the case of the man who gets up at dawn and goes to bed late at night, who plows and weeds, sows, and plants, until his hands and feet are thickly calloused in order to care properly for his parents, yet this man lacks a reputation for filial conduct. Why should this be so? Confucius replied,

> I surmise that he was personally not properly respectful in his relation with others, that his speech was not conciliatory, or that the expressions on his face indicated a lack of cordiality. The ancients had an expression that said: 'you give us clothes, you provide us with everything, but still we can never depend on you.' (29.4)

For Xunzi, respect is not only a fundamental moral requirement of a son in serving his living parents, but also the primary moral requirement of a son in the ceremony of mourning his dead parents. In Xunzi's opinion, to serve one's living parents is the beginning of rites and to send off one's dead parents is the end. A filial son, if he wants to offer proper service to his parents, has to attend fully to both the end and the beginning (19.16). Therefore, respect must continually be offered in the mourning ceremony for one's parents. Xunzi said:

> The general principles of mourning are that with each change the corpse is adorned, with each move it is taken farther away, and with the passage of time the ordinary course of life is resumed. Hence, the way of the dead is that if the corpse is not adorned, it becomes hideous, and if it is hideous, no grief is felt. If it is kept close at hand, one begins to scorn it; when having it close at hand makes it the object of scorn, one begins to weary of it; when one wearies of it, one becomes unmindful of one's duty to it; and if one becomes unmindful of one's duties, then one no longer shows proper respect. (19.12)

Otherwise, if in attending to the ceremonies of the funeral of one's revered parent, one shows neither grief nor respect, then one has conducted oneself as a beast would. The gentleman would be ashamed of such behavior.

Why must people give the same respect to the dead as to living parents? This is because, on the one hand, anybody's funeral is special and unrepeatable, and there is only one opportunity to treat the dead in a proper way. Beyond this, the funeral of a dead parent is the last chance for a son to express the greatest honor for his parent. On the other hand, to be generous on the occasion of birth and miserly at death is to be respectful of those that have consciousness, but disrespectful of those who lack consciousness. And to be respectful to those that have consciousness, but disrespectful of those who lack of consciousness is to follow a way that degenerates and to have a heart that rebels against Nature. As a gentleman, one would have a just and straight heart and be ashamed to deal with a shamed person with a rebellious heart (19.16); and so one should respect the dead with the same respect as the living. Only if in birth and death and at the end and the beginning people are treated the same will people's yearnings be satisfied and the highest expression of the piety of the filial son completed (19.10).

For Xunzi, filial piety is not only the moral responsibility, but also the moral obligation of the son. He used the examples of Yushun[18] and Xiaoyi[19] to explain this idea: both Yushun and Xiaoyi are filial sons of their parents; they observe their filial duties very well, but their parents do not like them and do not return their love. What should they do further? Should they stop their filial conduct in such a one-sided love relationship? The answer is that they should neither stop their filial conduct nor complain of their parents. To be filial to one's parents is one's obligation; one has no right to give up in any circumstances.

In Xunzi's thinking, filial piety was so important that he suggested that the custom laws should support sons in practising their filial piety in the following ways: if there is an octogenarian in a family, society should excuse one son's social service, such as military labour and so on. In a family with a nonagenarian, all the sons of the family should be excused from any social labour. Moreover, during the period of mourning for the father and the mother, the sons should be excused from social labour or services for three years. The *Li Ji* further developed Xunzi's idea by legalizing the privilege of the older:

> At court among parties of the same rank, the highest place was given to the oldest. Men of seventy years carried their staffs at the court. When the ruler questioned one of them, he made him sit on a mat. One of eighty years did not wait out the audience, and when the ruler would question him he went to his house. Thus the submission of a younger brother (and juniors generally) was recognized at the court.[20]

The other ethical manifestation of Xunzi's secular F–S relationship can be seen in his idea that the possible equality between the natural father and son is on the basis of inequality. Although absolute inequality between the father and the son was the mainstream of Xunzi's ethical thinking, perhaps in order to avoid the criticism of Confucian critics, such as Modi and Zhuangzi, he left some room for relative inequality. Both Zhuangzi and Mo Di had discussed the moral problem of obedience of a son to his father or his authority, and according to the testimony of the *Zhuangzi*, to consent to everything the parents say or do was regarded as unworthy and as flattery. In Mo Di's view, whoever wishes to achieve something in the world cannot do so without norms and standard, however, neither the parents, nor the teacher, nor the ruler can be taken as the norm for government, because only a few of them are humane. If everybody took their parents as a norm, they would in fact be taking inhumanity as a norm.

The equality between the father and the son can be expressed in the following ways: First, both the father and the son have their own moral responsibilities that need to be fulfilled; there is no excuse for either of them to avoid their moral duties. Both must complete their job according to the moral requirements that society prescribes for them. For example, the superior must be able to love those who are inferior to him, and the inferior must be able to honour and respect his superior. Otherwise, 'to occupy a superior position and yet be unable to love those inferior to him or to occupy an inferior position and to be fond of condemning his superior – this is the first way to bring certainty of dire need' (5.3). In terms of completion of moral duty, there is no difference between the father and the son.

Secondly, the father and the son must possess the same essential moral qualities or virtue. For example, truthfulness is the common virtue for both a good father and a good son:

> Heaven and Earth are indeed great, but were they to lack truthfulness, they could not trans-mute the myriad things. Sages to be sure are wise, but were they to lack truthfulness, they could not transmute the people. Fathers and sons naturally possess affection for each other, but were they to lack truthfulness, they would drift apart. The ruler being superior in posi-tion is honored, but were he to be untruthful, he would be considered base. (3.9c)

Maybe there are different moral duties provided for the varying and incompatible roles of the father and son; however, every person, irrespective of whether he is the father or the son must fulfill his particular moral duty when he plays any particular role.

Moreover, in terms of moral cultivation, the father and the son have the same oppor-tunity and will be judged by the same moral criteria. As men, father and son can choose either a high or a low level of moral life. If they cultivate themselves highly, they will each have the same opportunity to be employed by the ruler and to be given a high position in society. If they lack moral sense and cannot fulfill their moral responsibil-ities, they will both face the same punishment from society. Using Xunzi's own words, both father and son can avoid the death penalty by being filial, by respecting their elders, by being attentive, diligent, restrained, controlled, quick in exerting them-selves, and earnestly executing their tasks and duties and not daring to be indolent or haughty (4.7).

It must be admitted that Xunzi never mentioned the possibility of equality in term of moral rights between the father and the son. However, the equality between them is demonstrated through his discussion of the equal moral right of the noble-born and humble-born:

> Although they be the descendants of kings and dukes or knights and grand officers, if they are incapable of devotedly observing the requirements of ritual and moral principles, they should be relegated to the position of commoners. Although they be the descendants of commoners, if they accumulate culture and study, rectify their character and conduct, and are capable of devotedly observing the requirements of ritual principles and justice, they should brought to the ranks of a prime minister, knight, or grand officer. (9.1)

Although Xunzi clearly declared that everybody on the street could become a sage like Yu, he never proposed the idea that the son has the same moral right as his father. The equality between the father and the son is based neither on their moral right nor on their social status, but on their performing of moral duties and responsibilities. This means that Xunzi's view of equality between the father and the son is based on the inequality between them.

It is true that Xunzi did not advocate the possible equality between the father and the son, but he never denied the possibility of moral equality in this relationship, either. This leaves room for the possibility of both the father and the son to gain an equal posi-tion in society through their effort in learning and moral cultivation. For Xunzi, since morality is not inherent within human nature, both father and son need to undergo a process of learning and moral cultivation. The father's authority partly comes from his biological position, and partly from his prior learning of the sage's teaching. In fact, the power and authority of a father over his son depends on his role as the agent of the sage and the educator of the sage's teaching. In an ideal society, social position or status should correspond to the state of moral cultivation: 'the intelligent ruler examines relative inner power to assign precedence in official positions, thereby causing there to be no disorder' (8.6), so if the son cultivates morality better than his father, he should have the opportunity to be equal to, and even to exceed, his father's social status.

The authority–submission and mutual love moral relationship between the father and the son can be imputed to the family relationships between the elder and the younger brother as well as between the husband and the wife. Since this topic was discussed in the previous section, it is not necessary to repeat it here.

The manifestation of Xunzi's ethical father–son relationship in social and political relationships

As we have seen, Xunzi's natural F–S relationship is linked with not only the elder–younger brother, but also the ruler–subject relationship, and so the moral principle used to deal with this relationship should be a unitary principle that prevails within different familial as well as social and political relationships (9.15).

> The relationships between lord and minister, father and son, older and younger brothers, husband and wife, begin as they end and end as they begin, share with Heaven and Earth the same organizing principle, and endure in the same form through all eternity. Truly this may be described as the 'Great Foundation'. (9.15)

By following such a unitary principle, a man can easily deal with different circumstances. For example, when such a man unexpectedly encounters his lord, he devotes himself to observing the protocol appropriate to a minister and subject. When he meets a fellow villager, he makes it his object to employ all the courtesy due to age and accomplishment. When he encounters an older person, he devotes himself to observing the demeanour of a son or younger brother. When he meets a friend, he devotes himself to showing the appropriate courtesies and rules, polite refusal and yielding precedence. When he encounters someone of lower station or younger than himself, he devotes himself to the manner appropriate to guidance, instruction, magnanimity and tolerance (6.10).

The general principle behind different relationships is the same, even though it may be called by different names: to be able to employ ritual and moral principles in serving one's parents is called 'filial piety'; to be able to use them in serving one's elder brother is called 'brotherly affection'; to be able to use them in serving one's superiors is called 'obedience'; to be able to use them in commanding one's subordinates is called 'being lordly' (9.16a). Therefore, it is easy for Xunzi to transform the ethics of the natural F–S relationship into social and political relationships. H. D. R. Baker illustrates this point: by placing emphasis on the father's authority, Confucianism strengthens the father's domination; by placing emphasis on the son's filial piety, Confucianism strengthens the son's obedience. Both the father's authority and the son's filial piety are necessary for the family system to function effectively, but they also contribute to the development of people's submission and loyalty to the traditional authoritarian state.[21]

The ethical manifestation of the natural F–S in the social relationship can be seen in the relationship of teacher and disciple, old and young, and senior and junior. The ethical manifestation of the natural F–S in the political relationship can be seen in the relationship between ruler and minister, ruler and ruled, and superior and inferior. However, as the old–young and the senior–junior relationships are but an extension of the natural F–S, and the ruler–ruled and the superior–inferior relationships are a copy of the ruler–subject, the focus of discussion here will be only on the teacher–disciple and ruler–subject relationships.

A. The ethical manifestation of the teacher–disciple relationship   From Xunzi's point of view, the position of the teacher in both the social and political sense is very important. The ethical manifestation of the teacher–disciple relationship should be the same as that of the natural F–S relationship. Therefore, the absolute hierarchical order and patriarchal moral principles used to describe the natural F–S are appropriate to be used to describe the teacher–disciple relationship. Consequently, as respect and obedience are the two main virtues of the son they are likewise the important virtues of the student. Xunzi said: 'To discuss things in terms that do not agree with your teacher is called "rebellion." To teach in a fashion that does not correspond to what your teacher taught is called "subversion"' (27.79).

Why should the disciple respect and obey his teacher? Xunzi gave the following reasons: first, original human nature is not good but evil, and evil human nature can only be corrected by the instruction of the teacher (23.1a), in which the teacher is the representative of the ancient sages while his instruction is the explanation of their Way. Therefore, the teacher is necessary for everybody, including those who are talented and intelligent:

> Although a man may have fine talents and a mind with a discriminating intelligence, he must seek out a worthy teacher to serve and select good men as the friends with whom to associate. If he obtains a worthy teacher, then what he hears will be the Way of Yao, Shun and Yu, and Tang. (23.8)

In fact, from Xunzi's viewpoint, the more talents a man has, the more he needs to seek out a worthy teacher. Such a man faces more danger than other people: if a man who is intelligent lacks a teacher and model, he will certainly become a robber. If brave, he will surely become a murderer. If versatile, he will certainly produce disorder. If a precise investigator, he will surely create anomalous results. If a discriminator, he will certainly advance extravagant schemes. Accordingly, having a teacher and model is man's greatest treasure but lacking them his greatest calamity (2.4).

The teacher is guide and model, from whom people can learn righteousness and justice. He is the one who indicates the proper standard of deportment and the need to value what is at peace within; therefore, when one displays the required ritual in one's conduct and one's speech accords with the teacher's, the emotions will find peace in ritual. The more one's knowledge is like that of the teacher, the more chance one has of becoming a sage (2.11).

Finally, the teacher is not only a person who tells people what is right and wrong, but is one who perfects the rituals. Accordingly, Xunzi believed that without teachers no one knows the correct ritual, and without knowledge of ritual the individual will not be rectified (2.11).

How is it that the teacher can influence people? The most important reason is that human beings possess a faculty of wisdom. Although the 'inborn nature' of human beings – what is spontaneous from nature and cannot be learned (23.1c) – is evil in the sense that they cannot control it, because they have the faculty of wisdom, they can consider the temporal nature of things and think of the consequences of their actions (4.11); this makes it possible for them to be transformed through learning from the teacher and through the teacher's correction (8.11). Thus, through the faculty of wisdom, the influence of the teacher can reach the students.

Another reason for a teacher's possible influence on his student is the high significance of the individual's learning. Xunzi gave two reasons why learning is so important. First, learning is the only way to become a real human being: those who undertake learning become men, while those who neglect it become like wild beasts (1.8). Hence, learning is the only way for humans to escape the danger of being beasts. Secondly, learning is a necessary process for a person who wishes to be an ideal man: there are two purposes of learning, one is to create a scholar and the other is to create a sage (1.8); thus, only through the process of learning can one have a chance to be a sage or a scholar. Learning is so important that becoming a real man or an ideal man cannot take place without engaging in it, and the teacher is so important to the process of individual learning that without him no learning can be effectively completed. The teacher becomes, on the one hand, a compulsory force to ensure that the student becomes a real member of humankind, and on the other hand, reaches the level of sage – an ideal state of human being. Since both self-moral cultivation and social-moral education is so important for the transformation of humans' evil nature and the establishment of humans' acquired moral nature, through playing the most important role in the process of both individual moral cultivation and social moral education, the teacher influences the student profoundly. This why Xunzi declaimed that only those whose inborn nature has been transformed by their teacher and the model (*fa*), and those who have accumulated good form and learning, are the ones who are guided by the Way of ritual principles and moral duty so that they become gentlemen (23.1b).

Since a teacher is so important for both the individual and society, not only must disciples respect and obey their teachers, but also the whole of society and the state should treasure them:

> When a country is on the verge of a great florescence, it is certain to prize its teachers and give great importance to breadth of learning. If it does this, then laws and standards will be preserved. When a country is on the verge of decay, then it is sure to show contempt for teachers and slight masters. If it does this, then its people will be smug. If the people are smugly self-satisfied, then laws and standards will be allowed to go to ruin. (27.93)

In short, the teacher should be given a high position by both the individual and society; this is because the teacher is always linked to the real men and even the sage. Since the ancient sage-kings, the first generation of teachers, were not only the ancestors of teachers but were also linked with the rulers and good government, the teacher–disciple relationship is also linked with the ruler–subject relationship.

B. The ethical application of the natural father–son relationship in the ruler and subject relationship In the *Book of Xunzi*, another popular topic is the ethical relationship between the ruler and the subject. Why is it that the ruler–subject relationship occupies such an important place? Xunzi gave us three reasons: first, the state is the most powerful instrument for benefit in the world, while the ruler of men is in the most influential position of authority for benefit in the world (11.1a). Therefore the relationship between the ruler and the subject is important.

Secondly, to organize society is the only way for humans to survive and become the noblest species in the world; and in the organization of society, the sage plays a cardinal role: he is the parent of the people and the society must be organized in accordance with his invention of the moral principle. An ideal ruler must be a sage. Government administration, if it is under the control of a sage, should be an ideal government. Therefore, not only the moral position of the ruler, but also the relationship between the ruler and the minister is important.

Finally, in administering the state, both the ruler and the ministers play an important role: they are the managers of their people and also the moral model and teachers of their people. They have a duty to love and bring material benefits to the people; and also a responsibility to teach and instruct the people. Moreover, they should try their best to satisfy the people's spiritual needs. Therefore, harmony between the ruler and the subject is also important: the unity and cooperation between them are necessary for the order and peace of the society.

As noted in previous chapters, the ancient Chinese conceived the state on the model of the family. The ruler occupied the position of a parent, while the subjects were like children. The ruler should love and care for his subjects as well as nurture, teach and lead them. By contrast, the subjects should admire, emulate and follow the ruler, and respect and obey him. All these requirements of the Confucian tradition are also true of Xunzi.

In Xunzi's relationship between the ruler and the subject, the ethical requirement is similar to the ethics applied in the natural F–S relationship: on the one hand, the hierarchical order between the ruler and subject is absolute; there is no equality between the ruler and the subject: a subject can never oppose his ruler; he must always sacrifice himself for the good of his ruler in serving his lord. On the other hand, the moral relationship between the ruler and the minister is mutual. Both the ruler and the subjects must fulfill their own moral duties.

There is some slight difference between the ruler–subject relationship and the relationship between father and son. In the F–S relationship it is the son who takes responsibility for establishing and keeping the harmonious relationship between them, while in the ruler–ruled relationship, it is the ruler rather than the ruled who takes responsibility for the establishment of harmony between the two.

However, the responsibility of the ruler does not bring any further possible equality between the ruler and the subjects, but a strengthened power and authority of the ruler. Xunzi believed that two men of equal eminence cannot attend each other, and two men of the same low status cannot command each other—such is the norm of Heaven (9.3). Accordingly, the power and the position between the ruler and ruled cannot be equally distributed; it is necessary to establish the authority and power of the ruler.

There are two ways to ensure the authority and power of a ruler. First, the ruler must establish his authority and power by his own morality and wisdom; and secondly, it is necessary for him to expect that his subjects possess respect, obedience and submission as their virtues.

The most important thing for ruler establishing his power and authority is to gain morality and to be a benevolent government. Referring to the relationship between morality and the power of the governor, Xunzi gave the following declaration: if the ruler's humanity is the loftiest in the world, his justice will be the most admirable, and if his majesty is the most marvelous, he will have the greatest authority:

> His humanity being the loftiest is the cause of no one in the world being estranged from him. His justice being the most admirable is the cause of none failing to esteem him. His majesty being the most marvelous is the cause of no one in the world presuming to oppose him. His majesty permitting no opposition coupled with a way that wins the allegiance of others is the cause of his triumphing without having to wage war, of his gaining his objectives without resort to force, and of the world submitting to him without his armies exerting themselves. (9.9)

It is obvious that Xunzi, unlike Mengzi, was sure that morality has a power to ensure people have no enemies, and he linked morality with power and authority: if the sense of morality and justice is used to divide society into classes, concord will result. If there is concord between the classes, unity will result; if there is unity, great physical power will result; if there is great physical power, real strength will result (9.16a); if there is real strength, world order and peace will be realized.

The manifestation of morality for a ruler is to practise benevolent government. What are the signs of good government? A good governor, first of all, must promote the right principles and assign to each person a position of appropriate rank (9.12), and then, he must give honor to worthy men (27.2) and employ able men (9.12). He must select good and worthy men for office, promote those who are honest and reverent (9.4). More than that, he must put things in their proper position and grade them in terms of the moral force of their inner power (11.5b). And finally, he must reward filial piety and brotherly affection, gather under his protection orphans and widows, and offer assistance to those who are in poverty and need (9.4). He must provide benefit for and protect his people, and allow his people to be closely attached to him as if he were their own parent (10.5).

Why must the ruler practise good government? Xunzi believed that it is necessary for a ruler to be kind to the people, because the lord is the boat and his subjects the water. It is the water that both sustains the boat and capsizes it. Therefore, if the lord of men desires to be secure, no policy is as good as evenhanded government and the love of the people. If he desires glory, nothing is as effective as exalting ritual principles and treating scholars with strict observance of forms of respect. If he desires to establish his fame and meritorious accomplishments, nothing is as good as advancing the worthy and bringing the capable into one's service (9.4).

However, from Xunzi's point of view, to have only morality is insufficient for a good ruler; a good ruler must have wisdom – extra skills of government. As a Son of Heaven, the ruler must obtain morality and wisdom at the same time: 'Those lacking inner power shall be without honored status, those without ability should be without office' (9.12). The wisdom of the ruler or the skills of government includes the following aspects: (a) to execute in good order every act with proper ritual and with morality; (b) to hear proposals and makes decisions according to the proper categories; (c) to intelligently put everything in order down to the tip of the finest hair; (d) in promoting or dismissing, in responding to every change of circumstance, never to be at a loss (9.10). For Xunzi, if everybody who had achieved the above wisdom – skills of government – he would be treated as a sage-king, although he may not be on the throne:

> When a person cultivates the model of the Hundred Kings as easily as he distinguishes white and black; when he responds appropriately at every change of circumstances as easily as counting one, two; when he acts in accordance with the requirements of the indispensable points of ritual and is at ease with them as though he were merely moving his four limbs; when he seeks the occasion to establish the meritorious in his accomplishments as though he were proclaiming the four seasons; when with equality of government he harmonizes the common people to goodness and collects together the countless masses as though they were a single individual – then a person may be called a sage. (8.7)

It is clear that there is a strong consideration in Xunzi's thinking: a ruler must be not only a governor but also a model for his subjects and his people in both morality and wisdom. Like other early Confucians, Xunzi held the view that the superior should be the root and foundation of his subordinates. He argued that if the superior exhibits and elucidates acceptable standards, his subordinates will be orderly and manageable; if the superior is correct and sincere, his subordinates will be attentive and diligent; if the superior is impartial and right, his subordinates will be amenable and honest (18.1). The ruler is the model while the people are the reflection, in a sense that only if the model is upright will the reflection will be upright, otherwise, if the model is crooked so is the reflection (12.4). Therefore, it is the ruler and not the subject who should take chief responsibility for the establishment of a harmonious relationship. For establishing a harmonious relationship with one's subjects and his people and also for the sake of strengthening his power and authority, the ruler must cultivate both his wisdom and his morality.

Another important way to establish the power and the authority of the ruler is to foster the subjects' virtues of submission and obedience. For strengthening the power and authority of the ruler, Xunzi especially stressed the obedience and submission of the subjects. He indicated that anyone who acted as a minister or subordinate should offer remonstrance but not engage in vilification or fall into hatred inspired by jealousy; he should resent misdeeds, but should not display wrath (27.34).

To strengthen his idea of how important the virtues of respect and humility are in relationship to one's ruler, Xunzi invented methods by which the subject could retain favour, stay in office, and remain to the end without attracting any animosity. Six different conditions are listed in detail: (1) if the ruler bestows high rank on subject and exalts him, he should be respectful, take strict care to fulfill his duties, and be restrained. (2) If the ruler trusts and loves the subject, he should be careful, circumspect, and humble. (3) If the ruler gives the subject sole authority, he should hold fast to maintaining his responsibilities and oversee them meticulously. (4) If the ruler is at ease and friendly with a subject, he should be cautious of this closeness and not become corrupt. (5) If the ruler is distant and remote from a subject, the subject should strive for complete oneness with him but not oppose him. And (6) if the ruler diminishes and degrades the subject, he should be fearful and apprehensive but not harbor resentments. In short,

> When exalted, do not engage in boasting; when trusted, do not give cause for suspicion. When given heavy responsibilities, do not presume to keep them all for yourself. Whenever you come into an offer of wealth and benefits, you should consider that your good accomplishments do not justify them and accordingly must, with a due sense for what is right, offer polite refusals and defer to others better qualified before accepting the other. (7.2)

Some scholars maintain that this is not the way of the sage, and therefore argue that this idea does not belong to Xunzi because it is not in keeping with the logic of his thinking.[22] But the above idea of Xunzi is actually a logical deduction from his ethical ideas on the ruler–subject relationship. First, Xunzi strongly stressed the obedience and respect of the ruled for the ruler, which should even be carried on after the ruler's death. Xunzi insisted that, just as the respect of a son for his parents does not stop with the death of the parents, people should mourn their ruler for three years after his death.

Why was the practice of three year's mourning chosen for one's lord? Xunzi's answer is that a ruler can do more for his people than a parent can do for his child. The father can beget the child but cannot suckle it, and the mother can suckle the child but is unable to instruct and correct it. The lord, however, is not only able to feed his people, but is adept at teaching and correcting them (19.20). Because the ruler can bring more benevolence to his people than one's parent, one should return him an equal amount of respect and obedience, or at least the same as one would give one's parent. In order to show one's own serious respect and obedience to the ruler, it is necessary to exhibit extreme forms of conduct.

It is true that Xunzi's ideal subject will not blindly obey his ruler; if necessary, he will revolt against, even overthrow him for the sake of the ruler and the state. Xunzi encouraged subjects to 'follow the Way and not follow the lord' (13.2). This is why he says that to follow the mandate of one's commission for the profit of one's lord is called 'obedience'; to do so, but not for the profit of one's lord, is called 'toadying'; to contravene the mandate of one's commission for the benefit of one's lord is called 'loyalty'; and to contravene it but not for the benefit of one's lord, is called 'presumption' (13.2). However, not everybody can be an excellent subject who has efficient wisdom and ability to know exactly what conducts are the best for carrying forward the Way of the ancient sage. The excellent subjects who can deliver the true Way of the ancient sage, can do everything in a right way without any destruction of the Way and their life, and the above principle should be their ideal principle. However, for those whose wisdom and ability is not excellent and who cannot guarantee their conduct to be safe for both protecting the Way and their lives, it would be better to be a conservative in both persuading the ruler and breaking the rule. For Confucian scholars, the most important job is to enhance the Way of the ancient sages, but the task of enhancing the Way of the ancient sage is a difficult and dangerous one, especially when a scholar pursues a benighted lord to practise it. For a long-term benefit, the scholar-subject sometimes has to show the ruler even more extreme respect and obedience.

In short, as the country is nothing other than an enlarged form of family, the political relationship should be nothing other than an extension of the natural F–S relationship; the way of resolving conflict between the governor and the governed is equivalent to the way of dealing with the relationship between father and son. Consequently, benevolence and obedience are virtues that also characterize Xunzi's solution of the conflict between the ruler and the ruled, although, unlike in the F–S relationship where the son is held primarily responsible for resolving conflict, in the ruler–ruled relationship the chief responsibility for reducing tension and for solving conflict is on those who rule and govern. As the spiritual relationship between sage and common people is nearly the same as in the ruler and the ruled relationship, it is not necessary to provide a special discussion on the ethical manifestation of the spiritual relationship, such as sage and common people.

The Nature of Xunzi's Secular Ethical Father–Son Relationship

From the above discussion it can be seen that there are some general characteristics with respect to the nature of Xunzi's *secular* F–S relationship which will be discussed below.

Division according to ability and morality, and the nature of hierarchy in Xunzi's father–son relationship

Xunzi believes that the way to make the entire world self-sufficient lies in making clear social class divisions (10.7); therefore, division or distinction is the most important characteristic of Xunzi's political theory. What then is the meaning of distinction or division? The Chinese character for division is *fen*. It appears that *fen* in Xunzi's mind has three meanings: first, it is the classification of myriad things (10.1; 19.6); secondly, it means the differentiation of labour (10.1); and finally it means the distinction of social status (10.1; 27.22). These three definitions of *fen* are logically linked to each other and constitute the basis of the hierarchical character of Xunzi's secular F–S , relationship.

Xunzi says, 'The myriad things share the same world, but their embodied form is different. Although they have no intrinsic appropriateness, yet they maybe have different use to humanity: this is due to the natural order of things' (10.1). How can the myriad things be classified? The answer is that it is the sage who fulfills the task of assigning myriad things to their proper position (19.6). This means that differences and gradations exist not only in the natural world, but also in human society. Because nothing can escape gradation, the differentiation of people into different ranks or classes is inevitable. Although people seek the same things, they employ different methods in pursuit of them; although they have the same desires, they have different degrees of awareness concerning them (10.1). Because people have not only different faculties of wisdom, but also different abilities to develop their potential, this differentiation between the wise and the stupid, the able and the unable, is due to their inborn nature (10.1).

How then is it possible to differentiate people from each other? The best way, according to Xunzi, is to grade them according to moral duties and ritual principles: 'The *Ritual* contains the model for the primary social distinctions and categories used by analogical extension for the guiding rules and ordering norms of behaviour' (1.8).

Not only have moral duties to be fulfilled individually, there are also various necessary skills provided for each individual. However, even the ablest of humans cannot be expert in them all (10.1); therefore, the only way to resolve this problem is to divide social tasks into many parts and let each class undertake some part of them, thus everyone can share the benefits of society. This is called the division of social labour. Because the able and the wise can develop more of their abilities, they can undertake more social duties; but the less able and the people of average wisdom can only develop less potential and can undertake fewer tasks. Therefore, society should give tasks and duties to different classes of people in accordance with their ability and wisdom: the wiser and more able persons usually undertake the higher-level jobs, such as governance and management, while the average and below undertake the lower-level jobs. Since the wise and able men can do better and more government work, they should control the average; since the wise and able men become wise and able through their accumulation of knowledge, the men who have more knowledge and education should rule those who have less education.

From the differentiation of labour and the distinction of social status comes the hierarchical requirement of the ethical principle. Xunzi said,

> The graduated scale of humane conduct is to treat relatives in a manner befitting their relation, old friends as is appropriate to their friendship, the meritorious in terms of their accomplishment, and laborers in terms of their toil. The gradations of position in moral conduct are to treat the noble as befits their eminent position, the honorable with due honor, the worthy as accords with their worth, the old as is appropriate to their age, and those senior to oneself as is suitable to their seniority. (27.21)

From the above hierarchical illustration of Xunzi's thinking it is possible to infer that the most important aspect of the secular F–S relationship is hierarchy. Because every social relationship should be guided by the hierarchical principle, and the secular F–S relationship is the embodiment of all social relationships, hierarchy should permeate every relationship.

How can such a hierarchical nature be realized in a real society? Xunzi suggested that social division should be based on the potentiality of wisdom and moral effort of the individual. According to his viewpoint, people who have developed more of their abilities should rule those who have developed fewer. The more able man who has developed the most of his potentialities and has undertaken the most important work of society should be the ruler of that society: 'The inner power of the person must match his position; his position must match his emolument; his emolument must match his services to the state' (10.3a). This is the reason why, in the golden age, it was the sages rather than others who were the kings of their societies.

Nevertheless, Xunzi does not always adhere to this principle of 'division according to personal effort'. Sometimes, he prefers to insist on a contrary argument by stating that the gradation of ranks should be in accordance with people's social or economic positions, or according to age and gender (19.1c). He said 'that the young should serve the old, the base the noble, and the unworthy the worthy is the pervading moral rule throughout the world' (7.5). From this assertion, emerges the second element of Xunzi's ethic of the secular F–S relationship.

Division according to age and gender and the patriarchal nature of Xunzi's secular F–S relationship

Xunzi states that 'it is the meaning of ritual principles that there should be rankings according to nobility or baseness, disparities between the privileges of old and young, and modes to match these with poverty and wealth, insignificance and importance' (10.3a). What is the composition of nobility? According to Xunzi, the male is likened to heaven and the female to earth; heaven is always above and earth below. Therefore, the male should be noble like heaven and the female inferior like earth. So too with the F–S relationship: the father should be above and over his son and his son should be submissive to his father. The hierarchical character of Xunzi's secular F–S relationship is obviously a superior–inferior model. Baker's discussion gives us the evidence: ancestor worship serves to reinforce the unity of the family and, specifically, provides a ritual sanction to back up the generation/age/sex scheme of authority within the family. The principles of ancestor worship are to respect earlier generations (Generation), to give priority to eldest sons by keeping the tablets in the care of the senior line (Age), and to give no consideration to women unless they are the wives and mothers of men (Sex).[23]

There seems to be some contradiction here: how can a system of division which is in accordance with personal moral effort connect with one which is in accordance with social status such as age, social roles, sex, or wealth? According to the logic of Xunzi, there is no contradiction: inborn human nature is changeable through personal learning and social education, while for the common people knowledge mainly comes from one's personal effort in learning and education. However, both personal learning or individual moral cultivation and social education take time. Although the wise have perhaps learned more than the unwise at a particular time, generally speaking, the more time people spend on their study and education, the more they will achieve. Therefore, since the older have spent more time on their personal cultivation and have received more social education than the younger, they should have achieved more than the younger members of society. In the same way, a father being the older should have accumulated more knowledge and wisdom than the son. It is therefore reasonable to give the father authority to control his son. This is also the reason why social ranking must be based on age.

Here emerges a suggestion: the F–S relationship is not really the fundamental thing, since its importance rests on something else, i.e. the greater wisdom etc. of the father. And what is to happen in cases where a younger person is wiser or more knowledgeable than the older person? Does the normal rule about the dominance of the older then lapse? The proper answer might be thus: the F–S relationship acquires its significance in part from the fact that in the great majority of cases the father is wiser etc. than the son.

It is worth noting that this division only applies to the common mass, not to the ruler. Because the ruler should be the wise and able one, he should be a sage or at least a gentleman; therefore age for him is not a limitation.

We did not discuss the reason for division on gender, since all reason for the power of the father is applicable to the power of the male. Moreover, women were not engaged in the particular moral education that was aimed to support the moral government, therefore, women's moral cultivation was out of the calculation. Ho Chen[24] has also clearly exposed this condition of women in Confucianism:

> Women have duties but no rights . . . Household responsibilities cannot be assumed by men but all the tasks of managing the household are given to women. Out of fear that women might interfere with their concerns, men said women had no business outside of the home. This deprived women of their natural rights.[25]

According to the same logic, there is also a link between wealth, learning and education. Both personal learning and social education need the learner and people in education to have leisure time, but leisure cannot be gained without proper wealth. Wealth is therefore the precondition for both learning and education. To understand this, we have to understand Xunzi's concept of *li* – profit.

The character of giving consideration to both yi and li and the benevolent nature of Xunzi's secular father–son relationship

Li means profit or benefit and is closely linked to wealth. From Xunzi's point of view, 'A love of profit and the desire to obtain it belong to man's essential and inborn nature' (23.2a). Consequently, to provide enough material support for his family is the duty of a father, while to provide public profit and satisfy the essential needs of his people are the fundamental tasks of a government. For Xunzi, the senses of rightness and of profit are two things humans must possess. Although they were unable to get rid of the desire for profit in people, the ancient sages, such as Yao and Shun, were nonetheless able to persuade their people using *li yi* ('ritual principle' and 'morality') to control their desires of. Therefore, in Xunzi's thinking, neither *li* (ritual principle) nor *yi* (moral principle) is for or against human desires, but for satisfying human desires in a proper way, and so, *li yi* (rituals and morality) is linked to *li* (profit). Thus, his conclusion that 'human nature is evil' is not based on a belief that 'all human desires are evil', but is rather based on the condition that there are some improper human desires as well as some improper ways of pursuing or satisfying these human desires. These improper desires and the improper ways are the source and content of evil. Therefore, the ritual and moral principles are not aimed at eliminating human desires, but at nurturing them and supplying the proper means for their satisfaction (19.1a). Accordingly, to pursue one's proper benefit is reasonable and just. This is also the original aim of organizing society and formulating the principles of rites and morality. It is part of the inborn nature of human beings that they cannot but form societies. If they form a society in which there is no class division, strife will develop.

If there is strife, then there will be social disorder; if there is social disorder, there will be hardship (poverty) for all (10.4). 'This is precisely why it is unacceptable to neglect ritual and moral principles even for the shortest moment' (9.16a). In this sense, *yi* is equal to *li*, and justice is equal to benefit.

The admission of the rationality of proper benefit leads Xunzi to a situation that sets moral and ritual principles (*li yi*) on the basis of pragmatism. This pragmatic attitude of moral theory further leads to the following result: a mutual benevolent relationship in all familial and social and political contexts is built up. Because all moral and ritual principles are for the sake of nurturing and satisfying individual's desires, people should follow these principles on the precondition of mutual satisfaction and personal happiness. Consequently, something that benefits only one side but injures the other is unacceptable and unjust. Thus, benevolence becomes the theme of Xunzi's moral theory.

In the same way as earlier Confucians, Xunzi also stressed benevolent government and emphasized the importance of the virtue of benevolence in a ruler. Moreover, Xunzi especially stressed the mutual benevolence of various moral relationships. For example, he said, there must be a rule of respect in the relationship between the ruler and the minister; there must be affection in the F–S relationship; there must be harmony and submissiveness between brothers, and rejoicing between husband and wife. The son must be supported in his growth to maturity and old people must be provided with both material and spiritual nourishment.[26]

From such mutually benevolent relationships derive the mutual moral responsibilities of all relationships, for example, in the familial relationships, the father should love his son as well as the son his father; the husband must make his wife happy and the wife her husband; and the older brother must take care of and be kind to the younger brother, and the younger brother must show respect and submissiveness to his older brother. The same is true in the social political relationship: the young must be supported by the old for their growth and the old must be helped by the young for the nourishment of their old age; the teacher must help his student and the student must love and honor his teacher; the subject must honor his ruler and the ruler must respect his subject. In short, there is no moral responsibility that can be fulfilled by a one-sided moral relationship. Although it seems that in the relationship between father and son, the primary responsibility for harmony is laid on the shoulders of the son rather than the father, the tension between father and son is reduced through the filial piety which requires children to pay their father full service with a sincere and respectful attitude. However, unlike the later Confucians, who emphasize that the primary responsibility for a harmonious relation between father and son is on the latter, and try to say that the cause of any conflict between father and son is primarily due to the latter's attitude and behavior, Xunzi prefers to emphasize the responsibility for the harmony between father and son from both sides. Therefore, although Xunzi, like other traditional Chinese scholars, seldom mentions individual rights, it is possible to conclude from his attitude of mutual moral responsibilities that the individual's rights are probably a matter for both sides through the mutual fulfillment of their responsibilities. Xunzi said:

> Man has three patterns of behavior that certainly will reduce him to dire need. To occupy a superior position and yet be unable to love those inferior to him or to occupy an inferior position and to be fond of condemning his superiors . . . this is the first way to bring certainty of dire need. (5.8)

The pragmatic attitude of Xunzi to the relationship of *li* and *yi* or between benefit and morality also paved the way for the possibility of equality in moral cultivation among people. To investigate further, we start from the function and character of moral and ritual principles (*li yi*).

What is the function of *li yi*? Yan Ying, a famous minister of Qi and an elder contemporary of Confucius, provided one of the finest early rationales for the purpose and function of ritual by saying that:

> Ritual principles have the ability to govern the state since they are coeval with Heaven and Earth. That the lord issues commands and the minister discharges them, that the father is affectionately kind and the son dutiful, that the elder brother is loving and the younger brother reverent, that the husband is harmonious and the wife meek, and that the mother-in-law is affectionately kind and the daughter-in-law is docilely obedient are instances of ritual principles.[27]

What is the primary characteristic of *li yi*? According to Xunzi's theory that 'human nature is evil', human desire is limitless, but material goods are limited. For the sake of peaceful distribution, there must be a reasonable principle of division of benefit. There are two principles for the distribution of benefit; one is the principle of equal distribution; the other is the principle of unequal distribution. Xunzi chose the latter. He declared that if power and positions were equally distributed, then the result would be that no one's desires would be satisfied, and no one would be willing to follow the orders of another. If no one's desire can be satisfied properly, this will certainly lead to contention and conflict, which can only result in poverty. Therefore, unequal distribution is necessary: 'Two men of equal eminence cannot attend each other; two men of the same low status cannot command each other – such is the norm of Heaven' (9.3). Thus, hierarchy, gradation and order become the first and primary principle of social distinction and distribution.

However, there are many ways of organizing hierarchy, grade and order. Xunzi insists that it can be done first by patriarchal principles, then by age, and finally by the principle that the position can be taken as the status of division. Xunzi calls situations conflicting with these rules the three signs of misfortune: 'Man has three sure signs of misfortune: to be young and yet unwilling to serve one's elders; to be of humble origins and yet be unwilling to serve the noble; and to be lacking in worth yet be unwilling to serve the worthy' (5.8). Accordingly, inequality, hierarchy, patriarchy and 'back to the ancients' are the significant characteristics of Xunzi's theory. However, because 'human nature is evil', the moral and ritual principles cannot come from the inner nature, but from external learning and moral cultivation; everyone must gain *li yi* by personal moral effort. Therefore, the opportunity for learning and moral cultivation is equal for everybody. Moreover, because *li yi* serves the purpose of bringing more benefit to the whole society, every capable person in observing and practising *li yi* should have an equal opportunity to pursue their achievement in the whole of society so as to benefit society. If you are the ablest, you should be the ruler; if you are not the able one, you should be ruled. With respect to morality, as in the case of human nature, there is no distinction between people:

> Although they be the descendants of kings and dukes or knights and grand officers, if they are incapable of devotedly observing the requirements of ritual and moral principles, they should be relegated to the position of commoners. Although they be the descendants of commoners, if they accumulate culture and study, rectify their character and conduct, and are capable of devotedly observing the requirements of ritual principles and justice, they should be brought to the ranks of a prime minister, knight, or grand officer. (9.1)

Xunzi's pragmatic attitude can also be implemented through his theory of *dayi*, or the principle of greater justice, in which preferential choice of the greater or public profit is required. Since the satisfaction of one's desire is usually regarded as the benefit or profit of the individual, it is clear that the concept of *li yi* is closely linked with the satisfaction of human needs. For Xunzi, *li yi* is actually the protection or guarantee of the individual gaining his material benefit or spiritual profit. However, there are many kinds of benefits provided at the same time. They vary according to location, endurance, and longevity. There is therefore a division between greater and smaller benefits (*dali* and *xiaoli*), and a division between a greater and smaller amount of moral level.[28] Xunzi used *dayi* to describe the greater moral level and *xiaoyi* to describe the lesser moral level. The principle that can satisfy more desires and bring benefit to more people is called the principle of *dayi* or greater justice. The more benefit *yi* can provide the more needs it can satisfy; the more primary the principle the greater the *yi*. When conflicts occur between different benefits or moral conditions, people should choose the greater justice or *dayi* rather than *xiaoyi*. For example, submission to his ruler is the necessary moral requirement of a subject; however, when he knows that if he submits to his ruler, the whole country will be in danger, he must set aside his submission and choose against his ruler. There is a special section in *Xunzi* that discusses what is the most appropriate paths for a filial son. Xunzi said:

> Inside the home to be filial toward one's parents and outside the home to be properly courteous toward one's elders constitute the minimal standard of human conduct. To be obedient to superiors and to be reliable in one's dealing with inferiors constitute a higher standard of conduct. To follow the dictates of the Way rather than those of one's lord and follow the requirements of morality rather than the wishes of one's father constitute the highest standard of conduct. (29.1)

Xunzi illustrated this through three case studies of situations where a filial son should not follow his father's will. First, if a son by following the will of the father risks bringing peril to his family, whereas not following it would by contrast bring security. Secondly, if following his father's command would bring disgrace on his family, whereas not following it would bring honor. Finally, if obeying the father's command would cause him to act like a savage, whereas not obeying it would cultivate and improve him, then in not obeying it he acts with proper reverence. Hence, if it were morally possible to have followed the course, not to have done so would constitute being an improper son; if it were impossible to follow the course, to have done so would be disloyalty. This is summarized in the tradition: 'Follow the dictates of the Way rather than those of one's lord and follow the requirements of morality rather than the wishes of one's father' (29.2).

In the following story, Xunzi further explains what true filial piety and loyalty are. Duke Ai of Lu questioned Confucius. He said: 'Does a son by following the course of action mandated by his father behave filially? Does a minister by following the commands of his lord behave with integrity?' Three times he posed the same question, but Confucius did not reply. One of the famous disciples of Confucius, Zigong (520 BC–?), whose second name is Ci, did not understand why Confucius was not responding, so he asked, 'A son who follows his father's instructions is indeed filial and a minister who follows his lord's commands does indeed act with integrity. Why did the Master not reply thus?' Confucius replied,

> Ci, you are a petty man! You do not grasp the point! In the past, when a state of ten thousand chariots possessed four remonstrating servants, the border territories of that state would not be encroached upon. When a state of a thousand chariots had three remonstrating servants, its altars of soil and grain were not imperiled. When a family of a hundred chariots possessed two remonstrating servants, its ancestral shrine was not overturned. When a father had a remonstrating son, then nothing in his conduct lacked ritual principles. When a knight had remonstrating friends, he did not act against the requirements of morality. Accordingly, if a son merely follows his father, how is that son behaving filially? And, if a minister merely follows his lord, how is he behaving with integrity? You must carefully judge the manner of his 'following' before it can be described as 'filial' or as marked by 'integrity'. (29.3)

By this story, Xunzi tells us that true filial piety is not a son blindly following his father, but a son who can bring greater profit to his family and more glory and honor to his father; and true loyalty is not a subject unconditionally obeying his ruler, but a minister who can protect the greatest public good and keep his ruler from experiencing shame. It is clear that, on the one hand, compared to private interest, the public profit is more important, and this is why he says that to be filial toward one's parents constitutes the minimal standard of human conduct, but to be obedient to superiors and to be reliable in one's dealing with inferiors constitute a higher standard of conduct. On the other hand, compared to loyalty to one's ruler, to follow the requirement of morality is more important. This is why Xunzi said that 'to follow the dictates of the Way rather than those of one's lord and follow the requirements of morality rather than the wishes of one's father constitute the highest standard of conduct' (29.2).

From this analysis it can be seen that Xunzi's understanding of *yi* is quite different from Confucius' idea that 'the father conceals the misconduct of the son, and the son conceals the misconduct of the father' (18.2). Compared to the limitation of Confucius' content of *yi* by his focus on family consideration, Xunzi's *dayi* opened his moral content not only to family but also to public consideration, and this further leads Xunzi's moral theory to have both Confucian kinship and legalist rational characteristics, thereby making his moral theory more practicable.

The character of harmony according to order and the nature of graded love in the secular father–son relationship

For Xunzi, keeping society (from the smallest society of a family to the biggest society of a state) in a peaceful and harmonious state is the ideal and final goal of society. How can society be in a state of peace and harmony? The mark of a peaceful and harmonious state is that everything is in order and that there is neither collision nor conflict between its various parts. Therefore order is the precondition for keeping a family or a society or a state in a condition of harmony. The best way to realize such a state is in accordance with the Way of ritual principles. Xunzi said,

> Rites are the highest expression of order and discrimination, the root of strength in the state, the Way by which the majestic sway of authority is created, and the focus of merit and fame . . . If they proceed in accordance with the Way of ritual principles, then they will succeed; if they do not, then they will fail. (19.1d)

Why are rites the root of strength in the state? This is because there is nothing better than the solidarity of the people for keeping a state in a tranquil and secure condition. But the solidarity of the people is based on the creation and existence of authority. The establishment of majestic authority depends upon the generation of ritual principles. Rites are the Way by which the majestic sway of authority is created. Why can ritual principles create authority? This is because:

> Ritual principles have three roots. Heaven and earth are the roots of life. Forebears are the roots of kinship. Lord and teacher are the roots of order . . . Thus, rituals serve Heaven above and Earth below, pay honor to one's forebears, and exalt rulers and teachers, for these are the three roots of ritual principles. (19.2a)

In the establishment of majestic authority, punishment is necessary. Only if someone does not obey orders are punishments to be applied. Thus, when the ruler applies punishments to a single individual, the world becomes obedient. For this reason, although punishments and penalties are but seldom used, majestic authority spreads everywhere, like flowing water. Xunzi has the greatest esteem for the benevolence of government, but he never abandons the idea of punishment. He holds that punishment is the insurance of benevolent government. To explain his standpoint, he quotes an ancient saying: 'Let your majestic authority be stern and fierce, but do not wield it. Let your punishments be established, but do not use them' (19.1d [15.4]).

To create a family or a society or a state of harmony, mutual love is necessary. For Xunzi, because desire is the inherent nature of both father and son, then the essential proper desires of both father and son should be satisfied. Thus, to offer a proper rule system to satisfy the necessary desires of various social members is an essential duty of *li yi*. That is why the most important function of the principles of *li yi* are to apportion and nurture the desires of Men, and why the content of morality and justice is the responsibility of individuals.[29] The function of morality and justice is not only to satisfy desires of the father, ruler, husband, and elder brother, but also to protect the rights of the son, the minister, the wife and the younger brother. Accordingly, the relationship between father and son, ruler and minister, husband and wife, old and young are a mutual rather than a one-way relationship. Therefore, unlike later Confucians who emphasized the right of a father over his son, Xunzi insisted that both the father's and the son's essential needs should be satisfied.

Xunzi argued that both father and son are equally responsible for a harmonious family and that a harmonious F–S relationship needs the contribution of both the father and the son; while a son must be filial to his father, the father is required to be kind and benevolent to his son. However, this mutual love is still not an equal love, but a graded love. The love of the father is with authority and punishment, while the love of the son to his father should be with reverence and obedience. This graded love leads to a situation where the rights of the father and the responsibilities and duties of the son are constantly being stressed, but the responsibilities of the father and the rights of the son are seldom consciously mentioned in Xunzi's discussion.

For Xunzi, whether a person is a gentleman or a petty man does not depend on his role – for example, a father or a son, a ruler or a minister, a teacher or a student, older or younger – but rather depends on the degree of his moral cultivation. Although a ruler (or a father, a teacher, or an older) is supposed to be in a higher moral degree, there is a possibility for the minister, the son, the student and the younger to catch up with their superior in moral cultivation. Moreover, in political life, all people should have the same right and chance to be employed by the government according to their capacity and standard of morality. The government must offer opportunity and honor people entirely in the light of their level of morality and capacity rather than the background of their birth.

An interesting question arises: How can the idea of equality be produced on the basis of a gradation system? The logic of Xunzi in answering this question is as follows: the theory that 'human nature is evil' is like the twin edges of a sword; on the one hand, it produces equality and, on the other, requires a steady and strict system of principle in order to change evil into good. For Xunzi, if human beings want to hold the highest position over all other creatures, they must possess the following four characteristics: intelligence, virtue of *yi*, ability to govern and gradation. Gradation is the easiest and the most essential way to define human nature. However, Xunzi's positive attitude toward the enterprising spirit of humans pushed him to give everybody an equal chance to demonstrate the fruit of their effective moral effort, and to declare his political ideal of giving everybody their due according to their capacity and moral standards. Nonetheless, the essential gradation requirement in social relationships hindered the full development of Xunzi's idea of equality. Thus, as Heiner Roetz has recognized, Xunzi's central idea remains important and even topical today: the idea that social inequality, on the one hand, and the equality of all in terms of the safeguarding of their living and their equal deliverance from the fight for resources, on the other, are coupled with each other.[30]

CHAPTER SIX

Ethical Issues Concerning the Father–Son Relationship

This chapter highlights pivotal aspects of the cultural differences and similarities between Xunzi's and Pauline ethics. The argument will be illustrated through examining such issues as 'human nature and the F–S relationship', 'non-consequential and consequential evaluation of the F–S relationship', and 'spiritual and secular elements in the F–S relationship'.

Human Nature and the Father–Son Relationship

With respect to the ethical F–S relationship, the most crucial differences and similarities between Xunzi and Paul can be found in their understanding of human nature, to be discussed under the following headings:

Evil human nature and the salvation of human beings

Both Xunzi and Paul hold a similar idea on the original nature of human beings; that is, human inborn nature is not good. If people follow such an inborn nature, chaos and disorder will spread within society, and there will be no happiness and salvation for humankind. Paul declares that 'I know that nothing good lives in my sinful nature' (Rom 7:18), and that 'there is no-one righteous, not even one; there is no-one who understands, no-one who seeks God' (Rom 3:10–11), which leads him to conclude naturally that all human nature is the same, 'for all have sinned and fall short of the glory of God' (Rom 3:21). Xunzi states, 'All men possess one and the same nature: when hungry, they desire food; when cold, they desire to be warm; when exhausted from toil, they desire rest; and they all desire benefit and hate harm' (4.9); therefore, 'Human nature is evil; any good in humans is acquired by conscious exertion' (23.1a).

Although Paul and Xunzi have similar ideas in their understanding of human nature, when they discuss what human nature is composed of and why it becomes human beings' inborn nature, their answers are clearly differentiated. Xunzi uses a norm of '*e*' to describe this evil human nature. '*E*' in Chinese means 'evil', 'wicked' and 'bad'; the content of '*e*' includes inclining to prejudice, being 'prone to error', being 'perverse and rebellious' and not 'upright or orderly' (23.1b). Xunzi believes that the 'inborn human nature' is associated with chaos and tendencies to disorder; as a result of inborn natural inclination, human nature is evil. Xunzi's 'evil human nature' is an 'inborn nature', which embraces what is spontaneous from Nature, 'what cannot be learned, and what requires no application to master' (23.1c); it is linked to the essential qualities that are inherent within human nature which cannot be eliminated. These essential qualities include the desire to eat when hungry, the desire for warm clothing when cold, the desire for rest when weary (23.1e), and the desires of the ears and eyes, which are fond of sounds and colours (23.1a); it also involves the feeling of love of profit, the emotions of envy and hatred (23.1a), and so on. It is not possible to eliminate all these desires, feelings and emotions. This 'inborn nature' is associated with chaos and tendencies to disorder; therefore, if people follow and indulge in those un-eliminable desires, aggressiveness and greed are certain to develop.

By contrast, the Pauline content of sin embraces 'all the godlessness and wickedness of men who suppress the truth by their wickedness' (Rom 1:18): evil, greed and depravity (Rom 1: 29), which can be illustrated as follows:

1. 'Although they knew God, they neither glorified him as God nor gave thanks to him, but they became futile and their foolish hearts were darkened' (Rom 1:21), they would rather exchange the truth of God for a lie (Rom 1:25).
2. Although they claimed to be wise, they became fools (Rom 1:22).
3. They worshipped and served created things rather than the creator (Rom 1:25) and they exchanged the glory of the immortal God for images made to look like mortal man and birds and animals and reptiles (Rom 1:23).
4. They have sinful desires within their hearts, such as sexual impurity for the degrading of their bodies with one another (Rom 1:24), impurity and debauchery (Gal 5:19).
5. They have immoral feelings and wrongdoings in their worldly life, for instance, they are full of envy, murder, strife, deceit and malice and gossip (Rom 1:29), hatred, discord, jealousy, fits of rage, selfish ambition, dissensions, factions, drunkenness, orgies (Gal 5:20–1). In short, they are 'senseless, faithless, heartless, ruthless' (Rom 1:31); they are slanderers, God-haters, insolent, arrogant and boastful, and they disobey their parents (Rom 1:30).
6. The last but not least important consequence of sin is the death of the flesh or the perishable carnal body of human beings.

The above is indicative that in Pauline theology, sin is, first of all, something evil; it is linked to humans' departure from God, and at the same time sin has a worldly immoral connotation. Because of the immoral nature of sin, Paul sometimes encourages people to overcome sin by becoming good: 'Let us not become weary in doing good, for at the proper time we will reap a harvest if we do not give up. Therefore, as we have opportunity, let us do good to all people, especially to those who belong to the family of believers' (Gal 6:9–10).

Similarly to Xunzi, Paul also declares that it is impossible to escape from sinful human nature. The reason why humans cannot escape, Paul believes, is because of the fall of Adam – the first Man creature of God, who became separated from God: 'just as sin entered the world through one man, and death through sin, and in this way death came to all men, because all sinned' (Rom 5:12). Thus Pauline understanding of how and why 'human nature is sin' is not the same as Xunzi's 'human nature is evil'. The differences between Xunzi's 'human nature is evil' and Pauline 'sinful human nature' are explained below.

First, the content of '*e*', in Xunzi's view, is more closely linked to immoral conduct within various social relationships, while the content of the Pauline notion of sin is more akin to humans' religiously unjust behaviour or wrong attitude in their dealing with God. This difference leads Xunzi's ethical doctrine to be firmly grounded on the natural F–S relationship and its familial, social and political pattern, while Pauline teaching focused on religious belief concerning the divine father and divine son and their religious, political, and familial extensional relationships.

Secondly, while Xunzi uses 'undeletable inborn desire' to explain why 'human nature is evil', Paul offers 'the departure of Man from his creator' as the reason why 'human nature is sinful'. Connecting humans' desires to their inborn nature provides Xunzi with the possibility of regarding satisfaction of proper human needs as a necessary duty of his secular F–S relationship theory, and, at the same time, offers a social ethical theory on how to restrict extreme human desires. Admitting human sinful nature as the result of humans' separating themselves from God provides a necessary reason for the Pauline idea of humans' reunion with God, and gives the Pauline divine F–S relationship a religious base or theological foundation.

From the above analysis, it can be seen that the foundation of both Xunzi's *secular* F–S relationship and the Pauline *divine* F–S relationship is based on their understanding of human nature; it is their different understanding of human nature that paved the way for their different pursuits of ethical goals.

From Xunzi's point of view, men are born with desires which, if not satisfied, cannot but lead them to seek to satisfy them. If in seeking to satisfy their desires men observe no measure and apportion things without limits, then it would be impossible for them not to contend over the means to satisfy their desires, and such contention leads to disorder. Disorder leads to poverty (19.1a). Since human nature is evil and this evil nature could not only lead to terrible outcomes, but also lead to conflicts between people and chaos and disorder in society, seeking a suitable way to limit extreme human desires in order to change such an evil nature, and to build up an orderly and harmonious human secular society, thereby becomes the most important and final aim of Xunzi's ethical theory.

By contrast, in Pauline understanding, sinful human nature is caused by the departure of the human being from God; consequently, the target of Pauline religious ethics is to offer a solution for the separated condition between God and men, which is said to lead to the most fearful result: death – the end of an individual human life. To conquer death and to earn eternal life, one has to offer oneself to God: 'Do not offer the parts of your body to sin, as instruments of wickedness, but rather offer yourselves to God, as those who have been brought from death to life' (Rom 6:13). From this point of view it can be seen that to reunite with God is the only way for humans to overcome their fear of death and to win eternal life. This idea that sin is the separation of humans from God and the fearful result of sinful human nature is death sets Pauline ethics on a spiritual rather than a worldly basis. Therefore, how to live in Christian religious society when one is alive and how to earn a spiritual eternal life afterwards becomes the main theme of Pauline ethics.

The emphasis of spiritual transcendence makes Paul devote his attention to religious spiritual life. The religious spiritual life is a new separate life, different from the real social life people are living; the secular familial, social and political life for Paul are merely tools for a religious spiritual life, but the religious spiritual life – no matter in whatever familial, social and political background – should be the same. This enables Pauline teaching loosely to adhere to or to be relatively separated from its social background.

Compared with Pauline religious ethics, Xunzi's ethical theory is about the real secular familial, social and political life. His focus on people's day-to-day life and their secular relationships adheres to social life so tightly and enters worldly social and political life so deeply that the transcendental pursuit in his thinking leaves little space for further development. The result is that his theory cannot be easily free itself from its feudal social background; it is the immediate reflection of the Chinese feudal society and closely linked to feudal familial, social and political relationships. Therefore, in order to develop Xunzi's secular ethical theory into modern Confucian ethics, it is necessary to divide its universal value from its temporary or historical value and to add some new modern value.

In order to conquer and overcome human's evil/sinful nature, both Xunzi and Paul set up an ideal and perfect personality for human beings as their moral model and guide. Xunzi identifies this person as the sage, while Paul identifies him as Jesus Christ.

Both Paul's Christ and Xunzi's sage are regarded as the incarnation of goodness and righteousness, and the embodiment of wisdom and morality/justice. However, what the perfect personality meant to Paul and to Xunzi is different. By regarding death as one of the manifestations of sin, Paul gave Jesus a godlike perfect personality with eternal life. By regarding the immoral as the essential content of '*e*', Xunzi gives sages a feature as perfect moral model and guide of humans with moral immortality.

Xunzi occasionally discusses the highest state of a perfect human being (the sage) in the light of spiritual immortality, in which the sages use their perfect human wisdom to influence the operation of the universe and thereby become assistants and triad partners with Heaven and Earth (19.6; 9.15), clearly, then, the meaning of Xunzi's 'immortality' is totally different from Pauline 'eternal life'. For Paul, eternal life means the new life after death; but for Xunzi, neither physical nor spiritual life can exist after the death of the flesh. Then, his immortality is not a new life after death but a valuable moral principle which can guide humans to a happy and orderly moral life forever.

Paul's religious purpose in pursuit of spiritual life after death made it possible to pay more attention to religious relationships; while Xunzi's negation of spiritual life after death made it possible to focus on various human secular relationships. Paul's stress on Jesus' eternal life after his crucifixion made it possible to realize Christians' individual salvation through personal faith in Jesus Christ; while Xunzi's emphasis on the immortality of sages' words in their influence on human society made it possible to pay more attention to the benefit of the whole human society rather than the profit of individuals.

Desires, human nature and the way of transcendence

Both Xunzi and Paul consider desires as evidence of evil/sinful human nature. However, how desires are related to evil or sinful nature is explained differently in Pauline understanding and in Xunzi's theory. For Paul, evil desires link us with sin; while for Xunzi, it is the extreme desires and the wrong way of pursuing desires that compose '*e*'. From Xunzi's point of view, desires cannot be divided into good or evil, but only proper or extreme, and pursuit of the proper desire is fine if it is executed in a right way, while for Pauline teaching, desires can be divided into good and evil. Evil desires connect to sin or the body: 'But sin, seizing the opportunity afforded by the commandment, produced in me every kind of covetous desires' (Rom 7:8), while good desires connect to righteousness or the spirit: 'For I have desire to do what is good' (Rom 7:18).

It is clear that desire, in Paul's mind, has two different meanings: one is associated with physical needs and the other with the will of the person. A good desire is spiritual and leads people to good, while an evil desire is carnal and leads people only to evil: 'For in my inner being I delight in God's law, but I see another law at work in the members of my body, waging war against the law of my mind and making me a prisoner of the law of sin at work within my members' (Rom 7:22–3). Therefore, the struggle of the desires or the struggle between good and evil breaks out from time to time. As Paul says, 'live by the Spirit, and you will not gratify the desires of the sinful nature. For the sinful nature desires what is contrary to the Spirit, and the Spirit what is contrary to the sinful nature, they are in conflict with each other' (Gal 5:16–17). There is therefore no compromise between the good and evil desires, and people must give up the evil desires and pursue the good.

For Xunzi, extreme desires can be limited and proper desires can be sanctified through following moral principles, which are the work and purpose of ancient sages: 'They established the regulations contained within ritual and moral principles in order to apportion things, to nurture the desires of men, and to supply the means for satisfaction' (19.1a); thus can evil human nature be conquered and replaced by the acquired nature of goodness:

> 'Inborn nature' is what it is impossible for me to create but which I can nonetheless transform. 'Accumulated effort' consists in what I do not possess but can nonetheless create. It is by fixing the mind on the goal, devising ways and means to realize it, and effectuating it through the habituation of custom that the inborn nature is transformed. (8:11)

Therefore, unlike Paul, who divided desires into two totally different types, Xunzi did not see proper desires as separate from extreme desires. There is no distinction in quality, but only a change in quantity between proper and extreme desires. Here Xunzi justifies his concentration on morality: since the process of change in human nature is only a process of improving or evolution but not a process of revolution and can be realized by gradual self moral cultivation, it does not really need a saviour who is entirely outside of human nature. In other words, evil nature can be changed and improved simply by social moral education and self moral cultivation within human nature; good human nature is merely an acquired or cultivated moral nature within which the proper desires are properly satisfied; secular morality is at work since society can proceed satisfactorily by human personal effort and social education.

For Paul, sinful nature is separation from God, and is entirely alien to goodness and righteousness; hence the process of conquering sinful nature cannot be naturally realized by improving human nature itself, but must be realized by entirely uprooting the original human nature. This work can be done neither by individuals nor by political action, but only by faith in Christ and God. In other words, sinful human nature cannot be overcome except through faith in one man – Jesus Christ and his redemption. That is why it is not secular morality but moral theology that is at work in the Pauline F–S relationship.

Wisdom and the Ethical Father–Son Relationship

If human nature is evil or sinful, there is a question that needs to be answered by both Paul and Xunzi: how can be an inborn evil or sinful nature changed into good? To answer this question, we must examine their ideas on human wisdom.

Wisdom and the father–son theory

Unlike other early Confucians, who take wisdom or intelligence as one of the elements of virtue, Xunzi regards intelligence as the basis of moral establishment. For him, since human nature is evil, humans naturally do not like to work hard and to share benefits with others. However, because humans possess wisdom (*zhi*) – the faculty of intelligence – they are able to consider 'the long view of things and think of the consequences of their actions, they are apprehensive that they may lack means adequate to perpetuate their wealth' (4.11). For long-term benefit, humans choose moral and ritual principles as their rules for living.

Though like the ancient Greek philosophers in his emphasis on the 'faculty of intelligence', Xunzi nevertheless differs from them. The Greek philosophers regarded intelligence as the defining characteristic of a human being and saw obtaining knowledge and wisdom as the aim of human life, while Xunzi regarded morality rather than wisdom as the end of the human quest. Consequently, the most important thing Xunzi uses to distinguish human beings from animals is not wisdom but morality (5.4).

Wisdom is *zhi* in Xunzi's list of concepts, which is sometimes equal to 'awareness'. For example, when Xunzi discusses the differences between plants or trees and animals, he uses *zhi* to describe the common feature of animals, including humankind, which is actually a higher standard of life but a lower standard than morality and justice. In this sense, Xunzi uses morality rather than *zhi* to distinguish humans from animals: 'Fire and Water possess vital breath but have no life. Plants and trees possess life, but lack awareness. Birds and beasts have awareness, but lack a sense of morality and justice. Humans possess vital breath, life, and awareness, and add to them a sense of morality and justice' (9.16a). However, because the *zhi* of human beings includes not only awareness but also intelligence, as a mixture of all kinds of knowing and practising, the *zhi* of human beings is much higher than that of the animals; therefore, it can be called wisdom. In fact, *zhi* has many different translations in English: knowledge, the faculty of intelligence, perception and wisdom, by which people know what is good or bad for them and others.

For Xunzi, all human capacity and knowledge are due to the faculty of intelligence or wisdom. This wisdom is the insurance of human moral character. Although human nature is not good, the faculty of intelligence or wisdom within it can change this bad human nature into a moral one. And so wisdom is always linked to human morality (7.1). On many occasions, *zhi* is used by Xunzi as knowledge and ability of governing in dealing with political affairs, which is actually the mixture of intelligence and moral wisdom. We can see this from his emphasis on the skills and knowledge of government and capacity of the ruler: a ruler must possess the capacity and knowledge to ensure his authority; the higher the capacity and the better the knowledge he obtains, the greater the authority he will achieve. When a person cultivates the model of the Hundred Kings as easily as he distinguishes white from black; when he responds appropriately to every change of circumstances as easily as counting one, two; when he acts in accordance with the requirements of the indispensable points of ritual and is at ease with them as though he were merely moving his four limbs; when he seeks the occasion to establish the meritorious in his accomplishments as though he were proclaiming the four seasons; when with equality of government he harmonizes the common people to goodness and collects together the countless masses as though they were a single individual – then a person may be called a sage (8.7). In this sense, although Xunzi regarded morality rather than wisdom as the most important thing humans had to distinguish themselves from animals, human wisdom is also an important trait for ensuring the practise and realization of morality.

Like Xunzi, Paul regards wisdom as the endowed nature of humans, which comes from humans' imitation of God. God is full of wisdom; although human beings as imitators of God cannot have the same wisdom as God and, compared to God's supreme wisdom, theirs is always inferior and inefficient, humans certainly possess some kind of wisdom. It is this wisdom from God which constitutes the power of human beings in controlling and managing other creatures; it is also the right wisdom reflected from God which enables humans to know him and receive his salvation. However, unlike Xunzi, who regards human wisdom as the basis of moral sense as well as what distinguishes human beings from animals, Paul never regards human wisdom as the source of Christian faith; nor does he count it as the most important force and power in the establishment of his divine F–S relationship. This is because, though there are similarities between God's wisdom and human wisdom, human wisdom can never be superior but is always inferior and inefficient compared to the wisdom of God's supreme fullness of power and authority: 'The foolishness of God is wiser than man's wisdom, and the weakness of God is stronger than man's strength' (1 Cor 1:25). In addition, since 'the wisdom of this world is foolishness in God's sight' (1 Cor 3:19), then human wisdom, in Pauline thought, unlike that of Xunzi, becomes neither a base nor an important element in his religious ethical thinking. More than that, from the Pauline point of view, human wisdom can neither help human beings return to unity with God nor help people to earn an immortal life; rather, it simply further deepens the separation between humans and God. Therefore, it is not the wisdom of human beings but the wisdom of God which is more important.

Paul's emphasis on the distinction between God's supreme and humans' inferior wisdom has actually posed a new issue: what is the true reason for the human fall and separation from God?

From the Christian point of view, it is certainly because of Adam and Eve's disobedience. Paul also emphasizes this aspect. However, if we explore his thought at a deeper level, we may be able to draw the following conclusion: the separation from God is not only because of human disobedience, but also of because human's inferior wisdom which made the fall of humanity inevitable. As Paul indicated, Man, although created in the image of God, does not possess the same full and perfect wisdom as God. This means that God did not give Man the same full wisdom as himself when he created him; otherwise, the wisdom of Man would be as full as that of God. Because God did not give Man exactly the same wisdom as himself, humans' inefficient wisdom cannot offer the means fully to understand God; thus, misunderstanding the will of God and the wrongdoing of human beings are inevitable; in other words, the fall of Man is inevitable. This is decided not by Man's free will, but by God's creation. If the fall of Man is inevitable, the separation between God and Man will be also inevitable, and the sinfulness of human nature is certain.

It is true that Pauline teaching never presented his argument in this way, so some scholars may argue that this is not the view of Paul. Since Pauline teaching emphasized the distinction between God and Man – the full wisdom of God and lesser wisdom of Man, the power of God and the fear of Man, the supreme perfection of God and inferiority of Man – it is reasonable to draw such a conclusion from his concept of evil even if he did not explicitly attribute to the inevitability of Man's fall to it. This is because the notion of evil in Pauline understanding was not merely related to immoral behavior but also to imperfection and failure.

Although the fall of Man is inevitable, the salvation of Man in a sense of returning and union with God is still possible: Man's image of God's wisdom provides the possibility for human beings to return to and have union with him.

What then is the wisdom of God? God's wisdom is 'a wisdom that has been hidden and that God destined for our glory before time began' (1 Cor 2:7). More precisely, it is Jesus Christ and the Spirit of God: 'Christ, in whom are hidden all the treasures of wisdom and knowledge' (Col 2:3). God's wisdom cannot be revealed except by the Spirit: 'no-one knows the thought of God except the Spirit of God' (1 Cor 2:11); 'The Spirit searches all things, even the deep things of God' (1 Cor 2:10). Consequently, 'We have not received the spirit of the world but the Spirit who is from God, that we may understand what God has freely given us' (1 Cor 2:12). Because Christ is 'the power of God and the wisdom of God' (1 Cor 1:24), the greatest and most important wisdom Christian believers should possess is to know Jesus Christ and believe in God and Jesus.

From the above analysis it can be seen that, although both Xunzi and Paul held that human nature was evil, and both acknowledged that wisdom was part of human nature, their conclusions are totally different from each other. Xunzi's human wisdom becomes the base of his moral theory, while for Paul divine wisdom becomes the most important part of his Christian ethical thought. It is the emphasis on human wisdom that separates Xunzi's secular F–S relationship from Paul's divine one; while it is the emphasis on God's wisdom that leads Pauline ethics to be based on faith rather than morality. This can be seen from their different theories on the wisdom of humans' spiritual fathers: sage-kings and Abraham.

In Romans 4, Paul describes how Abraham became the father of all later believers by being justified by his faith in God. From Paul's point of view, it was by his witness to the divine law rather than anything else that Abraham became the father of the Jews, who are circumcised as well as the father of Gentiles, who are uncircumcised. Abraham's faithfulness may be illustrated on two points: Abraham was faithful in believing the promise that God would make him the father of many nations; and he believed in a God who gives life to the dead. David M. Hay and E. Elizabeth Johnson state this point explicitly: 'With Gen 17:15–21 and 18:9–15 in view, Paul can talk of Abraham displaying the strong faith that looked at the apparent impossibilities of his situation and yet still trusted completely in God to bring life (Isaac) out of death (his own body as good as dead and the deadness of Sarah's womb' (cf. 4:19).[1]

From Paul's interpretation of the narrative of Abraham, three arguments can be drawn out: (1) Abraham is an individual person who had strong faith and faithful hope in God's power of raising life from death; (2) through his wisdom of having faith he became the forefather of many nations; and (3) he is not only the father of Jews and Jewish Christians, but also the father of Gentiles and Gentile Christians.

Compared with the patriarchal character of Abraham's fatherhood, Xunzi's fatherhood of ancient sage-kings is a totally different vision. In his view, the ancient sage-kings included not only Yao, Shun and Yu, but also anyone who devised social principles and organized society for human beings. These ancient sage-kings earned their kingly positions through their moral cultivation and fullness of human wisdom. This understanding of the sage-kings enabled sagehood to have the following characteristics: (a) ancient sage-kings were not attached to a single person, but to a group of people. (b) The sages' fatherhood was neither because of their faith in an ultimate power beyond human beings and other creatures, nor because they belonged to divine beings, but because of their perfect personalities in both morality and wisdom, as well as their contribution to managing myriad things and organizing human society. (c) Although the sages are the fathers of all people in general, the term 'people', in Xunzi's mind, does not mean people of different races, but people who possess different endowments in both ability and wisdom, and people in different social positions.

It is clear that, first of all, Paul's fatherhood of Abraham moves from individual faith to Christian group belief, but Xunzi's fatherhood of sage-kings is derived from a group of people who possessed supreme human wisdom and the highest ability to form human society as a whole. The implication is that the individual is emphasized in Pauline tradition, but not in Xunzi's. The influence of sages on human society is profound. Nonetheless, this influence is worked out not only through their individual personality, but also through their discovery of the Way of Heaven and Earth; the moral principles used to guide human society are invented and achieved not by a particular individual but by a group of individuals. Neither individuals with normal wisdom and morality, nor a particular individual with excellent wisdom and morality, can on their own influence the whole of human collectivity. This leads Xunzi to lay extreme emphasis on the power of society rather than the power of an individual and to put enormous stress on social moral education and moral principles (*li* and *yi*) that are used to guide individual moral cultivation and social moral education. In this sense, what A. T. Nuyen concludes about the character of Confucian understanding of the relationship between society and individual is perhaps also true of Xunzi: rights, duties and responsibilities are not defined in terms of the individual but in terms of the relationship between the individual and his or her community.[2]

The more interesting point on discussion of wisdom is that Paul lays his emphasis on God's power and wisdom in raising a life from death through the power of faith, while Xunzi puts his special emphasis on the power and wisdom of learning and moral cultivation.

Through the emphasis of the power of faith, the importance of Jesus Christ is strengthened. Jesus Christ is humans' saviour, and only through faith in him can they receive God's glory and wisdom and gain an eternal life after death. Through the emphasis of the wisdom of learning, Xunzi puts more stress on the sage and the teacher. For him, learning is a matter of crucial importance: it is not only important for being a real man: 'Those who undertake learning become men; those who neglect it become as wild beasts' (1.8); it is also important for becoming a perfect man with fullness of knowledge and capacity. Only through learning and involving conscious effort can the original evil nature of man be overcome and the status of sage attained (1.8).

However, the aim of learning is to become a scholar, even a sage, and the content of learning is rituals and moral principles, which are inventions of the ancient sage. Unlike Jesus Christ, who is the Son and the incarnation of God, the sage, for Xunzi, is nothing more than the fullness of knowledge and capacity of human beings; hence the achievement of a sage can be attained through the personal accumulation of goodness: 'If you accumulate enough good to make whole your inner power, a divine clarity of intelligence will be naturally acquired and sage-like mind will be fully realized' (1.6). Nevertheless, learning cannot be completed without the help of teachers. The content of learning – the principles of humanity and justice which were invented by the ancient sage-kings – are difficult to understand without the interpretation of teachers. The duties of a teacher are (a) to offer the correct knowledge of the sage, (b) to resolve problems in the process of students' learning and to answer their questions, and (c) to provide a moral model for students: 'The teacher is one who indicates the proper standard of deportment and who values what is at peace with him' (2.11). Therefore, the teacher is important in offering the right knowledge of the ancient sage: 'If there is no teacher, people will not know which ritual is correct' (2.11); he is also important in rectifying individual students' wrongdoing as well as rectifying the wrong ritual: 'It is through ritual that the individual is rectified. It is by means of a teacher that ritual is rectified.' Moreover, the teacher is important in that he is the moral model for his students. In this sense, Xunzi concludes, 'In learning, no method is of more advantage than to be near a man of learning' (1.10); A 'sage is a person whose emotion finds peace in ritual and his knowledge is like that of his teacher' (2.11). Thus, the teacher is not only important in one's process of learning, but also important in one's moral cultivation: 'In summary, of all the methods of controlling the vital breath and nourishing the mind, none is more direct than proceeding according to ritual principles, none more essential than obtaining a good teacher' (2.4). In relation to the importance of the teacher, Xunzi advocates a proposal of esteeming the teacher: 'Thus, the gentleman esteems his teacher' (2.1).

The chief form of respect for the teacher in Xunzi is to follow one's teacher absolutely: 'When what your teacher says you say also, then your knowledge will be like that of your teacher' (2.11). By his objection to opposing one's teacher, Xunzi gives the teacher an absolute authority. Thus, through emphasis of the importance of learning, the absolute power and authority of the ancient sage-kings are transformed to the teacher. Paul's approach is different from Xunzi's transformation of power from the sage to the teacher. Although he occasionally discusses the importance of apostle and prophet and teacher, he never let the power of Jesus Christ be transfered to them. For him, no one except Jesus Christ can have the power and wisdom of God.

It is clear that Xunzi's secular ethical theory is developed along the following route: human nature is evil; however, humans have the wisdom to recognize their evil nature and to know what is good for their long-term benefit. Through the faculty of *zhi*, humans know the importance of moral principles and rituals, and the necessity of social moral education and the personal moral cultivation of individuals. The importance of moral principle and ritual leads to the importance of the sage (inventor of moral principle and rituals), and the importance of moral cultivation leads to the authority of the teacher. The route of Xunzi's theoretical development is different from that of Paul. Pauline ethical theory is developed along the following lines: human nature is sinful, and humans have neither the wisdom nor moral force to improve and thus change it. Only by faith in God through Jesus Christ can sinful nature be conquered and only when it has been conquered can humans earn eternal life.

These two different routes further strengthen the difference between Pauline and Xunzi's ethics. From his emphasis on the important role of morality in changing human evil nature and the importance of sage and teacher in moral cultivation and education, he confirms the importance of sage (inventor of moral principle and rituals) and teacher (the interpreter of the sage's invention) in social status, and thereby the hierarchical characteristic of Xunzi's secular F–S relationship between sage and common people, between teacher and students and *et al.* is further strengthened. From his emphasis on faith, Paul generated the importance of both the objective of religion (God) and the approach to this religious objective (Jesus Christ): because the Spirit of God and Jesus Christ can help us in our weakness (Rom 8:26) and faith in God must be realized through faith in Jesus Christ (Rom 3:22); therefore, both God and Jesus Christ are important for Christian believers. However, unlike sage and teacher, both God and Jesus Christ belong to Heaven rather than Earth; this hierarchy between God/Jesus and humans in the meantime evokes an equality between all humans in the secular society before God and Jesus Christ: there is no favourite before God; there is no difference between people in the eyes of God.

Faith/morality and Pauline and Xunzi's understandings of equality and hierarchy

Paul distinguishes between people on the ground of faith and this leads to a possibility of equality between people of different gender, age and social status. Gerd Theissen states: faith in the exalted Lord was an offer of advancement for everyone, whatever their existing social status. In Christ there was 'neither Jew nor Greek, neither slave nor free, neither male nor female' (Gal 3:28).[3] In contrast with Paul, Xunzi distinguished between people for the validation of morality and this resulted in the possible inequality of people of different gender, age and social status.

Nonetheless, as noted previously, there is a stream of equality in Xunzi's river of hierarchy and patriarchy; similarly, there is also a voice of hierarchy and patriarchy within Pauline equality. Therefore, although equality is the mainstream of Pauline religious ethics, while hierarchy and patriarchy are the mainstream of Xunzi's secular ethics, it is the combination of equality and inequality (hierarchy as well as patriarchy) rather than any single characteristic that composes the essential feature of both Xunzi's and Pauline F–S relationship.

Carolyn Osiek and David L. Balch have clearly noted the patriarchal and hierarchic characteristic of Pauline moral teaching. After examining some cases, they conclude that instead of being dynamic and dramatic, deutero-Pauline Christology becomes temporal and more intensely hierarchical, as do the ethics, which are no longer concerned with slaves' possible manumission, but focus on their suitably submissive role in the hierarchy of the (Roman) cosmos.[4] Indeed, the patriarchal and hierarchical characteristics of Pauline doctrine permeate every relationship, even spiritual and divine relationships. For example, Paul believes that Jesus 'is the image of the invisible God' and 'all things were created by him and for him. He is before all things, and in him all things hold together. And he is the head of the body, the church; he is the beginning and the firstborn from among the dead, so that in everything he might have the supremacy' (Col 1:15–18); this actually made the Jesus–Christian relationship a characteristic of hierarchy. Paul's description of the hierarchical order within the church is even more clearly stated: Jesus Christ is the head and cornerstone (Eph 2:20), all apostles are appointed first, prophets are second, teachers third, then workers of miracles, also those having gifts of healing, those able to help others, those with gifts of administration, and those speaking in different kinds of tongues (1 Cor 12:28). However, this hierarchical and patriarchal characteristic of Pauline doctrine mainly functions in the temporal or the worldly sphere rather than in the religious or spiritual sphere. From the standpoint of Pauline religious ethics, there is more of an echo of equality: albeit in many places Paul emphasized the inferiority of woman in the secular world, he nevertheless acknowledges the equality between man and woman in front of God; woman is not independent of man, nor man independent of woman; for woman came from man, so also is man born of woman. But everything comes from God (1 Cor 11:11–12). Although he stresses the obedience of children and slaves, he never forgets the rights God gave to children and slaves: 'Fathers, do not exasperate your children; instead, bring them up in the training and instruction of the Lord' (Eph 6:4); 'Masters, provide your slaves with what is right and fair, because you know that you also have a Master in heaven' (Col 4:1). The equal relationship among church members before God and through faith in Jesus Christ can be seen clearly from the following aspects:

First, although people can be different in terms of their innate qualities, jobs and roles, they are equal before God: 'There are different kinds of gifts, but the same Spirit. There are different kinds of service, but the same Lord. There are different kinds of working, but the same God works all of them in all men' (1 Cor 12:4–6); 'So neither he who plants nor he who waters is anything, but only God, who makes things grow' (1 Cor 3:7).

Secondly, as Christ's church is one body and everybody within it is a part of the whole body, there is no distinction between the superior and the inferior: 'For we were all baptized by one Spirit into one body – whether Jews or Greeks, slave or free– and we were all given the one Spirit to drink' (1 Cor 12:12). Although 'we have different gifts, according to the grace given us' (Rom 12:6), since everybody is one part of the body of Christ (1 Cor 12:27), 'there should be no division in the body, but that its parts should have equal concern for each other' (1 Cor 12:25). Therefore, people in the church can make different contributions according to their different gifts; for instance, if a man's gift is prophesying, let him use it in proportion to his faith. If it is serving, let him serve; if it is teaching, let him teach; if it is encouraging, let him encourage; if it is contributing to the needs of others, let him give generously; if it is leadership, let him govern diligently; if it is showing mercy, let him do it cheerfully (Rom 12:6–8). But they are no different before God.

Finally, because all Christians are sons of God through faith in Christ Jesus, and they are all one in Christ Jesus, then they are Abraham's seed and heirs according to the promise (Gal 3:26–9). Therefore, none of them live and die to themselves alone: 'If we live, we live to the Lord; and if we die, we die to the Lord. So, whether we live or die, we belong to the Lord' (Rom 14:7–8); they will be given an account of themselves to God (Rom 14:12). In the meantime, since every Christian is a child of God, and God had sent the Spirit of his Son into everybody's heart, every individual Christian can link to God personally and can contact God directly.

In short, although Pauline ethical theory accepts and even reinforces the basic structures of the patriarchal household, because Paul divides the world into two – the kingdom of God and the secular world, by putting equality into practice in the kingdom of God and hierarchy in the secular world, two contrary characteristics – equality and hierarchy can be separately practised in two different worlds without any conflict. Thus, within a patriarchal structure, it brings to bear Christian motivations of love and service;[5] a religious sense of equality was magically mixed together with the secular sense of hierarchy.

This Pauline understanding of equality between people is not perceivable in Xunzi's Confucian tradition, where the world is a unitary one and cannot be divided into two. The essential characteristic of the unitary world is hierarchical order or distinction; therefore the hierarchical order or distinction is absolute in Xunzi's opinion – there is no room left for an independent concept of equality standing side by side with hierarchy as in Pauline theory. However, Xunzi still talks about equality, which encompasses: (a) equality of human nature: Everybody desires a good life and wants to avoid a hard life. In this respect, there is no difference between people, neither between a father and his son, nor between a ruler and his subjects, neither between a teacher and his student, nor between a husband and his wife. (b) Equality before morality. Unlike Confucius, who divided people into three different groups – people with high intelligence, with middle intelligence, and the stupid – Xunzi declares that all human beings possess the same faculty of intelligence, which is inherited from Nature. In this sense, the ancient sage and the common people are the same. The difference between the sage and the common people is that the sages used their intelligence to observe the Way of Heaven and Earth consciously in order to bring benefit to the people and cultivate their morality fully; but the common people do not practise their intelligence. Therefore, everybody has the ability to pursue morality and everybody can take sagehood as their moral ideal or task of moral cultivation: since it is possible for every man to understand the substance of humanness, morality, the model of law, and rectitude and the ability to master their instruments (23.5a), therefore, every man can become a sage. (c) Equal opportunity employed by the government according to one's moral level. Xunzi insists that whether people are the descendants of kings and dukes or knights and grand officers, if they are incapable of devotedly observing the requirements of ritual and moral principles, they should be relegated to the position of commoners. Although people may be the descendants of commoners, if they accumulate culture and study and rectify their character and conduct, and if they are capable of devotedly observing the requirements of ritual principles and justice, they should be promoted to the ranks of prime minister, knight, or grand officer (9.1).

It is obvious that Xunzi pays much attention to potential equality among people in his doctrine. Nonetheless, because his idea of equality is merely linked to morality, and Xunzi's morality is established on the hierarchical order, his equality is actually based on inequality.

In summary, although the entire picture of Pauline ethics is hierarchical and patri-archal, he still leaves room for the possibility of moral equality; although Xunzi takes order and distinction as the basis of secular society, he allowed his ethics to embrace the pursuit of equal moral transcendence. In a similar way, although the 'new humanity' has transformed the entire equal relationship between Jews and Gentiles, Paul does not allow it to challenge the hierarchical and patriarchal structure of the believers' social, sexual and political relationships.[6] Although Paul had enhanced evolutional ideas and general values in the religious world, he could meanwhile let his ethics embrace hier-archy and patriarchy in the secular world by separating the religious world from the secular one.

Non-consequential and Consequential Evaluation of the Father–Son Relationship

The evaluation of the F–S relationship made by Xunzi and Paul is both consequential and non-consequential. In general, the Pauline evaluation leans more towards the non-consequential, while Xunzi's is more consequential. However, there are some consequential elements within the Pauline F–S relationship and some non-consequen-tial elements within that of Xunzi.

According to the *Dictionary of Western Philosophy, English–Chinese*, it is a general practice to divide moral theory into consequentialism and non-consequentialism. Consequentialism is also called teleological ethics and non-consequentialism non-tele-ological ethics. Consequentialism holds that the value of an action is determined entirely by its consequences and thus proposes that ethical life should be forward looking, that is, it should be concerned with maximizing the good and minimizing the bad consequences of actions.[7] And on the other hand, non-consequential ethics holds that the value of an action derives simply from intrinsic nature and thus proposes that ethical value should be primarily concerned with moral motive or moral intention.

Consequential evaluation as an essential characteristic of Xunzi's F–S relationship

Xunzi's consequential evaluation of the F–S relationship is closely related to his 'return or repay' theory. As some scholars have noted, the Chinese believe that reciprocity of actions – favour/reward between persons, or between humans and supernatural beings – should be as predictable as a cause–effect relationship: therefore, when a Chinese person acts, he normally anticipates a response or return.[8] As part of the Confucian tradition, Xunzi bases his understanding of the F–S relationship on consequential reasoning.

Consequentialism, in fact, is the foundation of Xunzi's establishment of the moral relationship between father and son. For the sake of continuation of his life after death, a father eagerly longs for his son's birth; for his own fame and reputation, a father instructs his son and gives him various education and moral training; and also in order to ensure that he will be loved during his old age and remembered after his lifetime, a father gives generous and unselfish love and kindness to his son. All these conditions indicate that the father loves his son partly for self-benefit. In the same way, in return for his parents' three years of fostering, a son is expected to give his father three years' mourning after the father's passing away; for his parents' rearing in his youth, a son should take care of his parents in their old age; to repay his parents' education and training, the son should respect his parents and obey them; moreover, for the sake of his own fame and reputation, he must give his parents filial love.

Such a reciprocal love based on consequential considerations can be seen more clearly in Xunzi's discussion of the necessity of 'three years' mourning' for the ruler of the state. His answer to the question 'why was the practice of mourning into the third year chosen for one's lord' is that the lord is the ruler of order and management, the source of good form and rational order, and the ideal of emotion and appearance. Moreover, he is the mother and father of his people (19.10). Why should the ruler of the state be treated as the father and mother of his people? This is because the ruler can bring more benefit to his people than a parent: although the father can beget the child, he cannot suckle it. The mother can suckle the child but is unable to instruct and correct it. The lord is not only able to feed his people, but is adept at teaching and correcting them. Therefore, it is indeed proper that all men should join together in exalting him above all others (19.10).

This consequential character of Xunzi's theory can also be seen from the social relationships between the old and the young, between the teacher and the student, and between friends. For example, the reason why the gentleman esteems his teacher and is intimate with his friend are because the teacher can correct one's wrongdoing and a friend can encourage one's doing good. Xunzi says: 'As of old, those who consider me to be in the wrong and are correct in doing so are my teachers; those who consider me to be in the right and correct are my friend[s]' (2.1). This means that whether or not one should regard an old person as one's teacher depends on whether this person has in fact corrected one's wrong behaviour. If he did not correct the youngster's wrongdoings, he is not worthy to be respected as a teacher even though he is old. In the same way, whether or not one should treat a person as a friend depends on his action of correction; if he cannot correct one's incorrect behaviour, he should not be treated as a one's real friend.

This consequential principle is also employed in the spiritual relationships between the ancient sage-kings and Confucian followers, and between the gentleman and the people. Xunzi says that the reason why Confucian followers (*ru*) must model themseves after the ancient kings and why the people must esteem the gentleman is because 'the ways of the ancient kings' are 'the guiding principles of humanity and justice, and the pattern of life' (4.11). If there were no gentleman, Heaven and Earth would lack any principle of order and ritual, and moral principles would have no guidelines: 'Above there would be no proper recognition of lord and leader; below there would be no proper relationship between father and son' (9.15). Obviously, it is the benefits that the ancient sage-kings brought to the people that gave them their authority and power over people, and the subsequent esteem and respect from the people.

For Xunzi, the consequences with regard to dealing with people in various relationships are common to everybody; accordingly, the gentleman is trustworthy and so desires other men's trust: he is loyal and so wants other men's affection; and he cultivates rectitude and makes orderly his management of situations and so desires that others should think well of him (4.8). However, there are still some non-consequential elements within this consequential theory. Xunzi clearly recognizes that returning goodness with goodness is not good enough; in order to avoid a bad result, people must first behave well without any consequential consideration. Thus, from a consequential motive a non-consequential love arises.

Xunzi uses the ruler–ruled relationship to illustrate his non-consequential argument: 'If the lord of men desires to be secure, no policy is as good as even-handed government and love of the people' (9.4). This non-consequential consideration is demonstrated more clearly in his discussion of the mutual requirement of various ethical relationships. Xunzi argues that ritual and moral principles are unitary principles applicable to different relationships, although it is given a different name in different relationships:

> To be able to employ ritual and moral principles in serving one's parents is called 'filial piety'. To be able to use them in serving one's elder brother is called 'brotherly affection'. To be able to use them in one's superior is called 'obedience'. To be able to use them in commanding one's subordinates is called 'being lordly'. (9.15)

This unitary principle can make people in different ranks act in accordance with the same spiritual requirement employed by particular principles provided for their special social roles: 'the lord acting as lord, the minister as minister, the father as father, son as son, the older brother as older brother, the younger brother as younger brother' (9.15). This spiritual requirement for different people is that everybody must fulfill their responsibilities unconditionally (9.17).

The most important demonstration of his non-consequential evaluation can be seen in his discussion of the selfless motive of the ancient sage in the process of his establishing the moral principles and rituals for humans: it is not for the sake of satisfying himself, but for the sake of bringing humans out of natural conflict and guiding them to live in an orderly and peaceful condition, that the ancient king 'acted to control them with regulations, ritual and moral principles, in order thereby to divide society into classes, creating therewith differences in age and youth, and the division of the wise from the stupid, the able from the incapable' (4.12).

Two things are clear: (1) the aim of the ancient sage in establishing rituals, moral principles and the distinction of people from each other is not for building up their own authority and power but for establishing a peaceful and harmonious human society; (2) the hierarchical distribution of moral duties and rights for people in different ranks is not for the oppression of some people by others, but for satisfying all the proper desires of all people. Therefore, to practise moral principles according to the role one is playing is important; to fulfill these moral duties and responsibilities completely and non-consequentially is more important. This non-consequential description of the sage is common in early Confucianism. As Julia Ching recognized: 'A sage is not only one with Heaven and Earth and all things, he is especially a man *for others*. He is the one who is first to worry about the world's worries, and last to enjoy its pleasure.'[9]

Pauline non-consequential-based ethical father–son relationship

Paul's religious F–S relationship is mainly non-consequential. The non-consequential value of Pauline religious ethics can be seen in the following ways. First, the love of the divine father is unconditional. God's love is fully self-giving, which depends upon neither the good deeds nor the beautiful souls of people:

> As he says in Hosea: I will call them 'my people' who are not my people; and I will call her 'my loved one' who is not my loved one, and it will happen that in the very place where it was said to them, 'you are not my people', they will be called 'sons of the living God'. (Rom 9:25–6)

As sunshine is given to thistles and thorns as well as to grass, God's love is given to sinners as well as those who do good deeds: 'for all have sinned and fall short of the glory of God, and are justified freely by this grace through the redemption that came by Christ Jesus' (Rom 3:23). Although people were sinful in terms of being endowed with original sin, which was spread from Adam, their first ancestor, and although by their sinful nature they ignored God's grace and power, rebelled against God the divine Father's will and thereby fell down into hell, God did not hate them and leave them alone in a miserable condition, but forgave them and carried on giving them a full heart of love: 'Just as you who were at one time disobedient to God have now received mercy as a result of their disobedience, so they too have now become disobedient in order that they too may now receive mercy as a result of God's mercy to you' (Rom 11:30). To save them, God even gave his only beloved Son as a sacrifice by death on a cross: 'Very rarely will anyone die for a righteous man, though for a good man someone might dare to die. But God demonstrates his love for us in this: while we were still sinners, Christ died for us' (Rom 5:7–8).

Secondly, the love of Jesus Christ to both God and sinful people is also non-consequential. To fulfill God's will and achieve people's salvation he was ready and willing to suffer earthly misery in a human form, and willingly and gladly to contribute his physical human life at a relatively young age: 'When we were still powerless, Christ died for the ungodly' (Rom 5:6); 'while we were still sinners, Christ died for us' (Rom 5:8).

Lastly, the response to God's self-giving love should be also unconditional: 'whatever other commandments there may be, they are summed up in this one rule: "Love your neighbour as yourself"' (Rom 13:9). 'Love your neighbour' includes three levels. First of all, love God and Jesus Christ and 'Never be lacking in zeal, but keep your spiritual fervour, serving the Lord' (Rom 12:11): 'in the view of God's mercy, to offer your bodies as living sacrifices, holy and pleasing to God – this is your spiritual act of worship' (Rom 12:1); show your sincere love of God since 'neither death nor life, neither angels nor demons, neither the present nor future, nor any powers, neither height nor depth, nor anything else in all creation, will be able to separate us from the love of God that is in Christ Jesus our Lord' (Rom 8:38–9). Secondly, 'Be devoted to one another in brotherly love. Honour one another above yourself' (Rom 12:11); 'Share with God's people who are in need. Practise hospitality' (Rom 12:13); and 'Be careful to do what is right in the eyes of everybody. If it is possible, as far as it depends on you, live at peace with everyone' (Rom 12:17–18). And finally, love your enemy. Although the divine Father will reward the good and punish the evil according to everybody's due on the final judgment day, as a human individual, nobody has any right to exercise judgment against others: 'Bless those who persecute you; bless and do not curse. Rejoice with those who rejoice; mourn those who mourn' (Rom 12:17–18). 'Do not repay anyone evil for evil' (Rom 12:17). 'Do not take revenge' (Rom 12:19), but 'On the contrary: if your enemy is hungry, feed him; if he is thirsty, give him something to drink' (Rom 12:20). Here, although the natural F–S relationship and its social political analogues are not particularly discussed in terms of non-consequentiality or a non-teleological sense, as the general response of people to God's self-giving love, a non-consequential attitude should be tenable for them.

All of this tells us that from the Pauline point of view, the only task for a pure Christian is to contribute love but not to expect any immediate repayment. Therefore, hoping and praying for God's blessing is not same as grounding one's belief on the basis of secular benefit.[10] On the contrary, belief in God not only usually generates secular benefit, but it may even bring about some secular political persecution. Thus, it can be concluded that the main characteristic of Christian love is non-consequential love.

Nonetheless, there are still some consequentialist features in the Pauline religious ethics. First, although *agape* is a self-giving and unconditional love, (a) there is still God's wrath and punishment for unbelievers: 'The wrath of God is being revealed from heaven against all the godlessness and wickedness of men who suppress the truth by their wickedness (Rom 1:18). 'For although they knew God, they neither glorified him as God nor gave thanks to him' (Rom. 1:21); 'Therefore God gave them over in the sinful desires of their hearts to sexual impurity for the degrading of their bodies with one another' (Rom 1:24); 'God gave them over to shameful lusts' (Rom 1:26). 'Since they did not think worthwhile to return the knowledge of God, he gave them over to a depraved mind, to do what ought not to be done' (Rom 1:28). (b) There is also God's judgment according to what people have done. To those who persist in doing good and seeking glory, honour and immortality, he will give eternal life. But for those who are self-seeking and reject the truth and follow evil, there will be wrath and anger. There will be trouble and distress for every human being who does evil (Rom 2:6–9). (c) God's forgiveness is not absolutely unconditional but is on the condition that Jesus Christ sacrificed his earthly life. Although Jesus himself was perfect, he had to receive punishment for releasing the sins that the people committed: 'God presented him as a sacrifice of atonement, through faith in his blood. He did this to demonstrate his justice, because in his forbearance he had left the sins committed beforehand unpunished' (Rom 3:25).

Secondly, although Jesus' descent and sacrifice were readily and willingly undertaken, there was also hope of ascending to the right hand of God and being king of the kings. Jesus Christ knew that 'in all things God works for the good of those who love him, who have been called according to his purpose' (Rom 8:28) and he knew that he was predestined to be a sin offering (Rom 8:3); he also knew that he would be raised from dead after his crucifixion and be at the right hand of God (Rom 8:34). This situation can be confirmed from what Jesus taught the people:

Blessed are the poor in spirit, for theirs is the kingdom of heaven.
Blessed are those who mourn, for they will be comforted.
Blessed are the meek, for they will inherit the earth.
Blessed are those who hunger and thirst for righteousness, for they will be filled.
Blessed are merciful, for they will be shown mercy.
Blessed are the pure in heart, for they will see God.
Blessed are the peacemakers, for they will be called sons of God.
Blessed are those who are persecuted because of righteousness, for theirs is the kingdom of heaven. (Matt 5:3–10)

Thirdly, the response of people to *agape* should be unconditional and without any expectation of secular benefit: 'share with God's people who are in need. Practise hospitality'; 'Bless those who persecute you; bless and not curse' (Rom 12:14); 'Do not repay anyone evil for evil' (Rom 12:17). The fear of God's wrath and punishment are still a precondition of people's faith: 'But they were broken off because of unbelief, and you stand by faith' (Rom 11:20). Moreover, hope of the reward of an eternal life and entering the kingdom of God is still people's purpose and the aim of their faith.

Finally, faith in Jesus Christ is also based on a benefit motivation: 'Anyone who trusts in him will never be put to shame' (Rom 10:11); if one was justified by his blood, one will be saved from God's wrath through him (Rom 5:9) and have now received reconciliation (Rom 5:11). More important, if we die with Christ, we believe that we will also live with him (Rom 6:8); people can have eternal life through faith in Jesus Christ: 'But if Christ is in you, your body is dead because of sin, yet your spirit is alive because of righteousness. And if the Spirit of him who raised Jesus from the dead is living in you, he who raised Christ from the dead will also give life to your mortal bodies through his Spirit, who lives in you' (Rom 8:9–11). Therefore, although from a secular standpoint the Pauline divine F–S relationship is built on a non-consequential base, in fact its consequential value is still emphasized and expected: if you want to have eternal life you have to believe in Jesus Christ; if you want to be set free from sin you have to become a slave of God (Rom 6:22–3). The consequential character of the Pauline divine F–S relationship can be also seen from Paul's discussion of secular relationships, for example, slave and master. Andrew T. Lincoln and A. J. M. Wedderburn have recognized this character clearly:

> In line with the expectations of the traditional codes, they (slaves) are enjoined to obey their masters and to serve with the proper attitudes of fear of their master's authority, integrity, wholeheartedness, and enthusiasm. Such attitudes, however, are to flow from their ultimate allegiance to Christ and they are reminded that they will be recompensed for their good service by the master at the final judgment. This is followed by a striking note of reciprocity in the call to masters to do the same to slaves as slaves are to do them. Their attitudes and actions are to be in the light of the relationship to the heavenly master which they have in common with their slaves. Specially, this should mean abandoning all attempts to manip-ulate, humiliate or frighten by threat. The mutual submission . . . is effectively reinforced by the reminder that the heavenly Master makes no partial judgments on the basis of social distinctions.[11]

Thus, the consequential element exists not only in the Pauline divine spiritual world, but also in his social secular world.

Combination of consequential and non-consequential evaluation in both Xunzi's and Pauline father–son relationship

From the above two sections' discussion, it can be seen that although there are essen-tial differences between Pauline religious and Xunzi secular ethical F–S theories, there are nevertheless some similarities: (a) both Xunzi and Paul reveal consequential as well as non-consequential moral evaluation on the ethical F–S relationship: while Xunzi's theory emphasizes the consequential value, it never ignores the value of the non-conse-quential. Meanwhile, although the Pauline Christian idea devotes more attention to non-consequential elements, it also leaves room for consequential evaluation. (2) The characteristics of coexistence of consequential and non-consequential moral evaluations of both Xunzi and Paul can be seen through their understanding of love, that is, *agape* for Paul and *ren* for Xunzi.

Just as *agape* and *ren* are respectively the heart and soul of both Christianity and Confucianism,[12] love is the same important theme in both Xunzi and Paul. Thus, an examination of them can therefore give us a general idea of how and why Xunzi's conse-quential as well as non-consequential values are different from Pauline non-consequential and consequential values.

The Xunzi's norm of *ren*, as it was used in earlier Confucianism, has three basic meanings: humanity, virtue and love. Because *ren* as love is more fundamental than *ren* as humanity and virtue, love is the heart of the heart and the soul of the soul.[13] Although Xunzi insists human nature is evil, he takes *ren* as the heart of his doctrine and, like Confucius, accepts love as the basis of the other two elements of *ren*, and by extension takes love as the basis of his F–S relationship.

It is commonly believed that 'within Christianity love has been explored and interpreted in a depth that goes beyond anything we find in other religions or in secular philosophies';[14] in the same way, love is the main theme and centre of Pauline teaching. In Pauline interpretation, God is the God of love, because he is full of self-giving love; Jesus Christ is an embodiment of love: on the one hand, in loving God, he was obedient to God's will in being put to death; on the other hand, in loving people, he contributed his life. All Christian believers are the agents of love; among them, 'to love God and Jesus' is the reply to God's self-giving love, 'to love one's parents' is the imitation of the loving God, 'to love one's neighbours' as one loves one's self is the direct response to God's self-giving love and to 'love one's enemies' is the extension of God's self-giving love.

However, love in Xunzi's secular ethical thinking is different from that in Pauline religious ethical thinking: *agape* in Pauline teaching is a universal love, while *ren* in Xunzi's theory is a graded love; and this different characteristic of *agape* and *ren* determines the chief characteristic of their consequential and non-consequential evaluation. For Xunzi, since *ren* is a graded love, it is an unequal love. Of the different sorts of love, the love between children and parents is the deepest and most primary: in emotion, the love for one's parents or children is the strongest; the love for one's other family members is less strong; the love for more distant relatives is less than the love for one's close family members; the love for one's neighbours is again less than the love for relatives; and finally the love for strangers is the least of all. It is clear that, for Xunzi, whether love is stronger or less strong totally depends on one's relation with the loved: the closer the relationship with the loved one, the deeper the feeling of love that will be given; this unequal graded love derives from reciprocal and consequential love.

However, since there is some selfless feeling and self-giving love within the natural F–S relationship, there is a potential to be developed out of a selfless and non-consequential love. The ancient sage-kings enlarged and extended this potential non-consequential love fully and ultimately, so that the sage–people relationship is an enlarged and extended natural F–S relationship with fully developed non-consequential love; thus, the consequential love between the natural father and his son was finally and entirely changed into unselfish love and non-consequential love. When this love is reflected onto social, secular and political relationships, its non-consequential character exerts its influence. This means that the natural F–S relationship can be moved upwards to a spiritual relationship, and the reciprocal and consequential can be developed and enhanced upwards to a non-consequential characteristic. This is the reason why, while consequential principles govern Xunzi's secular relationships, there is still room left for non-consequential love. More than that, from Xunzi's point of view, the strongest love should not be limited to parents, but should be transferred to the ruler and the sage; since the ruler and sage have actually provided broader benefit to people, people should return them more love and at least the same strength of love as they give to their parents. This gives Xunzi's graded love a universal characteristic. And this branch of universal love, which differentiated itself from the main graded love, is generated from its non-consequential character.

Unlike Xunzi's graded love, Pauline *agape* is an equal and universal love, in which, while loving God and Jesus Christ is a priority, there is no essential difference in quality between the love of God and the love of an enemy, between the love of the natural father and the love of the natural son, and between the love of the master and the love of the slave. All the love in family, social and political and religious relationships are a response to God's *agape*; therefore, unlike *ren*, which is derived from family love, *agape* is derived from divine love. This divine love is the response of God's self-giving love, in which the universal and non-consequential character is more basic than any other character. However, as the equal relationship is not entirely implemented through all secular relationships, in the family and social political relationships unbalanced love still prevails.

In summary, both the Pauline and Xunzi's F–S relationship reveal a non-consequential love as well as consequential love: although Xunzi focuses more on consequential love, non-consequential love is also emphasized in his ethical theory; although the chief characteristic of the Pauline divine F–S relationship is non-consequential, it still has some consequential characteristics.

Spiritual and Secular Elements in the Ethical Father–Son Relationship of both Xunzi and Paul

As noted earlier, neither Xunzi's nor Paul's ethical F–S relationship is limited in its essential secular or divine sense; both of them extended the original or primary pattern into a social political area and extended across it: Xunzi's ethical theory starts from the natural F–S relationship, then goes through its social and political analogues and finally reaches its spiritual manifestation; meanwhile Paul's religious ethical ideal starts from the divine F–S relationship, further spreads to its religious and spiritual pattern, then goes through its social and political manifestations and finally reaches the natural form of the F–S relationship.

This extension of the primary F–S pattern in both Xunzi and Paul encourages a transformation of various familial, social, political, religious and spiritual roles and also gives them a similar character of coexistence of the spiritual and secular elements.

The process of transformation in Xunzi's secular pattern may be regarded as transformation from family patriarchy to political hierarchy, while in the Pauline pattern it may be called transformation from divine monarchy to autocratic hierarchy. By such a transformation, Xunzi's secular F–S relationship surmounts its worldly nature and reaches into the spiritual arena, while the Pauline divine F–S relationship oversteps its separation from the reality of worldly life and descends from heaven to earth.

The transformation of the Pauline divine F–S relationship from spiritual to secular is completed through the sonship of Jesus. This term of sonship is used to express not only the 'divinity' of Christ, but also the unity between him and humans.[15] This divine relationship between God and Jesus is first transformed into the divine God–human relationship; and then turns to the spiritual relationship between Jesus and his believer, and between the apostle and church members; it further spreads to the secular political relationship between the ruler (the agent of God in worldly society) and the ruled and finally arrives at the various worldly familial and social relationships, such as the natural father–son, the husband–wife, the master–slave, the old–young and the teacher–student. In this transformation, the divine F–S relationship is the source or starting point, while the Jesus–disciple and the priest–church member relationships are the intermediate, and the various worldly relationships in politics, society and the family are the final. Thus, 'all service is finally rendered to the Lord himself, because, little by little, the human lords replace the heavenly one'.[16]

This characteristic of Pauline teaching can be also seen from his own role in relation to the church. As Donfried and Marshall have noted, Paul serves as both benefactor and authoritative leader to this new family in Christ, and it is essential that these functions continue in his absence. As these responsibilities are carried out by the leaders in their midst, the Thessalonian Christians are to esteem them 'very highly in love' (5:12).[17] In the light of this, they suggest:

> The intensity of the relationship between the founder and the believers is due to the fact that through their baptism they belong to one and the same eschatological family. Family structures, although transformed in Christ, are basic to the internal structure of the community and the community's relationship to the apostle. Because this is the case Paul can employ traditional kinship patterns in his association with the Thessalonians family; he is in solidarity with them as brother, father, nurse, orphan, or beloved.[18]

By contrast, the transformation of Xunzi's secular F–S relationship from its worldly form to its spiritual manifestation is completed through the figure of the sage. The sage in a Confucian context has two meanings: (1) by knowing the ways of Heaven and Earth and then employing this way of heaven and earth to invent the way of human society, the sage is called the assistant and the triad partner of Heaven and Earth. Therefore, a sage is a spiritual figure beyond ordinary human beings. (2) Sages are also real human beings who are no different from other humans in either their nature or their faculty of intelligence; they are neither gods nor the spiritual 'Sons of the God'. Since sages are men rather than God or Sons of God, the love they give to people is not the divine self-giving love but the enlarged parents' selfless love; therefore, the relationship between sage and common people is nothing but an imitation of the parent–child relationship.

As the ancient sages became kings after they organized society and invented the way of human society, they were actually the rulers of ancient societies and the teachers of the common people at the same time; therefore, if the spiritual F–S relationship between the sage and the common people was akin to the relationship between the parent and the child, the ruler–minister or the ruler–ruled and teacher–student relationships should also be analogues of the parent–child relationship. This is why the *Book of Rites* recommends the same relationship of filial obedience in other social relationships:

> The body is that which has been transmitted to us by our parents, dare any one allow himself to be irreverent in the employment of their legacy? If a man in his own house and privacy be not grave, he is not filial; if in serving his ruler, he be not loyal, he is not filial; if in discharging the duties of office, he be not brave, he is not filial; if with friends he be not sincere, he is not filial; if on the field of battle he be not brave, he is not filial. If he fails in these five things, the evil (of the disgrace) will reach his parents; dare he but reverently attend to them?[19]

The *Classic of Filial Piety* develops the idea and further asserts that the realization of social political order must begin with a child's filial attitude towards his/her parents.

It says:

> Now filial piety is the root of all virtues, and that from which all teaching comes . . . it commences with the service of parents; it proceeds to the service of the ruler; it is completed by the establishment of one's own personality. (Chapter 1)

> Yes, filial piety is the way of Heaven, the principle of Earth, and the practical duty of man. Heaven and Earth invariably pursue this course, and the people take it as their pattern. (Chapter 7)[20]

In Xunzi's view, the transformation from the secular to the spiritual is first from the natural F–S to various familial relationships, such as the older brother–younger brother or husband–wife; then to the social relationships, such as the old–young and the teacher–student; further to the political ruler–ruled or ruler–minister relationship, and finally to the spiritual relationships between *tiandi* and the sage, and between the sage and the people. In this transformation, the natural F–S relationship is a source and starting point; the various worldly familial, social and political relationships are the intermediate; and the *tiandi*–sage and the sage–people relationships are the end and final. Because this transformation is realized from the secular to the spiritual, the secular relationship is thus the source and root of the spiritual relationship.

Though Xunzi's theory and Pauline teaching reach their final goal by different approaches, yet both them are completed at the same socialization level. Through setting its source in God, the ruler's authority is established in Pauline teaching. Pope John XXIIII clearly realized this intention of Paul. He tried to develop this Pauline idea and further connect the authority of the ruler to God. He stated:

> Human society can be neither well ordered nor prosperous without the presence of those who, invested with legal authority, preserve its institutions and do all that is necessary to sponsor actively the interests of all its members. And they derive their authority from God, for, as St Paul teaches, 'there is no power but from God' . . . God has created men social by nature, and a society cannot 'hold together unless someone is in command to give effective direction and unity of purpose. Hence every civilized community must have a ruling authority, and this authority, no less than society itself, has its source in nature, and consequently has God for its author.' 'Government authority, therefore, is a postulate of the moral order and derives from God.'[21]

Through locating the root of the ruler into the natural father, the authority of the ruler is also established in Xunzi's doctrine: the lord is the most exalted in the state; the father is the most exalted in the family (14.7). More than that, by regarding the state as an enlarged family, the authority of the ruler is actually enlarged over the authority of the father in Xunzi's consideration: 'The state is the most powerful instrument for benefit in the world. The ruler of men is the most influential position of authority for benefit in the world' (11.1a), thus the state is more important than the family; thereby the ruler should be more important than a father.

Neither Xunzi nor Paul just discusses either the spiritual or secular element in their F–S relationship, but always both. Xunzi pays much attention to the secular F–S pattern, in which not only the natural F–S relationship but also its social and political extensions are focused; yet the spiritual relationship between *tiandi* and sage and between sage and common people are also under his focus. In a similar way, Paul does not confine his concerns merely to the divine F–S relationship, but also pays attention to its secular aspects, in which not only the religious relationship (priest–believer), but also the social/political and natural F–S relationships are also under discussion.

There are two manifestations of this combination of secular and spiritual elements: (1) the notion of the F–S relationship includes both spiritual demands and physical requirements. The concept of either father or son cannot be explained merely by a single physical or spiritual definition but by the combination of both. (2) The aims of both Xunzi's and Paul's discussion on the F–S relationship are not merely focused on secular or spiritual life, but the combination of transcendence of the secular life as well as the realization of the perfect spiritual life. However, these combinations in Xunzi's ethics are manifested differently from those of Paul.

First, the process of combination in Xunzi and Paul is different. In Xunzi the process of combination starts from the natural F–S relationship and finishes at its spiritual metaphor, and the other secular familial, social and political relationships are embraced in the middle. In the Pauline combination, the process starts from the divine F–S relationship and ends at its natural form; all other religious and spiritual F–S metaphors (although when we speak of God as a father we do so because of an analogy that we want to make with human fathers) and their political, social and familial analogues are included in the middle.

Secondly, although we have used the same word 'spiritual' to describe part of Pauline and Xunzi's ethics, the content of the spiritual F–S relationship in Xunzi's context and in Pauline letters is different. Neither Xunzi's *tiandi*–sage nor his sage–common people relationship is the same as Pauline God–Jesus and Jesus–Christian believers relationships. While Paul takes God as a supreme spiritual being, Xunzi regards Heaven and Earth as a natural process of operation; while Paul regards Jesus Christ as the incarnation of God, Xunzi's sage is regarded just as a perfect human being. Unlike Paul, who roots both social justice and righteousness and human salvation into God, the perfect invisible divine figure, Xunzi argues that it is the perfect human figure of the sage rather than any invisible force of Heaven and Earth that plays a subjective and active role in civilizing human society and makes people moral and good: although Heaven and Earth are the source of both the sage and myriad things, they did not intentionally and consciously do any moral work on either sage or human beings. Therefore, the function and influence of Heaven and Earth to humans cannot be completed without the assistance of the sage. The sage was not only the manager of the myriad things, but also the inventor of the Way of human society. Consequently, unlike the God–Jesus relationship, in which the F–S relationship is clear and conscious, the parent–children relationship between Heaven and the sage is obscure and veiled.

Thirdly, there is a tension between the spiritual and the secular element in Pauline teaching, but there is no such tension in Xunzi's secular F–S relationship. Unlike the Gospel of Luke, in which the tension between the secular and the spiritual relationships is distinctive: 'If anyone comes to me and does not hate his father and mother, his wife and children, his brothers and sisters – yes, even his own life – he cannot be my disciple' (Luke 14:26–7), it seems that Paul does not wish to enhance spiritual life at the expense of secular life. However, there is still a tension between this divine relationship and its secular analogues. When conflicts occur, the solution of Paul is to give priority to the divine F–S form. For example, although Paul especially emphasizes that 'each one should remain in the place in life that the Lord assigned to him and to which God has called him' (1 Cor 7:17) and 'each man, as responsible to God, should remain in the situation God called him to' (1 Cor 7:24), such as, if a woman has a husband who is not a believer, if he wants to live with her, she must not divorce him (1 Cor 7:13); Paul also insists that 'if the unbeliever leaves, let him do so. A believer man or woman is not bound in such circumstances; God has called us to live in peace' (1 Cor 7:15). This tells us that when there is conflict between the husband–wife and the God–believer relationships, the believer should care about the God–believer relationship first. The same thing would be true in the conflict between the God–believer and the natural F–S relationships.

By contrast, no tension exists in Xunzi's consideration of the F–S relationship. For Xunzi, the secular relationship is the incarnation or embodiment of the spiritual one; the spiritual F–S relationship is just an enlarged and extended form of the natural F–S pattern; the F–S relationship between Heaven and the sage and between the sage and the common people are exact extensions and reflections of the natural F–S relationship; therefore, the natural and spiritual F–S relationship can identify with each other. Hence, there is no contradiction and conflict but harmony between these two relationships.

As noted, this difference of Paul's tension and Xunzi's identity of the secular and spiritual F–S relationship comes from their different understandings of the relationship between people's social role and their social position. For a Christian, the role one plays in church or society is separate from one's religious or social position. In playing various social roles, people are perhaps different from each other; the son is different from his father, a wife her husband, a slave his master and a subject his ruler. However, this does not mean that these people have unequal positions before God. On the contrary, they are no different before God; all people who believe in God and Jesus Christ are sons of God; they will be all saved through their faith in God, and will all reach their heavenly father's kingdom through Jesus Christ. This means that in the mind of Paul, the social roles people play are not necessarily identical to their social statuses. In fact, the separation between the roles people play in society and their positions in the kingdom of God leads to a separation of the divine world from the secular one. Because the ethics prevailing in the secular world are not necessarily identical with those prevailing in the divine world, when they identify with each other there will be no tension but harmony between the two ethical systems; on the other hand, when they are contrary to each other, it is most likely that a tension will be produced.

This is clearly different from Xunzi's understanding. For him, since the social position is divided according to people's different roles, there is never a possible separation between people's roles and their positions. Since there is no separation but rather identification between social roles and social statuses in both secular and spiritual worlds, the ethical relationship in the secular world is the same as the ethical relationship in the spiritual world; therefore, it is possible to have no tension in the two different ethical spheres.

Finally, the difference between the Pauline emphasis on separation and Xunzi's stress on identification leads to their different understandings of the ideal of human life. For Paul, the ideal of human life is peace, while for Xunzi it is harmony.

In Pauline doctrine, peace is presented mainly with the following meanings: (a) a calm and quiet state of heart when humans return to reunion with God (1 Cor 1:3; 2 Cor 1:2; Gal 1:3; Eph 1:2, Phil 1:2; Col 1:2; 1 Thess 1:1; 2 Thess 1:2; 1 Tim 1:2; 2 Tim 1:2; Titus1:4); (b) a state of freedom from the war between God and man (Rom 5:1) and the struggle between one's good desire and evil desire (Rom 7:14–20; 8:1–11); and (c) the reconciliation between God and humans (Rom 5:9–11). Because of the Christian notion of separation, God and humans cannot avoid struggling with each other, but since they have been reconciled to each other through faith in Jesus Christ, there is peace between them: 'since we have been justified through faith, we have peace with God through our Lord Jesus Christ' (Rom 5:1); 'The God of peace will soon crush Satan under your feet' (Rom 16:20); 'Grace and peace to you from God and our Father and the Lord Jesus Christ' (2 Cor 1:2). Therefore, behind peace Paul emphasized the tension rather than the agreement between God and humans. Since peace comes after a war or a struggle, peaceful harmony means agreement or matching. This can be seen through his illustration of a peaceful and calm state of mind in which there are neither struggles between good and evil desires, nor conflicts between the body and the soul. In Pauline understanding, peace as well as grace is a gift that comes from God the Father and Jesus the Lord: 'Grace and peace to you from God our Father and from the Lord Jesus Christ' (Rom 1:7) because peace means a situation in which humans have been saved from God's wrath and reconciled with God. Avoiding separation and returning to union with God is the essential point for understanding the Pauline concept of peace and harmony.

This is totally different from Xunzi's understanding of harmony. The Chinese word for 'harmony' is *he*; in Xunzi's understanding *he* has three different meanings. First, *he* is to keep things in a proper order or to put them in a right place:

> The Ancient Kings acted to control them [desires] with regulations, ritual, and moral principles, in order thereby to divide society into classes, creating therewith differences in status between the noble and base, disparities between the privileges of age and youth, and the division of the wise from the stupid, the able from the incapable. All of this caused men to perform the duties of their station in life and each to receive his due; only after this had been done was the amount and substance of the emolument paid by grain made to fit their stations. This indeed is the Way to make the whole populace live together in harmony and unity. (4.12)

He is especially used to describe the regulations the sounds of music (20.1); a balance condition of compromise between different elements (2.4); and the unity of a mixture:

> When music is performed within the ancestral temple, lord and subject, high and low, listen to the music together and are united in feelings of reverence. When music is played in the private quarters of the home, father and son, elder and younger brother, listen to it together and are united in feelings of close kinship. When it is played in village meetings or clan halls, old and young listen to the music together and are joined in obedience. (20.1)

From the above meanings of harmony, it can be seen that the crucial meaning of harmony is not agreement or matching, but order and balance. This can be demonstrated by Xunzi's connection of *he* with *zhong*. *Zhonghe*, an important concept for Xunzi, is usually translated as 'the mean of due proportion'. Sometimes, *zhonghe* can be understood as a combined concept with two separated words: 'Thus musical performances are the greatest creator of uniformity in the world, the guiding line of the mean (*zhong*) and of harmony (*he*), and a necessary and inescapable expression of man's emotional nature' (20.1). In this case, *zhong* is to mean the highest ideal state of human conduct, while *he* harmony is to mean not only an ideal state of human conduct, but also an ideal condition of the universe. However, in most cases, *zhonghe* is used as a single concept by Xunzi. This is because the meaning of the 'mean' (*zhong*) and *he* (harmony) are identical to each other: the nature of moral and ritual principles is order and distinction, since the 'mean' (*zhong*) is correctly identified with ritual and moral principles (8.3), hence the nature of the 'mean' is also order and distinction. This is exactly what is meant by *he* (harmony).

He in Xunzi's view is mainly order or proper mixture. Order as the chief characteristic of harmony can also be seen from Xunzi's connection of rituals (*li*) and music (*yue*). He says that 'music embodies harmonies that can never be altered, just as ritual embodies principles of nature order that can never be changed. Music joins together what is common to all; ritual separates what is different' (20.3). For Xunzi, although there is a different function in music and rituals, the similarity between them is that they are both demonstrations of the unchangeable order. It is clear that Xunzi's harmony is an orderly mix of different elements rather than an identifying of them to each other.

The difference between Xunzi's taking harmony and Paul's taking peace as the ideal of life philosophies has influenced their understanding of the relationship between humans and the environment.

By claiming the identification between the Way of Heaven and Earth and the way of human beings, and attainable sagehood for common people, Xunzi gives humans the noblest position. However, this noble position is not given by a supernatural power, but must be earned by humans' own efforts through following the way of humanity and engaging in self-learning and moral cultivation. Because the way of humans is no different from the Way of Heaven and Earth, there is no difference between humankind and other creatures from nature; the relationship between myriad things and humans is one of equality – they have to coexist with each other and remain in an orderly harmonious relationship. In this sense, Xunzi not only stresses the harmony between various human groups or classes, but also between the humans and their environment: if humans want to multiply and increase their stock of domestic animals, they must nurture and breed them according to the seasons; if humans want the trees and plants to flourish, they must cut and plant them with the seasons:

> If it is the season when the grasses and trees are in the splendour of their flowering and sprouting new leaves, axes and halberds are not permitted in the mountain forest so as not to end their lives prematurely or to interrupt their maturation. If it is the season when the giant sea turtles, water lizards, fish, freshwater turtles, loach, and eels are depositing their

eggs, nets and poisons are not permitted in the marshes so as not to prematurely end their lives or to interrupt their maturation. (9.16b)

Thus, to explore the environment according to seasons and using the natural sources in a proper way comprises Xunzi's main idea of environment ethics.

This is totally different from the Pauline ethics of environment. From the Pauline perspective, everything is separated from each other: God is superior and humans are sinful; humans are the managers of the universe and the animals and other species are controlled by them. Therefore, not only does battle exist between God and humanity, but also between humans and the natural environment; thus a conqueror–conquered relationship occupies the mainstream of ethical relationships.

From the above analysis it can seen that the different ethical ideals in dealing with various human relationships within the environment actually reflects their different understanding of the nature of their primary model relationships. Therefore, in order to understand the crucial differences between Xunzi's and Pauline ethics, it is essential to interpret the nature of both Xunzi's and the Pauline central and primary model relationship correctly. From our discussion of their central and primary model relationships, that is, Pauline divine F–S and Xunzi secular F–S, some significances common to both Xunzi and Paul are worthy of note.

First, both offered an effective method for keeping society in order and for the improvement of the individual, that is, both lay stress on internal self-restraint and external social binding. For Paul, although affirming one's internal faith is more important than blindly following the external law, executing the external law is still important for a Christian believer; this effectively works, on the one hand, in making believers pursue a higher level of religious ideal and, on the other hand, keep their peaceful relationship with society and with other people who are not Christians. For Xunzi, following the external principle of rituals (*li*) is the most important thing for every individual: since human nature is evil and humans 'have a natural tendency to selfish, greedy, and quarrelsome' behaviour, people cannot ensure correctness without ritual. However, as humans 'also have a given ability to think' and to 'choose the most advantageous course, and act',[22] they, unlike animals, have a sense of morality, which on the one hand makes the organization of human society possible and, on the other, becomes the final aim of both society and the individual. Thus, although morality is, in some sense, alien to human nature, it can still be found in human nature; in other words, morality is also inherent in human nature and can be developed through moral self-cultivation. By emphasizing the contribution of both internal and external factors in the process of ensuring one's moral behaviour,[23] Xunzi stressed both self-cultivation from within and moral education from without; this characteristic has made his theory more reasonable and effective in both individual and social practices.

Moreover, both Paul and Xunzi's theories were based not only on high-level theoretical ideals but also on the requirements of their own concrete social requirement, and this made both of them more practicable. It has been remarked that Confucian teaching on the Five Relationships was composed of 'concrete values' as well as 'abstract values'.[24] This is also true of the household code as reflected in the Pauline literature, which on the one hand supplied concrete guidance for the Christian believers who lived in the first century period, and on the other hand, offered an abstract value of mutual love and differentiation. It is this unity between idealism and realism that made both the Xunzi and Pauline doctrine transcendent as well as secular.

CONCLUSION

Earlier chapters have explored the role of Xunzi's *secular* and Paul's *divine* F–S relationships in their own tradition, demonstrated their content and characteristics, and compared them from an ethical perspective. In this way divergences and similarities between these two distinctive philosophical and religious traditions have been illustrated.

Although both talk about the F–S relationship, the divergence between Xunzi and Pauline teaching in their arguments is fundamental and obvious: one is secular, the other is divine. Xunzi's discourse is based on, and confined to, a father-centred natural relationship, while Paul's is on, and to, a God-centred spiritual relationship. Because of this fundamental difference they present two different evaluation systems: a consequential standard is the main consideration in Xunzi's teaching, while non-consequential evaluation characterizes Pauline doctrine. They offer two different ethical ideals: peace is the highest value in Pauline doctrine, while harmony is the supreme target of Xunzi's ethics. They advocate two different ways of achieving their ethical ideal: moral learning and self-cultivation are the effective methods for Xunzi, while faith in God and Jesus Christ is the only permissible approach for Paul. They realize their ethical ideals by following two different routes: Xunzi starts from the natural F–S relationship, then extends it to family, social and political relationships and finally promotes it to the spiritual level, where Heaven and Earth (*tiandi*) and the sage and the common people come into an interactive relationship. Paul's route starts from the spiritual F–S relationship between God and Jesus and between Jesus and the Christian believer, and the subsequent transformations in religious, social and political relationships cause it gradually to move from heaven to earth and from the spiritual to the secular world, finally ending up with family relationships, especially the natural F–S relationship.

Notwithstanding the contrasts, the similarities between the Pauline *divine* and Xunzi's *secular* F–S relationship are more substantive than anticipated. In terms of the status of the relationship, F–S occupies a crucial as well as a central position in both Xunzi's and Pauline ethical thinking. The *divine* F–S, as has been argued, is the underlying relationship in Paul's religious ethics. The *natural* F–S relationship is one of the pillars supporting the whole Confucian world in Xunzi's ethical teaching.

The status between father and son in both Xunzi's and Pauline ethical teachings is unequal. The relationship between God the Father and Jesus the Son or between God the father and humans the sons in Pauline teaching is just as between the powerful and the powerless, while the relationship between a natural father and a natural son in Xunzi is like that between the authority and the subordinate; obedience, therefore, constitutes the chief virtue both for the divine son of Paul and for the natural son of Xunzi.

Both Paul and Xunzi adopt patriarchy as their cardinal ruling principle for their discussion of familial and social relationships. Although the important role of a female parent in relation to her child is also emphasized by Xunzi and Paul in their doctrines, the status of the male parent is higher than the female's. For Paul, woman was made from man and for man; for Xunzi, the male as Heaven is always on top, while the female, like the Earth, must always be underneath.

The central values of the Pauline *divine* and Xunzi's *natural* F–S relationship are extended widely and permeate into all their familial and social/religious and political and spiritual networks. The Pauline *divine* F–S is not only the model of various religious relationships (such as the apostle–disciple, priest–church member relationships), but also shapes various secular relationships, such as husband–wife, natural father–son and master–slave. Xunzi's *secular* F–S relationship not only includes secular relations, such as natural father–son, fictive father–son, elder–younger brother, husband–wife, and old–young, teacher–disciple, male–female in society and ruler–subject, ruler–ruled, senior–junior in politics, but also the spiritual relationships between Heaven and Earth and sage, and between sage and common humans.

Both hierarchy and equality are emphasized in the Pauline divine and Xunzi's secular F–S relationships at the same time. Neither Xunzi nor Paul propagates hierarchy at the cost of sacrificing equality. Xunzi emphasizes the order and distinction between father and son, between elder brother and younger brother and between ruler and subject, but still leaves room for the equality of everybody in terms of morality, especially in terms of moral self-cultivation and employment by the benevolent government through the individual's high standard of moral cultivation; Paul stresses not only the differentiation between God's wisdom and power and human's wisdom and ability, but also the difference between husband and wife, natural father and son, master and slave and ruler and citizen. He empowers the father, husband, master and ruler, and leaves obedience to the wife, son, slave and citizen, yet at the same time advocates equality of all before God.

Moreover both set up an ideal and perfect personality for human beings and establish a moral model to guide people's behaviour. Xunzi identifies this person as the sage, while Paul identifies him as Jesus Christ. Jesus Christ and the sage are not only mediators between humans and their spiritual sources, but also the models and guiders of humanity. Both Paul's Christ and Xunzi's sage are seen as the ideal personality of human beings; they are regarded as the incarnation of goodness and righteousness and the embodiment of wisdom and morality/justice: the Christian regards Jesus Christ especially as a model for personal imitation. Christian life has always referred to the imitation of Christ,[1] while the sages are considered to be those exceptional 'individuals who have known how to perfect their inborn nature and thus identify with the order of the world and apply themselves to accomplish it'.[2]

Finally, from a historical perspective, both Paul's and Xunzi's doctrine profoundly influenced their respective traditions and cultures, to their advantage as well as their disadvantage. Over two thousand years, especially in the Han dynasty (206 BC–220 ADY), Xunzi's doctrine of ritual, his enhancement of the ruler to an even higher position than the father, has influenced Chinese society so deeply that all ethical relationships in the family, society and politics were shaped under his influence.

Similarly, Pauline doctrine has influenced Christian society so profoundly that nobody in Christian history except Jesus Christ can rival Paul's historical status and influence.

Notwithstanding the above comparisons, some issues from which other significant questions have emerged are still worthy of further discussion:

Why do the two totally different cultures of Christianity and Confucianism adopt the F–S relationship (even if one is a real one and the other is merely a metaphor) as the crucial and foundational relationship for their ethical thinking? Does this mean that the F–S relationship or its metaphor can be applied as a primary relationship in some kinds of society?

Why do the entirely different types of F–S relationship manifest the same characteristics, such as hierarchy and patriarchy, but at the same time contain an emphasis on both sides of the relationship? Is it at all possible to conclude from the common characteristics that common values exist? If hierarchy and patriarchy are the common characteristics of Pauline *divine* and Xunzi's *secular* and their various forms of F–S relationship metaphors, is it possible to draw a conclusion that even in two totally different cultural systems some shared values do exist?

What elements caused both the doctrine of Xunzi and the teaching of Paul to influence their cultures and society for so long and so deeply? Are these elements common values that are available for both of them? Are there any common values implied in Xunzi and Pauline doctrines, which have made them function well in the past and which can still be employed in modern societies? Is there any possibility of integrating plural values from Xunzi's and Pauline ethical teachings into a new value system which can be used to modify traditional Chinese society to form a new modern one?

There are a variety of answers to these questions, but they are only starting points for further research and contemplation. First, if any common characteristics can be found in two totally different value systems, such as Xunzi's *secular* and Pauline *divine* F–S relationships, then it can probably easily be found between other less different or more similar value systems. For example, we might be able to find greater similarities between Greco-Roman and Chinese cultures than those we have found in Christian and Confucian ethics. Secondly, if similar characteristics can be found in different value systems, then a number of common values can perhaps be refined from such similarities. In other words, there may be common values underlying similar characteristics. Thirdly, if the premise that 'the similar characteristics between different values systems demonstrate their common values' is true, then the conclusion that 'the greater the number of similar characteristics shared by two value systems, the greater the number of common values they will share' is perhaps also true.

Accordingly, we can make three deductions: (1) some primary and fundamental values are shared by various, even totally different, societies, and the more primary and fundamental a value is, the more societies will share it. (2) The more primary and fundamental a value is, the more capable it is of being applied to, and employed by, different human societies. For example, many scholars have realized that the Bible has been interpreted by different cultures through different representative forms.[3] If a scholar can draw the conclusion that 'there is a common truth in the Bible' while recognizing that it has, in fact, been interpreted from different perspectives and represented within different forms of value system, then perhaps we can also conclude that a value which has repeatedly been presented in various different value systems should be a common value. (3) The more essential common values a tradition possesses, the deeper and longer influence it will offer to the society.

Bearing these deductions in mind, we can answer the questions we raised earlier in this way: the essential values that supported Xunzi's and Pauline ethics influencing their own traditions for a long period time are essentially the same, which can be briefly summarized as following.

First, they have both offered an effective method for keeping society in order and for the development of the individual. For example, both lay stress on internal self-restraint as well as on external social binding. For Paul, although affirming one's internal faith is more important than blindly following the external law, executing the external law is also important for a Christian believer; this effectively works in making believers pursue a higher level of religious ideal as well as in keeping their peaceful relationship with society and with other people who are not Christians. For Xunzi, following the external principle of rituals (*li*) and one's teacher is the most important thing for every individual: since human nature is evil and humans 'have a natural tendency to selfish, greedy, and quarrelsome' behaviour, therefore, without rituals, people cannot ensure correctness; without teachers, people cannot understand the correctness of rituals. However, as humans 'also have a given ability to think' and to 'choose the most advantageous course, and act',[4] by which they know that society is necessary for individual survival and morality is good at organizing an harmonious society; thus, although morality is not an innate part of human nature, it can still be developed through moral self-cultivation. By emphasizing the contribution of both internal and external factors in the process of ensuring moral behaviour,[5] Xunzi has stressed both self-cultivation from within and moral education from without.

Moreover, both theories were based not only on high-level theoretical ideals but also on the requirements of their own concrete social requirement, which made them both practicable. It has been remarked that Confucian teaching on the Five Relationships was composed of 'concrete values' as well as 'abstract values'.[6] This is also true of the household code as reflected in the Pauline literature, which supplied concrete guidance for the Christian believers who lived in the first century period on the one hand, and offered some abstract value of mutual love and differentiation for all people in the universe on the other. It is this unity between idealism and realism that made both Xunzi and Pauline doctrine transcendent as well as secular.

From the fact that both Paul and Xunzi regard the F–S relationship as the crucial and fundamental relationship of their ethical theories, it is perhaps reasonable to conclude that this is a primary and model relationship for all other social political relationships in all forms of human community that have a similar economical and political framework. Thus, how to establish a proper F–S relationship is perhaps a key point for the establishment of all other familial, social, political and spiritual relationships, in the past as well as today. In other words, if a society wishes to produce a new form of social–political network, it should start with the F–S relationship. The modernization of Chinese tradition should therefore also start from the modernization of the Confucian, especially Xunzi's F–S relationship.

However, how can Xunzi's F–S relationship be modernized if, as the common point of view has suggested, the essence of modernization is 'democracy, freedom and equality' and the traditional Confucian relationship – based on patriarchy and hierarchy – is entirely contrary to this spirit of modernization?

It has been claimed by some Western commentators that the reason why the question of human rights has dominated thought within the West for several decades, with much being made of the human rights record of Eastern cultures, is in part due to a lack of original thought within the East concerning such issues as individual rights and the supremacy of the monarch and authority within Confucian philosophy. Does this mean that Xunzi's hierarchical F–S ethical doctrine has no value at all?

Dissenting voices commenting on the Confucian idea of human rights and the supremacy of the monarch and authority have been raised by some modern scholars. William Theodore de Bary has pointed out that Confucian thought may well have been centuries ahead of its time in dealing with such issues as human rights.[7] Nuyen also challenges Huntington's conclusion that Confucian democracy is incompatible with liberal concepts and individual rights.[8] Nuyen believed that certain rights must be upheld if key Confucian ideals are to be obtained.[9] Tu Weiming further indicates that 'the Confucian personality ideals of *chun-tzu*, worthy and sage can be realized more fully in the liberal-democratic society than either in the traditional imperial-dictatorship or a modern authoritarian regime'.[10] From these researches, it can be further concluded that Xunzi's hierarchical F–S relationship probably still has relevance to modern Chinese society.

(1) Hierarchy and patriarchy still have meaning in modern Chinese society. It is true that values which were valid for a specific historical period are not necessarily valid for all history. Thus, historical values such as hierarchy and patriarchy are not necessarily still valid in modern Chinese society. Nonetheless, if the conditions supporting a particular historical value still existed today, that historical value would be available for today. Applying this opinion to Xunzi's *secular* F–S relationship, it can be seen that although the conditions to support the father and male's authority and power, which derived from the agricultural environment, have gradually changed in modern Chinese society, the conditions for the existence of hierarchical and patriarchal theory have not yet entirely disappeared. Although consciousness of equality has been planted into modern Chinese minds, the influence of ancient culture on them is still very strong; though the high hierarchical distinction between male and female, elder and young, father and son, and ruler and ruled has decreased so much that equality in the husband–wife relationship has even been established in some modern cities, there are nevertheless still some continuing conditions which support Xunzi's hierarchical and patriarchal F–S relationship. From an ideological point of view, where a custom has prevailed for thousands of years, agreement on the central status of the father and ruler in family and society is still very strong, and as a result the power and authority of the ruler in politics and the father in the family encounter little challenge. Both government officers and common citizens are used to the authority–obedience relationship between senior and junior and between ruler and ruled; both husband and wife and father and son are familiar with the authority of the husband and father; patriarchy is still the most popular model for most Chinese families, especially rural families. In spite of female advancement, since females have been accustomed to being governed by

males, the majority of women in Chinese society, especially in the countryside, lack consciousness of independence and equality; they are still used to depending on their husband's decisions on family matters and accept being in a secondary position in relation to their husbands. Thus, from both an ideological and a realistic standpoint, it is perhaps reasonable to say that hierarchy and patriarchy are still important in contemporary Chinese society, or at least that it is not yet out of fashion. It is possible to criticize this point of view as it compromises an ideal society, but as we have concluded, any theory, if it seeks to be practicable in a real society, must respond to the real situation of that society. Therefore it would be better if the theory were to correspond to the aspirations of the society we are currently living in.

(2) There is no absolute equality in any modern society even today. A. T. Nuyen argues that in spite of people having an equal start, for instance, having equal worth and equal potentiality, and even equal opportunity, they will still end up being different for various reasons; equality cannot be truly realized in real society. Therefore, equality should be understood along Aristotelian lines, that is, as having a 'horizontal aspect', where 'equals' should be treated equally, and a 'vertical aspect', where the 'unequal' should be treated unequally. Thus it can be argued that the unequal treatment of different people in Confucian society merely reflects the fact that they are unequal. If so, then what appears to be meritocracy and elitism could well be a commitment to equality: 'it is true that the hierarchical structure of the Confucian society assigns unequal powers and rewards. However, it does not follow that there is no commitment to the idea of equality.'[11]

(3) Beyond these musings, there are some special elements of objective truth within Xunzi's concepts of hierarchy that are still valuable to societies even today. Lin Yüsheng recognizes the significance of Confucian hierarchy in modern life. He says that considered simply as a form of family ethic, 'the central core of Confucian ethics, whose rules about correct conduct are based on a proper distinction between old and young, still has a positive significance for modern life'. This is because the model for this kind of family ethic, which is practised in the Chinese family, reflects the exercise of parental authority in a familial 'hierarchy' without oppression.[12] According to Lin, since the family order achieved by hierarchy is based on the principle and practice of 'empathetic reciprocity' among all members of the family, sustained by natural affection channeled through harmonizing rituals and customs, hierarchy in the Chinese family simply brings order and is non-oppressive. This is especially true of Xunzi's hierarchical F–S relationship.

There are two reasons that support this viewpoint. As noted, the target of Xunzi's ethical theory is to realize harmony among different familial, social, political and spiritual relationships, to establish a harmonious ethical relationship; this requires basing a relationship on consequential as well as non-consequential love and, moreover, requires a mutual response from both sides of a relationship. Xunzi called this mutual love between people *ren* (benevolence).

For Xunzi, the family is the natural place for the development of human moral feelings and genuine familial affection guided by the constant nature and unchangeable principle of *li*. The Confucian ideal of *li* (propriety) implies the observance of rights, not individual rights generally, but the rights of an individual in a certain social position.[13] In the process of moral development, individual moral cultivation is the most important element and respect for other people is the essential principle. As Lin has pointed out, 'classical Confucian thought originally contained the idea of respect for the individual person',[14] or in other words, respect for each other in Xunzi's F–S relationship is richer and more attainable. Thus, although authority is located on the side of father, elder brother, husband and ruler, to harmonize with the other side the authority side must show love and kindness to the lower side and practise moral and legal responsibility consciously; although sons, wives and younger brothers have fewer rights but more responsibilities compared to their fathers, husbands and elder brothers, they also have the same rights in cultivating their morality, and have the same right to be employed by the government for their achievement in learning and moral cultivation, and for their greater ability in practising beneficial government.

(4) Defenders of Confucianism typically insist that Confucianism is committed to the idea of equality at the most fundamental level, namely, equality of worth as human beings; in other words, there are good metaphysical reasons for social inequality and there is nothing wrong with inequality as long as one starts out with equality at the level of common humanity.[15] From this point of view, social differences in terms of rights and privileges are not evidence of a lack of commitment to equality at the social level. Instead, it can be argued that social differences are the inevitable outcome of putting the idea of equality to work; they are therefore just another dimension of equality.[16] If so, there is no problem in Xunzi practising hierarchy and patriarchy with non-oppression, but advocating proper love and equal responsibility within any single ethical relationship.

(5) More than that, there are deeper meanings within Xunzi's idea of hierarchy and patriarchy than the two concepts indicate in isolation. For extreme liberals and feminists, there is no difference between hierarchy and oppression or between patriarchy and discrimination. The essence of both is inequality. This standpoint stems from a determinedly individualistic attitude, which has little concern for ethics, or about the individual's responsibility to society.

Nonetheless, as noted, the essential nature of both Xunzi's hierarchy and patriarchy is distinction; the unequal relationship arising from age and social status and gender is merely the concrete manifestation of this distinction. The spirit of distinction aims to make it clear that the virtue of the individual, arising as it does from effort and courage of spirit, benefits both the individual and the other side of the relationship. The individual has responsibilities to their family and the community at large, which are repaid to the individual through the benefits of belonging to that family and community. There is a tacit agreement here that the two must be kept in balance: neither giving priority to the needs of family and community should produce tyranny over the individual, nor can the rights of the individual be allowed to take precedence over other people living within the family and society.

The concrete manifestation and expression of this distinction might change in the course of history, and the principles guiding a particular relationship may also change over time, for example, the kind of inequality between father–son, husband–wife and ruler–ruled changes. But the need for one individual to show responsibility to the other individual within a relationship, to the family and society, never changes; maintaining a distinction between different jobs and roles in family and society is also still strongly needed. Historical and social experience tell us that no society can run well without a proper distinction between social jobs and social roles, nor can family and society operate well without the full contribution of individual responsibility. In a well-run society and family, everybody should play a particular role and fulfill their own responsibilities in their particular social position.

(6) In addition, if we consider the precondition of Xunzi's principle of giving priority to the aged, the male, the father and the ruler, the fact that 'the Chinese recognized only the right of prince, right of patriarch, right of the ruler'[17] is also understandable. On the one hand, as Nuyen has recognized, in terms of power, it can hardly be expected that there is equality in any society; as long as there is differentiation of functions, every different role is given special power that other people do not have: for example, a police officer has a right to arrest people that others do not have. On the other hand, since Xunzi, like Confucianism in general, has explicitly endorsed equality of opportunity, particularly educational opportunity,[18] within the process of achieving power and authority, his hierarchical and patriarchal power of the father and husband and ruler is reasonable.

People argue that the basic meaning of the concept of hierarchy is inequality and the essential sense of patriarchy is gender discrimination, but if their meaning is translated into distinction and grade, then the whole content of these two concepts is changed. However, as noted, the spirit of Xunzi's hierarchy is not absolute inequality between ages and social status, but distinction according to moral cultivation and ability to promote benevolent government; furthermore, the essential core of Xunzi's patriarchy is not grade determined by gender but rather by leadership practised in the ancient Chinese family and society. Therefore, Xunzi's hierarchy and patriarchy have their own special meaning, and they do not completely match the modern concept of hierarchy or that of patriarchy. Therefore, when we use distinction and grade to describe Xunzi's hierarchy and leadership, or to describe Xunzi's understanding of patriarchy, the problem should be resolved. In this sense, it is reasonable to say that there are some values within Xunzi's hierarchical and patriarchal *secular* F–S relationship which can be shared with modern Chinese society.

Xunzi's hierarchical F–S relationship is still applicable in modern Chinese society, but since the problem of identifying society with the family, especially the state with the family, has been exposed and recognized by many people for some time, it is advisable to propose some revision of Xunzi's hierarchical F–S relationship.

Revision should involve merging Xunzi's notion of harmony and the Pauline concept of peace. As noted, the harmony ideal is closely connected to Xunzi's union theory, while the Pauline concept of peace is linked with his separation theory.

Pauline separation theory, from an ethical point of view, aims to make humans conscious of themselves individually, and make individuals independent and free from one another, which is good for the establishment of an individual independent personality and the development and fulfillment of individual faculties and potentialities. However, it can cause separation from God and each other, and can also make people feel isolated and lonely. Xunzi's union theory aims to establish a consciousness of human society and make people depend on each other, which is good for the establishment of a consciousness of unity and cohesion and a sense of belonging. Nonetheless, it is not good for the development of individual's independent personality.

As John B. Cobb Jr. recognized, since 'there is a chance that a wedding of Eastern and Western process thinking can successfully challenge the dominant philosophical traditions and provide the basis for new response to the enormous challenges humanity faces', 'the appropriation of process thought in both East and West seems to be a matter of human urgency'.[19]

Is it possible to merge these two theories' advantages and at the same time to get rid of their disadvantages? Is it possible to adopt Western methods while still holding to a Chinese 'essence'? It has been argued that uniting the two would enable each to enjoy harmony and have a sense of belonging;[20] it would allow all people to have an independent personality and to separate public affairs from private business. Perhaps using Xunzi's union of harmony to deal with family affairs while using Pauline peace to deal with social and political affairs is one possible way forward?

Obviously no firm answer to this question can be provided here, but nevertheless, the Confucian concept of harmony and the Christian idea of peace are closely connected to their highest ideals and are based on their central understanding of crucial familial social and political relationships. Kang Youwei has mentioned the close relationship between the Confucian family and the Confucian ideal of Grand Commonality, and believed that in order to fulfill the act with the traditional Confucian value of public-mindedness, the only way is to liberate people from a Chinese system of family. He said:

> We desire that men's nature shall all become perfect, that men's characters shall all become equal, that men's bodies shall all be nurtured . . . [That state in which] men's character are all developed, men's bodies are all hale, men's dispositions are all pacific and tolerant, and customs and morals are all beautiful, is what called Complete Peace and Equality. But there is no means by which to bring this about this way without abolishing the family.[21]

Wm Theodore De Bary discussed the possibility of 'harmony' as a key point to not only Confucian humane governance and consensual institutions but also to economic progress.[22] The concepts of harmony and peace would then become key points for understanding not only the differences between Xunzi's and Pauline F–S relationships, but also the advantages and disadvantages of Chinese as well as Western cultures.

Regarding the possibility of reformation and modernization of Chinese culture, some scholars hold a pessimistic view. For example, after examining the complex construction of Chinese culture, Sun Longji concluded that a fundamental problem exists within the Chinese way of thinking and life. However, there are many from both the old generation of scholars, such as Liang Shuming, Feng Youlan, Xiong Shili, Ma Yifu, Zhuang Junmai, Qianmu, Helin, Fang Dongmei, Tang Junyi, Mou Zongsan, Xu Fuguan and the new, such as Yao Xinzhong, Liu Xiaofeng, Jiao Guocheng, who have done much work on setting out the value and significance of Chinese culture to the world. Some of them have even considered the possibility of merging Chinese culture and Western culture, or integrating one with the other. There has been a special interest in the possible integration of Christianity and Confucianism by, as mentioned before, Chinese Christian scholars such as He Guanghu, Yang Huilin, and Liu Xiaofeng. Some of them, such as Tu Weiming and Cheng Zhongying, have even done detailed work on a possible proposal for the modernization of Chinese culture.

Some Western scholars have recognized this possibility of modification and modernization. Richard T. Amos says that those in China have to try their best to reconcile Confucian tradition with the dominant Western values. It is therefore possible to hope that the new democracies of 'Confucian' societies possess a shared value with Western Christian societies. Amos even suggests that, in view of the mutual dependent and coexistent relationship of world cultures, 'we in America have no choice but to try our best to reconcile our thin liberal democracy with the thicker conception of community promoted by Confucian thinking'.[23] More than that, even scholars who condemned Chinese culture still cannot deny the essential values within it. For example, although Sun Longji criticized Chinese culture, he still had to admit that Confucianism could function well in the sense of condensing the whole country together as one heart when led by a 'dynamic goal intention'.[24] The problem is not that the theory itself has no good function, but how it can be made to work and to function well. According to Sun Longji, the condensing function of Confucianism can only take place when either there is a 'dynamic goal intention' or when a sage is ruling. As there is neither a 'dynamic goal intention' within Chinese culture nor any likelihood of rule by a sage, the only way to reform Chinese society, for Sun, is to change its constitution of rule by the people into a constitution of rule by law.[25] Since emphasis on rituals is the main characteristic of Xunzi, perhaps his ideas of how to establish a ritual system can provide clues as to the way Confucianism can reform and modernize a society.

In summary, with respect to the reformation of the F–S relationship, notwithstanding the many attacks against its main manifestations in Confucian society, most attacks on Confucianism, especially those of the Chinese Communist Party, have been against a rigid feudal ideology that goes under the name of Confucianism, within which the original valuable spirit has faded away. As a tradition that has been handed down for more than two thousand years, there is undoubtedly value which can be further used to inspire the development of Chinese culture and society. The real Confucian value, despite its bad manifestations, cannot just be abandoned – that would be throwing out the baby with the bath water. Scholars in both the West and China have done excellent work in searching for a new ethic for both China and the world. Hans Küng's project of 'Global Ethics', Tu Weiming's 'Confucian Humanism', and He Huaihong's 'Minimalist Ethics' are prime examples. But more work needs to be done, and I suggest a reform of Chinese culture based on Confucian ideals, especially Xunzi's F–S relationship.

Research Scholarship in Christian and Confucian Studies

Although no systematic study directly on the topic of the comparison between Xunzi's and Paul's teachings on the father–son relationship is available, some relevant research has already been undertaken by both Chinese and Western scholars. The contributions by Chinese scholars to the topics relevant to the research detailed in this book can be divided into three groups: the first can be found in studies of Xunzi, the second contribution is in the area of the comparison of Confucianism and Christianity, and the last is research on the possible connections between the two cultures.

Owing to the comparatively small number of contemporary Chinese scholars interested in Xunzi in mainland China before the 1990s, most of the publications concerning Xunzi theories before that date were from Taiwanese scholars. According to my own research, no works were published on Xunzi's ideas in mainland China between 1950 and 1990, except for publications of Xunzi's own work. Even in Taiwan, most of the publications on Xunzi are interpretations of the text *Xunzi*, or at best, general studies on a particular subject of Xunzi, which are often quite different from other Confucians' ideas on the same topic. For example, the most popular topics of such Xunzi studies are discussions of his theory that 'human nature is evil' and his thinking on 'the division between Heaven and Humans'. Both on the mainland and in Taiwan, the scholarly interest in Xunzi studies is limited to the general characteristics of Xunzi, the differences between him and other Confucians, and his links with other academic groups. Seldom have scholars paid much attention to Xunzi's ethical theory in particular, with the exception of one book, which takes Xunzi's ethical theory as its main subject. Although more and more mainland Chinese scholars are gradually being attracted to Xunzi's theory, and studies of Xunzi in both mainland China and Taiwan are becoming more analytical, they still remain at a relatively elementary level. A look at publications in mainland China reveals the following books with broad themes: *The Origin of Xunzi Theory*,[1] *Xunzi and the Social Confucian Ideal*,[2] *A Good Combination of Confucianism and Legalism: The Story of Xunzi*,[3] *Xunzi and Modern Society*[4] and *Xunzi Studies*.[5] As scholars begin to appreciate the significance of Xunzi and his theory in Chinese cultural history, and his relevance to the modern age, more research has been published on Xunzi in recent years. They are not only general studies of Xunzi's theory, but they also address specific subjects, some of which are close to the theme of this volume. For example, a good number of books take the theory of humans (*ren*) or human nature (*renxing*) as their research title;[6] there is also a large number of books on Xunzi's theory of politics and his idea of *li* (rites or propriety) and *yi* (righteousness or justice); there are even some books directly related to Xunzi's ethical relationships.[7] Moreover, the position of Xunzi in Confucianism and in Chinese cultural history in general, and the relationships between Xunzi and other figures within and outside Confucianism, have also been discussed to some degree.[8] In short, Chinese scholars have done a considerable amount of essential research work on Xunzi's thinking.

The contribution of Chinese scholars to Christian studies and the comparison between Confucianism and Christianity is made mainly by Christian scholars, such as Zhao Zichen, Xu Baoqian, and Wu Leichuan, among others. They present rich ideas on Christian theory and also on how Christianity can be developed into a practicable religion within a Chinese cultural context. Moreover, New-Confucian scholars are focusing on comparative studies between Chinese culture, especially Confucianism, and Western culture. For example, Mou Zongsan, one of the most famous modern New-Confucians, produced an intensive discussion of the relationship between Confucianism and Christianity.[9] Earlier, Feng Youlan and Hu Shi did some work on the comparison between Chinese and Western culture.[10] There are also some new generation Chinese scholars who have begun to do such work.[11] However, most of the contributions to contemporary Chinese Christianity studies and the comparison between Confucianism and Christianity have been made by those scholars who live outside the mainland, in such places as Taiwan and Hong Kong. Generally speaking, Christian studies and comparative studies between Confucianism and Christianity are still a new theme for research in mainland China, but are beginning to gain momentum. Although Chinese scholars have been making great efforts in comparing Chinese and Western culture,[12] evidence of conflicts between Chinese and Western culture evoke greater necessity for comparative work between these two cultures. The limited number of comparative studies between Confucianism and Christianity make the current research very significant.

The contributions of Western scholars to the topics relevant to the thesis presented here can be divided into three kinds: Studies of Xunzi and Paul, studies of the background of both Pauline and Xunzi's teachings on the father-son relationship, and comparative studies between Confucianism and Christianity.

Two kinds of work have been done in Xunzi studies. One is translation and interpretation of the book of the *Xunzi*; the other is research on different topics of Xunzi's theory. At least two translations have been completed by Western scholars, notably the three-volume *Xunzi: A Translation and Study of the Complete Works* (John Knoblock, Stanford University Press, 1988–94); *The Works of Hsuntze* (Homer H. Dubs, Taibei: Wenzhi Chubanshe, 1972).

Apart from the above-mentioned source books, studies on Xunzi and his thought have also been published. For example: *The Chronology of Hsu-tzu* (J. J. L. Duyvendak, 1929); *Ethical Argumentation: A Study in Hsu Tzu's Moral Epistemology* (A. S. Cua, University of Hawaii Press, 1985); *Nature and Heaven in the Xunzi: A Study of the Tian Lun* (Edward J. Machle, State University of New York Press, 1993); *Virtue, Nature, and Moral Agency in the Xunzi* (T. C. Kline and P. J. Ivanhoe, Hackett Publishers, 2000); *Rituals of the Way: The Philosophy of Xunzi* (Paul Rakita Goldin, Open Court, 1999); and *Ritual and Religion in Xunzi* (T. C. Kline III, Seven Bridges Press, 2002). Some books directly related to the cultural background of Xunzi's father–son relationship also have been published, among which *Confucianism and the Family* (ed. Walter H. Slote and George A. DeVos) stands out.

Much work has been done in the field of comparative studies between Confucianism and Christianity. For example, John Berthrong, *All under Heaven: Transforming Paradigms in Confucian–Christian Dialogue* (SUNY Series in Chinese Philosophy and Culture, State University New York Press, 1994); Lionel M. Jensen, *Manufacturing Confucianism: Chinese Traditions and Universal Civilizations* (Duke University Press, 1997); Hans Kung and Julia Ching, *Christianity and Chinese Religions* (Bantam Doubleday Dell, 1989); Hwain Chang Lee, *Confucius, Christ and Co-partnership: Competing Liturgies for the Soul of Korean American Women* (University Press of America, 1994); Peter K. H. Lee (ed.), *Confucian–Christian Encounters in Historical and Contemporary Perspective* (Religious in Dialogue, Edwin Mellen Press, 1991); Denise Lardner Carmody and John Tully Carmody, *In the Path of the Masters: Understanding the Spirituality of Buddha, Confucius, Jesus, and Muhammad* (M. E. Sharpe, 1996); Xinzhong Yao, *Confucianism and Christianity: A Comparative Study of Jen and Agape* (Sussex Academic Press, 1996); and Stephen Uhalley, Jr. and Xiaoxin Wu (eds), *China and Christianity: Burdened Past, Hopeful Future* (M. E. Sharp, 2001). Comparative work has even been done at a person-to-person level. For example, Heup Young Kim, *Wang Yang-ming and Karl Barth: A Confucian–Christian Dialogue* (University of America, 1996); Kin Ming Au, *Paul Tillich and Chu Hsi: A Comparison of Their Views of the Human Condition* (Peter Lang, 2002). There are also some books and articles related not only to the general comparison between Chinese culture and Western culture, but also to the origins of Chinese tradition and Western tradition. For example, Steven Shankman, and Stephen W. Durrant, *Early China/Ancient Greece: Thinking through Comparisons* (State University of New York Press, 2002) is one such book.

More useful to the present volume is the research in the field of Christian studies and Pauline teaching studies. There is a significant number of books and articles about Christianity and the Pauline letters and publications on the particular subject of the father–son relationship; for example, on the Greco-Roman family, the Jewish family in antiquity and on family relationships in the NT and the OT. Although not so much research has been done directly on the father–son relationship,[13] especially Pauline teaching on that subject, there are many relevant studies on the relationships between husband and wife, master and slaves and the ruler and the ruled. For example, Halvor Moxnes (ed.), *Constructing Early Christian Family: Family as Social Reality and Metaphor* (Routledge, 1997); David L. Balch and Carolyn Osiek, *Family in the New Testament World: Household and House Churches* (Louisville, KY: Westminster/John Knox Press, 1997); Philip F. Esler, *The First Christians in Their Social World* (Routledge, 1994); Ellien T. Armour, *Deconstruction, Feminist Theology, and the Problem of Difference: Subverting the Race/Gender Divide* (Chicago: University of Chicago Press, 1999); Lari E. Borressen (ed.), *Image of God and Gender Models in Judeo-Christian Tradition* (Oslo: Solum, 1991); Elizabeth A. Castelli, 'Paul on Women and Gender', Ross Shepard Kraemer and Mary Rose D'Angelo (eds), *Women and Christian Origins* (Oxford University Press, 1999); Kathleen E. Corley, *Private Women, Public Meals: Social Conflict in Synoptic Tradition* (Peabody, MA: Hendrickson, 1993). Moreover, work on Christianity with regard to equality and democracy, and Christianity and the notion of hierarchy, has been done in relevant researches. For example, Richard P. Saller, *Patriarchy, Property, and Death in the Roman Family* (Cambridge University Press, 1994); Lone Fatum, 'Image of God and Glory of Man: Women in the Pauline Congregations';[14] Peter J. Haas (ed.), *Recovering the Role of Women: Power and Authority in Rabbinic Jewish Society* (Atlanta, GA: Scholar Press, 1992); Kittredgem Cynthia Briggs, *Community and Authority: The Rhetoric of Obedience in the Pauline Tradition* (Harvard Theological Studies 45, Harrisburg, PA: Trinity Press International, 1998); Elisabeth Castelli, *Imitation Paul: A Discourse of Power* (Louisville, KY: Westminster/John Knox Press, 1991); Sandra Hack Polaski, *Paul and the Discourse of Power* (Sheffield Academic Press, 1999).

Some researchers have highlighted the father–son relationship, especially the parent–child relationship. For example, *Children in English Society*,[15] *Australian Childhood: A History* (Allen & Unwin, 1997); Margaret Mead, *Culture and Commitment: A Study of the Generation Gap* (Bodley Head, 1970); Jeffery Grentell-Hill (ed.), *Growing up in Wales, 1895–1939* (Gomer, 1996); Thomas E. Jordan, *The Degeneracy Crisis and Victorian Youth* (Albany, NY: State University of New York Press, 1993); Linda A. Pollock, *Forgotten Children: Parent–Children relations from 1500 to 1900* (Cambridge University Press, 1983); Lloyd de Mause (ed.), *The History of Childhood: The Evolution of Parent–Child Relationship as a Factor in History* (London: Souvenir Press, 1974), and John Sommerville, *The Rise and Fall of Childhood* (Beverly Hills/London/New Delhi: Sage Publications, 1982). However, most of these books refer to modern society. Some of them, though referring to historical data, are concerned with the parent–child relationship alone, but there are no books that take this relationship as the basis of a social relational network, and to my knowledge, no one has conducted research in relation to other social familial, social and political relationships.[16] Thus, Halvor Moxnes comments:

> Strangely enough, although 'family' is such an important topic in Christianity, there have been few comprehensive studies of family in early Christianity. There has been much interest in certain aspects, in particular in ethical issues concerning marriage or the so called 'household' codes, but much less in the social behaviour and forms of family as a social institution among early Christians.[17]

Although many publications have resulted from both Chinese and Western studies of Confucianism and Christianity, based on a comparison between Chinese culture and Western culture, as far as Xunzi's theory and Pauline teaching go there are still some limitations to these achievements. First of all, there are no directly significant achievements on the topic of the F–S relationship in Xunzi, nor even any book that is devoted to the Confucian F–S relationship either in China or in the West. Neither Xunzi's F–S relationship nor Xunzi's ethical theory has yet entered the arena of systematical discussion.

Next, although many scholars have already made considerable contributions on Pauline moral teachings, and even on the Pauline F–S relationship, the F–S relationship is not the main focus of their research and, as a result, it has not been discussed systematically. Therefore, it is safe to say that seldom do Pauline scholars pay enough attention to the important functions of the Pauline divine F–S relationship in Christian ethics and Christian social life.

Neither Chinese nor Western scholars have developed systematic discussions of the divine F–S as the origin of Pauline ethical relationships or the kinship F–S relationship as the cornerstone of Xunzi ethical thinking. So far as I am aware, few scholars have ever tried to understand Paul's and Xunzi's ethical ideas in the way they are presented here. No discussion either of the disciple–master relationship or of the ruler–ruled relationship has been conducted in the framework of the F–S relationship; nor has this framework been consciously used to further elucidate Xunzi's and Pauline teachings.

Finally, no comparison has ever been undertaken between Confucianism and Christianity from the point of view of the relationship between the divine F–S and the secular F–S relationships and their analogues, and no comparison between Pauline ethical teaching and Xunzi's moral theory has been attempted.

In conclusion, in terms of comparing the divine F–S relationship with the secular F–S relationship, Xunzi with Paul and earlier Confucianism with the NT, the arguments and presentation put forward in this book shed new light on this important concept, and is of distinct significance to our appreciation of the differences and similarities between Chinese and Western cultures.

Glossary

bi	Female ancestor.
bian	Differentiation.
bizu	Female and male ancestors.
cheng	Truthfulness, loyalty, sincerity, honesty.
chun-tzu = *junzi*	Gentleman.
Ci	First name of Zigong, one of the famous disciples of Confucius.
dali	Greater benefits.
Dao	The way.
dayi	Greater justice.
e	Evil, bad, not good, wicked.
fa	Law, model.
fang	Following or obeying.
fen	Distinction.
fu	Father.
fu	An honorary title for an older male; an honorific term for addressing males; the meaning of origin.
fù	Male parent; address for all former generations.
guojia	One's country or state.
Hanfeizi	One of the most representative proponents of Chinese Legalism.
he	Harmony.
Ji Kangzi	One of disciples of Confucius.
jia	Family, household, home.
jiao	Cross, to imply sexual intercourse between male and female.
jiating	Family, household.
jiazu	Kinship clan.
jie	A sample of kings with immortal virtue.
jingli	Plan and pattern.
Jixia	A place in Qi State in the Pre-Qin period, a famous academic palace.
junzi	Gentleman, cultivated man.
kaobi	Female ancestor.
Kun	Earth means mother.
lao	Older in age; old people; a gentle word for the death of people;

	someone who has rich experience; to name a thing that has existed for a long time; original or former.
lei	Categories.
li	Rituals, propriety, rites.
Li	Principle of natural existence, or the Way as the 'plan and pattern' of reality; also, profit, benefit.
Li Ji	*The Book of Rites.*
li ji	Principle of morality and justice.
min	Normal people.
ming	Names.
Mo Di	The founder of Mohism.
Mozi	Mohist.
quedang	City or community.
qian	Sky, father.
ren	Benevolence and humanity, magnanimity, compassion, human-heartedness.
renxing	Human nature.
Ru	Confucianism.
Ru classic	Confucian classic.
Ru jia	Confucianism.
Ru person	Confucians.
Ru philosophers	Confucian philosophers.
Ru tradition	Confucian tradition.
sheng	Produce, birth.
shengren	Sage.
shenzu	Male ancestor.
Shi Jing	*The Book of Songs, The Book of Poetry.*
shu	Do not do to others what you yourself do not like.
Shuowei Jiezi	Explanation and analysis of words, the first Chinese dictionary, which was edited in AD 100.
Tao = Dao	The way of the universe or the law of nature.
Three Bonds	Three main relationships: ruler–subject, father–son, husband–wife.
ti	Brother's love.
tian	Heaven.
tian ren he yi	A theory to integrate Heaven and human beings together that regards humans as sharing the same nature as the universe.
tian sheng. *zheng min*	Heaven gives birth to thousands of people.
tiandao	The Way of Heaven.
tiande	Heavenly virtue, the power of nature.
tiandi	Heaven and Earth.
wei	Acquired human nature or man-made human nature.

wulun	Five relationships: ruler–subject; father–son; husband–wife; elder brother–younger brother; and friends.
xiao	Filial piety.
Xiao Jing	*Classic of Filial Piety.*

Notes

Preface

1 See *Confucian China and Its Fate* (University of California Press, 1965).

2 *Zhongguo Wenhua de Shenceng Jiegou* (Xianggang: Jixianshe, 1983).

3 See *Songming Lixue yu Zhengzhi Wenhua* (Taibei: Yunchen Wenhua Shiye gufen youxian gongsi, 2004).

4 *Centrality and Commonality: an Essay on Confucian Religiousness* (Albany, NY: State University of New York Press, 1989).

5 See *Qishi yu Zhexue de Zhengzhi Chongtu* (Xianggang: Daofeng Shushe, 2001).

6 Quoted from Jin Zhongshu, 'Du Xianshi Qianmu Xiansheng Zuihou de Xinsheng – *Zhongguo Wenhua dui Renlei Weilai Keyou de Gongxian*', in *Guoji Ruxue Yanjiu*, Volume I (Renmin Chubanshe, 1995), p. 52.

7 Daniel J. Cook and Henry Rosemount, Jr (eds), *Goffried Wilhelm Leibniz, Writings on China* (Chicago and La Salle: Open Court Publishing Company, 1994), p. 10. Also in Günter Wohlfahrt, 'Modernity and Postmodernism: Some Philosophical Remarks on the Necessity of an East-West Dialogue', in Karl-Heinz Pohl (ed.), *Chinese Thought in a Global Context: A Dialogue between China and Western Philosophical Approaches* (Brill, 1999), pp. 24–5.

8 See Tu Weiming, Dongya Jiazhi yu Duoyuan Xiandaixing (Zhongguo Shehui Kexue Chubanshe, 2001), p. 4.

9 Cf. Kant, Jasche-Logik § 6, quoted after Wohlfahrt 'Modernity and Postmodernism', p. 24.

10 Pohl (ed.), *Chinese Thought in a Global Context*, p. xi.

11 Robert Young, *Intercultural Communication: Pragmatics, Genealogy, Deconstruction* (Clevedon, Avon, England: Multilingual Matters, 1996), p. 154.

12 Pohl (ed.), *Chinese Thought in a Global Context*, p. x.

13 Quoted from Fritjof Capra, *The Tao of Physics* (USA: Shambhala Publications, Inc., 1992), p. 10.

14 Xinzhong Yao, *Confucianism and Christianity: A Comparative Study of Jen and Agape* (Brighton & Pontland: Sussex Academic Press, 1996), pp. 1–2.

15 Archie J. Balm, 'Standards for comparative philosophy', in H. D. Lewis (ed.), *Philosophy: East and West* (Bombay: Blackie & Son Ltd, 1976), pp. 81–94.

16 Matteo Ricci, *China in the Sixteenth Century: The Journals of Mathew Ricci: 1583–1610*, Louis J. Gallagher (trans.) (New York: Random House, 1953), pp. 110–11.

17 Longxi Zhang, 'Translating culture: China and the West', in Karl-Heinz Pohl (ed.), *Chinese Thought in a Global Context*, p. 41.

18 Leibniz, *Novissima sinica* (1699), quoted in Longxi Zhang, ibid., p. 39.

19 Arthur O. Lovejoy, *Essays in the History of Ideas* (Baltimore: Johns Hopkins University Press, 1948), p. 105

20 Julia Ching, *Confucianism and Christianity: a Comparative Study* (New York: Kodansha International, 1977), p. xvi.

21 Xinzhong Yao: 'Knowledge and Interpretation: A hermeneutical Study of Wisdom in Early

Confucian and Israelite Traditions' (in *Journal of Chinese Philosophy*, Vol. 32, issue 2, 2005, Blackwell Publishing), p. 298

22 Gavin Flood, *Beyond Phenomenology: Rethinking the Study of Religion* (London and New York: Cassell, 1999), p. 1.

23 Martin Heidegger, *Being and Time*, John Macquarrie and Edward Robinson (trans.) (Oxford: Blackwell, 1962), p. 153.

24 Xinzhong Yao, 'Knowledge and Interpretation', p. 299.

INTRODUCTION   The Relationship at the Centre of Confucian Thinking and Christian Ethics

1   See Adolf von Harnack, *What is Christianity?* Lecture 7 (Williams & Norgate, 1901); see also James D. G. Dunn, *Jesus and the Spirit* (London: SCM Press LTD, 1975), p. 14.

2   Walter H. Slote, 'Psychocultural Dynamics within the Confucian Family', in Walter H. Slote and George A. DeVos (eds), *Confucianism and the Family* (New York: State University of Press, 1998), p. 37.

3   Fung Yu-lan, *A Short History of Chinese Philosophy*, edited by Derk Bodde (New York: Macmillan Co., 1948), p. 21.

4   Julia Ching, *Confucianism and Christianity* (New York: Kodansha International, 1977), pp. 96–7.

5   See 'The Roman Family: Ideal and Metaphor', in *Constructing Early Christian Families: Family as Social Reality and Metaphor* (London and New York: Routledge, 1997), pp. 1 and 103.

6   Athenag. *leg.* 32 (Schoedel, 78–80); in Michael Penn, 'Performing Family: Ritual Kissing and the Construction of Early Christian Kinship', *Journal of Early Christian Studies*, Vol. 10, 2002, p. 170.

7   *Passio Andreae* 12, MacDonald 338–40, in Andrew S. Jacobs, 'A Family Affair: Marriage, Class, and Ethics in the Apocryphal Acts of the Apostles', *Journal of Early Christian Studies*, Vol. 7, 1999, p. 129.

8   'Introduction: The Humanistic Chinese Mind', in Charles A. Moore (ed.), *The Chinese Mind* (The University Press of Hawaii, first edition 1967), p. 5.

9   David K. Jordan, 'Filial Piety in Taiwanese Popular Thought', in Walter H. Slote and George A. DeVos (eds), *Confucianism and the Family* (New York: State University Press, 1998), p. 267.

10 Heiner Foetz, *Confucian Ethics of the Axial Age: A Reconstruction under the Aspect of the Breakthrough toward Postconventional Thinking* (State University of New York Press, 1993), pp. 53–66.

11 Foetz, *Confucian Ethics of the Axial Age*, p. 53.

12 J. D. Cohen (ed.), *The Jewish Family in Antiquity* (Scholars Press, 1993), pp. 67, 69.

13 See 'Family Structure in Gnostic Religion', in Halvor Moxnes (ed.), *Constructing Early Families*, p. 237.

14 Note: in this book neither Xunzi's theory nor Pauline doctrine is limited to a certain version, all chapters and letters under their name are included.

15 J. K. Fairbank, *The United States and China* (Cambridge, MA: Harvard University Press, 1948), pp. 59–60.

16 Walter H. Slote, 'Psychocultural Dynamics within the Confucian Family', in Slote and De Vos (eds), *Confucianism and the Family*, p. 37.

17 Tu Weiming: 'Confucius and Confucianism', ibid., p. 3.

18 George A. De Vos, 'A Cross-Cultural Perspective: The Japanese Family as a Unit in Moral

Socialization', in Philip A. Cowan (ed.), *Family, Self and Society: Toward a New Agenda for Family Research* (Erlbaum Assoc., Hilldale, NJ, 1993), p. 329

19 Cf. Keith Ward, *Religion and Creation* (Oxford 1996); W. L. Craig and Q. Smith, *Theism, Atheism and Big Bang Cosmology* (Oxford, 1995); Paul Badham, *The Contemporary Challenge of Modernist Theology* (Cardiff, 1998).

20 Research at the Alister Hardy Religious Experience Research Centre, Lampeter, suggests that between 31% and 49% of people report such experiences.

21 Liang Qichao, 'Qingdai Xueshu Gangyao' 25, in *Liang Qichao Xuanji*, Vol. 2 (Zhongguo Guangbo Dianshi Chubanshe, 1992).

22 Tan Sitong, 'Ren xue' 29, in *Tan Sitong Quanji*, Vol. 2 (Zhonghua shu jiu, 1981).

23 Zhuxi, *Zhuzi Yulei*, Vol. 137, edited by Li Jingde (Song Dynasty), Volume IV (Yuelu Shuyuan, 1997), p. 2937.

24 Hu Shi, *Zhongguo Zhonggu Sixiangshi Changbian*, Anhui Jiaoyu Chubanshe, 1999, pp. 262–4.

25 See Han Deming, *Xunzi yu Rujia de Shehui Lixiang*, Qilu Shushe, 2001, pp. 427–549.

26 Li Zehou, 'Xun Yiyong Jiyao', in *Zhongguo Gudai Sixiang Shilun* (Beijing: Renmin Chubanshe, 1985). See also Zhang shuguang, *Waiwang Zhixue: Xunzi he Zhongguo Wenhua* (Henan daxue Chubanshe, 1997), pp. 5–6.

27 Xunzi's surname is Xun, his first name Kuang, and his second name Qing.

28 Knoblock, *Xunzi, A Translation and Study of the Complete Works*, 1988, Vol. I, p. vii.

29 H. H. Dubs, *HSUNTZE: The Moulder of Ancient Confucianism* (London: W. C. Arthur Probsthain, 1927), p. xiii.

30 Weiming Tu, 'Confucius and Confucianism', in Slote and Devos (eds), *Confucianism and the Family*, p. 17.

31 Knoblock, *Xunzi*, Vol. 3, p. 274.

32 C. K. Barrett: *From First Adam to Last: A Study in Pauline Theology* (London: Adam & Charles Black, 1962), p. 3.

33 K. Armstrong, *The First Christian: Saint Paul's Impact on Christianity* (London: Pan, 1983), pp. 12 and 13.

34 C. K. Barrett, *From First Adam to Last*, p. 3.

35 James D. G. Dunn, *The Theology of Paul the Apostle* (Grand Rapids, Michigan/ Cambridge: William B. Eerdmans Publishing Company, 1998), p. 3

36 Jeffrey L. Sheler: 'Reassessing an Apostle' in *U.S. News & World Report* 126.13, April 5, 1999), p. 55.

37 Robert L. Reymond, *Paul: Missionary Theologian: A Survey of his Missionary Labour and Theology* (Mentor, first published in 2000 and reprinted in 2002 by Christina Focus Publications, Geanies House, Fearn, Ross-shire, Scotland), p. 10.

38 Neil Elliott, *Liberating Paul: The Justice of God and the Politics of the Apostle* (Sheffield: Sheffield Academic Press, 1995), p. 4.

39 Elliott, *Liberating Paul*, pp. 5–9.

40 From the start of the twentieth century, Wrede began to call Paul 'the second founder of Christianity' (William Wrede, *Paul*, London: Green, 1907), p. 179.

41 David Wenham, *Paul: Follower of Jesus or Founder of Christianity* (Grand Rapids/Cambridge: William B. Eerdmans Publishing Company, 1995), p. 3.

42 George Arthur Buttrick (ed.), *The Interpreter's Dictionary of the Bible: An Illustrated Encyclopedia* (Abingdon Press, 1962), p. 681.

43 E. R. Dodds, 'Introduction: where did all this madness come from?' in John G. Gager, *Reinventing Paul* (Oxford University Press, 2000), p. 3.

44 Hui Jixing examines this situation of the Neo-Confucians in his book *Xunzi yu Zhongguo Wenhua* (Guiyang: Guizhou Renmin Chubanshe, 1996), pp. 37–44.

45 H. H. Dubs, *HSUNTZE: The Moulder of Ancient Confucianism* (London: W. C. Arthur Probsthain, 1927), p. xiii.

46 Guo Moruo, 'Xunzi Pipan', in *Shi Pipan Shu* (Beijing: Renmin Chubanshe, 1954).

47 Joubert, Stephan J. 'Managing the Household: Paul as Paterfamilias of the Christian household group in Corinth', in Philip F. Esler (ed.), *Modelling Early Christianity: Social-Scientific Studies of the New Testament in its Context* (London/New York: Routledge, 1995), p. 216.

48 James D. G. Dunn, 'Diversity in Paul', in Dan Cohn-Sherbok and John M. Court (eds), *Religious Diversity in the Graeco-Roman World: A Survey of Recent Scholarship* (Sheffield: Sheffield Academic Press, 2001), p. 107.

49 See W. S. Campbell, 'Millennial Optimism for Jewish-Christian Dialogue', in *The Future of Christian–Jewish Dialogue*, edited by Dan Cohn-Sherbok (Lampeter, UK: Mellen, 1999), pp. 217–37.

50 Han Demin, *Xunzi yu Rujia Shehui Lixiang* (Qilu Shushe, 2001), p. 19.

51 Chen Yinke, *Jinming guan conggao erbian: Feng Youlan's Zhongguo Zhexueshi Diaocha Baogao(2)* (Shanghai Guji Chubanshe, 1980).

52 Gerd Theissen, *Essays on Corinth: The Social Setting of Pauline Christianity*, edited and translated by John H. Schütz (T&T Clark Limited, 1975), pp. 35–6.

53 For instance, Bernadette J. Brooten's 'Paul and the Law. How Complete was the Departure?' is an example, see *The Princeton Seminary Bulletin*, Supplementary Issue, No. 1, 1990, pp. 71–89.

54 George Arthur Buttrick (ed.), *The Interpreters Dictionary of the Bible* (Nashville: Abingdon Press, 1962), p. 689.

55 Buttrick (ed.), *The Interpreters Dictionary of the Bible*, p. 689.

56 Alexander Jones, *The Jerusalem Bible* (London: Darton, Longman & Todd, 1966), p. 252.

57 Knoblock, *Xunzi, A Translation and Study of the Completed Work*, Vol. I, 1988, p. 212.

58 Liu Xiang's 'preface to the *Sun Qing Xinshu*' in ibid., Vol. III, 1994, p. 271.

59 Jones, *The Jerusalem Bible*, p. 251.

60 Ibid., pp. 251–2.

61 Buttrick (ed.), *The Interpreters Dictionary of the Bible*, p. 688.

62 Ibid., p. 688.

ONE   The Origin of Xunzi's Secular Father–Son Relationship

1 These are Xia Dynasty (2070?–1600? BCE), Shang Dynasty (1600–1046 BCE) and Zhou Dynasty (1046–256 BCE), especially the Western Zhou Dynasty (1046–771 BCE).

2 Han Demin, *Xunzi yu Rujia de Shehui Lixiang* (Jinan: Qilu shushe, 2001), p. 171.

3 Arthur F. Wright, *Confucianism and Chinese Civilization* (Stanford University Press), p. x.

4 See Xiao Qunzhong, *Xiao yu Zhongguo Shehui* (Beijing: Renmin Chubanshe, 2001), pp. 18–19.

5 Benjam Schwartz, *The World of Thought in Ancient China* (Cambridge, MA: Harvard University Press, 1985), pp. 20–1.

6 Patricia Buckley Ebrey, *Confucianism and Family Rituals in Imperial China: A Social History of Writing About Rites* (Princeton, NJ: Princeton University Press, 1991), p. 15.

7 Zha Chang-guo, 'First Exploration on the Meaning of Filial Piety of the Western Zhou Period', in *Zhongguoshi Yanjiu*, No. 3, 1993.

8 Walter H. Slote, 'Psychocultural Dynamics within the Confucian Family', in *Confucianism*

and the Family, edited by Walter H. Slote and George A. DeVos (State University of New York Press, 1998), pp. 37–8.

9 He Ping, 'Xiaodao de Qiyuan yu Xiaoxing's Zuizao Tichu', in *Nankai Daxue Xuebao*, 2nd edn, 1988.

10 See 'Long and strong is the Trailing Plant' in *Translation of Confucian Classics: The Book of Songs*, A Chinese–English Bilingual Edition (Shandong Friendship Press, 1999).

11 Zha Chang-guo, 'Lun Chunqiu zhi "Xiao" fei Zunqin', in *Anqing Shifan Xueyuan Xuebao*, No. 4, 1993.

12 Zhou Yutong, 'Xiao yu Shengzhiqi Chongbai', in *Zhou Yu-tong Jingxueshi Lunzhu xuan ji* (Shanghai Renmin Press, 1983), pp. 71, 77.

13 Song Jinlan, 'Xiao de Wenhua Neiyun jiqi Shanbian', in *Qinghai Shehui Kexue*, No. 3, 1994.

14 Guo Moruo, *Zhongguo Gudai Shehui Yanjiu* (Kexue Chubanshe, 1960), p. 252.

15 Xiao Qunzhong, *Xiao yu Zhongguo Wenhua* (Beijing: Renmin Chubanshe, 2001), p. 22.

16 'Have Pity on Me' in *The Temple Hymns*, see *Translations of Confucian Classics: The Book of Songs* (Shandong Friendship Press, 1999), p. 907.

17 'The First Presence at Court' in *The Temple Hymns*. See *Translations of Confucian Classics: The Book of Songs* (Shandong Friendship Press, 1999), p. 901.

18 'The Chain of Undulating Hills' in the *Great Odes*. See *Translations of Confucian Classics: The Book of Songs* (Shandong Friendship Press, 1999), p. 769.

19 *The Sacrificial Odes of Shang, Ode 2*, see The *Book of Poetry*, in *The Sacred Books of the East*, edited by F. Max Müller, translated by James Legge (reprinted by Motilal Banarsidass, 1970), p. 306.

20 *The Book of Mengzi*, 4A:26.

21 *The Li Ki*, BK. IX, 8, translated by James Legge, in *The Sacred Book of China*, part III, in F. Max Müller (ed.), *Sacred Books of the East*, Vol. XXVII (Delhi: Motilal Banarsidass, first published by the Oxford University Press, 1968, reprinted in 1985), pp. 430–1.

22 R. F. Winch, *The Modern Family* (New York, Holt, Rinehart and Winston, 1963), pp. 36–7.

23 Hsieh Yuwei, 'Filial Piety and Chinese Society', in Charles A. Moore (ed.) *The Chinese Mind* (The University Press of Hawaii, Honolulu, Paperback Edition, 1967, 1977), pp. 171, 174.

24 The Chinese version of 'Ground Course' is *dadao*, the greatest Way, which means the perfect and most harmonious principle.

25 Book VII, The 'Li Yun' of *The Li Ki*, translated by James Legge, in *The Sacred Book of China*, part III, in F. Max Müller (ed.), *Sacred Books of the East*, Vol. XXVII, pp. 364–5.

26 Book XXIV, 'Ai Kung Wan', *The Li Ki*, translated by James Legge, in *The Sacred Book of China*, part IV, in F. Max Müller (ed.), *Sacred Books of the East*, Vol. XXVIII, p. 269.

27 Jiao Guocheng, *Zhongguo Gudai Renwu Guanxi Lun* (Renmin Daxue Chubanshe), p. 58.

28 Fei Xiaotong, *Native Land China* (Sanlian Shudian, 1985), p. 34.

29 Walter H. Slote, 'Psychocultural Dynamics within the Confucian Family', in *Confucianism and the Family*, edited by Slote and A. DeVos (State University of New York Press, 1998), pp. 37–8.

30 Han Demin, *Xunzi yu Rujia de Shehui Lixiang* (Qilu shushe, 2001), p. 151.

31 John Knoblock, *Xunzi*, 1988, p. 53.

32 *Xiao Jing*, Ch. ix (Zhonghua Shuju, 1996), p. 19.

33 Chen Lai, *Ancient Religions and Morality* (Sanlian Shudian, 1996), p. 30.

34 Heiner Roetz, *Confucian Ethics of the Axial Age* (Albany: State University of New York Press, 1993), p. 53.

35 For example, Tang Xuewei declared that Confucius linked the practice of filial piety with political action (in *Xianqin Xiaodao Yanjiu*, Wenjin Chubanshe, 1992), p. 181, whereas, Xiao Qunzhong holds a different opinion that in the thought of Confucius, although there are some connections between filial piety (*Xiao*) and loyalty (*Zhong*), they are actually different concepts: while filial piety belongs to family ethics, loyalty belongs to political ethics (see Xiao Qunzhong, 2001), p. 41.

36 Weiming Tu, 'Probing the "Three Bonds" and "Five Relationships"', in Walter H. Slote and George A. De Vos (eds), *Confucianism and the Family* (State University of New York Press, 1998), p. 127.

37 'Li Yun', SECT. II., 19. Translated by James Legge, in *The Sacred Book of China*, part III, in F. Max Müller (ed.), *Sacred Books of the East*, Vol. XXVII, p. 379–80.

38 Lin Yüsheng, 'Creative Transformation of Chinese Tradition', in *Chinese Thought in a Global Context*, edited by Karl-Heinz Pohl (Brill, 1999), p. 85.

39 According to Homer H. Dubs, Quedang means city or community. See *The Works of Huntze* (Confucius Publishing Co., 1972), p. 124

40 See Han Demin, *Xunzi*, 2001, pp. 149–50.

41 Ibid., 2001, pp. 167–8.

42 'Ki I' in *The Li ki*, XXI, Sect II, 11, translated by James Legge, in F. Max Müller (ed.), *Sacred Books of the East*, Vol. XXVIII, p. 226.

43 James Legge, 'Ki I' in *The Li ki*, 1968, p. 226.

44 *XiaoJing*, chap. 1 (Zhonghua Shuju, 1996), p. 1.

45 Hui Jixing, *Xunzi and Chinese culture* (Guizhou Renmin Chubanshe, 1996), p. 21.

46 Hsieh Yuwei, 'Filial Piety and Chinese Society', in *The Chinese Mind* (ed. by Charles A. Moore, The University Press of Hawaii, Honolulu, 1967), p. 174.

47 Wing-Tsit Chan, 'Chinese Theory and Practice, with Special Reference to Humanism', in Karl-Heinz Pohl, *Chinese Thought in a Global Context*, p. 12.

48 David S. Nivision, 'Husu Tzu and Cuang Tzu', in Henry Rosemont, Jr. (ed.), *Chinese Texts and Philosophical Contexts: Essays Dedicated to Angus C. Graham* (La Salle, Illinois: Open Court, 1991), p. 129.

49 *Dao De Jing*, Chap. 25, in James Legge (trans), *The Text of Taoism* (New York: Dover, 1962), p. 68.

50 Paul Goldin, *Rituals of the Way: The Philosophy of Xunzi* (Chicago: Open Court, 1999), p. 98.

51 Robert Eno: *The Confucian Creation of Heaven: Philosophy and the Defense of Ritual Mastery* (Albany, SUNY Series in Chinese Philosophy and Culture, 1990), p. 272.

52 Kurits Hagen: 'Xunzi's Use of Zhengming', in *Asian Philosophy*, Vol. 12, No. 1, 2002, p. 39.

53 Li Shenzhi, 'Reflections on the Concept of the Unity of Heaven and Man', in Karl-Heinz Pohl (ed.), *Chinese Thought in a Global Context* (Brill, 1999), p. 115.

54 John Knoblack, *Xunzi: A Translation and Study of the Complete Works*, Vol. III, pp. 3–4.

55 Although 'The commentaries of the Book of Changes' is considered as a production of later Confucians after Xunzi, it is in fact a reflection of Pre-Qin Confucian doctrine; it is reasonable therefore to trace this as a source.

56 'Shuogua' , see Richard Rutt, *Zhouyi: The Book of Changes* (Curzon, 1996), p. 447.

57 'Xugua', see Richard Rutt, *Zhouyi: The Book of Changes* (Curzon, 1996), p. 451.

58 Yao was an ancient Sage-King who established a model of benevolent government enhanced by Confucianism; Jie was an ancient bad king who practised cruel government.

59 Jiao Guocheng, *Zhongguo Lunlixue Tonglun* (Vol. 1) (Shangxi Jiaoyu Chubanshe, 1997), p. 82.

60 Ibid., p. 6.

61 Cho-Yun Hsü discusses the possibility that Xunzi was influenced by both Daoism and Mohism in his article 'The Unfolding of Early Confucianism: The Evolution from

Confucius to Hsün-Tzu', in *Confucianism: The Dynamics of Tradition*, edited by Irene Eber (New York: Macmillan Publishing Company, 1986), pp. 33–4.

62 John Knoblock, *Xunzi: A Translation and Study of the Complete Works* (Stanford University Press, 1990), Vol. I, p. 184.

63 *Zhuangzi*, 22 *Zhibeiyou*, 7.23ab. The relevant English translation can be seen in James R. Ware, *The Sayings of Chuang Tzu* (Confucius Publishing Co., 1971), p. 262.

64 *Guanzi*, *Neiye*, 16.2b.

65 Homer H. Dubs gives a detailed discussion on the different perceptions of the essential human nature in Xunzi and Mencius in 'Mencius and Hsutze on Human Nature', in *Philosophy East and West*, 6, 1965, pp. 213–22. However, some scholars, such as Philip J. Ivanhoe believe that Dubs misunderstood Xunzi's theory of human nature. In *Confucian Moral Self Cultivation*, *The Rockwell Lecture Series 3* (New York Peter Lang, 1993), pp. 39–40.

66 Philip J. Ivanhoe, *Confucian Moral Self Cultivation*, *The Rockwell Lecture Series 3* (New York: Peter Lang, 1993), p. 37.

67 Lu Debin, 'Xunzi Zhexue zai Rujia Fazhan Guocheng zhong de Diwei he Zuoyong', in *Zhongguo Zhexueshi*, period 3, 1997; also in *Zhongguo Renmin Daxue Baokan Fuyin Ziliao: Zhongguo Zhexue*, volume 3, 1998, pp. 60–2.

68 Mou Zongsan, *Daode Lixiang Zhuyi* (Taibei: Xuesheng, 1982, fifth edition), see also Fang Keli and Li Jinquan (eds), *Xiandai Xin Rujia Xuean* (Beijing: Shenhuikexue Chubanshe, 1995), Vol. 3, p. 529.

69 Weiming Tu, 'Confucius and Confucianism', in *Confucianism and the Family*, edited by Walter H. Slote and Geoge A. De Vos (State University of New York Press, 1998), p. 17.

70 Hui Jixing, *Xunzi and Confucian Culture*, p. 73.

71 See 'Book XL. Kwan I' of *The Li Ki*, translated by James Legge, in *The Sacred Book of China*, part IV, in F. Max Müller (ed.), *Sacred Books of the East*, Vol. XXVIII, p. 423.

72 Wei-Ming Tu, Confucius and Confucianism, see *Confucianism and the Family*, edited by Walter H. Slote and George A. De Vos, p. 17.

TWO   Sources and Background of the Pauline Divine Father–Son Relationship

1 John Stambaugh and David Balch, *The Social World of the First Christians* (London: SPCK, 1986), p. 44.

2 See Brian S. Rosner (ed.), *Understanding Paul's Ethics: Twentieth Century Approaches* (Grand Rapids, MI: William B. Eerdmans Publishing Company, 1995), p. 10.

3 Joseph Klausner, *From Jesus to Paul* (trans. Williams F. Stinespring, London: George Allen & Unwin Ltd, 1946), p. 14.

4 William S. Campbell, 'All God's Beloved in Rome: Jewish Roots and Christian Identity', Paper presented at the Studiorum Novi Testamenti Societas annual meeting, Tel Aviv, August 2000, in *Celebrating Romans*, edited by Sheila McGinn (Grand Rapids, MI: Eerdmans, 2004), pp. 67–82.

5 Adolf von Harnack, *The Mission and Expansion of Christianity in the First Three Centuries* (New York: Harper, 1961), pp. 60–4.

6 James Dunn, 'The Status and Contribution of Paul', in *The Future of Jewish-Christian Dialogue*, edited by Dan Cohn-Sherbok (Toronto Studies in Theology, Vol. 80, Lampeter: The Edwin Mellen Press, 1999), p. 172.

7 Wayne A. Meeks, *The First Urban Christians: The Social World of the Apostle Paul* (2nd edition, New Haven and London: Yale University Press, 2003), p. 87.

8 John G. Gager, *Reinventing Paul* (Oxford University Press, 2000), p. 147.

9   Peter Balla, *The Child–Parent Relationship in the New Testament and its Environment* (Tübingen, Mohr Siebeck, 2003), p. 10.

10 J. D. Cohen (ed.), *The Jewish Family in Antiquity* (Atlanta, GA: Scholars Press, 1993), p. 65.

11 Peter Balla, *The Child–Parent Relationship*, pp. 355–6.

12 Craig A. Evans and Stanley E. Porter (eds), *Dictionary of New Testament Background* (InterVarsity Press, 2000), p. 355.

13 Philo is the most prominent of those Jewish authors who were deeply acculturated to Hellenism. The basis of his thought was and remained the Jewish Bible, but his life was at the same time deeply committed to the faith of his ancestors; his understanding of the parent–child relationship is still a model of Jewish thinking.

14 J. D. Cohen (ed.), *The Jewish Family in Antiquity*, p. 65.

15 Tessa Rajak, 'The Jewish Community and Its Boundaries', in Judith Lieu, John North and Tessa Rajak (eds), *The Jews Among Pagans and Christianity in the Roman Empire* (London and New York: Routledge, 1992), p. 13.

16 J. D. Cohen (ed.), *The Jewish Family in Antiquity*, p. 65.

17 Evans and Porter (eds), *Dictionary of New Testament Background*, p. 355.

18 'Jewish Mothers and Daughters in the Greco-Roman World', in Cohen (ed.), *The Jewish Family in Antiquity*, p. 110.

19 Josephus *Against Apion* II. 201, trs., Thackeray (London: Printed by W. Bowyer for the author, sold by Whiston, 1737).

20 B. Brooten, *Women Leaders in the Ancient Synagogue* (Brown Judaic Studies 36, Chico, California. 1982). Also in Tessa Rajak 'The Jewish Community and its Boundaries', in Judith Lieu, John North and Tessa Rajak (eds.), *The Jews Among Pagans and Christianity in the Roman Empire*, p. 22.

21 R. van Bremen, 'Women and Wealth', in A. Cameron and A. Kuhrt (eds.), *Images of Women in Antiquity* (London and Sydney, 1983), pp. 223–42. See also Tessa Rajak, 'The Jewish Community and its Boundaries', in Lieu, North and Rajak (eds.), *The Jews Among Pagans and Christianity in the Roman Empire*, pp. 23–5.

22 Some female theologians dive into this field and seek out much valuable fruit. See E. Schüssler Fiorenza, *In Memory of Her: A Feminist Theological Reconstruction of Christian Origins* (New York: Crossroad: London: SCM Press, 1983). Bernadette Brooten, *Women Leaders in the Ancient Synagague* (Brown Judaic Studies 36, Chico, California: Scholars Press, 1982).

23 There is, nevertheless, co-existence of patriarchy and equality in the Pauline idea of the male and female relationship. As Kathleen E. Corley has noted, in antiquity we can find tendencies toward more equality or more mutual appreciation. See *Private Women, Public Meal: Social Conflict in the Synoptic Tradition* (Peabody, MA: Hendrickson, 1993), pp. 78–9. This also occurs in the Pauline texts. Under God and Jesus Christ, men and women, a number of times, are treated equally and mutually.

24 E.g. Schüssler Fiorenza, *In Memory of Her*; see also Kathy Ehrensperger, *That We May be Mutually Encouraged: Feminism and the New Perspective in Pauline Studies* (T&T Clark International, 2004), p. 40.

25 Evans and Porter (eds), *Dictionary of New Testament Background*, pp. 359–7.

26 Stephen C. Barton, 'The Relativisation of Family Ties in the Jewish and Graeco-Roman Traditions', in Halvor Moxnes (ed.), *Constucting Early Christian Families* (Routledge, 1997), p. 82.

27 See *Constucting Early Christian Families* (Routledge, 1997), p. 4.

28 Moxnes (ed.), *Constucting Early Christian Families*, p. 98.

29 Evans and Porter (eds), *Dictionary of New Testament Background*, p. 355.

30 Andrew T. Lincoln, 'The Household Code and Wisdom Mode of Colossians' in *Journal for Study of the New Testament*, issue 74, 1999, p. 100.

31 See Kathy Ehrensperger, *That we May Be Mutually Encouraged: Feminism and the New Perspective in Pauline Studies* (New York/London: T&T Clark International, 2004), p. 50.

32 Paul van Buren, *According to the Scripture: The Origin of the Church's Old Testament* (Grand Rapids, MI: Eerdmans, 1998), p. 26.

33 Troels Engberg-Pedersen (ed.), *Paul in His Hellenistic Context* (T&T Clark, Edinburgh, 1994), p. xx.

34 David E. Aune, *Greco-Roman Literature and the New Testament* (Atlanta, GA: Scholars Press, 1988), pp. 25–33. Balla gives a more detailed discussion of the Platonic and Aristotelian background to the Christian household. See *The Child–Parent Relationship in the New Testament and its Environment*, pp. 7–9.

35 Adolf von Harnack, *The Mission and Expansion of Christianity in the First Three Centuries* (New York: Harper, 1961), p. 74.

36 *The Interpreter's Dictionary of the Bible* (Nashville: Abingdon Press, 1976), Vol. 3, p. 688.

37 Martin Hengel, 'The Pre-Christian Paul', in Judith Lieu (ed.), *The Jews among Pagans and Christians in the Roman Empire* (Routledge, 1992), p. 30.

38 Emiel Eyben discusses this power of the father in 'Fathers and Sons', see Beryl Rawson (ed.), *Marriage, Divorce, and Children in Ancient Rome* (Oxford: Clarendon Paperbacks, 1996), pp. 114–43.

39 Carolyn Osiek and David L. Balch, *Families in the New Testament World: Households and House Churches* (Louisville, Kentucky: Westminster John Knox Press, 1997), p. 38.

40 Aristotle, *Politics 1.5* (1259a35–1260b20, passim); also Osiek and Balch, *Families in the New Testament World*, p. 55.

41 Eva Marie Lassen, 'The Roman Family: Ideal and Metaphor', in Halvor Moxnes (ed.), *Constructing Early Christian Families: Family as Social Reality and Metaphor* (London and New York: Routledge, 1997), p. 104.

42 Keith R. Bradley, *Discovering the Roman Family: Studies in Roman Social History* (Oxford: Oxford University Press, 1991). Suzanne Dixon, *The Roman Family* (Baltimore: Johns Hopkins University Press, 1992).

43 See Richard P. Saller, *Patriarchy, Property and Death in the Roman Family* (Cambridge University Press, 1994), pp. 79–83.

44 Ibid.

45 Eyben, Emiel: 'Fathers and Sons', in Rawson Beryl (ed.), *Marriage, Divorce, and Children in Ancient Rome* (Oxford: Clarendon Press, 1996), p. 115. Osiek and Balch discuss the custom in Greco-Roman society of infanticide or the exposure of children in *Families in the New Testament World: Households and House Churches*, pp. 65–7.

46 Richard P. Saller, *Patriarchy, Property and Death in the Roman Family* (Cambridge University Press, 1994), pp. 102–3.

47 Evans and Porter (eds): *Dictionary of New Testament Background*, p. 359.

48 Veyne 1987:16–17, 18.29; see also Saller, *Patriarchy, Property and Death in the Roman Family*, p. 104.

49 Eyben, Emiel: 'Fathers and Sons', in Rawson Beryl (ed.), *Marriage, Divorce, and Children in Ancient Rome* (Oxford: Clarendon Press, 1996), pp. 117–18.

50 J. D. Cohen (ed.), *The Jewish Family in Antiquity* (Scholars Press, 1993), p. 62.

51 Halvor Moxnes (ed.), *Constructing Early Christian Families*, 1997, p. 4.

52 Balsdon, quoted in Richard P. Saller, *Patriarchy, Property and Death in the Roman Family* (Cambridge University Press, 1994), pp. 105–6.

53 Eva Marie Lassen, 'The Roman Family: Ideal and Metaphor', in Moxnes (ed.), *Constructing Early Christian Families*, 1997, pp. 112–13.

54 Richard P. Saller, *Patriarchy, Property and Death in the Roman Family* (Cambridge University Press, 1994), p. 102.

55 Cicero, Off.1.54, also in Saller, *Patriarchy, Property and Death in the Roman Family*, p. 102.

56 Evans and Porter (eds), *Dictionary of New Testament Background*, p. 353.

57 Saller, *Patriarchy, Property and Death in the Roman Family*, p. 72.

58 Ibid., p. 43.

59 Gerd Theissen, *Social Reality and the Early Christians: Theology, Ethics, and the World of the New Testament*, translated by Margaret Kohl (Edinburgh: T&T Clark, 1992), p. 194.

60 Osiek and Balch, *Families in the New Testament World*, pp. 53–4, pp. 38–9.

61 There is a description of the debate on the status of the Roman father in Saller's *Patriarchy, Property and Death in the Roman Family*, p. 106.

62 Lassen Eva Marie, 'The Roman Family: Ideal and Metaphor', in Moxnes, *Constructing Early Christian Families*, p. 114.

63 Eva Marie Lassen insists that Roman family metaphor was in many aspects dissimilar to that introduced by the first Christians. Whereas the Roman family signaled hierarchical power relationships, the Christian family metaphors were used to describe inter-human relationships; their function was primarily to create equality and a new sense of belonging (Ibid., pp. 114–15).

64 G. H. C. Macgregor and A. C. Purdy, *Jew and Greek: Tutors Unto Christ – the Jewish and Hellenistic Background of the New Testament* (Edinburgh: The Saint Andrew Press, 1959), p. 195.

65 David E. Aune (ed.), *Greco-Roman Literature and the New Testament* (Scholars Press, 1988), pp. 35–6.

66 L. Hartman investigates Martin Dibelius' construct in his article 'Some Unorthodox Thoughts on the "Household-Code Form"' in Jacob Neusner, Ernest S. Frerichs, Peder Borgen and Richard Horsley (eds), *The Social World of Formative Christianity and Judaism* (Philadephia: Fortress Press, 1988), p. 220.

67 K. Weidinger, *Die Haustafeln: Ein Stück urchristlicher Paranese*, Untersuchungen zum Neuen Testament 14 (Leipzig: J. C. Hinrichs, 1928).

68 David E. Aune (ed.), *Greco-Roman Literature and the New Testament* (Scholars Press, 1988), p. 27.

69 Evans and Porter (eds), *Dictionary of New Testament Background*, p. 353.

70 K. Berger, 'Hellenistic Gattungen im Neuen Testament', in *Aufstieg und Niedergang der romischen Welt 2.25.2* (New York and Berlin: Walter de Gruyter, 1984), pp. 1031–432, also in L. Hartman 'Some Unorthodox Thoughts on the "Household-Code Form"', in Jacob Neusner and Ernest S. Frerichs (eds), *The Social World of Formative Christianity and Judaism* (Philadephia: Fortress Press), p. 221.

71 David E. Aune, *Greco-Roman Literature and the New Testament*, p. 28.

72 G. H. C. Macgregor and A. C. Purdy, *Jew and Greek*, p. 189.

73 Von Lips, Hermann, *Glaube-Gemeinde-Amt: Zum Verstandnis der Ordination in den Pastoralbriefen* (Gottingen: Vandenhoeck & Ruprecht, 1979), p. 126. Also in Stephan J. Joubert, 'Managing the Household: Paul as Paterfamilias of the Christian Household Group in Corinth', in Philip F. Esler (ed.), *Modelling Early Christianity*, p. 213.

74 John H. Elliott, *What is Social-Scientific Criticism?* (Minneapolis: Fortress Press, 1993), p. 85.

75 Stephan J. Joubert, 'Managing the Household: Paul as Paterfamilias of the Christian Household Group in Corinth' in Philip F. Esler (ed.), *Modelling Early Christianity*, p. 213.

76 Andrew S. Jacobs and Rebecca Krawiec, 'Fathers Know Best? Christian Families in the Age of Asceticism', in *Journal of Early Christian Studies*, Vol. II, 2003, p. 260.

77 W. K. Lacey, 'Patria Potestas' in Beryl Rawson (ed.), *The Family in Ancient Rome: New Perspectives* (Ithaca: Cornell University Press, 1987), p. 140.

78 Suzanne Dixon, 'The Sentimental Ideal of the Roman Family', in Beryl Rawson (ed.), *Marriage, Divorce and Children in Ancient Rome* (Oxford: Clarendon Press, 1991), pp. 99–113.

79 Halvor Moxnes, *Constructing Early Christian Families: Family as Social Reality and Metaphor* (London: Routledge, 1997), p. 5.

80 Karl Olav Sandnes, 'Equality within Patriarchal Structures: Some New Testament Perspectives on the Christian Fellowship as a Brother-sisterhood and a Family', in Moxnes, *Constructing Early Christian Families*, pp. 150–65.

81 W. D. Davies, *Paul and Rabbinic Judaism* (London, 1962), p. 136.

82 Lars Hartman, 'Code and Context: A Few Reflections on the Parenesis of Col 3:6–4:1', in Brian S. Rosner (ed.), *Understanding Paul's Ethics: Twentieth Century Approaches* (Grand Rapids, Michigan: William B. Eerdmans Publishing Company, The Paternoster Press, 1995), p. 179.

83 Richard N. Longenecker: 'New Testament Social Ethics for Today', in Brian S. Rosner (ed.), *Understanding Paul's Ethics*, p. 345.

84 Robert M. Grant, *Paul in the Roman World: the Conflict at Corinth* (London and Leiden: Westminster John Knox Press, 1989), pp. 3–4.

85 Joachim Jeremias, *The Central Message of the New Testament* (New York: Charles Scribner's Sons, 1965), p. 9.

86 This concept of 'paternity' has been challenged by some; Paul Smith, for example insists that the term 'Mother' is equally acceptable (See *Is it Okay to call God 'Mother'*, Peabody: Hendrickson Publishers, Inc., 1993), but concedes the historical necessity of 'father'.

87 T. W. Manson, *The Teaching of Jesus* (Cambridge, 1931), pp. 90ff.

88 Jeremias, *The Central Message of the New Testament*, pp. 14–6.

89 Jeremias, *The Central Message of the New Testament*, p. 17.

90 Martina Gnadt, 'Abba Isn't Daddy – Aspekte einer feministische-befreiungstheologische Revision des Abba Jesus', in Luise Schottroff and Marie-Theres Wacher (eds), *Von der Wurze getragen: Christlich-feminische Exegese in Auseinanderstzung mit Antijudaismus* (Leiden: Brill, 1995), pp. 115–31.

91 James Barr, 'Abba Isn't Daddy', *The Journal of Theological Studies*, Vol. 39, 1988, pp. 29–47.

92 See *Is It Okay to Call God 'Mother'* (Peabody: Hendrickson Publishers, Inc. 1993), pp. 96–7, note 21.

93 Jeremias, *The Central Message of the New Testament*, pp. 22–3.

94 Balla, *The Child–Parent Relationship in the New Testament and its Environment*, pp. 117–18.

95 Moxnes (ed.), *Constructing Early Christian Families*, p. 35.

96 Carolyn Osiek and David L. Balch, *Families in the New Testament World: Households and House Churches* (Louisville, Kentucky: Westminster John Knox Press, 1997), p. 124.

97 Andrew S. Jacobs, 'Let Him Guard Pietas: Early Christian Exegesis and the Ascetic Family', in *Journal of Early Christian Studies*, Vol. II, 2003, pp. 266–7.

98 See Stephen Barton, *Discipleship*, 80, and Raymond E. Brown, *Mary in the New Testament* (Philadelphia: Fortress Press, 1978), pp. 61–4.

99 Gerd Theissen, 'The Wandering Radicals: Light Shed by the Sociology of Literature on the Early Transmission of Jesus Sayings', in David G. Horrell (ed.), *Social-Scientific Approaches to New Testament Interpretation* (Edinburgh: T&T Clark, 1999), p. 100.

100 Theissen, 'The Wandering Radicals', p. 101 and 102.

101 John M. G. Barclay, 'The Family as the Bearer of Religion in Judaism and Early Christianity', in Moxnes, *Constructing Early Christian Families*, p. 73.

102 Karl Olav Sandnes, 'Equality within Patriarchal structures', in ibid., p. 151.

103 K. Schäfer, *Gemeinde als 'Bruderschaft', Ein Beitrag zum Kirchenverstandnis des Paulus*, Europeische Hochschuschriften XXIII/333 (Bern: Peter Lang, 1989), pp. 19, 37, 353–5, 358, 369, 443–4.

104 Balla, *The Child–Parent Relationship in the New Testament and its Environment*, p. 158, p. 150.

105 E. Schüssler Fiorenza, *In Memory of Her, A Feminist Theological Reconstruction of Christian Origins* (New York: Crossroad, 1983).

106 David E. Aune (ed.), *Greco-Roman Literature and the New Testament* (Scholars Press, 1988), pp. 33–4.

107 Karl Olav Sandnes, 'Equality within Patriarchal Structure: Some New Testament Perspectives on the Christian fellowship as a brother or sister and family', in Moxnes, *Constructing Early Christian Families*, p. 151.

108 Gerd Theissen, *Social Reality and the Early Christians: Theology, Ethics, and the World of the New Testament*, trans. Margaret Kohl (Edinburgh: T&T Clark, 1993), p. viii.

109 H. Moxnes, 'Social Integration and the Problem of Gender in St Paul's Letters', *ST* 43:99–113, also Karl Olav Sandnes, 'Equality Within Patriarchal Structures', in Moxnes, *Constructing Early Christian Families*, p. 162.

110 Reidar Aasgaard, 'Brotherhood in Plutarch and Paul: Its Role and Character', in ibid., p. 176.

111 Daniel Boyarin, *A Radical Jew: Paul and the Politics of Identity* (Berkeley: University of California Press, 1994), p. 181.

112 'What is Family?' in Moxnes (ed.), *Constructing Early Christian Families*, p. 36.

113 Bruce J. Malina, *The Social World of Jesus and the Gospels* (London: Routledge, 1996), p. 109.

114 Robert L. Reymond, *Paul: Missionary Theologian: A Survey of his Missionary Labours and Theology* (Mentor, first published in 2000 and reprinted in 2002 by Christian Focus Publications), p. 330.

115 See *The Interpreter's Dictionary of the Bible*, edited by George Arthur Buttrick (Abingdon Press, 1962), volume 3, p. 692.

116 James D. G. Dunn, *The Theology of Paul the Apostle*, p. 81.

117 Ibid., p. 91.

118 David E. Aune, 'Human nature and Ethics: Issues and Problems', in Troels Engberg-Pedersen (ed.), *Paul in His Hellenistic Context*, p. 299.

THREE Classification of the Father–Son Relationship

1 Kinship is a word which is an abstraction relating to the network of relationships based upon birth (either real or fictive) and marriage. See K. C. Hanson, 'BTB Readers Guide: Kinship', *BTB* 24, pp. 183–94, 1994. Also see Halvor Moxnes, 'What is Family', in his book (ed.), *Constructing Early Christian Families: Family as Social Reality and Metaphor* (London: Routledge, 1997), p. 17.

2 *Theological Dictionary of the New Testament*, edited by Gerhard Friedrich, translator and editor: Geoffrey W. Bromiley, D. Litt., D. D. (WM. B. Eerdmans Publishing Company, 1972), Vol. VIII, pp. 334– 9.

3 Friedrich (ed.), *Theological Dictionary of the New Testament*, Vol. VIII, pp. 340–4.

4 Ibid., p. 334.

5 Ibid., Vol. V, p. 948.

6 *Theological Lexicon of the New Testament*, translated and edited by James D. Ernest (Hendrickson Publishers, 1994), Vol. 2, p. 233.

7 Friedrich (ed.), *Theological Dictionary of the New Testament*, Vol. V, p. 963.

8 Abraham is the original believer in God, and Israel and later believers are his successors in belief; therefore, if he is the father of Israel and later believers, it means that all later believers are the sons of former believers.

9 David G. Horrell, 'Leadership Patterns and the Development of Ideology', in *Social-Scientific Approaches to New Testament Interpretation* (T&T Clark, 1999), p. 330.

10 Halvor Moxnes confirms that Paul's exhortations in Rom 12:3–16 are bound together by a thematic unity – he is concerned for the social relations within the community of believers. See Troels Engberg-Pedersen, *Paul in His Hellenistic Context* (T&T Clark, 1994), p. 219.

11 Stowers, *Rereading of Romans*, 219–22. See also Carolyn Osiek and David L. Balch (eds), *Family in the New Testament World: Households and House Churches* (Louisville, Kentucky: Westminister John Knox Press, 1997), p. 177.

12 R. A. Campbell, *The Elders: Seniority within Earliest Christianity* (Edinburgh: T&T Clark, 1994), pp. 210–16.

13 Horrell, 'Leadership Patterns and the Development of Ideology', p. 330.

14 Stephan J. Joubert, 'Managing the Household in Paul', in Philip F. Esler (ed.), *Modelling Early Christianity* (Routledge, 1995), p. 216.

15 Halvor, Moxnes, 'What is Family', in *Constructing Early Christian Families*, p. 26.

16 M. Y. MacDonald, *The Pauline Churches: A Socio-historical Study of Institutionalization in the Pauline and Deutero-Pauline Writings*, SNTSM60 (Cambridge: Cambridge University Press, 1988), p. 214.

17 *The source of Chinese Words* (Shangwu Yinshuguan, 1995), pp. 419, 1066. From the usage of Son (zi) in Chinese tradition, we can see that the position of son in Chinese culture is higher than in ancient Greek society. As *fu*, sometimes *zi* could also be used as a respectable address or title for a male.

18 *Chambers 20th Century Dictionary*, edited by E. M. Kirkpatrick (W & R Chambers Ltd, 1983), p. 459 and p. 1233.

19 John Knoblock, *Xunzi: A Translation and Study of the Complete Works* (Stanford University Press, 1994), Volume I, p. 69.

20 *The Doctrine of the Mean*, chap. 26.9, in *The Four Books*, English translation and notes by James Legge, D.D., L. L. D (Taibei: Culture Book Co., 1992), p. 100.

21 Dong Zhongshu, *Chuqiu Fanlu Yizheng* (Zhonghua Shuju, 1992), p. 354 and p. 402.

22 Ibid., p. 318. Also in Xinzhong Yao, *An Introduction to Confucianism* (Cambridge University Press, 2000), p. 145.

23 Moxnes says that relations between parents and small children are characterized by care and concern on the part of the parents. In *Constructing Early Christian Families*, p. 33.

24 According to Moxnes, the commandment 'honour thy father and mother' is directed towards situations in which parents are old and need help (Mark 7:9–13; Matt 15:6–9). It is towards adult sons and daughters that the hierarchical and patriarchal character of the family becomes most visible. See 'What is Family', in ibid., p. 34.

25 Osiek and Balch discuss the teacher–children relationship and the authority of prophets. See *Family in the New Testament World*, pp. 156–73.

26 *Family in the New Testament World: Households and House Churches*, by Carolyn Osiek and David L. Balch (eds), p. 41.

27 According Osiek and Balch, 'The patron functions as a kind of surrogate father, and the patronage system is a way of replicating kinship systems. The patron must provide some material benefits to the client, but most important to the benefits for social advancement is that the client gives proper deference to the patron, as well as the pouring on of attributed honor, and the performance of certain actions that contribute to the support of the patron, especially help in any way that the patron might need'. See *Family in the New Testament World: Households and House Churches*, p. 39.

28 John Knoblock, *Xunzi: A Translation and Study of the Complete Works* (Stanford University Press, 1994), p. 87.

29 Han demin, *Xunzi* 2001, p. 178.

30 See 'Development and Modern Significance', in Silke Krieger and Rolf Trauzettel (eds),

Confucianism and the Modernization of China (v. Hase & Koehler verlag, Mainz, 1991), pp. 97–9.

31 This idea is based on Gerd Theissen's idea of four different motives in the principle of loving one's enemy.

32 Maccrice Hutton , *The Greek Point of View* (London, 1925), p. 104.

FOUR The Pauline Ethical Father–Son Relationship

1 Brian S. Rosner (ed.), *Understanding Paul's Ethics* (Grand Rapids/ Michigan: William B. Eerdmans Publishing Company, 1995), p. 4.

2 See J. Paul Sampley, *Walking between the Times: Paul's Moral Reasoning* (Minneapolis: Fortress Press, 1991), p. 3.

3 James D. G. Dunn, *The Theology of Paul the Apostle* (Grand Rapids, Michigan Cambridge, U.K: William B. Eerdmans Publishing Company, 1998), p. 28.

4 Brian S. Rosner, *Understanding Paul's Ethics: Twentieth Century Approaches* (Grand Rapids, Michigan: William B. Eerdmans Publishing Company, The Paternoster Press, 1995), p. 17.

5 *The New International Webster's Comprehensive Dictionary of the English Language* (Deluxe Encyclopedic Edition, 1996), p. 373.

6 C. K. Barrett, *On Paul: Essays on His Life, Work and Influence in the Early Church* (London and New York: T&T Clark, A Continuum Imprint, 2003), p. 67.

7 James D. G. Dunn, *The Theology of Paul the Apostle*, pp. 251–2.

8 Dunn gives a detailed examination on how important the father–son relationship between God and Jesus is in the sense that it existed before all things were created. See *The Theology of Paul the Apostle*, pp. 267–8.

9 *The New International Webster's Comprehensive Dictionary of the English Language* (Deluxe Encyclopedic Edition, 1996), p. 436.

10 John M. G. Barclay, 'The Family as the Bearer of Religion in Judaism and Early Christianity', in Halvor Moxnes (ed.), *Constructing Early Christian Families: Family as Social Reality and Metaphors* (London: Routledge, 1997), pp. 66–79.

11 D. D. Newman Smyth, *Christian Ethics* (T&T Clark, Edinburgh, 1893), 2nd edition, p. 18.

12 William Wrede, quoted from Leander E. Keck, 'Rethinking "New Testament Ethics"', in *Journal of Biblical Literature*, Vol. 115, 1996, p. 3.

13 Dunn, *The Theology of Paul the Apostle*, p. 42.

14 C. K. Barrett, *On Paul: Essays on His Life, Work and Influence in the Early Church* (T&T Clark, 2003), p. 180.

15 Carolyn Osiek and David L Balch, *Families in the New Testament World: Household and House churches* (Louisville, Kentucky: Westminster John Knox Press, 1997), p. 157.

16 Barrett, *On Paul: Essays on His Life, Work and Influence in the Early Church*, p. 181.

17 Brian S. Rosner, *Understanding Paul's Ethics: Twentieth Century Approaches* (Grand Rapids, Michigan: William B. Eerdmans Publishing Company, The Paternoster Press, 1995), p. 21.

18 Balla, *The Child–Parent Relationship in the New Testament and its Environment*, p. 117.

19 James D. G. Dunn, *The Theology of Paul the Apostle*, p. 29.

20 Robert L. Reymond gives a survey on the oneness of God see *Paul: Missionary Theologian: A Survey of His Missionary Labours and Theology* (Mentor, 2002), pp. 311–12.

21 See Henri Blocher, 'Divine Immutability', in Nigel M. de S. Cameron (ed.), *The Power and Weakness of God* (Edinburgh: Rutherford House Books, 1991), p. 14.

22 Dunn, *The Theology of Paul the Apostle*, p. 31.

23　Ibid., pp. 39–40

24　R. P. Martin, *Reconciliation: A Study of Paul's Theology* (London: Marshall, Morgan and Scott/ Atlanta: John Knox, 1981), pp. 103–7.

25　C. K. Barrett, *On Paul: Essays on His Life, Work and Influence in the Early Church* (London/ New York: T&T Clark, A Continuum imprint, 2003), p. 70.

26　Brad Eastman, *'The Significance of Grace in Letters of Paul'*, Studies in Biblical Literature 11 (New York, Washington, D.C.: Peter Lang, 1999), p. 2.

27　Dunn, *The Theology of Paul the Apostle*, p. 48.

28　Hermann Häring gives a discussion on human's image of God in 'From Divine Human to Human God', in Hans-Georg Ziebertz, Friedrich Schweitzer, Hermann Häring and Don Browing (eds), *The Human Image of God* (Leiden and Boston: Brill, 2001), pp. 3–28.

29　In *Understanding Paul's Ethics: Twentieth Century Approaches* (William B. Eerdmans Publishing Company Grand Rapids, Michigan, The Paternoster Press, 1995), p. 12 and note 31.

30　R. Bultmann, *Jesus and the Word* (ET, London, 1935), p. 84.

31　In 'The Crucified God', p. 205, quoted by David Cook in 'Weak Church, Weak God: the Charge of Anthropomorphism', in Nigel M. de S. Cameron *The Power and Weakness of God* (Edinburgh: Rutherford House Books, 1990), p. 82.

32　Robert L. Reymond, *Paul: Missionary Theologian* (Mentor, 2002), p. 343.

33　Reymond demonstrates the correlation of love with every facet of new obedience in his book, *Paul: Missionary Theologian*, p. 417.

34　R. Bultmann, *Jesus and the Word*, ET; London, 1935, also C. K. Barrett: *On Paul: Essays on His Life, Work and Influence in the Early Church* (London/ New York: T&T Clark Continuum imprint, 2003), p.180.

35　Gustaf Aulen, *Christus Victor*, mentioned by G. B. Caird in *Principalities and Powers* (Oxford at the Clarendon Press, 1956), p. vii.

36　Morna D. Hooker, *Pauline Pieces* (London: Epworth Press, 1979), p. 60.

37　Reymond, *Paul: Missionary Theologian*, p. 388.

38　Ibid., p. 318.

39　Reymond discusses the Sacrifice of Jesus Christ in the expiatory sense, in the propitiatory sense, and in the reconciling and redemptive and destructive senses (in *Paul: Missionary Theologian*, pp. 388–404)

40　Xinzhong Yao, *Confucianism and Christianity: A Comparative Study of Jen and Agape* (Sussex Academic Press, 1996), p. 114.

41　Reymond, *Paul: Missionary Theologian*, p. 418.

42　F. F. Bruce, *Paul: Apostle of the Heart Set Free* (Grand Rapids: Eerdmans, 1996, reprint of 1977), p. 192.

43　Reymond, *Paul: Missionary Theologian*, p. 417.

44　Gerd Theissen, *Social Reality and the Early Christians Theology, Ethics, and the World of the New Testament*, trans. Margaret Kohl (Edinburgh: T&T Clark, 1992), p. 115.

45　William S. Campbell, 'Millennial Optimism for Jewish–Christian Dialogue', in Dan Cohn-Sherbok (ed.), *The Future of Jewish–Christian Dialogue* (Toronto Studies in Theology, Volume 80, Lewiston/Lampeter: The Edwin Mellen Press, 1999), p. 227.

46　C. H. Dodd, *The Epistle to the Romans* (London: Hodder & Stoughton, 1932).

47　Brian S. Rosner, *Understanding Paul's Ethics: Twentieth Century Approaches* (Grand Rapids, Michigan: William B. Eerdmans Publishing Company, The Paternoster Press, 1995), pp. 12–13.

48　Carolyn Osiek, 'Philippians', in E. Schüssler Fiorenza, A. Brock and S. Matthews (eds), *A*

Feminist Commentary, Vol. 2 of *Searching the Scripture* (New York: Crossroad, 1994), p. 246.

49 Max Weber, *Economy and Society: An Outline of Interpretive Sociology*, Vol.1, edited by G. Roth and C. Wittich (Berkeley and Los Angeles, CA: University of California Press), pp. 212–301.

50 B. Holmberg, *Paul and Power: The Structure of Authority in the Primitive Church as Reflected in the Pauline Epistle* (Lund: C.W.K. Gleerup, 1978), p. 155.

51 David G. Horrell, 'Leadership Patterns and the Development of Ideology in Early Christianity', in his book (ed.), *Social-Scientific Approaches to New Testament* (T&T Clark, 1999), p. 317.

52 R. A. Campbell, *The Elders: Seniority within Earliest Christianity* (Edinburgh, T&T Clark, 1994), p. 126.

53 Clarke, *Secular and Christian Leadership in Corinth*, pp. 118, 112.

54 David G. Horrell, 'Leadership Patterns and the Development of Ideology in Early Christianity', in his book (ed.), *Social-Scientific Approaches to New Testament*, p. 326.

55 Kathy Ehrensperger, '"Be Imitators of Me as I am of Christ': A Hidden discourse of Power and Domination in Paul', in *Lexington Theological Journal*, Vol. 38/4, Winter 2003, pp. 241–61.

56 David G. Horrell, 'Leadership Patterns', p. 328.

57 Richards A. Horsley (ed.), *Paul and Politics* (Trinity Press International, 2000).

58 Robert A. Atkins, *Egalitarian Community: Ethnography and Exegesis* (Tuscaloosa and London: University of Alabama Press, 1991), p. 186.

59 Robin Scroggs, 'The Earliest Christian Communities as Sectarian Movement', in David G. Horrell (ed.), *Social-Scientific Approaches to New Testament Interpretation*, p. 75.

60 Dunn, *The Theology of Paul the Apostle*, p. 701.

61 Stephan J. Joubert, 'Paul as broker for the heavenly patrons', in Esler, *Modelling Early Christianity*, p. 217.

62 Carolyn Osiek and David L. Balch, *Families in the New Testament World: Households and House Churches* (Louisville, Kentucky: Westminster John Knox Press, 1997), p. 54.

63 Osiek and Balch, *Families in the New Testament World*, pp. 47–9.

64 Horrell, 'Leadership Patterns', p. 323

65 W. Klassen, 'Musonius Rufus, Jesus, and Paul', see also Justin J. Meggitt, *Paul, Poverty and Survival* (Edinburgh: T&T Clark, 1998), p. 184.

66 Stephan J. Joubert, 'Managing the Household: Paul as paterfamilias of the Christian household group in Corinth', in *Modelling Early Christianity: Social-Scientific studies of the New Testament in its context* (London and New York: Routledge, 1995), pp. 213–23.

67 Jerome. H. Neyrey, *Paul in Other Words: A Cultural Reading of His letters* (Louisville: Westminster/John Knox Press, 1990), pp. 38–9.

68 Ehrensperger, ' "Be Imitators of Me as I am of Christ, p. 248.

69 Richard A. Horsley, 'Krister Stendahl's Challenge to Pauline Studies', in *Paul and Politics* edited by Richard A Horsley (Trinity Press International, 2000), p. 13.

70 Bruce W. Winter, 'Civil Litigation in Secular Corinth and the Church', in Brian S. Rosner (ed.), *Understanding Paul's Ethics: Twentieth Century Approaches* (Grand Rapids, Michigan: Willam B. Eerdmans Publishing Company, The Paternoster Press, Carlisle, 1995), p. 85.

71 Amy-Jill Levine (ed.), *A Feminist Companion to the Deutero-Pauline Epistles* (London/ New York: T&T Clark International, A Continuum Imprint, 2003), p. 1.

72 Neil Elliott, *Liberating Paul: the Justice of God and the Politics of the Apostle* (Sheffield Academic Press, 1994), p. 10.

73 Susan Faludi, *Backlash: the Undeclared War against American Women* (New York: Crown, 1991), p. 233.

74 Justin J. Meggitt, 'Appendix 1: Paul's Social Conservatism: Slavery, Women and the State', in *Paul, Poverty and Survival* (T&T Clark, 1998), p. 181.

75 M. Y. MacDonald, *The Pauline Churches: A Socio-historical Study of Institutionalization in the*

Pauline and Deutero-Pauline Writings, SNTSMS60 (Cambridge University Press, 1988), pp. 121–2.

76 Dunn, *The Theology of Paul the Apostle*, p. 700.

77 G. Theissen, *The Social Setting of Pauline Christianity*, tr. J. H. Schütz (Edinburgh: T&T Clark, 1982), p. 107.

78 MacDonald, *The Pauline Churches*, pp. 102–22.

79 Horrell, 'Leadership Patterns', p. 329.

80 J. Gnilka, *Das Evangelium nach Markus* (EKKNT II/2, 1979, Zürich: Benziger Verlag; Neukirchen- Vluyn: Neukirchener Verlag), p. 148.

81 Baller, *The Child–Parent Relationship in the New Testament and Its Environment*, p. 125.

82 I. S. Gilbus, 'Family Structures in Gnostic Religion', in Halvor Moxnes, p. 235.

83 Balla, *The Child–Parent Relationship in the New Testament and its Environment*, p. 161.

84 Craig A. Evans (eds), *Dictionary of New Testament Background* (Illinois and Leicester, England: Inter-Varsity Press), p. 357.

85 Blackstone, *Commentaries on the Law of England* (5th edn, Oxford, 1765), p. 442. See also in Ivy Pichbech and Margaret Hewitt, *Children in English Society* (London: Routledge & Kegan Paul, 1973), p. 362.

86 Pichbech and Hewitt, *Children in English Society*, pp. 362–3.

87 Ibid., p. 363.

88 Howard Thurman, *The Creative Encounter* (New York: Harper and Row, 1954), p. 152.

89 Thomas R. Schreiner, *The Law and Its Fulfillment: a Pauline Theology of Law* (Baker Books, 1993), p. 14.

90 Gerd Theissen, *The Social Setting of Pauline Christianity*, ed. and trans. by J. H. Schütz (Edinburgh: T&T Clark, 1982), p. 107.

91 Jacques Gernet, *The China and the Christian Impact: a Conflict of Cultures*, trans. by Janet Lloyd (Cambridge University Press, 1985), p. 140.

FIVE   Xunzi's Ethical Father–Son Relationship

1 See Y. P. Mei, 'The Basis of Social, Ethical, and Spiritual Values', in Charles A. Moore (ed.), *The Chinese Mind* (Honolulu: The University Press of Hawaii, 1967), pp. 149–66.

2 See Patricia Buckley Ebrey, *Confucianism and Family Rituals in Imperial China: A Social History of Writing about Rites* (Princeton, NJ: Princeton University Press, 1991), p. 26. For more about the development of Xunzi's idea including his idea of *li*, see Hsü, ChoYun, 'The Unfolding of Early Confucianism: The Evolution from Confucius to Hsün-tzu', in Irene Eber (ed.), *Confucianism: The Dynamics of Tradition* (London: Collier Macmillan Publishers), pp. 23–37.

3 A. S. Cua has discussed the two main functions of *li*: one is the establishment of order and the other harmony. See his book: *Moral Vision and Tradition: Essays in Chinese Ethics* (Washington, D.C.: The Catholic University of America Press 1998), p. 3.

4 Patricia Buckley Ebrey, *Confucianism and Family Rituals in Imperial China* (Princeton, NJ: Princeton University Press, 1991), p. 26.

5 John H. Berthrong, *Transformations of the Confucian Way* (Boulder, Colorado: Westview Press, 1998), p. 33.

6 Fung Yu-lan, 1948, p. 100. See also Julia Ching: 'What Is Confucian Spirituality?' in Irene Eber (ed.), *Confucianism: The Dynamics of Tradition* (New York: Macmillan Publishing Company, 1986), p. 67.

7 Tu Weiming, *Centrality and Commonality: An Essay on Chung-Yung* (Honolulu: University of Hawaii Press, 1976), pp. 75–99. Also in Ebrey, *Confucianism and Family Rituals in Imperial China*, p. 27.

8   Xinzhong Yao, *An Introduction on Confucianism* (Cambridge University, 2000), p. 171.

9   D. C. Lau, *The Analects* (Harmondsworth and New York: Penguin Books, 1979), pp. 38–9.

10 Ibid., p. 40.

11 For reference discussion see Henry Jr. Rosemont, 'State and Society in the Hsün Tzu: A Philosophical commentary' (in *Monumenta Seria* 29, 1970–71, pp. 38–78); Weiming Tu, "Probing the 'Three Bonds' and 'Five Relationships'", see Walter H. Slote and George A. De Vos (eds), *Confucianism and the Family* (Albany: State University of New York Press, 1998), pp. 121–36.

12 Edward J. Machle gives a general discussion on the relationship among *tiandi, shengren* and common people in 'The Mind and the "Shen-Ming" in Xunzi'. See *Journal of Chinese Philosophy* 19, No. 4, 1992, pp. 361–86.

13 ChoYun Hsü, 'The Unfolding of Early Confucianism: The Evolution from Confucius to Hsün-tzu', in Irene Eber (ed.), *Confucianism: The Dynamics of Tradition* (Simon & Schuster, 1986), p. 34.

14 For details see Chapter One, the philosophical root of Xunzi's father–son relationship.

15 See ChoYun Hsü, 'The Unfolding of Early Confucianism', 1986, pp. 34–5.

16 John Knoblock, *Xunzi: A Translation and Study of the Complete Works* (Stanford, California: Stanford University Press, Vol. 1, 1990), p. 75.

17 Heiner Roetz discusses this sort of father–son relationship in *Confucian Ethics of the Axial Age* (Albany: State University of New York Press, 1993), pp. 53–7.

18 Shun was an ancient sage king of the three dynasties advocated by Confucianism. He established the Yu dynasty by his virtues, and most especially by his distinctive virtue of filial piety to his parents and benevolent government.

19 *Xiaoyi* was also a person who established a good reputation by his filial piety to his parents.

20 *The Li Ki* gives an evident for this. In 'Ki I' in Book XXI, sect II, 16, In *The Sacred Book of China*, part IV (James Legge, trans.), in F. Max Müller (ed.), *Sacred Books of the East*, p. 230.

21 H. D. R. Baker, *Chinese Family and Kinship* (London: Macmillan, 1979), p. 91.

22 This was first put forward in Guo Moruo, *Shi Pipan Shu*. See Zhang Zainian, *Zhongguo Zhexueshi Shiliaoxue* (Sanlian Shudian, 1982), p. 75.

23 Baker, *Chinese Family and Kinship*, p. 91.

24 Wife of Liu Shipei, a leading feminist who championed a blend of anarchism and communism for the liberation of women.

25 Ho Chen, 'Nüzi fuchou lun', see *Tianyi bao*, No. 3 (10), 7–13, trans. by Peter Zarrow; also see W. M. Theodore de Bary, *Confucianism and Human Rights*, pp. 2–3.

26 My translation is different from that of John Knoblock. His translation is: 'Where [ritual] is not obtained, between lord and minister there is no honored position, between father and son is no affection; between elder and younger brother no submissiveness, and between husband and wife no rejoicing. Through it, the young grow to maturity, and the old acquire nourishment' (27.31).

27 *Chuqiu Zuozhuan*, Zhaogong year 26, in Yang Bojun (ed.), *Chunqiu Zuozhuan Yizhu* (1–4), Volume 4 (Zhonghua Shuju, 1981), pp. 1480–1.

28 In my opinion, Xunzi's concept of *yi* can be divided into at least four levels: the highest level is the level of natural law; the second level is the way of human beings; the third level is the principle and doctrine of morality; and the last level is individual virtue.

29 Heiner Roetz gives a discussion on Xunzi's understanding of justice and social order in *Confucian Ethics of the Axial Age* (State University of New York Press, 1993), pp. 69–70.

30 Ibid., p. 71.

SIX Ethical Issues Concerning the Father–Son Relationship

1 David M. Hay and E. Elizabeth Johnson (eds), *Paul Theology Volume III: Romans* (Minneapolis: Fortress Press, 1995), p. 153.

2 See 'Confucianism and Citizenship', *Asian Philosophy*, Vol. 12, No. 2, 2002, p. 132.

3 Gerd Theissen, *Social Reality and the Early Christian: Theology, Ethics, and the World of the New Testament*, trans. by Margaret Kohl (T&T Clark, 1992), p. 194.

4 Carolyn Osiek and David L. Balch, *Families in the New Testament World: Households and House Churches* (Westminster John Knox Press, 1997), pp. 182–3.

5 Andrew T. Lincoln, A. J. M. Wedderburn, *New Testament Theology: The Theology of the Later Pauline Letters* (Cambridge University Press, 1993), pp. 122–3.

6 Elaine Pagels, 'Paul and Women: A Response to Recent Discussion' in *Journal of the American Academy of Religion* 42, 1974, p. 545.

7 *Dictionary of Western Philosophy: English–Chinese*, edited by Nicholas Bunnin and Jiyuan Yu (Bejing: Renmin Press, 2001), p. 189.

8 Lien-sheng Yang, 'The Concept of Pao as Basis for Social Relationships in China', in *Chinese Thought and Institutions*, ed. J. K. Fairbank (The University of Chicago Press, 1957), p. 291.

9 Julia Ching, *Confucianism and Christianity: A Comparative Study* (Kodansha International, 1977), p. 10.

10 A similar idea can be seen in Xunzi's thought: worship of the ghosts of ancestors is not for their blessing but for showing one's respect and memory of them.

11 Andrew T. Lincoln, A. J. M. Wedderburn, *New Testament Theology: The Theology of the Later Pauline Letters* (Cambridge University Press, 1993), p. 124.

12 Xinzhong Yao, *Confucianism and Christianity: A Comparative Study of Jen and Agape* (Sussex Academic Press, 1999), p. 67.

13 Ibid., p. 75.

14 John Macquarrie, *In Search of Humanity – A Theological and Philosophical Approach* (New York: Crossroad, 1982), p. 172.

15 Morna D. Hooker, *Pauline Pieces* (London: Epworth Press, 1979), p. 66.

16 Osiek and Balch, *Families in the New Testament World*, p. 184.

17 Karl P. Donfried, I. Howard Marshall, *New Testament Theology: The Theology of the Short Pauline Letters* (Cambridge University Press, 1993), p. 62.

18 Ibid., p. 60.

19 The Li KI, Bk. XXI, Sect. II, 11. See James Legge (trans.), *The Sacred Books of China*, Part IV, in F. Max Müller (ed.), *Sacred Books of the East*, Vol. XXVIII, 1968, p. 226.

20 Hu Pinsheng, *Xiaojing Yizhu* (Beijing: Zhonghua Shuju Chubanshe, 1996), p. 12.

21 Pope John XXIIII, 'Pacem in Terris', in *Proclaiming Justice and Peace*, edited by Michael Walsh and Brian Davies (Caford: Collins, 1984), pp. 54–5.

22 David S. Nivison, *The Way of Confucianism: Investigations in Chinese Philosophy*, edited with an introduction by Bryan W. Van Norden (Chicago and La Salle: Open Court, 1996), p. 47.

23 A. S. Cua, *Moral Vision and Tradition: Essays in Chinese Ethics* (Washington, D.C.: The Catholic University of America Press, 1998), p. 101.

24 Ch. Perelman and L. Olbrechts-Tyteca, *The New Rhetoric: A Treatise on Argumentation* (Notre Dame: University of Notre Dame Press, 1969), p. 79.

CONCLUSION

1 Julia Ching, *Confucianism and Christianity: A Comparative Study* (Kodansha International, 1977), p. 79.

2 Jacques Gernet, *China and the Christian Impact: A Conflict of Culture*, translated by Janet Lloyd (Cambridge University Press, 1985), p. 158.

3 A typical example can be seen in Yoe Khiok-khng (K. K) (ed.), *Navigating Romans through Cultures* (Edinburgh: T&T Clark, 2004,), in *Romans Through History and Cultures Series*.

4 David S. Nivison, *The Way of Confucianism: Investigations in Chinese Philosophy*, edited with an introduction by Bryan W. Van Norden (Chicago and La Salle: Open Court, 1996), p. 47.

5 A. S. Cua, *Moral Vision and Tradition: Essays in Chinese Ethics* (Washington, D.C.: The Catholic University of America Press, 1998), p. 101.

6 Ch. Perelman and L. Olbrechts-Tyteca, *The New Rhetoric: A Treatise on Argumentation* (Notre Dame: University of Notre Dame Press, 1969), p. 79.

7 See William Theodore De Bary and Tu Weiming (eds), *Confucianism and Human Rights* (New York: Columbia University Press, 1998), pp. 1–26.

8 *Copenhagen Journal of Asia Studies*, 14, 2000, pp. 130–51.

9 See 'Confucianism and the Idea of Citizenship', in *Asian Philosophy*, Vol. 12. No. 2, 2002, p. 130.

10 Weiming Tu, 'Human Rights as Confucian Moral Discourse', in William Theodore De Bary & Tu Weiming (eds), *Confucianism and Human Rights* (New York: Columbia University Press, 1998), p. 303.

11 A. T. Nuyen, 'Confucianism and the idea of Citizenship', in *Asian Philosophy*, Vol. 12, No. 2, 2002, p. 131.

12 Lin Yüsheng, 'Creative Transformation of Chinese Tradition', in Karl-Heinz Pohl (ed.), *Chinese Thought in A Global Context* (Brill, 1999), p. 87.

13 Nuyen, 'Confucianism and the Idea of Citizenship', p. 130.

14 Lin Yüsheng: 'Creative Transformation of Chinese Tradition', in Karl-Heinz Pohl (ed.), *Chinese Thought in A Global Context* (Brill, 1999), p. 88.

15 Nuyen: 'Confucianism and the Idea of Equality', p. 61.

16 Ibid.

17 D. W. K. Kwok: 'On the Rites and Rights of Being Human', in De Bary and Weiming Tu, *Confucianism and Human Rights*, p. 90.

18 Nuyen: 'Confucianism and Idea of Citizenship', p. 131.

19 John B. Cobb Jr., 'Chinese Philosophy and Process Thought', in *Journal of Chinese Philosophy*, Vol. 32, issue 2, July, 2005, p. 170.

20 The Rev Father Vincent Shih observes: 'the dependence of individuals on the group and the submission of the group to tradition . . . rendered the individual members of a traditional society incapable of accepting anything new'. See *Histoire de l'expédition chrétienne*, Introduction, p. 49; also Jacques Gernet, *The China and the Christian Impact*, trans. Janet Lloyd (Cambridge University Press, 1985), p. 2.

21 Lawrence G. Thompson, *Ta T'ung Shu: The One-World Philosophy of K'ang Yu-wei* (London: George Allen and Unwin, 1958), p. 183.

22 In Wm. Theodore De Bary and Tu Weiming (eds), *Confucianism and Human Rights*, p. xiii.

23 Richard T. Amos: 'Confucian Doctrine and Social Progress', in International Association Committee: *International Confucianism Studies*, Vol. III (Zhongguo Sheke Chubanshe, 1997), p. 289.

24 Sun Longji, *Zhongguo Wenhua de Shenceng Jiegou* (Xianggang: Jixianshe,1987), p. 67–70.

25 Ibid., p.70.

APPENDIX Research Scholarship in Christian and Confucian Studies

1 Ma Jigao, *Xun xue yuan liu* (Shanghai Guji Chubanshe, 2000).

2 Han, Demin, *Xunzi yu Rujia de Shehui Lixiang* (Jinan: Qi Lu Shushe, 2001).

3 An Jiazheng, *He bi ru fa: Xunzi di gu shi* (Beijing: Huawen Chubanshe, 1997).

4 Xiong Liangzhi and Zhuang Jian, *Xunzi yu xian dai she hui* (Chengdu: Sichuan Renmin Chubanshe, 1995).

5 Yang Yunru and Chen Dengyuan, *Xunzi yan jiu* (Shanghai: Shanghai shudian, 1992).

6 For example, Zhao Shilin, 'Xunzi de Renxinglun Xintan' (in *Zhexue Yanjiu*, Vol. 10, 1999), pp. 60–9. Yezhou and Xingyan, 'Lun Xunzi Renxing Lilun' (in *Huabei Dianli Xueyuan Xuebao*, No. 4, 1997); Liu fenquan and Yulejun, 'Meng Xun Renlun Bijiao' (in Jinan Daxue Xuebao, Vol. 7, No. 2, 1997). Huang Baoxian, 'Meng Xun Renxing Lun Bijiao' (in *Guanzi Xuekan*, No. 2, 1995). Liu Guirong, Liu Jingwei and Liyong, 'Xunzi de Renxinglun jiqi Yanbian' (in *Baoding Shifan Xueyuan Xuebao*, Jan. 2002).

7 For example, Liao Mingchun, 'Lun Xunzi de Junmin Guanxi Shuo' in *Zhongguo Wenhua Yanjiu* Summer, 1997, total No. 18, pp. 41–4.

8 Lu Debin's 'Xunzi Zhexue zai Rujia Fazhan Guocheng zhong de Diwei yu Zuoyong' (in *Zhongguo Zhexueshi*, No. 3, 1997) is one example; Hui Jixing's *Xunzi yu Zhongguo Wenhua* (Guiyang: Guizhou Renmin Chubanshe, 1996) is another.

9 Mou Zongsan often interpreted Chinese philosophy by contrasting it with Western philosophy or Christian understanding. This characteristic can be seen in *Caixing yu Xuanli* (Taibei: Xuesheng, 1985) and his *Zhongguo Zhexue de Tezhi* (Hongkong: Rensheng, 1963).

10 Both Feng and Hu graduated from American universities, and both interpreted Chinese philosophy by way of Western research. When they did their research work, they had already done the comparison between Chinese culture and Western culture.

11 For example, Feng Tianyu, a professor of Wuhan University, published his article 'Liulun Zhongxi Renwen Qingshen' (in *Zhongguo Shehui Kexue*, No. 1, 1997), pp. 16–24. Deng Xianhui published his article titled 'Xunzi Xing e Lun yu Nicai Quanli Yizhi zhi Bijiao' (in *Zhonghua Wenhua Luntan*, No. 1, 1997), pp. 89–95.

12 For example, He Guanghu has published a series books in this subject. See He Guanhu, Xu Zhiwei, *Duihua: Ru Shi Dao yu Jidujiao* (Beijing: Shehui Kexue Wenxian Chubanshe, 1998); *Duihua 2: Ru Shi Dao yu Jidujiao* (Beijing: Shehui Kexue Wenxian Chubanshe, 2001). Luo Bingxiang, Zhao Dunhua, *Jidujiao yu Zhongxi Wenhua* (Beijing Daxue Chubanshe, 2000).

13 With the exception of James Barr, '"Abba, Father" and the familiarity of Jesus' Speech' (in *Theology Today* 91, 1988), pp. 173–9 and 'Abba isn't Daddy' (in *Journal of Theological Studies* 39, 1988).

14 In Kari E. Borresen (ed.), *Image of God and Gender Models in Judeo-Christian Tradition* (Oslo: Solum, 1991), pp. 56–137.

15 Ivy Pinchbeck and Margaret Hewitt, *Children in English Society*, volumes I & II (London: Routledge & Kegan Paul and Toronto: Toronto Press, 1973).

16 Except Peter Pampe, 'Family' in Church and Society of New Testament Times' (in *Affirmation*, Union Theological Seminary in Virginia, 5: 1–20, 1992) and Carolyn Osiek, 'The Family in Early Christianity: "Family Values" Revisited' (in *Catholic Biblical Quarterly*, 58:1–24, 1996).

17 Moxnes (ed.), *Constructing Early Christian Families*, p. 1. Jerome H. Neyrey also points to the need for further studies of the family and role of the *paterfamilias*, namely, the ways in

which the first Christians regarded and treated each other as family, in 'Loss of Wealth, Loss of Family and Loss of Honour', in Esler (ed.), *Modelling Early Christianity*, pp. 139–58.

Bibliography

Christianity and Western Culture

Source Books

Aristotle, *Politics* (Cambridge, MA: Harvard University Press; London: Heinemann, 1932).

Buttrick, George Arthur (ed.), *The Interpreter's Dictionary of the Bible* (Nashville: Abingdon Press, 1962).

Evans, Craig A. & Porter, Stanley E. (eds), *Dictionary of New Testament Background* (Downers Grove, IL and Leicester: InterVarsity Press, 2000).

Ernest, James D. (trans. and ed.), *Theological Lexicon of the New Testament* (Peabody, Mass.: Hendrickson Publishers, 1994), Vol. 2.

Jones, Alexander (ed.), *The Jerusalem Bible* (General, London: Darton, Longman & Todd, 1966).

Josephus, Flavius, *Against Apio*, trans. A. Thackeray (London: Printed by W. Bowyer for the author, 1737).

Kittel, Gerhard (ed.), *Theological Dictionary of the New Testament*, Translator and Editor: Geoffrey, W. Bromiley (W.M.B. Eerdmans Publishing Company, 1964).

Books and Articles

Aichele, George, 'Jesus Uncanny "Family Scene"' in *Journal for the Study of the New Testament*, issue 74, 1999, pp. 29–49.

Allen, Prudence, *The Concept of Woman: The Aristotelian Revolution, 750 BC–AD 1250* (Grand Rapids: Eerdmans, 1996).

Arendt, Hannah, *The Origins of Totalitarianism* (New York: Harcourt Brace Jovanovich, 1979, reprint of *The Burden of Our Time* (London: Secker & Warburg, 1951).

Armstrong, K., *The First Christian: Saint Paul's Impact on Christianity* (London: Pan, 1983).

Armour, Ellien T., *Descontruction, Feminist Theology, and the Problem of Difference: Subverting the Race/Gender Divide* (Chicago: University of Chicago Press, 1999).

Aune, David E., *Greco-Roman Literature and the New Testament* (Scholars Press, Atlanta, Georgia, 1988).

——'Human Nature and Ethics: Issues and Problems', in Troels Engberg-Pedersen (ed.), *Paul in His Hellenistic Context* (Edinburgh: T&T Clark, 1994), pp. 291–312.

Balch, David L., *Let Wives Be Submissive: The Domestic Code in 1 Peter* (Chico, CA: Scholars Press, 1981)

—— (ed.) with Osiek, Carolyn, *Families in the New Testament World: Household and House Churches* (Louisville, KY: Westminster/John Knox Press, 1997).

Balla, Peter, *The Child–Parent Relationship in the New Testament and Its Environment* (Tübingen: Mohr Siebek, 2004).

Barclay, John M. G., 'The Family as the Bearer of Religion in Judaism and Early Christianity', in Halvor Moxnes (ed.), *Constructing Early Christian Families: Family as Social Reality and Metaphor* (London and New York: Routledge, 1997), pp. 66–80.

——, *Jews in the Mediterranean Diaspora: From Alexander to Trajan (323BCE–117CE)* (Edinburgh: T&T Clark, 1996).

Barr, James: 'Abba Isn't Daddy', *The Journal of Theological Studies*, Vol. 39, 1988, pp. 28–47.

——, '"Abba, Father" and the Familiarity of Jesus' Speech', in *Theology Today* 91 (1988), pp. 173–9.

Barrett, C. K., *From First Adam to Last: A Study in Pauline Theology* (London: Adam & Charles Black, 1962).

——, *Paul: An Introduction to His Thought* (Louisville, KY: Westminster/John Knox, 1994).

——, ed., *On Paul: Essays on His Life, Work and Influence in the Early Church* (London/New York: A Continuum Imprint, T&T Clark, 2003).

Barton, Stephen C. (ed.), *Family in Theological Perspective* (Edinburgh: T&T Clark, 1996).

——, 'The Relativisation of Family Ties in the Jewish and Graeco-Roman Traditions', in Moxnes Halvor, *Constucting Early Christian Families* (London and New York: Routledge, 1997), pp. 81–100.

Beker, J. Christian, *Paul the Apostle: The Triumph of God in Life and Thought* (Edinburgh: T&T Clark, 1980).

Benhabib, Seyla, *Situating the Self: Gender, Community, and Postmodernism in Contemporary Ethics* (New York: Routledge, 1992).

Blustein, J., *Parents and Children: The Ethics of the Family* (New York: Oxford University Press, 1982).

Bornkamm, Günther, *Paul*, trans. D. M. G. Stalker (New York: Harper & Row, 1971).

Borresen, Kari E. (ed.), *Image of God and Gender Models in Judeo-Christian Tradition* (Oslo: Solum, 1991).

Boyarin, Daniel, *A Radical Jew: Paul and the Politics of Identity* (Berkley: University of California Press, 1994).

Bradley, Keith R., *Discovering the Roman Family: Studies in Roman Social History* (Oxford University Press, 1991).

Bremen, R. van, 'Women and Wealth' in A. Cameron and A. Kuhrt (eds), *Images of Women in Antiquity* (London and Canberra: Croom Helm, 1983), pp. 223–42.

Briggs, Kittredgem Cynthia, *Community and Authority: The Rhetoric of Obedience in the Pauline Tradition*, Harvard Theological Studies 45 (Harrisburg, PA: Trinity Press International, 1998).

Brown, Raymond E., *An Introduction to the New Testament* (New York/Doubleday: Anchor Bible Reference Library, 1997).

Brooten, Bernadette J., 'Paul and the Law. How Complete was the Departure?' in *The Princeton Seminary Bulletin*, Supplementary Issue, No. 1 (1990): 71–89.

Brown, Raymond E., *Mary in the New Testament* (Philadelphia: Fortress Press, 1978).

——, *An Introduction to the New Testament* (New York: Doubleday, 1997).

Brown, Joanne Carlson and Bohn, Carole R. (eds), *Christianity, Patriarchy, and abuse: A Feminist Critique* (New York: Pilgrim, 1989).

Bruce, F. F., *Paul: Apostle of the Heart Set Free* (Grand Rapids: Eerdmans, 1996).

Bultmann, R., *Jesus and the Word* (ET; London, Ivor Nicholsom Watson, 1935).

Caird, G. B., *Principalities and Powers* (Oxford at the Clarendon Press, 1956).

Cameron, A. and Kuhrt, A. (eds), *Images of Women in Antiquity* (London and Sydney: Routledge, 1993).

Campbell, William S., 'All God's Beloved in Rome: Jewish Roots and Christian Identity' (Paper presented at the Studiorum Novi Testamenti Societas annual meeting, Tel Aviv, Aug. 2000) in Sheila E. McGinn (ed.), *Celebrating Romans* (Grand Rapids, MI: Eerdmans, 2004), pp. 67–82.

——, *Divergent Images of Paul and His Mission*, in Christina Grenholm, and Daniel Patte (eds), *Reading Israel in Romans: Legitimacy and Plausibility of Divergent Interpretations* (Harrisburg, PA: Trinity Press International 2000), pp. 187–211.

——, *Paul's Gospel in an intercultural context: Jew and Gentile in the letter to the Romans* (Berlin: Peter Lang, 1992).

——, 'Millennial Optimism for Jewish–Christian Dialogue', in *The Future of Jewish-Christian Dialogue*, edited by Dan Cohn-Sherbok, Toronto Studies in Theology, Vol. 80 (The Edwin Mellen Press, 1999), pp. 239–65.

——, 'The Contribution of Tradition to Paul's theology', in *1 and 2 Corinthians*, Vol. 2 of *Pauline Theology*, edited by David M. Hay (Minneapolis: Fortress,1993), pp. 234–54.

Campbell, R. A., *The Elders: Seniority within Earliest Christianity* (Edinburgh: T & T Clark, 1994).

Carney, T. F., *The Shape of the Past: Model and Antiquity* (Lawrence, KA: Coronado, 1975).

Casey, P. Maurice, 'General, Generic and Indefinite: the Use of the Term "Son of Man" in Aramaic Sources and in the Teaching of Jesus', in *Journal for the Study of the New Testament* Issue 29, 1987, pp. 21–56.

Castelli, Elizabeth A., *Imitation Paul: A Discourse of Power* (Louisville: Westminster/ John Knox, 1991).

——, 'Paul on Women and Gender', in Ross Shepard Kraemer and Mary Rose (eds), *Women and Christian Origins* (Oxford: Oxford University Press, 1999), pp. 221–35.

——, 'Romans', in Elisabeth Schüssler Fiorenza, A. Brock, and S. Mathews (eds), *Searching the Scriptures: A Feminist Commentary*, Vol. 2 (London: SCM Press, 1995), pp. 272–300.

Clarke, Andrew D., *Secular and Christian Leadership in Corinth: A Socio-Historical and Exegetical Study of 1 Corinthians 1–6* (E. J. Brill, 1993).

Cohen, J. D. (ed.), *The Jewish Family in Antiquity* (Atlanta, GA: Scholars Press, 1993)

Cohn-Sherbok, Dan (ed.), *The Future of Jewish–Christian Dialogue*, Toronto Studies in Theology, Volume 80 (Lampeter: The Edwin Mellen Press, 1999).

Collins, John J., *Between Athens and Jerusalem: Jewish Identity in the Hellenistic Diapora* (New York: Crossroad, 1986).

——, *Jewish Wisdom in the Hellenistic Age* (Louisville: Westminster/John Knox, 1997).

Connolly, Peter (ed.), *Approaches to the Study of Religion*, Foreword by Ninian Smart (London and New York: Cassell, 1999).

Corley, Kathleen E., *Private Women, Public Meal: Social Conflict in the Synoptic Tradition* (Peabody, MA: Hendrickson, 1993).

Cone, James H., *Black Theology and Black Power* (New York: Seabury, 1969).

——, *A Black Theology of Liberation* (Philadelphia: Lippincott, 1970).

Corley, Kathleen E., *Private Women, Public Meal: Social Conflict in Synoptic Tradition* (Peabody, MA: Hendrickson, 1993)

Dahl, Nils A., *Studies in Paul: Theology for the Early Christian Mission* (Minneapolis: Augsburg, 1977).

Daniel Migliore (ed.), *The Church and Israel: Romans 9–11* (Princeton, NJ: Princeton Theology Seminary, 1990).

Darrel, J. Doughty, 'Citizens of Heaven: Philippians 3.2–21', in *N. T. Studies*, Vol. 41, 1995, pp. 102–22.

Davies, W. D., *Jewish and Pauline Studies* (Philadephia: Fortress, 1984).

——, *Paul and Rabbinic Judaism: Some Rabbbinic Elements in Pauline Theology* (London: SPCK, 1948).

Denney James, *The Death of Christ* (London: Hodder & Stoughton, 1900).

Derrida, Jacques, *Writing and Difference*, translated with an introduction and additional notes by Alan Bass (London: Routledge & Kegan Paul Ltd, 1978).

Dixon, Suzanne, *The Roman Family* (Baltimore: Johns Hopkins University Press, 1992).

——, 'The Sentimental Ideal of the Roman Family', in Beryl Rawson (ed.), *Marriage, Divorce and Children in Ancient Rome* (Oxford: Clarendon Press, 1991), pp. 99–113.

Dodd, C. H., *The Epistle to the Romans* (London: Hodder & Stoughton, 1932).

Dodds, E. R., 'Introduction: where did all this madness come from?' in John G. Gager, *Reinventing Paul* (Oxford University Press, 2000).

Donfried, Karl P. & Marshall, I. Howard, *New Testament Theology: The Theology of the Short Pauline letters* (Cambridge University Press, 1993).

—— (eds), *Judaism and Christianity in First-Century Rome* (Grand Rapids: William B. Eerdmans, 1998).

Dunn, James D. G., *Jesus and the Spirit* (London: SCM Press ltd, 1975).

——, *Jesus, Paul and the Law: Studies in Mark and Galatians* (London: SPCK, 1990).

—— (ed.), *Paul and the Mosaic Law* (Tübingen: Mohr, 1996).

——, *The Theology of Paul the Apostle* (Michigan/Cambridge, UK: William B. Eerdmans Publishing Company, 1998).

——, 'The Status and Contribution of Paul', in Dan Cohn-Sherbok (ed.), *The Future of Jewish-Christian Dialogue*, Toronto Studies in Theology, Volume 80 (Lampeter: The Edwin Mellen Press, 1999), pp. 169–82.

——, 'Diversity in Paul', in Dan Cohn–Sherbok and John M. Court (eds), *Religious Diversity in the Graeco-Roman World: A survey of Recent Scholarship* (Sheffield: Sheffield Academic Press, 2001).

Duling, Dennis G., 'The Matthean Brotherhood and Marginal Scribal Leadership', in Philip F. Esler (ed.), *Modelling Early Christianity* (London and New York: Routledge, 1995), pp. 159–82.

Dungan, David L., *The Saying of Jesus in the Churches of Paul* (Oxford: Basil Blackwell, 1971).

Eastman, Brad, *The Significance of Grace in Letters of Paul*, Studies in Biblical Literature 11 (New York Washington, D.C.: Peter Lang, 1999).

Ehrensperger, Kathy, *That We May Be Mutually Encouraged: Feminism and the New Perspective in Pauline Studies* (New York/London: T&T Clark International, 2004).

——, '"Be Imitators of Me as I am of Christ": A Hidden Discourse of Power and Domination in Paul', in *Lexington Theological Journal*, Vol. 38/4, Winter 2003, pp. 241–61.

Eisenstadt, S. N. and Roniger, L., *Patrons, Clients and Friends: Interpersonal Relations and the Structure of Trust in Society* (Cambridge University Press, 1984).

Elliott, John H., *What Is Social-Scientific Criticism?* (Minneapolis: Fortress Press, 1993).

Elliott, Neil, *Liberating Paul: The Justice of God and the Politics of the Apostle* (Sheffield: Sheffield Academic Press, 1995)

Ellis, E. Earle, *Paul's Use of the Old Testament* (Edinburgh and Grand Rapids: W. B. Eerdmans Publishers Co., 1957).

Engberg-Pedersen, Troels (ed.), *Paul Beyond the Judaism/Hellenism Divide* (Louisville: Westminster John Knox, 2001).

—— (ed.), *Paul in His Hellenistic Context: Studies in the New Testament and Its World* (Edinburgh: T&T Clark, 1994).

English, Jane, 'What Do Grown Children Owe Their Parents?' in Christina Hoff Sommers (ed.), *Vice and Virtue in Everyday Life* (San Diego: Harcourt Brace Jovanovich, 1985), pp. 682–9.

Esler, Philip F. (ed.), *Modelling Early Christianity: Social Scientific Studies of the New Testament in its Context* (London and New York: Routledge, 1995).

——, *The First Christians in Their Social World* (London and New York: Routledge, 1994).

Eyben, Emiel, 'Fathers and Sons', in Beryl Rawson (ed.), *Marriage, Divorce, and Children in Ancient Rome* (Oxford: Clarendon Press, 1996).

Faludi, Susan, *Backlash: The Undeclared War against American Women* (New York: Crown, 1991).

Fatum, Lone, 'Image of God and Glory of Man: Women in the Pauline Congregations', in Kari E. Borresen (ed.), *Image of God and Gender Models in Judeo-Christian Tradition* (Oslo: Solum, 1991), pp. 56–137.

Finkel, A. & Frizzel, L. (eds), *Standing Before God: Studies on Prayer in Scriptures and in Tradition with Essays, In Honour of John M. Oesterricher* (New York: Ktav Publishing house, 1981).

Fiorenza, E. Schüssler, *In Memory of Her: A Feminist Theological Reconstruction of Christian Origins* (New York/ Crossroad/ London: SCM Press, 1983).

—— (eds), *A Feminist Commentary*, Vol. 2 of *Searching the Scriptures* (New York: Crossroad, 1994)

——, *Rhetoric and Ethic: The Politics of Biblical Studies* (Minneapolis: Fortress, 1999).

Fretheim, Terence E. & Thompson Curtis L. (eds), *God, Evil, and Suffering: Essays in Honor of Paul R.. Sponheim*, Word & World Luther Seminary St. Paul (Minnesota, 2000).

Gager, John G., 'Paul's Contradictions ——, can they be resolved?' in *Bible Review* 14 (Dec. 1998): pp. 32–9.

——, *Reinventing Paul* (Oxford: Oxford University Press, 2000).

Gardner, Jane F. & Wiedemann, Thomas, *The Roman Household: A Source Book* (London and New York: Routledge, 1991).

Garnet, Paul, 'The Baptism of Jesus and the Son of Man Idea', in *Journal for the Study of the New Testament*, Issue 9, 1980, pp. 49–65.

Gill, Robin, *The Cambridge Companion to Christian Ethics* (Cambridge University Press, 2001).

Gilhus, I. S., 'Family Structure in Gnostic Religion', in Halvor Moxnes (ed.), *Constructing Early Families* (London and New York: Routledge, 1997), pp. 235–49.

Grant, Robert M., *Paul in the Roman World: The Conflict at Corinth* (London and Leiden: Westminster/ John Knox Press, 1989)

Grant, Michael, *Saint Paul* (New York: Charles Scrbner's Sons, 1976).

Gnadt, Martina, 'Abba Isn't Daddy – Aspekte einer feministische – befreiungstheologische Revision des Abba Jesu', in Luise Schottroff and Marie-Theres Wacher (eds), *Von der Wurzee getragen: Christlich-feminische Exegese in Auseinanderstzung mit Antijudaismus* (Leiden: Brill, 1995), pp. 115–31.

Grenholm, Christina and Patte, Daniel (eds), *Reading Israel in Romans: Legitimacy and Plausibility of Divergent Interpretations* (Harrisburg, PA: Trinity Press International, 2000).

Grey, Mary, *Introducing Feminist Images of God* (Sheffield: Sheffield Academic Press, 2001).

——, *The Wisdom of Fools? Seeking Revelation for Today* (London: SPCK, 1993).

Haas, Peter J. (ed.), *Recovering the Role of Women: Power and Authority in Rabbinic Jewish Society* (Atlanta: Scholar Press, 1992).

Hanson, A. T., *The Pastoral Epistles*, NCBC (London: Marshall, Morgan & Scott, 1982).

Harnack, Adolf von, *The Mission and Expansion of Christianity in the First Three Centuries* (New York: Harper, 1961).

——, 'The Old Testament in the Pauline Letters and in the Pauline Church', in Brian S. Rosner (ed.), *Understanding Paul's Ethics* (Grand Rapids, Michigan: William B Eerdmans Publishing Company, 1995), pp. 27–49.

——, *What is Christianity?* lecture 7 and Lecture X (Williams & Norgate, 1901).

Hartman, L., 'Some Unorthodox Thoughts on the "Household-Code Form"' in Jacob Neusner,

Ernest S. Frerichs, Peder Borgen & Richard Horsley (eds), *The Social World of Formative Christianity and Judaism* (Philadephia: Fortress Press, 1988), pp. 219–32.

——, 'Code and Context: A Few Reflections on the Parenesis of Col 3:6–4:1', in Brian S. Rosner (ed.), *Understanding Paul's Ethics: Twentieth Century Approaches* (Michigan: The Paternoster Press, 1995), pp. 177–91.

Hay, David M. and Johnson, E. Elizabeth (eds), *Paul Theology, Volume III: Romans* (Minneapolis: Fortress Press, 1995).

—— (ed.), *1 and 2 Corinthians*, Vol. 2 of *Pauline Theology* (Minneapolis: Fortress, 1993).

Heidegger, Martin, *Being and Tine*, trans. John Macquarrie and Edward Robinson (Oxford: Blackwell, 1962).

Hengel, Martin, *Judaism and Hellenism: Studies in Their Encounter in Palestine during the Early Hellenistic Period*, translated by John Bowden, 2 vols (Philadephia: Fortress, 1981).

——, *The Charismatic Leader and His Followers* (Edinburgh: T&T Clark, 1981).

——, 'The Pre-Christian Paul', in Judith Lieu, John North and Tess Rajak, *The Jews Among Pagans and Christianity in the Roman Empire* (London and New York: Routledge, 1992), pp. 29–52.

——, *The Charismatic Leader and His Followers* (Edinburgh: T&T Clark, 1981).

Heschel, Araham J., *God in Search of Man: A Philosophy of Judaism* (New York: Garrar, Strauss & Cudahy, 1955).

Heyward, Carter, *The Redemption of God: A Theology of Mutual Relation* (Washington, D.C.: University of America Press, 1982).

——, *Touching Our Strength: The Erotic as Power and Love of God* (San Francisco: Harper & Row, 1989).

Hills, Judian V. et al. (eds), *Common Life in Early Church: Essays Honoring Graydon F. Snyder* (Harrisburg, PA: Trinity International, 1998).

Hill, David, 'Son and Servant: An Essay on Matthean Christology', in *Journal for the Study of the New Testament*, Issue 6, 1980, pp. 2–16.

Holmberg, B., *Paul and Power: The Structure of Authority in the Primitive Church as Reflected in the Pauline Epistle* (Lund: C. W. K. Gleerup, 1978).

Hooker, Morna D., and S. G. Wilson (eds), *Paul and Paulinism: Essays in honour of C. K. Barrett* (London SPCK, 1982).

Hooker, Morna D., *Pauline Pieces* (London: Epworth Press, 1979).

Horbury, William, *Jews and Christians in Contact and Controversy* (Edinburgh: T&T Clark, 1998).

Horrell, David G. (ed.), *Social-Scientific Approaches to New Testament Interpretation* (Edinburgh: T&T Clark, 1999).

——, 'Leadership Patterns and the Development of Ideology in Early Christianity', in *Social-Scientific Approaches to New Testament* (Edinburgh: T&T Clark, 1999).

Horsley, Richard A. (ed.), *Paul and Politics: Ekklesia, Israel, Imperium, Interpretation* (Harrisburg, PA: Trinity Press International, 2000).

—— (ed.), *Paul and the Roman Imperial Order* (Harrisburg/London/ New York: Trinity Press International, 2004).

Hutton, Maurice, *The Greek Point of View* (London, New York, Harcourt: Brace and Co., 1925).

Jacobs, Andrew S., ' "Let Him Guard Pietas": Early Christian Exegesis and the Ascetic Family', in Journal of *Early Christian Studies*, Vol. II, 2003, pp. 265–81.

——, 'A Family Affair: Marriage, Class, and Ethics in the Apocryphal Acts of the Apostle', in Journal of *Early Christian Studies*, Vol. 7, 1999, pp. 105–38.

Jewett, Robert, *Christian Tolerance: Paul's Message to the Modern Church* (Philadelphia: Westminster, 1982).

——, 'Fathers Knows Best? Christian Families in the Age of Asceticism', in Journal of *Early Christian Studies*, Vol. II, 2003, pp. 257–63.

Jeremias, Joachim, *The Central Message of The New Testament* (New York: Charles Scribner's Sons, 1965).

Johnson, E. Elizabeth, *The Function of Apocalyptic and Wisdom Traditions in Romans 9–11*, SBL Dissertation series 109 (Atlanta: Scholars Press, 1989).

Joubert, Stephan J., 'Managing the Household: Paul as Paterfamilias of the Christian household group in Corinth', in Philip F. Esler (ed.), *Modelling Early Christianity: Social Scientific Studies of the New Testament in its Context* (London and New York: Routledge, 1995), pp. 213–23.

Judge, Edwin A., 'Interpreting New Testament Ideas', in Brian S. Rosner (ed.), *Understanding Paul's Ethics: Twentieth Century Approaches* (Grand Rapids, Michigan: The Paternoster Press, 1995), pp. 75–84.

Juel, Donald, *Messianic Exegesis: Christological Interpretation of the Old Testament in Early Christianity* (Philadephia: Fortress, 1988).

Keck, Leander E., *Paul and His Letters* (Philadephia: Fortress, 1979).

——, 'Rethinking "New Testament Ethics"', in *Journal of Biblical Literature*, Vol. 115, 1996, pp. 3–16.

Keesmaat, Sylvia C., *Paul and His Story: (Re)Interpreting the Exodus Tradition* (Sheffield: Sheffield Academic Press, 1999).

Khiok-khng, Yoe (ed.), *Navigating Romans through Cultures* (Edinburgh: T&T Clark, 2004).

Kittredge, Cynthia Briggs, *Community and Authority: The Rhetoric of Obedience in the Pauline Tradition*, Harvard Theological Studies 45 (Harrisburg, PA: Trinity Press International, 1998).

Kociumbas, Jan, *Australian Childhood: A History* (St. Leonards, NSW: Allen & Unwin, 1997).

Klausner, Joseph, *From Jesus to Paul*, trans. Williams F. Stinespring (London: George Allen & Unwin Ltd, 1946).

Knight, George A. F., *Christ the Centre* (Edinburgh: Handsel, 1999).

Kraemer, Ross Shepard, *Her Share of the Blessing: Women's Religions among Pagans, Jews, and Christians in the Greco-Roman World* (New York: Oxford University Press, 1992).

——, 'Jewish Mothers and Daughters in the Greco-Roman World', in S. J. D. Cohen, *The Jewish Family in Antiquity* (Atlanta, Georgia: Scholar Press, 1993), pp. 89–112.

—— (eds.), *Women and Christian Origins* (Oxford University Press, 1999).

Lacey, W. K., 'Patria Potestas', in Beryl Rawson (ed.), *The Family in Ancient Rome: New Perspectives* (Ithaca: Cornell University Press, 1987), pp. 121–44.

Lassen, Eva Marie, 'The Roman Family: Ideal and Metaphor' in Halvor Moxnes (ed.), *Constructing Early Christian Families: Family as Social Reality and Metaphor* (London and New York, Routledge, 1997), pp. 103–20.

Levine, Amy-Jill (ed.), *A Feminist Companion to the Deutero-Pauline Epistles* (London/New York: T&T Clark International, A Continuum Imprint, 2003).

Lieu, Judith and North, John and Rajak, Tessa (eds), *The Jews Among Pagans and Christianity in the Roman Empire* (London and New York: Routledge, 1992).

Lincoln, Andrew T., *New Testament Theology: The Theology of the Later Pauline Letters* (Cambridge University Press, 1993).

——, 'The Household Code and Wisdom Mode of Colossians,' in *Journal for the Study of the New Testament*, issue 74, 1999, pp. 93–112.

——, 'The Use of the OT in Ephesians', in *Journal for the Study of the New Testament*, issue 14, 1982, pp.16–57.

Lohse, Eduard, 'The Church in Everyday Life: Consideration of the Theological Basis of Ethics in the New Testament', in Brian S. Rosner (ed.), *Understanding Paul's Ethics: Twentieth Century Approaches* (Grand Rapids, Michigan: William B Eerdmans Publishing Company, the Paternoster Press, 1995), pp. 251–65.

Maccoby, Hyam, *The Mythmaker: Paul and the Invention of Christianity* (New York: Harper & Row, 1986).

MacDonald, M. Y., *The Pauline Churches: A Socio-historical Study of Institutionalization in the Pauline and Deutero-Pauline Writings* (Cambridge: Cambridge University Press, 1988).

Macgregor, G. H. C. and Purdy, A.C., *Jew and Greek: Tutors Unto Christ – The Jewish and Hellenistic Background of the New Testament* (Edinburgh: The Saint Andrew Press, 1959).

MacIntyre, Alistair, *A Short History of Ethics* (London: Routledge & Kegan Paul Ltd, 1968).

Mack, Burton L., *The Lost Gospel: The Book of Q & Christian Origins* (San Francisco, CA: HarperSanFrancisco, 1993).

Macquarrie, John, *In Search of Humanity – A Theological and Philosophical Approach* (New York: Crossroad, 1982).

Malina, Bruce J., *The Social World of Jesus and the Gospels* (London: Routledge, 1996).

—— (eds), *Social-Science, Commentary on the Synoptic Gospels* (Minneapolis: Fortress Press, 2003).

——, Judaism, Hellenism and the Birth of Christianity, in *Paul Beyond the Judaism/Hellenism Divide* (Louisville: Westminster John Knox, 2001), pp. 17–28.

Manson, T. W., *The Teaching of Jesus* (Cambridge: The University Press, 1931).

Martin, Dale B., 'Paul and the Judaism/Hellenism Dichotomy: Toward a Social History of the Question', in Troels Engberg-Pedersen (ed.), *Paul beyond the Judaism/ Hellenism Divide* (Louisville: Westminster John Knox, 2001), pp. 29–61.

——, 'Slavery and the Ancient Jewish Family', in S. J. D. Cohen, *The Jewish Family in Antiquity* (Atlanta, Georgia: Scholar Press, 1993), pp. 113–29.

Martin, R. P.: *Reconciliation: A Study of Paul's Theology* (London: Marshall, Morgan and Scott; Atlanta: John Knox, 1981).

Mause, Lloyd de, *The History of Childhood: The Evolution of Parent-Child Relationship as a Factor in History* (A Condor Book Souvenir Press [E & A] Ltd, 1974).

Meeks, Wayne A., *The First Urban Christians: The Social World of the Apostle Paul*, 2nd edn (New Haven: Yale University Press, 1983, 2003).

——, *The Origins of Christian Morality: The First Two Centuries* (New Haven: Yale University Press, 1993).

——, *The Writing of St. Paul* (New York: Norton, 1972).

——, 'Understanding Early Christian Ethics', in *Journal of Biblical Literature*, Vol. 105/1, 1986, pp. 3–11.

Meggitt, Justin J., *Paul, Poverty and Survival* (T&T Clark, Edinburgh, 1998).

——, 'Appendix 1: Paul's Social Conservatism: Slavery, Women and the State', in *Paul, Poverty and Survival* (Edinburgh: T&T Clark, 1998), pp. 181–8.

Michel, Otto, et al. (eds), *Studies on the Jewish Background of the New Testament* (Assen: Van Gorcum, 1969).

Migliore, Daniel (ed.), *The Church and Israel: Romans 9–11* (Princeton Seminary Bullentin, Suppl. Issue No. 1, 1990).

Miller, James C., *The Obedience of Faith, the Eschatological People of God, and the Purpose of Romans* (Atlanta: Society of Bible Literature, 2000).

Mitchell, Margaret M., *Paul and the Rhetoric of Reconciliation: An Exegetical Investigation of the Language and Composition of 1 Corinthians* (Tübingen: Mohr. 1991).

Moxnes, Halvor, *Theology in Conflict: Studies in Paul's Understanding of God in* Romans, Supplements to Novum Testamentum 53 (Leiden: Brill, 1980).

—— (ed.) *Constructing Early Christian Families: Family as Social Reality and Metaphor* (London and New York: Routledge, 1997).

——, 'Honor, Shame, and the Outside World in Paul's Letter to the Romans', in *Constructing Early Christian Families: Family as Social Reality and Metaphos* (London and New York: Routledge, 1997), pp. 207–18.

——, 'What is Family? Problems in Constructing Early Christian Families', in *Constucting Early Christian Families*, 1997, pp. 13–41.

——, 'The Quest for Honor and the Unity of the Community in Romans 12 and in the Orations of Dio Chrysostom', in Troels Engberg-Pedersen (ed.), *Paul in His Hellenistic Context* (Edinburgh: T&T Clark, 1994), pp. 203–30.

Nanos, Mark D., *The Irony of Galatians: Paul's Letter in First-Century Context* (Minneapolis: Fortress, 2002).

——, *The Mystery of Romans: The Jewish Context of Paul's Letter to the Romans* (Minneapolis: Fortress, 1996).

Nathan, Geoffry, *The Family in Late Antiquity: The Rise of Christianity and the Endurance of Tradition* (London: Routledge, 2000).

Neusner, Jacob, and Bruce Chilton, *The Intellectual Foundations of Christian and Jewish Discourse: The Philosophy of Religious Argument* (London: Routledge, 1997).

Neusner, Jacob and Ernest S. Frerichs, Peder Borgen and Richard Horsley, *The Social World of Formative Christianity and Judaism* (Philadephia: Fortress Press, 1988).

Neyrey, Jerome H., *Paul, in other Words: A Cultural Reading of His Letters* (Louisville: Westminster/ John Knox Press, 1990).

——, 'Loss of Wealth, Loss of Family and Loss of Honour', in P. F. Esler (ed.), *Modelling Early Christianity: Social-Scientific Studies of the New Testament in its Context* (London: Routledge, 1995), pp. 139–58.

Northcott, Michael S., 'Sociological Approaches', in *Approaches to the Study of Religion*, edited by Peter Connolly, Foreword by Ninian Smart (London and New York: Cassell, 1999), pp. 193–225.

Osiek, Carolyn, 'Philippians', in E. Schüsser Fiorenza, A. Brock, and S. Matthews (eds), *A Feminist Commentary*, Vol. 2 of *Searching the Scriptures* (London: SCM Press, 1994), pp. 237–49.

——, 'The Family in Early Christianity: "Family Values" Revisited', *Catholic Biblical Quarterly*, Vol. 58, No. 1, 1996, pp. 1–24.

—— (eds), *Family in the New Testament World: Households and House Churches* (Louiseville, Kentucky: Westminster/John Knox Press, 1997).

Pampe, Peter, 'Family' in Church and Society of New Testament Times' in *Affirmation* (Union Theological Seminary in Virginia, 5, 1992), pp. 1–20.

Panther, Margaret Mead, *Culture and Commitment: A Study of the Generation Gap* (London: Panther, 1972).

Parkes, Graham (ed.), *Heidegger and Asian Thought* (Hawaii, 1987).

Parkin, Tim G., *Demography and Roman Society* (Baltimore: Johns Hopkins University Press, 1992).

Penn, Michael, 'Performing Family: Ritual Kissing and the Construction of Early Christian Kinship', in *Journal of Early Christian Studies*, Vol. 10, 2002, pp. 151–74.

Peristiany, J. G., 'Honour and Shame: Mediterranean Family Structure', in J. G. Peristiany and Julian Pitt-Rivers (eds), *Honour and Grace in Anthropology* (Cambridge University Press, 1992).

Pinchbeck, Ivy and Hewitt, Margaret, *Children in English Society*, Vols. I & II (London: Routledge & Kegan Paul; Toronto: Toronto Press, 1973).

Polaski, Sandra Hack, *Paul and the Discourse of Power* (Sheffield: Sheffield Academic Press, 1999).

Pollock, Linda A., *Forgotten Children: Parent–Children relations from 1500 to 1900* (Cambridge University Press, 1983).

Pomeroy, Sarah B., *Goddesses, Whores, Wives and Slaves: Women in Classical Antiquity* (New York: Schocken, 1975).

Pope John XXIIII, *Pacem in Terris*, See *Proclaiming Justice and Peace*, edited by Michael Walsh and Brian Davies (Collins, 1984).

Porter, Stanley E. (ed.), *The Pauline Canon* (Leiden/ Boston: Brill, 2004).

Räisänen, Heikki, *Paul and the Law* (Philadelphia: Fortress, 1983).

Rajak, Tessa: 'The Jewish Community and its Boundaries', in Judith Lieu, John North and Tessa Rajak (eds), *The Jews Among Pagans and Christianity in the Roman Empire* (London and New York: Routledge, 1992), pp. 9–28.

Rawson, Beryl (ed.), *The Family in Ancient Rome: New Perspectives* (London & Sydney: Croom Helm, 1986).

——, 'The Roman Family', in (ed.), *The Family in Ancient Rome: New Perspective* (London & Sydney: Croom Helm, 1986), pp. 1–57.

Reymond, Robert L., *Paul: Missionary Theologian: A Survey of his Missionary Labour and Theology* (Mentor, first published in 2000 and reprinted in 2002 by Christina Focus Publications, Geanies House, Fearn, Ross-shire, Scotland).

Reasoner, Mark, *The Strong and the Weak: Romans 14:1–15:13 in Context*, Society for New Testament Studies Monograph Series 103 (Cambridge: Cambridge University Press, 1999).

Reinhartz, Adele, 'Parent and Children: A Philonic Perspective', in S. J. D. Cohen (ed.), *The Jewish Family in Antiquity* (Atlanta, GA: Scholar Press, 1993), pp. 61–88.

Ricoeur, Paul: *The Symbolism of Evil* (Boston: Beacon, 1969).

Ridderbos, Herman, *Paul: An Outline of His Theology*, Translated by John R. DeWitt (Grand Rapids: Eerdmans, 1975; London, SPCK, 1977).

Riesner, Rainer, *Paul's Early Period: Chronology, Mission Strategy, Theology*, translated by Doug Stott (Grand Rapids: Eerdmans, 1998).

Rohrbaugh, Richard L., 'Legitimation Sonship – a Test of Honour', in Philip F. Esler (ed.), *Modelling Early Christianity: Social-Scientific Studies of the New Testament in its Context* (London and New York: Routledge, 1995), pp. 183–97.

Rosner, Brian S. (ed.), *Understanding Paul's Ethics: Twentieth Century Approaches* (Grand Rapids, Michigan: William B. Eerdmans Publishing Company, the Paternoster Press, 1995).

Ruddick, Sara, *Maternal Thinking: Toward a Politics of Peace* (Boston: Beacon, 1989).

Ruether, Rosemary Radford and Eleanor McLaughlin (eds.), *Women of Spirit: Female Leadership in the Jewish and Christian Traditions* (New York: Simon & Schuster, 1979).

Sadler, William Alan, *Personality and Religion: The Role of Religion in Personality Development* (London: S.C.M. Press, 1970).

Saller, Richard P., *Patriarchy, Property and Death in the Roman Family* (Cambridge University Press, 1994).

——, *Personal Patronage under the Early Empire* (Cambridge University Press, 1982).

Sampley, J. Paul, *Walking between the Times: Paul's Moral Reasoning* (Minneapolis: Fortress Press, 1991).

Sanders, E. P., *Paul and Palestinian Judaism: A Comparison of Patterns of Religion* (Philadelphia: Fortress, 1977).

Sandnes, Karl Olav, 'Equality within Patriarchal Structures: Some New Testament Perspectives on the Christian Fellowship as a Brother-sisterhood and a Family', in Halvor Moxnes, *Constructing Early Christian Families* (Routledge, 1997), pp. 150–65.

Schafer, K., *Gemeinde als 'Bruderschaft', Ein Beitrag zum Kirchenverstandnis des Paulus*, Europeische Hochschuschriften XXIII/333 (Bern: Peter Lang, 1989).

Schreiner, Thomas R., *The Law and Its Fulfillment: A Pauline Theology of Law* (Grand Rapids, MI: Baker Books, 1993).

Schwartz, Daniel R., *Studies in the Jewish Background of Christianity* (Tübingen: Mohr, 1992).

Schottroff, Luise, "'Not Many Powerful': Approaches to a Sociology of Early Christianity", in David G. Horrell (ed.), *Social-Scientific Approaches to New Testament Interpretation* (Edinburgh: T&T Clark, 1999), pp. 275–88.

Scroggs, Robin, 'The Earliest Christian Communities as Sectarian Movement', in David G. Horrell (ed.), *Social-Scientific Approaches to New Testament Interpretation* (Edinburgh: T&T Clark, 1999), pp. 69–92.

Seeberg, Alfred, 'Moral Teaching: The Existence and Contents of "the Way"', in Brian S. Rosner (ed), *Understanding Paul's Ethics: Twentieth Century Approaches* (Grand Rapids, Michigan: William B. Eerdmans Publishing Company; The Paternoster Press, 1995), pp. 155–75.

Sheler, Jeffrey L., 'Reassessing an Apostle' in *U.S. News & World Report* 126.13, April 5, 1999.

Simmons, A. J., *Moral Principles and Political Obligations* (Princeton, NJ: Princeton University Press, 1979).

Simon, Marcel & Longerecher, Richard, *The Christology of Early Christianity* (Naperville, IL, A. R. Allenson, 1970).

Simon Marcel: 'On Some Aspects of Early Christian Soteriology', in Eric J. Sharpe and John R. Hinnells (eds), *Man and His Salvation* (Manchester: Manchester University Press, 1973), pp. 263–79.

Smith, Paul R., *Is it Okay to Call God 'Mother': Considering the Feminine Face of God* (Peabody: Hendrickson Publishers, 1993).

Smyth, D. D. Newman: *Christian Ethics* (Edinburgh: T&T Clark, 1893, second edition).

Sommerville, John: *The Rise and Fall of Childhood* (Beverly Hills/London/New Delhi: Sage Publications, 1982).

Srowers, Stanley K., *A Rereading of Romans: Justice, Jews, and Gentiles* (New Haven: Yale University Press, 1994).

Stacey, W. David, *The Pauline View of Man: in Relation to its Judaic and Hellenistic Background* (London: Macmillan & Co Ltd, 1956).

Stambaugh, John and Balch, David, *The Social World of the First Christians* (London: SPCK, 1986).

Stott, John, *The Cross of Christ* (Downers Grove, IL: InterVarsity, 1986).

Talbert, Charles H., 'Paul, Judaism, and the Revisionists', in *Catholic Biblical Quarterly*, 63.1, 2001: 1–22.

Theissen, Gerd: *Essays on Corinth: The Social Setting of Pauline Christianity*, edited and translated by John H. Schütz (Edinburgh: T&T Clark Limited, 1982).

——, *Social Reality and the Early Christians: Theology, Ethics, and the World of the New Testament*, trans. Margaret Kohl (Edinburgh: T&T Clark, 1993).

——, 'The Wandering Radicals: Light Shed by the Sociology of Literature on the Early Transmission of Jesus Sayings', in David G. Horrell (ed.), *Social-Scientific Approaches to New Testament Interpretation* (Edinburgh: T&T Clark, 1999), pp. 93–122.

Thurman, Howard, *The Creative Encounter* (New York: Harper and Row, 1954).

Tackett, Christopher, 'The present Son of Man', in *Journal for the Study of the New Testament*, issue 14, 1982, pp. 58–81.

——, *Jesus and the Disinherited* (Nashville: Abingdon Press, 1949).

Tomson, Peter J., *Paul and the Jewish Law: Halakha in the letters of the Apostle to the Gentles* (Minneapolis: Fortress, 1990).

Towner, P. H., *The Goal of Our Instruction: The Structure of Theology and Ethics in the Pastoral Epistles* (Sheffield: JSOT Press, 1989).

Verner, D. C., *The Household of God: The Social World of the Pastoral Epistles*, SBLDS71 (Chico, CA: Scholars Press, 1983).

Van, Buren Paul, *According to the Scripture: The Origin of the Church's Old Testament* (Grand Rapids: Eerdmans, 1998).

Wallace-Hardrill, Andrew (ed.), *Patronage in Ancient Society*, Leicester–Nottingham Studies in Ancient Society (London and New York: Routledge, 1989).

Watson, Francis B., *Paul, Judaism and the Gentiles: A Sociological Approach* (Cambridge: Cambridge University Press, 1986).

Weber, Max, *Economy and Society: An Outline of Interpretive Sociology*, Vol. 1, G. Roth and C. Wittich (eds), (Berkeley and Los Angeles, CA: University of California Press).

Weidinger, K., *Die Haustafeln: Ein Stück urchristlicher Paranese*, Untersuchungen zum Neuen Testament 14 (Leipzig: J.C. Hinrichs, 1928).

Wenham, David, *Paul: Follower of Jesus or Founder of Christianity* (Grand Rapids/ Cambridge: William B. Eerdmans Publishing Company, 1995).

Westermann, William L., *Slave System of Greek and Roman Antiquity*, Memoirs of the American Philosophy Society 40 (Philadelphia: American Philosophical Society, 1955).

Wire, Antoinette C., *The Corinthian Women Prophets: A Reconstruction through Paul's Rhetoric* (Minneapolis: Fortress Press, 1990).

Winkler, John, *The Constraints of Desires: The Anthropology of Sex and Gender in Ancient Greece* (New York: Routledge, 1990).

Winch, R. F., *The Modern Family* (New York: Holt, Rinehart and Winston, 1963).

Winter, Bruce W., 'Civil Litigation in Secular Corinth and the Church', in Brian S. Rosner (ed.), *Understanding Paul's Ethics: Twentieth Century Approaches* (Grand Rapids, Michigan: William B. Eerdmans Publishing Company, The Paternoster Press, Carlisle, 1995), pp. 85–103.

Witherington, B., *Women in the Earliest Churches* (Cambridge: Cambridge University Press, 1988).

Wrede, William, *Paul* (London: Green, 1907).

Wright, N. T., *Christian Origins and the Question of God* (Minneapolis: Fortress Press, 1992).

——, *What Saint Paul Really Said: Was Paul of Tarsus the Real Founder of Christianity?* (Grand Rapids, MI: W. B. Eerdmans Pub. Co., 1997).

——, *The Climax of the Covenant: Christ and the Law in Pauline Theology* (Minneapolis: Fortress Press, 1992).

Wood, Diana (ed.), 'The Father and the Children', in *The Church and Childhood* (Oxford: Blackwell, 1994), pp. 1–27.

Yarbrough, O. Larry, 'Parents and Children in the Jewish Family of Antiquity', in Shaye J. D. Cohen (ed.), *The Jewish Family in Antiquity* (Atlanta, GA: Scholar Press, 1993), pp. 39–60.

Zhou Fuchen, *Xifang Lunlixue Mingzhu Xuandu* (I) (Beijing: Shangwu Yinshuguan, 1987).

Ziesler, John, *Paul's Letter to the Romans* (London: SCM, 1989).

——, *Pauline Christianity* (Oxford and New York: Oxford University Press, 1983, revised edition, 1990).

Confucianism and Chinese culture

Source Books

Ci Yuan (Shanghai: Shangwu Yinshuguan, 1995).

Confucian Analects, in the *The Four Books*, Chinese–English version with English translation and Notes by James Legge, D.D., LL.D. (Taibei: Culture Book Co., reprinted, 1992).

Oxford Advanced Learner's English–Chinese Dictionary (Shanghai: The Commercial Press and Oxford University Press, 1997).

The Book of Changes, in Richard Rutt, *Zhouyi: The Book of Changes* (Surrey: Curzon, 1996).

The Book of Songs, in *Translation of Confucian Classic: The Book of Songs*, A Chinese–English Bilingual Edition (Jinan: Shandong Friendship Press, 1999).

Xiaojing (Beijing: Zhonghua Shuju Chubanshe, 1996).

Xiaojing Yizhu, edited by Hu Pinsheng (Beijing: Zhonghua Shuju Chubanshe, 1996).

The Li Ki, translated by James Legge, in *The Sacred Book of China*, part III, in F. Max Müller (ed.), *Sacred Books of the East*, Vol. XXVII (Delhi: Motilal Banarsidass, reprinted 1968, reprinted in 1985).

The Book of Mengzi, in the *The Four Books*, Chinese–English version with English translation and Notes by James Legge, D.D., LL.D. (Taibei: Culture Book Co., 1992).

The Doctrine of the Mean, in the *The Four Books*, Chinese–English version with English translation and Notes by James Legge, D.D., LL.D. (Taibei: Culture Book Co., 1992).

The Book of Great Learning, in the *The Four Books*, Chinese–English version with English translation and Notes by James Legge, D.D., LL.D. (Taibei: Culture Book Co., 1992).

Dong Zhongshu: *Chuqiu Fanlu Yizheng* (Beijing: Zhonghua Shuju, 1992).

Dubs, Homer H. (trans.): *The works of Hsutze* (Taibei: Wenzhi Chubanshe, 1972, reprint in 1977, New York: AMS Press).

Guanzi Jiaoshi (Changsha: Yuelu Shushe, 1996).

Knoblock, John, *Xunzi: A Translation and Study of the Complete Works*, Vol. I (Stanford University Press, California, 1988).

——, *Xunzi: A Translation and Study of the Complete Works*, Vol. II (California, Stanford University Press, 1990).

——, *Xunzi: A Translation and Study of the Complete Works*, Vol. III (California: Stanford University Press, 1994).

Li Jingde (ed.), *Zhuzi Yulei*, Vol. 137 (Yuelu Shuyuan, 1997).

Ware, James R. (trans.), *The Sayings of Chuang Tzu* (Taiwan: Confucian Publishing Co., 1983 reprinted).

Yang Bojun (ed.), *Chunqiu Zuozhuan Yizhu* (1–4), Vol. 4 (Beijing: Zhonghua Shuju, 1981).

Books and Articles

Amos, Richard T.: 'Confucian Doctrine and Social Progress', in International Association Committee (ed.), *Guoji ruxue yanjiu*, Vol. III (Beijing: Zhongguo Shehui Kexue Chubanshe, 1997), pp. 289–302.

An Jiazheng, *Hebi Ru Fa : Xunzi di Gu shi* (Beijing: Huawen Chubanshe, 1997).

Au Kin Ming, *Paul Tillich and Chu Hsi: A Comparison of Their Views of Human Condition* (New York: Peter Lang, 2002).

Balm, Archie J., 'Standards for comparative philosophy', in H. D. Lewis (ed.), *Philosophy: East and West* (Bombay: Blackie & Son Ltd, 1976), pp. 81–94.

Baker, H. D. R., *Chinese Family and Kinship* (London: Macmillan, 1979).

Bell, D. A., 'Democracy with Chinese Characteristics: a Political Proposal for the Post-Communist Era', in *Philosophy East and West*, 49, pp. 451–91.

Berthrong, John, *All Under Heaven: Transforming Paradigms in Confucian-Christian Dialogue*, in *Sunny Series in Chinese Philosophy & Culture* (Albany: State University New York Press, 1994).

Berthrong, John H., *Transformations of The Confucian Way* (Boulder, Colo: Westview Press, 1998).

Bilsky, Lester James, *The State Religion of Ancient China* (Taibei: Chinese Association for Folklore, 1975).

Bloom, Irene, 'Mencian Argument on Human Nature', *Philosophy East and West*, 44, No. 1, 1994, pp. 19–53.

——, Human Nature and Biological Nature in Mencius, in *Philosophy East and West*, 47, No. 1, 1997, pp. 21–32.

Breiner, S. J., 'Child abuse Patterns: Comparison of Ancient Western Civilization and Traditional China', in *Analytic Psychotherapy and Psychopathology* 2, 1985.

Capra, Fritjof, *The Tao of Physics: an Exploration of the Parallels between Modern and Eastern Mysticism* (London: Flamingo, 1992), 3rd ed.

Carmody, Denise Lardner and Carmody, John Tully, *In the Path of the Masters: Understanding the Spirituality of Buddha, Confucius, Jesus, and Muhammad* (Armonk, NY: M.E. Sharpe, 1996).

Chan Wing-Tsit, 'Chinese Theory and Practice, with Special Reference to Humanism', in Charles A. Moore (ed.), *The Chinese Mind: Essays of Chinese Philosophy and Culture* (Honolulu: The University Press of Hawaii, 1968), pp. 11–30.

Chen Lai, *Gudai Zongjiao yu Lunli* (Beijing: Sanlian Shudian, 1996).

Chen Yinke, *Jinming guan conggao erbian – Feng Youlan's Zhongguo Zhexueshi Diaocha Baogao (2)* (Shanghai Guji Chubanshe, 1980).

Cheng Chung-ying, 'Transforming Confucian Virtues into Human rights', in William Theodore De Bary & Tu Weiming (eds), *Confucianism and Human Rights* (New York: Columbia University Press, 1998), pp. 142–53.

——, *Zhongguo Zhexue de Xiandaihua yu Shijiehua* (Taibei: Lianjing Chuban Shiye Gongsi, 1985.

——, *Zhongguo Xiandaihua de Zhexue Xingsi* (Taibei: Dongda Tushu Gongsi, 1988).

——, *Zhongxi Zhexue de Huimian yu Duihua* (Taibei: Wenjin Chubanshe, 1994).

——, *Shiji Zhijiao de Jueze: Lun Zhongxi Zhexue de Huitong yu Ronghe* (Shanghai: Zhishi Chubanshe, 1991).

——, 'Chinese Philosophy: A Characterization', in Arne Naess and Alastair Hannay (eds), *Invitation to Chinese Philosophy* (Oslo: Universitetsforlaget, 1972).

Ching, Julia: *Confucianism and Christianity: A Comparative Study*, New York: Kodansha International, 1977.

——, 'What Is Confucian Spirituality?', in Irene Eber (ed.), *Confucianism: The Dynamics of Tradition* (New York: Macmillan Publishing Company, 1986), pp. 63–80.

Colegrave, Sukie, *The Spirit of the Valley: Androgyny and Chinese thought* (London: Virago, 1979).

Collier, Andrew, *Christianity and Marxism: A Philosophy Contribution to their Reconciliation* (London; New York: Routledge, 2001).

Cook, Daniel J. and Henry Rosemount, Jr (eds.), *Goffried Wilhelm Leibniz, Writings on China* (Chicago and La Salle: Open Court, 1994).

Cowan, Philip A. (ed.), *Family, Self and Society: Toward a New Agenda for Family Research* (Hilldale, NJ: Erlbaum Assoc., 1993).

Cua, A. S., *Ethical Argumentation: A Study in Hsu Tzu's Moral Epistemology* (Honolulu: University of Hawaii Press, 1985).

——, *Moral Vision and Tradition: Essays in Chinese Ethics* (Washington, D.C.: The Catholic University of America Press, 1998).

——, 'The Conceptual Aspect of Hsün Tzu's Philosophy of Human nature', in *Philosophy East and West*, 27, 70. 4, 1977, pp. 373–90.

——, 'The Quasi-Empirical Aspect of Hsün Tsu's Philosophy of Human Nature', *Philosophy East and West*, 28, No. 1, 1980, pp. 3–20.

——, 'Hsün Tzu and the Unity of Virtues', in *Journal of Chinese Philosophy*, 14, No. 4, 1987, pp. 381–400.

De Bary, William Theodore and Tu Weiming (eds), *Confucianism and Human Rights* (New York: Columbia University Press, 1998).

De Bary, William Theodore (eds.), *Sources of Chinese Tradition* (New York: Columbia University Press, 1960), Vol. 2.

DeVos, George A, 'A Cross-Cultural Perspective: The Japanese Family as a unit in Moral Socialization', in Philip A. Cowan (ed.), *Family, Self and Society: Toward a New Agenda for Family Research* (Hilldale, NJ: Erlbaum Assoc., 1993), pp. 329–80.

Deng Xianhui:'Xunzi Xingelun yu Nicai Quanli Yizhi zhi Bijiao', in *Zhonghua Wenhua Luntan*, No. 1, 1997, pp. 89–95.

Dubs, Homer H.: *HSUNTZE: The Moulder of Ancient Confucianism* (London, 1927)

——, 'Mencius and HSUNTZE on Human Nature', in *Philosophy East and West*, 6, 1956, pp. 213–22.

Eber, Irene (ed.), *Confucianism: The Dynamics of Tradition* (Simon & Schuster: 1986).

Ebrey, Patricia Buckley, *Confucianism and Family Rituals in Imperial China: A Social History of Writing about Rites* (Princeton, NJ: Princeton University Press, 1991).

Eno, Robert, *The Confucian Creation of Heaven: Philosophy and the Defense of Ritual Mastery* (Albany: SUNY Series in Chinese Philosophy and Culture, 1990).

Fairbank, J. K. (ed.), *Chinese Thought and Institutions* (Chicago: The University Press, 1957).

——, *The United States and China* (Cambridge, MA: Harvard University Press, 1948).

Fang Keli and Li Jinquan (eds), *Xiandai Xin Rujia Xuean* (Beijing: Shenhui Kexue Chubanshe, 1995), Vol. 3.

Fei Xiaotong, *Xiangtu Zhongguo* (Hongkong: Sanlian Shudian, 1991).

Feng Tianyu, 'Lüelun Zhongxi Renwen Jingshen', in *Zhongguo Shehui Kexue*, No. 1, 1997, pp. 16–24.

Fingarette, Herbert, *Confucius – the Secular as Sacred* (Harper Torchbooks, Harper & Row, 1972).

Foetz, Heiner, *Confucian Ethics of the Axial Age: A Reconstruction under the Aspect of the Breakthrough toward Postconventional Thinking* (New York: State University Press, 1993).

Fung, Yu-lan, *A Short History of Chinese Philosophy*, edited. by Derk Bodde (New York: Macmillan Co., 1948).

Gao Jishun, 'Shilun Xunzi Lifa Sixiang de Dute Xingge', in *Guanzi Xuekan*, Vol. 4, 1994, pp. 14–19.

Gernet, Jacques, *China and the Christian Impact*: *A Conflict of Cultures*, translated by Janet Lloyd (Cambridge: University Press, 1985).

Goldin, Paul Rakita, *Rituals of the Way: The Philosophy of Xunzi* (Chicago: Open Court 1999).

Guo Moruo, 'Xunzi Pipan', in *Shi Pipan Shu* (Beijing: Renmin Chubanshe, 1954).

——, *Zhongguo Gudai Shehui Yanjiu* (Beijing: Kexue Chubanshe, 1960).

Hagen, Kurits: 'Xunzi's Use of Zhengming', in *Asian Philosophy*, Vol. 12, No. 1, 2002, pp. 35–51.

Han Demin, *Xunzi yu Rujia Shehui Lixiang* (Jinan: Qilu Shushe, 2001).

Hansen, Chad, *A Daoist Theory of Chinese Thought* (New York: Oxford University Press, 1992).

He Guanhu, Xu Zhiwei (eds), *Duihua: Ru Shi Dao yu Jidujiao* (Beijing: Shehui Kexue Wenxian Chubanshe, 1998).

——, *Duihua 2: Ru Shi Dao yu Jidujiao* (Beijing: Shehui Kexue Wenxian Chubanshe, 2001).

He Huaihong, *Shengtai Lunli Jingshen Ziyuan ye Zhexue jichu* (Baoding: Heibei Daxue Chubanshe, 2002).

He Ping, 'Xiaodao de Qiyuan yu Xiaoxing de Zuizao Tichu', in *Nankai Xuebao*, 2nd edn, 1988.

He Xinquan, *Ruxue yu Xiandai Minzhu* (Zhongguo shehui kexue chubanshe, 2001).

Holzman, Donald, 'Filial Piety in Ancient and Early Medieval China: Its Perennity and Its

Importance in the Cult of the Emperor'. Paper presented at the conference on the Nature of State and Society in Medieval China, August 16–18, 1980.

Hsieh Yuwei: 'Filial Piety and Chinese Society', in Charles A. Moore (ed.), *The Chinese Mind* (The University Press of Hawaii, Honolulu, first edition, 1967), pp. 167–87.

Hsu, Francis L. K., *Under the Ancestors Shadow: Chinese Culture and Personality* (London: Routlege & Kegan Paul, 1949).

——, *Clan, Caste, and Club* (Princeton, NJ; Toronto; London; New York: D. Van Nostrand Company, Inc., 1963).

——, 'Confucianism in Comparative Context', in Walter H. Slote and George A. DeVos, *Confucianism and the Family* (State University of New York Press, 1998), pp. 53–71.

Hsü, ChoYun, 'The Unfolding of Early Confucianism: The Evolution from Confucius to Hsün-tzu', in Irene Eber (ed.), *Confucianism: The Dynamics of Tradition* (Simon & Schuster, 1986), pp. 23–37.

——, 'Thinking and Learning in Early Confucianism', *Journal of Chinese Philosophy*, 17, No. 4, 1990, pp. 473–94.

——, 'A Happy Symmetry: Xunzi's Ethical Thought', in *Journal of the American Academy of Religion*, 59, No. 2, 1991, pp. 309–22.

——, *Confucian Moral Self Cultivation*, The Rockwell Series Lecture 3 (New York: Peter Lang, 1993).

——, 'Human Nature and Moral Understanding in Xunzi', in *International Philosophical Quarterly* 34, No. 2, 1994, pp. 167–76.

Hu Shi, *Zhongguo Zhonggu Sixiangshi Changbian* (Anhui Jiaoyu Chubanshe, 1999).

Huang Baoxian,'Meng Xun Renxinglun Bijiao', in *Guanzi Xuekan*, No. 2, 1995, pp. 31–4.

Hui Jixing, *Xunzi he Zhongguo Wenhua* (Guiyang: Guizhou Renmin Chubanshe, 1996).

Huntington, S., '"Democracy" Third Wave', in *Journal of Democracy*, 2, 1991, pp. 15–26.

Inada, Keeneth K., 'the Cosmological Basis of Chinese Ethical Discourse' in *Journal of Chinese Philosophy*, Vol. 32, Issue 1, April, 2005, pp. 35–46.

Ivanhoe, Philip J., *Confucian Moral Self Cultivation* (New York: Peter Lang, 1993).

Jensen, Lionel M., *Manufacturing Confucianism: Chinese Traditions and Universal Civilizations* (Durham: Duke University Press, 1997).

Jiao Guocheng, *Zhongguo gudai renwo guanxi lun* (Renmin Daxue Chubanshe, 1991).

——, *Zhongguo Lunlixue Tonglun* (Shangxi Jiaoyu Chubanshe, 1997).

Jin Zhongshu, 'Du Xianshi Qianmu Xiansheng Zuihou de Xinsheng – *Zhongguo Wenhua dui Renlei Weilai Keyou de Gongxian*', in *Guoji Ruxue Yanjiu*, Vol. 1 (Renmin Chubanshe, 1995), pp. 23–61.

Jordan, David K, 'Filial Piety in Taiwanese Popular Thought', in Slote, Walter H. and De Vos, George A., *Confucianism and the Family* (State University of New York Press, 1998), pp. 267–83.

Jr., John B. Cobb, 'Chinese Philosophy and Process Thought', in *Journal of Chinese Philosophy*, Vol. 32, Issue 2, July, 2005, pp. 163–70.

Kim, Heup Young, *Wang Yang-ming and Karl Barth: A Confucian–Christian Dialogue* (Lanham, MD: University of America, 1996).

Kline, T. C. and Ivanhoe, P. J., *Virtue, Nature, and Moral Agency in the Xunzi* (Indianapolis: Hackett Pub., 2000).

Kline III, T. C., *Ritual and Religion in Xunzi* (Seven Bridges Press, 2002).

Krieger, Silke & Trauzettel, Rolf (eds), *Confucianism and the Modernization of China* (Mainz: v. Hase & Koehler verlag, 1991).

Kubin, Wolfgan: '"Only the Chinese Understanding China' – The Problem of East–West Understanding", in Karl-Heinz Pohl (ed.), *Chinese Thought in a Global Context: A Dialogue between China and Western Philosophy Approaches* (Leiden; Boston, MA: Brill, 1999), pp. 46–57.

Küng, Hans, *Global Responsibility: in Search of a New Ethic* (New York: Crossroad Pub. Co., 1991).

———, *A Global Ethic: The Declaration of the Parliament of the World's Religions* (New York: Continuum, 1993).

———, *A Global Ethic for Global Politics and Economics* (New York: Oxford University Press, 1998).

Küng, Hans and Ching, Julia, *Christianity and Chinese Religions* (New York: Bantam Doubleday Dell Pub., 1989).

Kurtis, Hagen, 'Xunzi's use of Zhengming: Naming as a Constructive Project', in *Asian Philosophy*, Vol. 12, No. 1, 2002, pp. 35–51.

Kwok, D. W. K., 'On the Rites and Rights of Being Human', in De Bary & Weiming Tu: *Confucianism and Human Rights* (New York: Columbia University Press, 1998), pp. 83–93.

Lau, D. C., *The Analects* (Harmondsworth; New York: Penguin Books, 1979).

Lee, Cheuk-yin, 'The dichotomy of Loyalty and Filial piety in Confucianism: Historical Development and Modern Significance', in *Confucianism and the Modernization of China*, Silke Krieger & Rolf Trauzettel (eds) (Mainz: v. Hase & Koehler verlag, 1991).

Lee, Hwain Chang, *Confucius, Christ and Co-partnership: Competing Liturgies for the Soul of Korean American Women* (Lanham: University Press of America, 1994).

Lee, Peter K. H. (ed.), *Confucian–Christian Encounters in Historical and Contemporary Perspective* (Religious in Dialogue) (Lewiston, NY: E. Mellen Press, 1991).

Levenson, Joseph R., *Confucian China and its Modern Fate* (Berkeley and Los Angeles, California: University of California Press, 1965).

Lewis, D. J., 'The *Guanxi* system: An Inquiry into Chinese Conservatism in the Face of Legal and Ideological Reform' Paper presented to 7th Annual Conference of the Chinese Law Program at the Chinese University of Hong Kong (The Chinese University Press, 1988).

Lewis, H. D. (ed.), *Philosophy: East and West* (Bombay: Blackie & Son Ltd, 1976).

Li Zehou, 'Xun Yiyong Jiyao', in *Zhongguo Gudai Sixiang Shilun* (Beijing: Renmin Chubanshe, 1985).

———, 'Human Nature and Human Future: A Combination of Marx and Confucius', in Karl-Heinz Pohl, *Chinese Thought in A Global Context: A Dialogue Between China and Western Philosophical Approaches* (Brill, 1999), pp. 129–44.

Liao Mingchun, 'Lun Xunzi de Junmin Guanxi Shuo', in *Zhongguo Wenhua Yanjiu*, Summer, 1997, total No. 18, pp. 41–4.

Liang Qichao, 'Qingdai Xueshu Gangyao' 25, in *Liang Qichao Xuanji*, Vol. 2 (Zhongguo Guangbo Dianshi Chubanshe, 1992).

Liang Shuoming, *Dongxi Wenhua jiqi Zhexue* (Beijing: Shangwu Yinshuguan, 2003).

Lin Yüsheng, 'Creative Transformation of Chinese Tradition', in Karl-Heinz Pohl (ed.), *Chinese Thought in A Global Context* (Brill, 1999), pp. 73–114.

———, (ed. and trans.), *The Wisdom of Confucius* (Random House, 1938, reprinted in Taibei: Zhengzhong Shuju, 1992).

———, 'Concealing the Misconduct of One's Own Father: Confucius and Plato on a question of filial piety', *Journal of Chinese Philosophy*, 21(2), June 1994.

Lovejoy, Arthur O., *Essays in the History of Ideas* (Baltimore: Johns Hopkins University Press, 1948).

Lovin, Robin W. and Reynolds, Frank E. (eds), *Cosmogony and Ethical Order: New Studies in Comparative Ethics* (Chicago: University of Chicago Press, 1985).

Liu Fenquan, Yu Lejun, 'Meng Xun Renxue Bijiao', in *Jinan Daxue Xuebao*, Vol. 7, No. 2, 1997.

Liu Guirong, Liu Jingwei and Li Yong, 'Xunzi de Renxinglun jiqi Yanbian', in *Baoding Shifan Xueyuan Xuebao*, Jan. 2002.

Liu Xiaofeng, *Xiandaixing Shehui Lilun Xulun: Xiandaixing yu Xiandai Zhongguo* (Xianggang: Niujin Daxue Chubanshe, 1996).

——, *Dao yu Yan: Huaxia Wenhua yu Jidujiao Wenhua Xiangyu* (Shanghai: Sanlian Chubanshe,1995).

——, *Qishi yu Zhexue de Zhengzhi Chongtu* (Xianggang: Daofeng Shushe, 2001).

Lovin, Robin W. and Reynolds, Frank E. (eds), *Cosmogony and Ethical Order: New Studies in Comparative Ethics* (Chicago: University of Chicago Press, 1985).

Lu Debin, 'Shilun Xunzi Zhexue zai Ruxue Fazhan zhong de Diwei he Yiyi', in *Guoguo Zhexueshi*, period 3, 1997, pp. 41–8.

Luo Bingxiang, Zhao Dunhua, *Jidujiao yu Zhongxi Wenhua* (Beijing Daxue Chubanshe, 2000).

Ma Jigao, *Xunxue yuanliu* (Shanghai Guji Chubanshe, 2000).

Machle, Edward J., *Nature and Heaven in the Xunzi: A Study of the Tian Lun* (Albany: State University of New York Press, 1993).

——, 'The Mind and the "Shen-Ming" in Xunzi', in *Journal of Chinese Philosophy* 19, No. 4, 1992, pp. 361–86.

Mei, Y. P., 'The Basis of Social, Ethical, and Spiritual Values', in Charles A. Moore (ed.), *The Chinese Mind* (Honolulu: The University Press of Hawaii, 1967), pp. 149–66.

——, 'HsünTzu's theory of Education', in Qinghua Xuebao, No. 2, 1961, pp. 361–79

Milgram, Stanley S., *Obedience to Authority: an Experimental View* (New York, Harper & Row, 1974).

Milner, Anthony & Quilty, Mary (eds), *Comparing Cultures* (Melbourne: Oxford University Press, 1996).

Moore, Charles A. (ed.), *The Chinese Mind* (The University Press of Hawaii, first edition 1967).

Mou Zongsan, *Caixing yu Xuanli* (Taibei: Xuesheng, 1985).

——, *Zhongguo Zhexue de Tezhi* (Hongkong: Rensheng, 1963).

——, *Daode Lixiang Zhuyi* (Taibei: Xuesheng, 1982, fifth edition).

Naess, Arne and Hannay, Alastair (eds), *Invitation to Chinese Philosophy* (Oslo: Universitetsforlaget, 1972).

Nivision, David S., 'Hsun Tzu and Cuang Tzu', in Henry Rosemont, Jr. (ed.), *Chinese Texts and Philosophical Contexts: Essays Dedicated to Angus C. Graham* (La Salle, Illinois: Open Court, 1991), pp.129–42.

——, *The Way of Confucianism: Investigations in Chinese Philosophy*, edited with an introduction by Bryan W. Van Norden (Chicago and La Salle: Open Court, 1996).

Nuyen, A. T, 'Confucianism and the Idea of Citizenship', in *Asia Philosophy*, Vol. 12, No. 2, 2002, pp. 127–39.

——, 'Confucianism and the Idea of Equality', in *Asian Philosophy*, Vol. 11, No. 2, 2001, pp. 61–71.

Parks, Graham (ed.), *Heidegger and Asian Thought* (Honolulu: University of Hawaii Press, 1987).

Perelman Ch., Olbrechts-Tyteca, L., *The New Rhetoric: A Treatise on Argumentation* (Notre Dame: University of Notre Dame Press, 1969).

Pohl, Karl-Heinz (ed.), *Chinese Thought in A Global Context: A Dialogue between China and Western Philosophical Approaches* (Leiden; Boston, MA: Brill, 1999).

Qian Mu, *Zhongguo hechu qu?* (Taibei: Lianhe Yuekan Zazhishe, 1986).

——, *Shijie Jushi yu Zhongguo Wenhua* (Taibei: Dongda tushu gongsi, 1977).

——, *Traditional Government in Imperial China: A Critical Analysis* (Hong Kong: Chinese University Press, 1982).

Ricci, Matteo, *China in the Sixteenth Century: The Journals of Mathew Ricci: 1583–1610*, trans. Louis J. Gallagher (New York: Random House, 1953).

Rosemont, Henry, Jr., 'State and Society in the Hsün Tzu: A Philosophical commentary', *Monumenta Seria* 29, 1970–71, pp. 38–78.

Russel, Bertrand, *The Problem of China* (London: George Allen & Unwin Ltd., 1922).

Schwartz, Benjamin, *'The World of Thought in Ancient China'* (Cambridge, MA: Harvard University Press, 1985).

Shankman, Steven and Durrant, Stephen W., *Early China/Ancient Greece: Thinking through Comparisons* (Albany: State University of New York Press, 2002).

Sim, Luke J., with James T Bretzke, S. J., 'The Notion of "Sincerity" (Cheng) in the Confucian Classics', *Journal of Chinese Philosophy*, 21, No. 2, 1994, pp. 179–212.

Slote, Walter H, 'Psychocultural Dynamics within the Confucian Family', in Slote, Walter H. and De Vos, George A. (eds), *Confucianism and the Family* (New York: State University of Press, 1998), pp. 37–51.

Slote, Walter H. and DeVos, George A. (eds), *Confucianism and the Family* (New York, State University of Press, 1998).

Song, Jinlan, 'Xiao de Wenhua Neiyun jiqi Tanbian', in *Qinghai Shehui* Kexuee, No. 3, 1994.

Song, Young-Bae, 'Crisis of Cultural Identity in East Asia: On the Meaning of Confucian Ethics in the Age of Globalization ', in *Asia Philosophy*, Vol. 12, No. 2, 2002, pp. 109–25.

Sun, Longji, *Zhongguo Wenhua de Shenceng Jiegou* (Xianggang: Jixianshe, 1987).

Tan, Sitong, 'Ren Xue' 29, in *Tan Sitong Quanji*, Vol. 2 (Zhonghua shu jiu, 1981).

Tang, Xuewei, *Xianqin Xiaodao Yanjiu* (Taibei: Wenjin Press, 1992).

Thompson, Lawrence G., *Chinese Religion: An Introduction* (Belmont: Wadsworth Publishing Company, 1996).

——, *Ta T'ung Shu: The One-World Philosophy of K'ang Yu-wei* (London: George Allen and Unwin, 1958).

Tu, Weiming, *Centrality and Commonality: An Essay on Chung-Yung* (Honolulu: University of Hawaii Press, 1976).

——, *Centrality and Commonality: an Essay on Confucian Religiousness* (Albany, NY: State University of New York Press, 1989).

——, 'Confucius and Confucianism', in Walter H. Slote and Geoge A. DeVos (eds), *Confucianism and the Family* (Albany: State University of New York Press, 1998), pp. 3–36

——, "Probing the 'Three Bonds' and 'Five Relationships'", see Walter H. Slote and George A. De Vos (eds), *Confucianism and the Family* (Albany: State University of New York Press, 1998), pp. 121–36.

——, 'Human Rights as Confucian Moral Discourse', in William Theodore De Bary & Tu Weiming (eds), *Confucianism and Human Rights* (New York, Columbia University Press, 1998), pp. 297–307.

——, *Confucian Traditions in East Asian Modernity: Moral Education and Economic Culture in Japan and the Four Mini-Dragons* (Cambridge, MA: Harvard University Press, 1996).

——, *China in Transformation* (Cambridge, MA: Harvard University Press, 1994).

Uhalley, Stephen Jr. and Wu Xiaoxin, *China and Christianity: Burdened Past, Hopeful Future* (Armonk, NY: M. E. Sharpe, 2001).

Williams, S. W., 'The Worship of Ancestors among the Chinese', *China Repository* 18 (1849).

Winch, R. F., *The Modern Family* (New York: Rinehart and Winston, 1963).

Wright, A. F. (ed.), *The Confucian Persuasion* (Stanford, California: Stanford University Press, 1960).

Wohlfahrt, Günter, 'Modernity and Postmodernism: Some Philosophical Remarks on the Necessity of an East–West Dialogue', in Karl-Heinz Pohl (ed.), *Chinese Thought in A Global Context: A Dialogue between China and Western Philosophical Approaches* (Brill, 1999), pp. 14–28.

Xiao Qunzhong, *Xiao yu Zhongguo Shehui* (Beijing: Renmin Press, 2001).

Xiong Liangzhi and Zhuang Jian, *Xunzi yu Xiandai Shehui* (Chengdu: Sichuan Renmin Chubanshe, 1995).

Xu Fuguan, *Zhongguo Sixiangshi Lunji Xubian* (Taibei: Shibao Wenhua Chuban Shiye Youxian Gongsi, 1982).

——, *Zhongguo Sixiangshi Lunji* (Taibei: Xuesheng, 1983).

Yang Huilin, *Shengyan Renyan: Shenxue Quanshixue* (Shanghai: Shanghai Yiwen Chubanshe, 2002).

Yang Yunru and others, *Xunzi Yan Jiu* (Shanghai: Shanghai Shudian, 1992).

Yao Xinzhong, *An Introduction to Confucianism* (Cambridge: Cambridge University Press, 2000).

——, *Confucianism and Christianity: A Comparative Study of Jen and Agape* (Brighton: Sussex Academic Press, 1996).

——, 'Knowledge and Interpretation: A hermeneutical Study of Wisdom in Early Confucian and Israelite Traditions', in *Journal of Chinese Philosophy*, Vol. 32, issue 2, 2005 (Blackwell Publishing), pp. 297–311.

Yearley, Lee H., 'Hsün Tzu on the Mind: His Atempted Synthesis of Confucianism and Taoism', *Journal of Asian Studies*, 39, No. 3, 1980, pp. 415–80.

——, 'A Confucian Crisis: Mencius Two Cosmogonies and Their Ethics', in Robin W. Lovin and Frank E. Reynolds (eds), *Cosmogony and Ethical Order: New Studies in Comparative Ethics* (Chicago: University of Chicago Press, 1985), pp. 310–27.

Ye Zhou, Xing Yan, 'Lun Xunzi Renxing Lilun', in *Huabei Dianli Xueyuan Xuebao*, No. 4, 1997.

Young, Robert, *Intercultural Communication: Pragmatics, Genealogy, Deconstruction* (Clevedon, Avon, England: Multilingual Matters, 1996).

Yü Yingshi, *Songming Lixue yu Zhengzhi Wenhua* (Taibei: Yunchen Wenhua Shiye Gufen Youxian Gongsi, 2004).

Zha Chang-guo, 'Lun Chunqiu zhi *Xiao* fei Zunqin, in *Anqing Shifan Xueyuan* Xuebao, 4th period, 1993.

——, 'Xizhou Xiaoyi Chutan', in *Zhongguoshi Yanjiu*, period 2, 1993.

Zhang Longxi: 'Translating culture: China and the West', in Karl-Heinz Pohl (ed.), *Chinese Thought in a Global Context: A Dialogue between Chinese and Western Philosophical Approaches* (Leiden; Boston, MA: Brill, 1999), pp. 29–48.

Zhang Shuguang, *Waiwang Zhixue: Xunzi he Zhongguo Wenhua* (Henan Daxue Chubanshe, 1997).

Zhao Shilin, 'Xunzi de Renxinglun Xintan', in *Zhexue Yanjiu*, No. 10, 1999, pp. 60–8.

Zhou Fucheng, *Xifang Lunlixue Mingzhu Xuandu* (I) (Beijing: Shangwu Yinshuguan, 1987).

Zhou Yütong, 'Xiao yu Shengzhiqi Chongbai', in *Zhou Yu-tong Jingxueshi Lunzhu Xuanji* (Shanghai Renmin Press, 1983).

Zhu Lan, 'Lun Xiao wei Ren zhi Ben', in *Zhongguo Zhexueshi*, period 2, 1999, pp. 46–9.

Index